THE WAGE-PRICE ISSUE

A Theoretical Analysis

by WILLIAM G. BOWEN

GREENWOOD PRESS, PUBLISHERS
NEW YORK

FOREWORD

Although very few people are experts on the impact of wage- and price-setting institutions on inflation, many have expressed strong opinions on the subject. Union leaders and industrialists, for example, are commonly at odds about the forces which account for movements of wages and prices. There are differences too among political leaders and government officials as well as among social scientists. The tendency is strong, unfortunately, to marshal facts which best support deep-seated convictions rather than to use them to question where the truth may lie. Many people know many things about the wage-price issue, and much of what people know is simply not true. Certainly, research in this controversial area is of vital importance.

Knowledge is gained by gathering facts and learning to interpret them meaningfully. Theories allow one to determine what facts are relevant and thus worth gathering. And analysis permits one to fit facts into a meaningful theoretical framework. Actually, our knowledge about such things as "cost-push," "demand-pull," or "creeping" inflation is quite limited. In part, the reason may be the dearth of empirical facts about the wage-price issue. But, an even more important reason for the unsatisfactory state of our knowledge in this area is the lack of an appropriate system of thought for analysis of the subject.

In this volume Dr. Bowen offers a system for analysis of wage-price relationships. His aim is not to assemble a mass of facts nor to place the blame for inflation on any particular group or interest, but to outline the logical steps which should be taken to arrive at an objective appraisal. He makes a critical analysis of existing studies, and shows how the various pieces of the wage-price puzzle can fit together. Other writings have dealt with particular aspects of the subject, such as, for example, the impact of unions on wages or the kinds of monetary policies needed for dealing with cost inflation. But this volume, we believe, is the first attempt to present a broad theoretical analysis of wage-price relationships in modern economic society.

In contrast to many theoretical works, Dr. Bowen's analysis is clear and understandable even for the layman. Thus, this volume can help the businessman, the union leader, the banker and the journalist as well as the professional economist to develop his thinking on this very vital issue. Those who already have strong convictions about who is responsible for inflation may find this book sobering, and, hopefully, enlightening as well. Those who have been more perplexed than convinced and who want to deepen their understanding of the wage-price issue should find it most rewarding.

The sponsorship of this study has been a new departure for the Section. In the past its projects have been concerned largely with empirical research, reports on policy operations, and analyses of experience in dealing with problems in the field of labor economics and industrial relations at home and abroad. This is the first project to be concerned exclusively with a system of analysis. It is, in our judgment, an outstanding contribution to knowledge. And, it provides a sound foundation for future projects by Professor Bowen and his associates which will deal more empirically with the behavior of wages and salaries.

FREDERICK HARBISON, DIRECTOR
INDUSTRIAL RELATIONS SECTION
PRINCETON UNIVERSITY

November 1, 1959

PREFACE

One of the most frequent criticisms of the economist is that he often spends his time investigating problems which, while interesting to fellow members of his rather exclusive profession, are not particularly important to society as a whole. Whatever may be the validity of this criticism in general, it certainly does not apply to the subject matter under discussion here. A strong case can be made for the proposition that the entire problem of the inflationary impact of our wage- and price-setting institutions constitutes one of the most important economic issues of our time. My own interest in this subject stems from an awareness of how very important it is that the public policies designed to deal with the various aspects of the wage-price issue be based on careful investigation and analysis.

However, while the central problem of this study has, so to speak, been "taken from society," the same cannot be said of its methodology. In looking over the vast array of popular and scholarly writings germane to the wage-price issue, it is difficult to avoid the feeling that in our pursuit of this elusive topic we have been guilty of that typical American malady of impatience. We have tried to "catch the culprit" before we understood the nature and magnitude of the problem, and we have tried to understand the problem before understanding its constituent elements. It is my conviction that this impetuous mode of attack has outlived its usefulness and that at this juncture what we need is a more detached and systematic analysis that will help us arrange the various parts of the wage-price puzzle into a more coherent whole.

For reasons that are explained in some detail in the introductory chapter, I have become convinced that any systematic investigation of the wage-price issue must begin with a detailed analysis of certain theoretical questions and thus have concentrated my efforts in this area. Certain important empirical and public policy questions have, therefore, been declared outside the scope of this study. As a consequence, it is necessary to warn the reader that this inquiry neither assigns the "blame" for inflation to any particular group nor contains any simple policy prescriptions which will "solve" the wage-price issue. Instead, this study is dedicated to the more humble—and yet at the same time more fundamental—task of providing a theoretical framework within which these ultimate questions can fruitfully be explored.

From what has been said above, it is comparatively easy to infer that this book is designed primarily for persons possessing a rather broad interest in the wage-price controversy. However, it is hoped that certain sections will prove useful to the individual who has an especially strong interest in specific topics such as the usefulness of distinguishing amongst "types" of inflation, the impact of the union on wages, and the role of the monetary environment in the cost-inflation process.

The fact that this book does cover a wide terrain has one additional implication that should at least be mentioned: specialists in particular areas of economics (such as wage theory or price behavior) may encounter a certain amount of material with which they are already familiar. While a determined effort has been made to keep such material to a minimum, it must be remembered that this difficulty is in large measure an inherent by-product of any effort to fuse the individual facets of the wage-price issue into a comprehensible whole, and thus cannot be avoided altogether.

I should now like to mention a few of the many friends who have been especially helpful in the preparation of this study. My first debt is to my Princeton colleagues in general and, in particular, to Richard A. Lester, who has been a constant source of advice and encouragement. In addition, William J. Baumol, Lester V. Chandler, and Richard E. Quandt have painstakingly read the manuscript in whole or in part and have contributed many useful suggestions. The manuscript has also benefited greatly from a careful reading by Edgar O. Edwards of Rice Institute and Kenyon E. Poole of Northwestern University. Needless to say, none of these men should bear any onus for whatever faults remain.

My wife has very graciously undertaken the arduous task of putting the footnotes in proper order and has contributed her skills to the over-all project in countless other ways.

Finally, I should like to express my appreciation to the Ford Foundation and to the Industrial Relations Section of Princeton University for the financial support which made this study possible. Mrs. John Vliet has done a splendid job of typing the main part of the manuscript, and her work has been very ably supplemented by the entire secretarial staff of the Industrial Relations Section.

WILLIAM G. BOWEN

Princeton, New Jersey
April 29, 1959

CONTENTS

CONTENTS

Part III. The Cost and Price Determination Assertions

Part IV. The Monetary Policy Assertion

Part V.   Conclusions

ILLUSTRATIONS

THE WAGE-PRICE ISSUE
A Theoretical Analysis

1. Introduction

The Subject and Its Importance

The purpose of this study is to cast some measure of additional illumination on a widely discussed, highly controversial, and poorly defined subject—which, for want of a better shorthand expression, will be referred to simply as "the wage-price issue." In brief, this "issue" encompasses the whole complex of questions involved in the allegation that the wage- and price-setting institutions of the contemporary American economy impart an upward bias to the price level.

There is certainly no denying the importance of this subject. It would be hard to exaggerate the widespread interest in the over-all problem of inflation and in the more specialized possibility that our wage- and price-setting institutions themselves exert strong upward pressure on prices. Professor Paul Samuelson, in his widely used economics textbook, tells us: "It is hardly too much to say that this price-wage question is the biggest unsolved economic problem of our time. . . . A wage and price policy for full employment—that is America's greatest problem and challenge."[1] Indeed, so much attention has been lavished on various facets of this subject in professional economic journals, in the popular press, in the halls of Congress, and in the publications of labor leaders and industry spokesmen that it is manifestly unnecessary to belabor the importance of the wage-price issue any further.[2]

[1] P. A. Samuelson, *Economics: An Introductory Analysis* (4th ed.; New York: McGraw-Hill, 1958), p. 360.

[2] It is revealing to note that even Galbraith's recent attempt to debunk the significance of most problems economists find interesting does not deny the real importance of the inflation issue. See J. K. Galbraith, *The Affluent Society* (Boston: Houghton-Mifflin, 1958), p. 250.

3

The much more interesting and significant question is: *why* this great interest in wage-price relationships? The most basic answer to this query is, of course, that there is no single explanation or rationale. However, those interested in the wage-price issue can be categorized—albeit roughly—into two main camps.

The first and by far the most populous camp is rather easily identified. It consists of that substantial segment of the public who simply possess a strong dislike for inflation regardless of its source. The size and significance of this group stems directly from the fact that price stability is an important objective in our society and any situation or combination of circumstances threatening price stability is considered a major public policy problem. In an area fraught with controversy this is one point on which there is remarkable unanimity. It is important to remember that whereas the direct brunt of other undesirable economic phenomena (such as unemployment) is often heavily concentrated on certain sectors of society, almost everyone feels himself directly affected by increases in the price level.

This anti-inflation group is, of course, far from homogeneous and includes a number of significantly different viewpoints. Consequently, it is helpful to subdivide this broad category into: (1) those who are adversely affected personally by inflation (for example, pensioners and others whose money incomes are relatively fixed); (2) those who feel that inflation is bad for the country in that it is inequitable and may be harmful to economic growth; and (3) those who simply do not realize that inflation may be in their own economic interest—that is, many may not see the connection between rising money incomes and rising prices, and so may assume that their own money incomes are independent of movements of the general price level. It may well be that the tendency of this latter group to

4

see only the "bad" side of inflation provides much of the public support for anti-inflationary policies.

Prior to the end of World War II, this general fear of inflation manifested itself mainly in concern with the level of governmental spending and with the management of the money supply. One of the most significant developments in the postwar period has been the tendency for this anti-inflationary sentiment to spill over into the area of micro-economic behavior as well. This increasing concern over the role of modes of wage and price determination in the inflationary process seems to be the product of a number of interacting influences: (1) an increasing awareness of the potential significance of micro-economic institutions in general and of the union in particular; (2) the adoption of "full" employment policies and the recognition of the potential impact of such policies on the behavior of various wage- and price-setting institutions; (3) the existence of increases in the price level in the absence of obvious inflationary pressures from the demand side; and (4) the natural inclination of our society to expect better and better performance from the economic system.

This last point requires brief elaboration. It is important to note that it is not just the economic data and the characteristics of the economy which are susceptible to change—the public's conception of what constitutes an economic problem may also vary over time. In fact, it seems perfectly reasonable to suppose that the standards by which we judge the performance of our economy are ever-rising. That is, the public seems to be demanding continually better records of achievement from both economists and the economy itself. Whereas a 1 to 3 per cent per annum increase in the price level might not have been regarded as an important economic problem in the recent past, it is so regarded today. And, as the public's tolerance of inflation narrows we should expect increasing attention to be devoted to structural features of our economy (such as the modes of wage determination) which may stimulate even a slow rate of increase in the price level. It is at least encouraging to think that some portion of the increasing interest in wage-price relationships is attributable to nothing more dangerous than rising expectations.

So much for those who belong in the anti-inflation camp. The second main group possessing a strong interest in the wage-price controversy consists of those who are less worried about the consequences of inflation than they are about the consequences of the actions that may be taken in an effort to halt gradual inflations. For instance, some labor leaders are worried that the public image of "wage inflation" may inspire strong anti-union legislation. Similarly, businessmen may fear that the government will attempt to regulate "administered prices." Furthermore, some economists and Congressmen are concerned that public pressure for anti-inflationary measures will stimulate government policies which will in turn interfere with the attainment of other important economic objectives, such as high-level employment and a sufficiently rapid rate of growth.[3]

In short, some of the interest in the wage-price issue stems directly from the fear that gradual inflation will panic us into making some very costly mistakes. A failure to understand the "causes" of gradual increases in the price level may lead to the adoption of measures which will do more harm than good. Consequently, even those prepared to view a mild inflation with considerable equanimity are quite properly concerned with the issues involved in the wage-price controversy.

[3] Numerous expressions of this point of view are contained in (United States Congress, Joint Economic Committee) *January 1959 Economic Report of the President: Hearings* . . . , 86th Cong., 1st Sess., 1959. See, in particular, the repeated comments made by Senator Douglas.

Appraising the Wage-Price Issue: Some Difficulties

The acknowledged importance of the wage-price issue has led, naturally enough, to the investment of a tremendous amount of time and energy in this area. And yet, in spite of the great amount of attention lavished on this subject, it is safe to say that most people regard the mass of existent literature as something less than satisfactory. In fact, apart from the question of the importance of the subject, there is probably more unanimity on the proposition that the available literature leaves much to be desired than there is on any other proposition germane to the wage-price issue.

The main generic difficulty with the existent literature is that much of it is either too general or too specific. On the one hand, there are a number of article- or chapter-length writings which sketch the process of wage- or cost-inflation in very broad terms but which fail to go into the individual components of this process in sufficient detail. Such important considerations as the factors influencing the level of money wages are frequently given very little attention. On the other hand, there have been a number of rather detailed inquiries into specific aspects of the wage-price issue (such as the impact of unions on wages) which suffer from the lack of an over-all conception of the inflationary process. This latter category might also be stretched to include numerous polemics designed to fix the "blame" for inflation on one group or another.

In order to appreciate the methodology used throughout this book it is now necessary to consider some of the factors which account for the unsatisfactory state of the existent literature. The general point of view adopted here is that the reasons for the inadequacies which exist are bound up to a considerable extent with certain difficulties inherent in the subject itself. The vast outpouring of effort in this area by many well-known and highly competent men certainly serves as evidence in support of this position.

The first inherent difficulty is simply that the questions which comprise the wage-price issue involve the whole of the economy and many complex areas of economics. That is, it is hard to analyze the allegation that our contemporary wage- and price-setting institutions impart an upward bias to the price level without becoming embroiled in micro-economic wage theory, the theory of the firm in general and price theory in particular, monetary theory, and aggregative income analysis.

A second, closely-related, source of difficulty is that the questions in the wage, price, and monetary areas cannot be neatly tied off from one another but are interdependent to a large degree. For example, it is hard (impossible?) to appraise the impact of the union on the general price level without a careful analysis of the effect of costs on price behavior and of the reaction of the monetary-fiscal authorities to initial changes in the level of employment and prices. Because of this interdependence, efforts to deal with a single aspect of this subject are not likely to meet with much success.

The existence of serious obstacles to empirical work has also impeded efforts to investigate various facets of the wage-price issue. There is no denying the necessity of empirical work in this area—a priori reasoning simply cannot tell us much about magnitudes. However, identification problems make it very difficult to deduce much from data which are readily available. For instance, a simple comparison of wage and price indices can tell us very little indeed. An equi-proportionate increase in wages and prices is compatible with any one of at least three hypotheses: (1) that wages pushed up prices, (2) that prices pulled up wages, or (3) that some third factor affected both wages and prices. Conclusion: macro-economic data of this type are by themselves of limited usefulness.

The fourth difficulty is of a quite different sort. The great importance of the wage-price issue to various special groups has served to encourage quests for "culprits" and quick "solutions"—and yet the complex nature of the subject makes the successful attainment of these objectives extremely unlikely. It is both paradoxical and unfortunate that a subject which requires as much patience and detailed analysis as this one is also so emotionally charged that a premium is put on dogmatic assertion and quick, simple answers.

Finally, it is necessary to mention the contribution which the confusion between "is" and "ought" propositions has made to the unsatisfactory state of much of the existent literature. The strong ethical overtones which have characterized so much of the discussion of this subject (the "right" to wage increases in line with general increases in productivity, the need to protect the "integrity" of the dollar, the profit "greed" of corporations) have tended to obscure the need for careful analyses of how various economic institutions in fact function.

General Approach and Plan of the Book

In light of the above difficulties, how are we to proceed? The first and most basic methodological conviction undergirding this book is that the wage-price issue has been "debated" long enough and that the time is now ripe for more systematic investigations which, while less exciting, are also potentially more rewarding.

If wage-price relationships are to be studied rather than just debated, it is absolutely necessary to recognize that anything purporting to be a complete analysis of this problem must concern itself with three broad sets of questions: (1) the theoretical set which includes such problems as the nature and origins of inflation, the factors influencing individual wage, price, and employment decisions, and the role of the monetary environment in shaping these decisions; (2) the empirical set which includes the broad problem of statistical inference and the arduous task of collecting and analyzing data in order to estimate the quantitative magnitudes involved; and (3) the public policy set which includes the questions of the criteria on the basis of which policy decisions are or should be made and the total implications of various proposed solutions.

This particular study does *not* purport to be a complete analysis of the wage-price issue, but is limited to the first, or theoretical, set of questions. The decision to concentrate limited resources on this aspect is based on the conviction that a more systematic investigation of the underlying theoretical issues is a necessary prelude to a successful assault on the empirical and public policy questions.

Within the theoretical area, the approach of this book is based on three additional convictions: first, that it is necessary to avoid an extreme amount of aggregation and instead to invest a significant portion of research time in understanding the behavior patterns of the ultimate decision-making units involved—namely, the firm, the union, the government (Federal Reserve and Congress), households as spenders and households as suppliers of services; second, that an adequate understanding of the behavior of these decision-making units requires considerable patience and can come only from a rather detailed analysis; third, that it is necessary to avoid excessive compartmentalization of the economic process and to concentrate instead on understanding the links which connect wage, price, and employment decisions.

Stated briefly, the conviction here is that our most pressing need in this area is for a careful, systematic assembly job that will tie together what we know and can find out about wage determination, cost determination, price determination, and the impact of monetary and fiscal policies in each of these categories. Of course, in the process of assembling we inevitably discover parts which are missing and parts which in their present form are not quite satisfactory for our purposes. Consequently, this study is devoted to: (1) rethinking and refining certain individual building blocks (such as the theory of wage determination) where this is necessary to render them more usable, and (2) combining and assembling these individual building blocks into a more coherent whole.

Organizationally, this inquiry is divided into five parts. Part I is devoted to an analysis of certain key links which inextricably bind the wage-price issue to the general theory of inflation. In the following chapter we examine several of the most basic questions in this area: What is inflation? How does inflation originate? Is there more than one type of inflation? With what brand of inflation is the wage-price issue concerned? Then, in Chapter 3, we investigate in some detail one particular model of the inflationary process—namely, the familiar "dilemma model," in which it is asserted that "spontaneous" increases in labor costs instigate a train of events which force society (and especially the monetary authorities) to choose between inflation and unemployment. This basic model is at the very heart of the wage-price issue, and the remainder of the book is devoted to exploring the questions raised by this schema.

Part II concentrates on the wage determination aspects of the dilemma model. In this part an attempt is made: to evaluate the probable effect of various economic factors —productivity, excess demand for labor, ability-to-pay, cost of living, and wage comparisons—on the magnitude of wage adjustments; to appraise the significance of certain institutional factors such as unionization and the characteristics of the wage-setting process; to describe the way in which these factors interact within the individual firm; and, finally, to analyze the factors which influence the behavior of "the general wage level."

Part III deals with the cost and price determination

aspects of the dilemma model. In this part an examination of the links which connect wage adjustments, unit labor costs, and unit total costs is followed by an analysis of micro-economic price theory in general, and the impact of costs on prices in particular. The cost-plus pricing controversy is very briefly reviewed, and an attempt is made to analyze the way in which considerations such as public opinion and uncertainty modify the picture of price behavior derived from the traditional theory of the firm. Finally, more aggregative models of price behavior are appraised, and the proximate determinants of variations in the general price level are discussed.

Part IV is devoted to an analysis of the monetary policy questions which arise out of the dilemma model. Here the main issues discussed include: the general role played by the monetary environment in translating wage adjustments into changes in aggregate monetary demand; the "natural" barriers to inflation which operate in spite of an "elastic" monetary policy; the widely debated issue of the effectiveness or *modus operandi* of a restrictive monetary policy; and the significance of governmental interest in the level of employment for price movements.

Finally, in Part V, an attempt is made to draw together some of the main findings which stem from the preceding chapters and to offer a few observations on the general problems of affixing the "responsibility" for inflation and "solving" the wage-price issue.

The reader is now forewarned—at least to some extent—of what to expect from this study. This inquiry certainly makes no pretense of "solving" the wage-price issue (whatever that may mean), nor does it pretend to provide such "fundamental" data as the volume of unemployment needed to permit price stability. Instead, this study offers more humble fare in the form of a general discussion of certain theoretical problems which constitute the roots of the wage-price issue.

PART 1
The Wage-Price Issue and the General Theory of Inflation

2. The Nature and Origins of Inflation

One conclusion emerges clearly from the preceding chapter: much of the contemporary interest in our wage- and price-setting institutions stems directly from the growing tendency to associate these institutions with an awesome word—"inflation." Consequently, there is a clear mandate to begin the substantive part of this study with some brief comments on inflation in general and the links which connect the wage-price issue with this more general topic.

This particular chapter is concerned with two of the more obvious links between the wage-price issue and the general theory of inflation: first, there is the question of just what the key concept "inflation" means; secondly, there is the question of how the "type" of inflation involved in the wage-price controversy is supposed to originate and in what ways this type of inflation differs from other members of the inflation family. Answers to both these questions are necessary prerequisites to the much more detailed discussion of the "dilemma model" of the inflationary process which comes in Chapter 3 and which serves as the organizational cornerstone of the entire study.

The Definition of Inflation

What is "inflation"? Anyone who thinks that the answer to this question is clear and unambiguous is invited to try a simple experiment—interrogate a group of people possessing at least some general interest in economics and then note the diversity of their replies. And, this lack of consensus is by no means restricted to "the untrained." Even in the technical writings of economists there is a surprising lack of unanimity, and much resulting confusion. As Bach has quite aptly pointed out: "One reason why arguments about inflation so often get nowhere except

15

around in a circle is that the disputants so often fail to define the term. . . ."[1]

It is, of course, naïve to expect every term to have an unequivocal meaning and pointless to debate the "rightness" or "wrongness" of alternative definitions—the important criterion is usefulness. Nonetheless, it is absolutely essential that whatever meaning is assigned such an important concept as inflation be both carefully chosen and clearly stated. After all, the definition selected can determine final answers to important questions.[2]

For the purpose of this study, it seems most sensible to define inflation simply as an increase in the general level of prices, as measured by some composite statistic such as the Consumer Price Index. The main advantages of this definition are: (1) it is simple and unequivocal; (2) it is in accord with common usage;[3] and (3) it is sufficiently non-restrictive to permit modification by appropriate adjectives if this is desired as a means of distinguishing special cases.

In order to avoid any possible misunderstanding, it is necessary to note several things that this definition does

[1] G. L. Bach, *Inflation: A Study in Economics, Ethics, and Politics* (Providence: Brown University Press, 1958), p. 6.

[2] This point is well illustrated by a recent statement made by Mr. W. C. Mullendore: "We cannot answer the question of whether wage raises cause inflation until we know what inflation is. Inflation, in my book, is an increase in the supply of the media of exchange, money and bank deposits, brought about through the perversion of the power of issue and through misuse and abuse of credit." (W. C. Mullendore, "Are Wages Inflationary?—II," *Management Record*, XIX, August 1957, p. 272). Thus it is no surprise when Mullendore concludes: "Inflation's source is not the bargaining table." The source of inflation simply has to be the monetary authorities on the basis of his definition.

[3] See, for example: Samuelson, *Economics* . . . , 1958, p. 268; Bach, *Inflation* . . . , 1958, p. 6; and L. V. Chandler, *The Economics of Money and Banking* (rev. ed.; New York: Harper, 1953), pp. 130ff.

not do. First of all, it does not require that the increase in prices be of a certain magnitude in order to qualify as a bona fide inflation. Some authors have preferred to indentify inflation with "considerable and sudden variations of the value of money."[4] The main disadvantage of this treatment is that it becomes very hard to know where to draw the line separating inflations from non-inflations—precision is more difficult or arbitrariness more troublesome once the clear guidepost of a zero increase in the price index is cast aside. Consequently, it seems more useful to classify an increase in the price level of *any* magnitude as an inflation. The degree of inflation can then be noted separately, either by numerical means (usually the most satisfactory treatment) or by the use of such adjectives as "creeping" and "galloping."

Secondly, the definition used in this study is concerned solely with price behavior in the commodity markets and ignores the factor markets altogether. This treatment has been criticized by Bent Hansen, who argues that a major weakness of Keynesian inflation analyses is their disregard of the possible existence of excess demand in the labor market.[5] Hansen then proposes the following definition:

> We may say that a *monetary pressure of inflation* exists if there is monetary excess demand in either the composite commodity-market or the composite factor-market, or in both these composite markets, so long as neither of them exhibits monetary excess supply.[6]

The main disadvantage of the factor-market aspect of Hansen's definition is that it permits conclusions which

[4] George N. Halm, *Monetary Theory: A Modern Treatment of the Essentials of Money and Banking* (2d ed.; Philadelphia: The Blakiston Company, 1946), pp. 16-17.

[5] Bent Hansen, *A Study in the Theory of Inflation* (New York: Rinehart & Co., Inc., 1951), pp. 18-20.

[6] *Ibid.*, p. 20.

17

differ radically from common usage. For example, on his definition, a situation of constant prices and rising wages would be classed as "inflation," whereas rising prices accompanied by unemployment would not be so designated. And yet, the constant price-rising wage situation is often thought of as the norm for public policy, and certainly does not carry all the unpleasant connotations of inflation; on the other hand, the rising price-unemployment situation entails the same diminution in the purchasing power of the monetary unit generally regarded as the hallmark of all inflations—the fact that unemployment also exists merely means that the public has an additional problem with which to wrestle.

The main advantage of Hansen's treatment is that it very properly emphasizes the necessity of including a careful analysis of factor market behavior in any investigation of inflation. However, there is no reason why this cannot be done without sacrificing the rising-commodity-price definition of inflation.

The third—and in many ways most important—negative by-product of the inflation definition used in this study is that it does not specify the "cause" or "origin" of inflation. The advantages of this omission will be made more clear in the following section, where the complex question of "inflation-types" is explored in some detail. For the present, it is sufficient to note that the failure to leave this question open is one of the most telling objections to defining inflation either as an increase in the quantity of money or in terms of excess demands for commodities and factors of production.

Finally, it must be emphasized that the term "inflation," as used here, has no moral connotations at all. Whether inflation is good or bad can be decided only in specific contexts where an evaluation of the costs of inflation per se can be weighed against the costs of preventing inflation.

18

"Types" of Inflation

It used to be that when an author interested in the subject of price behavior had explained what he meant by "inflation" his definitional chores were at an end. This is certainly not true today. The recent and amazingly rapid proliferation of inflation "types" has made it unfashionable to speak simply of "inflation." Instead, one must specify whether he means "cost inflation," "demand inflation," "excess-demand inflation," "wage inflation," "money inflation," "structural inflation," "log-rolling inflation," "speculative inflation," "bottleneck inflation," "buyers' inflation," "sellers' inflation," "mark-up inflation," "administered-price inflation," and so on.

The introduction of some measure of order into this apparent chaos most assuredly constitutes an early imperative for anyone desirous of making sense out of the wage-price controversy. The key question is quite obvious: with what brand of inflation is the wage-price issue concerned? Unfortunately, the answer to this question is considerably less obvious than is commonly thought—in fact, there is no really satisfactory answer for the simple reason that the inflation types listed above have not been invested with precise meanings. Nonetheless, the fact that so much of the wage-price issue has been carried on in these terms requires that we at least wrestle with this question.

Perhaps the best way to start is by emphasizing that the wage-price issue is *not* concerned with inflations which are triggered by an increase in aggregate demand at a time when resources are already fully employed. Instead, the wage-price issue is concerned with inflationary pressures generated by our wage- and price-setting institutions in the absence of general excess demand. It is exceedingly difficult to be any more specific than this—and, it is far from clear that there is much advantage to be gained from being more specific!

However, as a concession to the popularity of the inflation types mentioned above, it is possible to go on and say that the "type" of inflation involved in the wage-price discussion has come to be known as "wage inflation," "cost inflation," or "sellers' inflation." For a statement of this kind to be worth anything, it is, of course, necessary to take an additional step and explore the meaning of these terms. The next part of this chapter is devoted to this task. Then, at the end of the chapter, a few comments are offered concerning the usefulness of such typologies.[7]

A Framework for Classifying the Origins of Inflation

The easiest way to analyze the meaning of the popular inflation typologies is by constructing a framework into which such distinctions as "cost inflation" versus "demand inflation" can be inserted. The outline of this framework is depicted in Figure 1. For the moment it is convenient to ignore the arrows and concentrate on the main outline which begins with the word "INFLATION."

The first basic distinction to be drawn concerns the nature of the product market within which price increases occur. The total increase in the over-all price index used to measure the extent of inflation can (conceptually, at least) be divided into: (A) price increases which are induced by the appearance of excess demand in markets whose characteristics approximate the requirements of perfect competition; and (B) price increases which occur in the non-perfectly competitive sector of the economy—sometimes referred to as the "administered price" sector. Within the perfectly competitive sector (for reasons

[7] Thus, the two remaining parts of this chapter are addressed primarily to those who desire to grapple with this inflation-type terminology, and who wish to consider the meaning and significance of the various classification schemes currently in use. Readers who have no direct interest in these inflation typologies may want to skip over this material.

THE NATURE AND ORIGINS OF INFLATION

Figure 1

THE ORIGINS OF INFLATION: A FRAMEWORK FOR CLASSIFICATION

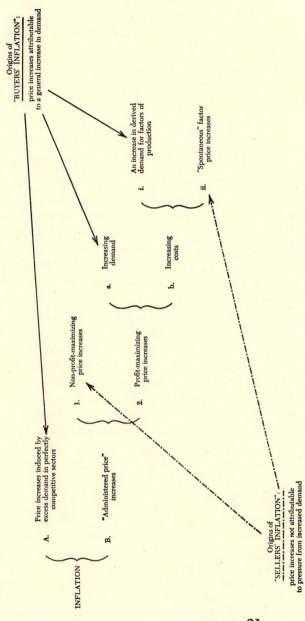

which will be made clear subsequently, it is convenient to include within this sector only those enterprises which both sell and buy in perfectly competitive markets), prices will increase if and only if there is an excess of demand over supply at non-inflationary prices. It is, of course, possible to take an additional step and distinguish between excess demand brought about by a shift in the demand curve and excess demand brought about by a shift in the supply curve. However, this distinction is not of overriding importance for the present discussion, and so, in the interests of keeping Figure 1 relatively uncluttered, we have avoided placing subheadings under A.

Within the "administered price" sector, the situation is sufficiently complex to necessitate three pairs of subheadings. First of all, "administered price" increases can be subdivided into: (1) non-profit-maximizing price increases; and (2) profit-maximizing price increases. The non-profit-maximizing group is meant to include mainly those price increases which stem directly from governmental action rather than from the unaided decisions of private individuals pursuing their own self-interest outside the political arena. This category would include, for example, higher farm prices resulting from higher government supports and higher prices on imported commodities attributable to an increase in tariff barriers. An inflation which originated in one of the above ways might be termed a "governmentally-induced inflation." The non-profit-maximizing category can also include the rather peculiar possibility that private price-setters simply elect to raise prices to the upper limit of their "zone of relative indifference" in the absence of changes in the cost or demand situation.[8]

[8] This possibility has been suggested by Gardiner Means (U.S. Senate, Committee on the Judiciary, Subcommittee on Anti-trust and Monopoly, *Administered Prices; Hearings, Part I*, 85th Cong., 1st Sess., 1957, p. 84). The full quotation from Means is as follows: ". . . With the discretion implicit in administered prices,

Within the private sector, "profit-maximizing price increases" seem much more plausible. Actually, to avoid becoming prematurely embroiled in the debate as to whether firms do or do not seek to "maximize" profits, the designation of this category can be modified to read: "profit-*increasing* price increases." The important point is that price adjustments designed to maximize (or to increase) profits may result from two main sources—and so it is now convenient to make a further distinction between price increases which are attributable to: (a) increasing demand; and (b) increasing costs.

It is at this juncture that the most popular inflation-typology comes to the fore—namely, the "cost inflation" versus "demand inflation" dichotomy. Professors Hart

---

it would be possible to have a rise of prices without a prior increase in the public demand for goods. . . . If there were no excess in buying power, business enterprises could decide to raise their prices within the area of discretion [zone of relative indifference] so as to increase their unit profit margins. This could lead to a considerable rise in the price level without an initial increase in buying power, simply as a result of decisions by price makers to move their prices to the upper margin of their respective areas of discretion. . . . In this manner, the area of discretion implicit in administered prices could lead to creeping inflation without an initial impetus from fiscal and monetary expansion, while fiscal and monetary expansion might serve to maintain employment only at successively higher price levels. I suggest that we could properly call this type of inflation administrative inflation in contrast to the traditional monetary inflation which arises from too much money chasing too few goods." While it is certainly possible that price-setters behave in accord with Dr. Means' hypothesis, it seems rather unlikely that any significant number would do so—and, it is for this reason that this possibility was referred to as "rather peculiar" in the text. After all, why should a firm raise prices in the absence of pressures from either the demand or cost side unless higher prices were simply preferred on per se grounds? And, in view of the public opprobrium which follows price increases, it is hard to believe that businessmen would prefer higher prices on an other-things-being-equal basis.

and Brown popularized this distinction by emphasizing that inflation is a two-sided process, resulting partly from the upward "pull" of demand on prices and partly from the "push" of increasing costs.[9] The present-day acceptance of this dichotomy is illustrated by the following, rather typical, quotation:

> We distinguish, nowadays, two kinds of inflation according to their origin: demand-induced inflation, which is due to an excess of effective demand over supply; and cost-induced inflation, which is due to wage increases, leading in their turn to inflation of prices if the employers succeed in passing the increase in labour costs on to the consumers.[10]

The main criticism to be levied at the cost-demand inflation categorization is that it leaves unanswered—in fact, unasked—the basic question of the origin of cost increases. The important point here is that the demand for labor is a derived demand, and so an increase in the demand for a product may be reflected in the factor markets as an increase in the demand for labor or other factors, and may thus result in higher factor costs which are in turn translated into higher commodity prices.[11]

Consequently, it is necessary to take one additional step and to distinguish between: (i) higher costs attributable

[9] Albert G. Hart and E. Cary Brown, *Financing Defense* (New York: The Twentieth Century Fund, 1951), p. 6. See also Albert G. Hart, *Defense Without Inflation* (New York: The Twentieth Century Fund, 1951), pp. 59-71.

[10] Valentin F. Wagner, "Wage Policy and Full Employment," *The Theory of Wage Determination*, ed., John T. Dunlop (London: Macmillan & Co. Ltd., 1957), p. 89.

[11] It should be remembered that higher factor prices mean increasing costs only if increases in productivity fail to offset increasing factor prices. However, in the interests of simplicity, the productivity consideration is not discussed in this chapter. The significance of productivity movements is examined in considerable detail in subsequent chapters.

to an increase in the derived demand for factors of production, and (ii) higher costs attributable to "spontaneous" factor price increases. The modifier "spontaneous" was originally suggested by Keynes,[12] and is used to encompass all increases in factor prices *not* attributable to an increase in the demand for factors relative to the supply. For instance, if a trade union succeeded in raising wages in spite of unemployment in the firm or industry concerned, this would be a spontaneous factor price increase. It is in this way that "wage inflation" presumably originates.

The individual categories making up the framework to be used in interpreting inflation-types have now all been described. Inflation may originate in any one of the five "terminal" categories—that is, those categories which have no further subdivisions.

It is now time to see how certain of these categories can be grouped together to make composite inflation-types. Professor Lerner's recent distinction between "buyers' inflation" and "sellers' inflation" provides the best starting point. Lerner distinguishes between inflations which result from competition among buyers for goods in which excess demand bids up prices and price increases which result from the pressure of sellers even though they find it hard to sell.[13]

For reasons which will be explained below, it is best to eliminate the phrase "excess demand" from Professor Lerner's schema and instead to speak of "buyers' inflation"

[12] John Maynard Keynes, *A Treatise on Money* (New York: Harcourt Brace, 1930), Vol. I, pp. 167-168.

[13] Abba P. Lerner, "Inflationary Depression and the Regulation of Administered Prices," *The Relationship of Prices to Economic Stability and Growth; Compendium of Papers Submitted by Panelists Appearing before the Joint Economic Committee,* 85th Cong., 2d Sess., 1958, p. 258. [Cited hereafter as: Joint Economic Committee, *Compendium on Prices and Economic Stability,* 1958.]

25

simply as an increase in the price index attributable to the pressure exerted by a general increase in monetary demand. Defined in this way, buyers' inflation may originate in any or all of the three categories indicated by the solid arrows in Figure 1. That is, a general increase in monetary demand (which arises, let us say, from a war-induced increase in government spending) will usually mean an increased demand for the produce of both the perfectly competitive sector and the administered price sector, as well as an increase in the derived demand for labor and other productive factors.

It is now apparent that several other inflation-types listed in the opening paragraph of this section are but sub-types or special cases of buyers' inflation. "Bottleneck inflation," for instance, arises because of a concentration of demand in a particular sector of an economy characterized by imperfect mobility of factors. Similarly, "speculative inflation" of the sort which occurred at the time of the outbreak of the Korean War is nothing but buyers' inflation brought about by a particular set of circumstances—namely, by an increase in demand precipitated by the fear of imminent shortages and price increases.

Turning now to "sellers' inflation," the first point to note is that this brand of inflation cannot originate in the perfectly competitive sector of the economy.[14] The very possibility of a price increase stemming from a source other than excess demand presupposes the existence of monopoly clements in some markets. In an economy characterized by universal perfect competition, no individual

[14] However, this is true only so long as the perfectly competitive sector is defined with reference to the character of competition in *factor* as well as product markets. If the only requirement for membership in this sector were perfect competition in the product market, then a "spontaneous" increase in costs might bring about an upward shift of supply schedules and thus initiate "sellers' inflation."

or aggregate of individuals could exercise the discretion over price movements implicit in the sellers' inflation hypothesis.

Within the non-perfectly competitive area of the economy, sellers' inflation might originate in either of the two categories indicated by the broken arrows in Figure 1. Actually, however, sellers' inflation is usually envisioned as gaining its impetus from "spontaneous" wage increases which exceed productivity improvements.

It is now necessary to say a word about the relationship between the buyers' and sellers' inflation terminology on the one hand, and another important attempt to classify inflations into two broad categories—namely, the "induced"–"spontaneous" dichotomy, which was devised initially by J. M. Keynes, and which has been espoused more recently by Bent Hansen.[15] "Induced" price increases are those called forth by excess demand, whereas "spontaneous" price increases are all others. In essence, there seems to be little or no difference between this distinction and the buyers'-sellers' inflation schema. However, the key phrase used by Professor Hansen in distinguishing between "induced" and "spontaneous" price increases—namely, "excess demand"—can be both troublesome and misleading.

The main difficulty is simply that the concept of excess demand (which is clearly defined in the case of a perfectly competitive market as the difference between the quantity demanded and the quantity supplied at a given price) loses its essential clarity when carried over to imperfect markets. A basic characteristic of price setting under con-

[15] See: Keynes, *Treatise on Money*, 1930, Vol. I, pp. 167-168; Bent Hansen, *Study in the Theory of Inflation*, 1951, p. 15; Bent Hansen, "Full Employment and Wage Stability," *Theory of Wage Determination*, ed. Dunlop, 1957, pp. 76-77; and Bent Hansen, "Fiscal Policy and Wage Policy," trans., R. Spink, *International Economic Papers*, I (1951), p. 69.

ditions of imperfect competition is the absence of a supply schedule, and in such circumstances it is hard to know what *excess* demand means.[16]

A second, closely related, source of confusion is that the excess demand concept can be used in a variety of senses. In the preceding discussion, this phrase has been used solely as a shorthand expression for the supply-demand situation within a perfectly competitive market. However, "excess demand" can also be used in a more aggregative sense to denote a general economy-wide disparity between the purchasing intentions of buyers and the ability of sellers to satisfy these demands.

In spite of these difficulties with the excess demand concept, it is nonetheless true that, in spirit at least, Bent Hansen's distinction bears a very, very close resemblance to Professor Lerner's schema. In a similar vein, the popular division between demand and cost inflation *can* be construed to mean essentially the same thing as the buyers'-sellers' inflation model. All that is necessary is to reserve the phrase "cost inflation" for situations in which rising costs are attributable to "spontaneous" factor price in-

[16] Hansen has made an effort to interpret the concept of excess demand in the context of an imperfectly competitive market. Thus he says: "Such a simple demand-and-supply diagram does not exist when perfect competition does not hold sway, but the concept of excess demand is easily formed, as the difference between the quantity which is in demand and the quantity which is supplied at the price chosen by the monopolist (monopsonist)." (*A Study in the Theory of Inflation*, 1951, p. 3.) However, it is exceedingly difficult to understand how, on this definition, *ex ante* excess demand in an imperfectly competitive market could ever be anything other than zero. This is because at the price chosen by the monopolist the quantity supplied will equal the quantity demanded at that price. The quantity supplied will differ from the quantity demanded (on an *ex ante* basis) only if the price-setter elects to make at least partial use of some non-price rationing or allocation scheme.

creases rather than to the general upward pull of rising demand.

So much for nomenclature. The important point to keep in mind is that the wage-price issue is concerned mainly with the possibility of a slow but steady inflation stemming from "spontaneous" factor price increases rather than from an exogenously inspired increase in aggregate demand. The remainder of this study is devoted to exploring this particular source of inflation and the mechanism by which such factor price increases are alleged to result in a rising commodity price level.

Comments on the Classifications

While à full evaluation of the utility of such distinctions as cost inflation versus demand inflation cannot be attempted here, there are a few general comments which are appropriate at this juncture.[17]

In general terms, the basic shortcoming of the inflation classifications described above is that there are serious and perhaps insurmountable obstacles in the path of anyone who attempts to fit a particular inflation into its proper pigeonhole.

The first and most fundamental difficulty is that there are no known criteria that will enable us to decide how much of any particular price increase represents a contribution to "buyers' inflation" (or "cost inflation") and how much represents a contribution to "sellers' inflation" (or "demand inflation"). The most obvious source of this difficulty is the fact that under conditions of imperfect competition the cost and demand schedules are likely to be quite interdependent. Perhaps a specific illustration will help clarify the significance of this point.

[17] For a more detailed appraisal of such classification schemes plus a suggestion for an alternative approach, see my " 'Cost Inflation' versus 'Demand Inflation': A Useful Dictinction?" *Southern Economic Journal*, January 1960.

Suppose we are concerned with the behavior of a particular unionized industry (such as steel or autos) and observe that between time 1 and time 2 there has been an increase in unit labor costs, prices charged, and quantity sold. Even if we could ignore the very real possibility that a portion of the cost increase was brought on by the increase in demand, it would be exceedingly difficult to decide how much of the price increase was cost-induced and how much was demand-induced.[18] However, the real fun begins when we try to split the cost increase into demand-induced and "spontaneous" components.

Surely no one would deny that both the pressure for wage increases exerted by a union on an employer and the willingness of the employer to accede to this pressure are greatly influenced by the strength of demand in the product market. At the same time, it is equally clear that the size of the resulting change in costs depends not only on the derived demand for labor (and other factors of production) but also on such important additional considerations as the nature of organization on the supplier side of the factor markets. In short, while it is obvious that demand conditions influence costs, it is equally obvious that anyone trying to separate out that portion of the cost increase attributable to increased demand faces a truly Herculean task!

A second, equally serious, drawback of the classification scheme developed above is its failure to pay sufficient attention to what might be called the "index" nature of inflation. That is, at the outset of this chapter, it was em-

---

[18] And the problems here are not solely empirical. Even if the problem of identifying shifts in demand from shifts in costs were solved, the fact that the resultant price change depends not only on the amount the curves shift but also on the *slope* of the curves means that it is impossible to make a neat conceptual distinction between the cost-induced and demand-induced categories. For an elaboration of this point, see my article on inflation types (*Southern Economic Journal*, January 1960).

phasized that the word "inflation" refers to the upward movement of a price index composed of many individual prices and weights. It can be very misleading to think of inflation either as an increase in a single "typical" price or as a uniform increase in a great number of prices. And, once it is recognized that an inflation is the statistical outcome of a number of possibly divergent sorts of price behavior, it is easy to develop a dislike for such all-inclusive and pretentious terms as "cost inflation" and "demand inflation."

It is, of course, obvious that when we try to deal with the plethora of prices that make up an inflation index the difficulties noted above are multiplied accordingly. However, this is by no means the end of the story. The various prices which make up an inflation index are related in diverse ways, and can certainly not be thought of as independent of one another. As a consequence, numerous additional difficulties arise to block attempts to distinguish between "cost inflation" and "demand inflation."

For one thing, a certain cost-induced price increase (assuming, for the sake of argument, that it were possible to make such an identification) may also bring about certain demand-induced price increases via the income side of factor price adjustments. To illustrate, wage increases may raise money incomes as well as costs and so may lead to a bidding up of certain other prices (e.g., food prices) as a direct result of increased demand.

Furthermore, there is apt to be a strong "kick-back" from increases in the cost-of-living index (regardless of their source) to factor price behavior. The existence of formal "escalator clauses" is only the most visible manifestation of the influence which product price movements exert on costs and then back on prices. How second- and third-round price increases of this sort are to be categorized is, to put it mildly, hard to say.

The final, and perhaps most important, way in which

the individual prices which constitute the inflation index are related is via the general monetary environment. Without going into great detail, it is clear that the attitudes and policies of the Federal Reserve constitute an important intervening variable between initial pressures on prices and the ultimate change in the general price level.

As an illustration, let us suppose there is an initial increase in prices in a particular sector of the economy and that we are somehow miraculously able to identify this price pressure as cost-induced. This initial upward pressure on prices can result in (a) an offsetting reduction in other prices; (b) a decrease in output and employment; (c) an upward movement of the whole price level; or (d) some combination of the above. Which of these possible eventualities comes to pass depends not only on certain micro-economic considerations (such as price and income elasticities of demand and the rigidity of costs and prices in the downward direction) but also on the state of the money markets and the policies adopted by the monetary and fiscal authorities. Consequently, it is extremely difficult to see what criteria could possibly serve to divide the eventual change in the over-all price index between the "cost inflation" and "demand inflation" categories.

The main conclusion to be drawn from the foregoing comments is quite clear. The inflation categories described earlier cannot be used as a way of identifying any particular inflationary episode. The reason is simply that these concepts have not been defined in a way that is simultaneously testable and useful. It is this basic inadequacy of the concepts themselves which no doubt explains why, in spite of the great interest in this topic, no one has succeeded in separating any given inflation into its constituent parts.[19] And, given the total absence of any ap-

[19] Two of the more valiant attempts at empirical work in this area have been made by Gardiner Means (see his testimony before the Senate Subcommittee on Antitrust and Monopoly of the Committee on the Judiciary, *Hearings on Administered Prices,*

parent solutions to these basic conceptual difficulties, there is little reason to expect future efforts to meet with better success.

However, the inadequacy of these classifications as a way of labeling inflations does not mean that all attempts to distinguish types of inflation have involved a total waste of resources. Classification schemes of the sort described in this chapter have two important merits. First of all, efforts to classify inflations serve the extremely useful function of forcing us to recognize the existence of a number of potential sources of inflation, and thus warn us against thinking about all inflations in terms of such a narrow conceptual framework as "too much money chasing too few goods." It is certainly important to recognize that, just as "there are unions and there are unions," so "there are inflations and there are inflations"—and that it may be unwise to try to deal with all upward pressures on the price level in the same manner.

Secondly, attention is focused on the modes of wage and price determination which characterize various sectors of our economy. This has the advantage of emphasizing that changes in the price level depend not only on certain broad considerations, such as monetary policy and the temperature of the cold war, but also on the contemporary wage- and price-setting institutions through which variations in aggregate monetary demand are mediated. Consequently, we are encouraged to analyze the inflation problem in micro- as well as macro-economic terms. The remainder of this book represents one attempt to apply this important methodological proposition.

Part I, 1957, pp. 85ff.) and Richard Selden (*Journal of Political Economy*, February 1959, pp. 1-20). However, there are a number of rather obvious and serious shortcomings implicit in the methodology used by both of these authors.

3. THE DILEMMA MODEL OF THE INFLATIONARY PROCESS

In the preceding chapter an attempt was made to define inflation, to classify the various sources of inflation, and to identify the "type" of inflation at the root of the wage-price issue. The task of this chapter is to move from the question of the origins of inflation to a consideration of the nature of the inflationary *process*. As Gardner Ackley has quite properly observed: "Too much of our thinking about inflation has concentrated on how it starts rather than on how it proceeds."[1]

At the outset, it is helpful to note that there exists no generally accepted model of the inflationary process—and that there are good reasons for this void. The basic reason is simply that there is no such thing as *the* inflationary process. Rather, there are a great variety of inflationary processes. And, this is certainly not surprising in light of: (1) the fact that it is impossible to discuss the inflationary process independently of the question of the origins of inflation, and (2) the variety of potential inflation-sources described in the preceding chapter. It seems perfectly reasonable to expect the inflationary process following a substantial increment in defense spending unmatched by rising tax revenues to differ significantly from the train of events following on the heels of a spontaneous increase in costs originating in a specific sector of the economy.

Furthermore, even when the initial impetus is identical, economies (or the same economy at different points of time) may respond in diverse ways if the structure of economic relations within the economies differs significantly. In short, the specific characteristics of any given

---

[1] "A Third Approach to the Analysis and Control of Inflation," Joint Economic Committee, *Compendium on Prices and Economic Stability*, 1958, p. 630.

inflationary process will depend on both the nature of the initial stimulus and the structure of economic relations within the economy at the moment of time when the stimulus is felt. Consequently, the various members of the inflation family should not be expected to resemble each other too closely.

Having made the proper obeisances to the complexity and variety of inflationary processes, it is now time to turn to the main business of this chapter, and to examine in some detail both the nature and the implications of *one* particular model of the inflationary process.

The "Dilemma Model" in General

While it would certainly be improper to minimize the broad scope of the wage-price issue and the wide diversity of approaches to the general question of the inflationary impact of our contemporary wage- and price-setting institutions, it would be equally improper to fail to recognize the strong "central tendency" of at least the theoretical aspects of the discussion. Much of the discussion on all sides of this issue has taken place within a very simple and rather well-defined framework which may be called the "dilemma model." In fact, this basic model has become so familiar that it has found its way into a number of recent economics textbooks as well as into the pages of some newspapers and magazines.

Even though many authors choose to add their own trappings, it is not difficult to describe the skeleton of the "dilemma model." The essence of this model consists of simple assertions about wage determination, cost and price determination, and monetary policy. These assertions can be summarized as follows:

(1) *Wage determination.* The strong unions in our society succeed in raising wages faster than productivity in general can advance.

(2) *Cost and price determination.* The increases in unit labor costs and unit total costs which result from the wage determination process in turn encourage producers to increase product prices.

(3) *Monetary policy.* The monetary authorities are then faced with a difficult choice. If they increase the supply of money by following an "elastic" credit policy they will have "justified" the higher price level and set the stage for yet another increase in unit labor costs and prices. On the other hand, if they try to fight the incipient inflation by preventing the money supply from expanding, at some point a decrease in employment will ensue since businesses and individuals will lack the financial resources necessary to buy all the goods and services available at the higher price level.

This model leads to the conclusion that free collective bargaining, stable prices, and full employment are incompatible. Society must choose among these things and cannot have all three simultaneously. It is for this reason that this formulation of the problem is referred to as the "dilemma model."[2]

Before proceeding further, a word should be said about some of the major variants of this basic dilemma model. In general, there have been two routes taken to the dilemma conclusion. One approach starts with the assertion that wages will increase more rapidly than productivity, and ends with a discussion of the monetary *reaction* to the re-

[2] This model (or some variation) is discussed in many, many writings on the wage-price issue. Perhaps the most succinct and clear statement is: "The Uneasy Triangle," *The Economist*, August 9, 1952, pp. 322-323; August 16, 1952, pp. 376-378; and August 23, 1952, pp. 434-435. For a much more thorough and sophisticated treatment of the various ways in which full employment and price stability can be said to be incompatible, see Bent Hansen, *The Economic Theory of Fiscal Policy*, trans., P. E. Burke (Cambridge, Mass.: Harvard University Press, 1958), especially Chaps. I and XVII.

sultant situation. This, of course, is the approach outlined above. An extreme version of this approach is the assertion of J. R. Hicks that we are now on a Labour Standard. The essence of Hicks' argument seems to be that under the gold standard monetary conditions were "laid down from outside" and the money wage level adjusted itself to this condition. Today, however, the monetary system has become more elastic, so that it accommodates itself to changes in wages rather than the other way around. Thus Hicks says: "It is hardly an exaggeration to say that instead of being on a Gold Standard, we are on a Labour Standard."[3] It should be noted that Hicks' conclusion depends not just on a discretionary monetary system, but on a system sworn to maintain full employment—and able to make good on its promise.

The second main route to the dilemma conclusion has started with either the assumption of a government guarantee of "full employment at whatever cost" or at least an initially high level of employment. From this starting point two paths have been followed. One group has argued that the goals of full employment and price stability are inherently incompatible, quite apart from the existence of strong unions.[4] The argument here is that, in our imperfect and somewhat rigid economy, any approach to full employment will be accompanied by rising prices because of the existence of bottlenecks and the lack of perfect factor mobility.

Another group of writers has also started from the full

[3] "Economic Foundations of Wage Policy," *Economic Journal,* LXV (September 1955), p. 391.

[4] Rees is perhaps the main spokesman for this viewpoint (see his review of Lindblom's *Unions and Capitalism* in *Journal of Political Economy,* June 1950, p. 260). For a more technical discussion of this possibility, couched in terms of the shape of cost schedules, see Alvin H. Hansen, *Monetary Theory and Fiscal Policy* (New York: McGraw-Hill, 1949), pp. 99-114.

37

employment assumption but has *not* by-passed unions en route to the dilemma conclusion. Beveridge, for example, stresses the danger that under a full employment program the bargaining power of unions will be so strong as to force higher and higher labor costs on employers.[5] The key point in this view is that the upward pressure of wages is the *result* of the full employment program rather than of the strength of unions per se.

It is apparent that the existence of these two main routes or approaches to the dilemma conclusion stems from the inter-relatedness of the three aspects or categories of assertions that constitute the basic model—wage behavior, price policies, and the monetary environment. This connectedness is a major source of analytical difficulty in this area and will command considerable attention in the following chapters.

One final variation on the dilemma model must be mentioned before leaving this section. There has been increasing dissatisfaction with the special attention lavished on unions in the basic model, and some authors have suggested that pressure groups in general should be assigned the part customarily played by the trade unions. It is argued that any pressure group, including enterprise monopoly and the farm bloc, could bring about the same result as unions if it were able to force an arbitrary increase in its rate of remuneration.[6]

A Closer Look at the Dilemma Model

The dilemma model serves as the organizational cornerstone for the remainder of the book. Consequently, a some-

[5] Sir William H. Beveridge, *Full Employment in a Free Society* (New York: W. W. Norton, 1945), pp. 43-44.

[6] See Gardiner Means, Senate Subcommittee on Antitrust and Monopoly of the Committee on the Judiciary, *Hearings on Administered Prices*, 1957; and Rees, *Journal of Political Economy*, June 1950.

what closer and more detailed examination of the characteristics and implications of this model constitutes the next order of business.[7] It is hoped that this more careful scrutiny will serve: (1) to provide a clearer understanding of just what the dilemma model is saying and what explicit and implicit assumptions are involved, and (2) to suggest various ways in which the separate assertions which comprise the model are related. It must be emphasized that the following discussion is confined to ferreting out the assumptions and behavior patterns which undergird the dilemma model, and that *no attempt is made to pass judgment on the validity of these assumptions.* Such an evaluation is the task of subsequent chapters.

Since a description of all the variants of the dilemma model described above would be both somewhat repetitious and wasteful of space, the ensuing discussion deals only with the variant in which inflationary pressures originate at the collective bargaining table and are then transmitted throughout the economy via the reactions of firms and the monetary authorities. Needless to say, the decision to describe this variant in no way implies prior acceptance of the thesis that it is the parties to wage determination—and especially the unions—who are in some sense "responsible" for peacetime inflation.

It is convenient to begin by listing some of the more general assumptions about the structure of the economy which are implicit in the dilemma model: (1) The industrial organization of the economy can be thought of as consisting of a single, fully-integrated firm charging a single price for its product and paying a single wage to its employees; (2) the wage is set by collective bargaining between the firm and a single union; (3) the price is set by

[7] The reader who already has an acquaintance with the detailed workings of the dilemma model may wish to skip over this section and proceed directly to the "Comments and Questions Inspired by the Dilemma Model," pp. 53-60.

the unilateral action of the firm; (4) Government economic activity is confined to the exercise of monetary policy by a single monetary authority; and (5) the economy is closed—that is, there are no foreign economic transactions of any sort.[8]

The time has now come to embark on a step-by-step analysis of the development of the dilemma model. At the outset, it is useful to think of the dilemma process as if it were neatly divisible into four chronological stages, each containing a certain number of periods.[9] The reasons for this division and the characteristics of each stage will be explained in due course.

The Dilemma Model: Stage I

At the start of the dilemma process, it is assumed that the economy is enjoying high-level employment and stable prices—and that there are no exogenous forces contributing to any alteration in either the level of employment or prices when the first period begins.

The first event of the first period is the wage negotiation between the union and the firm. The wage determination assertion in the dilemma model reveals the outcome of the negotiation—namely, that wages increase faster than productivity. However, the key word "productivity" has

[8] Other assumptions (in the main, of a more behavioral sort) will be listed as we proceed. It should be noted that not all the assumptions made in this discussion are implicit in the dilemma model in the sense that they are absolutely required by it. In some cases, any one of a group of assumptions would serve equally well. In brief, the purpose of this discussion is to state *sufficient* conditions for the conclusions of the dilemma model, and not all of these conditions are *necessary*.

[9] In the following discussion, the word "period" is used rather loosely to connote a segment of time within a broad "Stage" of the model. In general, a period can be thought of as the length of time between wage negotiations. That is, each wage negotiation begins a new period.

not as yet been defined. Probably the most satisfactory procedure is to follow common usage and define "productivity" as a simple arithmetic ratio in which total output is the numerator and total man-hours worked is the denominator—in brief, productivity equals average output per unit of labor input.

The most obvious and direct result of a wage hike in excess of the improvement in output per man-hour is an increase in the firm's unit labor costs. And, on the *assumption* that labor costs are the sole element in variable costs (as well as in total costs if profit is regarded as a residual rather than as a cost item), it follows that unit variable costs increase in the same proportion as wage increases outstrip productivity gains.

We come now to the price determination hypothesis of the dilemma model. While any number of price policy equations are consistent with the assertion that prices increase when unit costs rise, perhaps the most common assumption is that prices are set by adding a fixed percentage mark-up to unit costs. In the present context, this price-setting formula will grind out a price increase proportionate to the initial increase in unit labor costs.

This brings us to the monetary assertion of the dilemma model. Whereas the wage and price determination assertions were fairly straightforward, the monetary policy assertion promises to be much more troublesome. There are three reasons for this: (1) we are not told what general line the monetary authorities will take, but rather are given a choice between an elastic credit policy and a tight credit policy; (2) we are not told how the monetary authorities carry out whatever decision they arrive at; and (3) we are not told just how whatever mechanism they elect in order to carry out whatever policy they have decided on succeeds in achieving its objective. In short, we are given a large area of discretion and are forced to improvise.

However, before tackling this problem it is necessary to

note that the monetary policy assertion is incomplete in yet another respect. Another special assumption is needed before the banking system's potential refusal to supply more credit is a significant factor in the inflationary process. To understand the nature of this special assumption as well as the general problem of the monetary aspects of the dilemma process, it is necessary to consider the financing problems which arise as a consequence of the initial increase in costs and prices. The root of this financing problem is, of course, that if reductions in employment or output are to be avoided, the economy in general will have to obtain larger transaction balances.[10]

The important point is that this need for higher transaction balances can be met in one of two ways: first, by the drawing down of idle or excess balances currently held at the commercial bank;[11] and, second, by borrowing. The special assumption needed to make central bank monetary

[10] The identity of the specific groups within the economy which initially encounter a financing problem will depend on such considerations as the temporal distribution of receipts and disbursements as well as the speed with which higher prices reach the consumer sector. Suppose, for instance, that the firm responds to the higher labor costs by marking up the prices of goods already produced and in stock as well as goods in process. In this case, higher prices are likely to reach the consumer before higher wages, and so it will be the consumer group that will first encounter a need for larger transaction balances. On the other hand, the firm may attach the price increase only to the units of product which will actually be produced at higher cost. If this happens, it will be the firm that will face a financing problem, since it will have to meet a higher wage bill before realizing the potentially higher gross receipts which may eventually result from the decision to increase prices. At this juncture, it is not necessary to speculate as to which of these possibilities is the more likely.

[11] For the sake of convenience it is assumed that the banking system consists of but a single commercial bank and a single central bank (the latter being charged with sole responsibility for the effectuation of monetary policy).

policy relevant at this stage of the inflationary process is now clear. Whatever group is initially faced with the need for larger transaction balances can *not* have idle balances which it is willing to draw down in order to meet the additional financing requirements. Having added this assumption to our list, let us now return to the task of spelling out the monetary policy assertion of the dilemma model.

The first decision to be made concerns the general tenor or direction of central bank policy. As was noted above, the dilemma model does not supply a uni-directional answer here (as it did in the case of the wage and price determination assertions) but instead provides a choice between two alternatives—an elastic or a tight credit policy—each of which is alleged to have its own consequences, namely, inflation and unemployment, respectively. In the absence of more precise directions, it seems reasonable to assume that the first stage of the dilemma process is characterized by an elastic monetary policy.

During the elastic monetary policy stage (which constitutes Stage I of the model), it is assumed that the central bank permits the commercial bank to finance the higher level of costs and prices. Given this basic assumption, the problems of the manner in which the policy is effectuated and the way in which the firm and union are affected by the actions of the central bank are of lessened significance. The central bank can effectuate its elastic monetary policy by either doing nothing if the commercial bank already has excess reserves, or by providing the bank with additional reserves if this happens to be necessary. As far as the effect on the firm is concerned, an elastic monetary policy, almost by definition, has a minimal effect since it means that credit policy is adapted to the "needs of the trade" or to the preferences of industry.

Our discussion of the behavior of wage-setters, price-setters, and the monetary authorities during the first period of the dilemma model is now complete. However, before summarizing the events which have transpired thus far, it is necessary to comment briefly on one problem which has not been mentioned heretofore. This is the problem of what has been happening on the consumer side of the economy. While the aggregate spending aspects of the inflationary process are assigned little or no role in the usual discussions of the dilemma model, it seems safe to suppose that the proponents of this model do not envision any shortage of aggregate demand arising to check upward movements of wages and prices *so long as the monetary authorities play a permissive role* and do not prevent the money supply from increasing. Hence, let us assume that during the elastic credit stage of the dilemma model all units produced by the firm are sold. The key question is whether or not this assumption is consistent with the rest of the dilemma model.

The only answer to this question is that there is no reason why it cannot be consistent. Two additional assumptions will insure consistency, and at this stage of the discussion assumptions are cheap. First, assume the existence of a sort of Say's Law economy in which people as consumers plan to spend the entirety of their incomes on the single composite product available. Second, assume that profit recipients expect an income during the period equal to the expected rate of profit per unit of product multiplied by the number of units they plan to produce, and also that the profit recipients are willing and able to finance their consumer purchases from preexisting balances until their profits start to arrive.

Given these two assumptions, it follows that the dollar volume of intended spending (aggregate monetary demand) will be exactly equal to the dollar value of the goods produced during the period (aggregate supply). This is because in the simple model under discussion here, aggregate demand and aggregate supply are just two different ways of looking at total income. The dollar volume of spending equals the sum of worker and profit income—and this sum must equal the dollar value of output since the price per unit consists solely of wage cost per unit and profit per unit.

Thus far our discussion has centered on but a single period of the dilemma process—the first period of Stage I. During this period, the wage rate increased more rapidly than productivity, and the firm responded by raising its price to compensate itself for the higher wage costs. The promise of higher costs and prices required the private sector to seek additional funds from the banking system; and, since the central bank elected to follow an elastic credit policy, this need for additional financing was met by the extension of new loans. All goods produced during the period were sold, and there was no change in the number of man-hours worked. The money incomes of both workers and profit recipients increased in proportion to the increase in the money wage, whereas the real incomes of both groups increased only in proportion to the improvement in output per man-hour.

This brings us to the second period of the dilemma process. Again, the wage negotiation is the first item on the agenda. Since the employment situation is unchanged and since the attempt of the workers in the previous period to secure a larger share of the real national product was frustrated by the subsequent price rise, it is likely that the union will again press for wage increases in excess of productivity gains. And, if the workers were able to make good their demands in the first period, it is reasonable to expect them to enjoy an equal measure of success this time, especially since the firm sustained no ill effects as a consequence of granting the previous wage increase. Hence, it is assumed that the union again succeeds in negotiating a wage increase in excess of the productivity gain. Since there is no reason to suppose that the firm will

45

suddenly abandon its cost-plus pricing formula, prices will again go up. And, since the monetary authorities are assumed to pursue an "easy" money policy throughout Stage I, no difficulty is encountered in financing the higher level of wages and prices. Assuming that the above assumptions concerning the spending habits of the community continue to hold, the same level of employment will be maintained and all output produced will be sold. Thus, the events of the second period closely parallel the events of the first period, and happenings in the subsequent periods of Stage I can be expected to follow this same pattern.

The elastic credit stage of the dilemma model can now be characterized as follows: wages and money incomes rise at the same percentage rate per period; productivity and prices rise at somewhat slower rates; employment is maintained at the initial level; and there is no change in the distribution of real income as both real wage and real profit income rise at the same rate as productivity. In short, the elastic monetary policy stage is characterized by steady inflation but no unemployment, with the excess of wage increases over productivity gains as the parameter determining the rate of inflation.

The Dilemma Model: Stage II

The first period of Stage II begins just as the preceding periods. The wage negotiation takes place, and the bargainers—having had no trouble with the monetary authorities thus far—agree on a wage adjustment which exceeds the improvement in output per man-hour. Unit costs thus increase, and prices are then raised according to the dictates of the cost-plus pricing formula.

However, when the private sector turns to the banking system for assistance in financing the higher level of wages and prices, a new element is injected into the trend of events. For the first time the firm experiences difficulty in obtaining the desired funds. After watching prices climb steadily throughout Stage I, the central bank has finally decided that the time has come to combat this inflation by the only means available to it in the present model— namely, by exerting pressure on the reserve position of the commercial bank, thereby limiting the amount of funds that the commercial bank can lend.

Suppose that the central bank operates on the commercial bank's reserve position so as to prevent the commercial bank from increasing its loans beyond the level reached at the close of the previous period (the last period of Stage I).[12] The effect of the central bank's anti-inflationary program (regardless of its precise characteristics)[13] is, of course, to prevent either the firm from financing the newest increment to its wage bill or the consumer sector from purchasing all the available output at the

[12] At this juncture, it should be noted that this restriction on the commercial bank's ability (or willingness) to extend credit may have occurred as a consequence of any number of possible "operations" by the central bank, ranging from an increase in the reserve requirement to a simple refusal to supply additional reserves to the commercial bank. This latter, "do-nothing," measure would have the desired effect if, at the close of Stage I, the commercial bank were completely "loaned up" in the sense that any excess reserves it might have possessed at the start of the inflationary process had by now been exhausted. The important point illustrated by this possibility is that the central bank's intent cannot always be deduced from its overt actions—what it deliberately chooses not to do can be equally as important as what it does. What may appear to be a passive policy may in actuality represent a strong, positive program. For a lengthy discussion of this problem of determining the intended policy of the monetary authorities from their overt actions, see Robert V. Roosa, *Federal Reserve Operations in the Money and Government Securities Markets* (New York: Federal Reserve Bank of New York, 1956), especially pp. 100-105.

[13] Throughout this chapter the possibility and significance of higher interest rates are neglected.

higher prices. Consequently, something has got to give—and, in the simple model being considered here, that something is the volume of employment. If it was the firm which was unable to obtain the needed funds, then there will be a direct reduction in man-hours worked as the firm endeavors to bring its wage bill down to the size that can be financed.[14] If it was the consumer sector that was unable to obtain needed funds, there will first be a reduction in demand and then a cut in employment.

This reduction in hours worked will, in turn, bring about a reduction in worker income, in the number of units of product produced, and thus in total profit income as well (since profit per unit is rigidly fixed by the cost-plus pricing convention). The key question is what effect these happenings will have on behavior in subsequent periods. In the most general terms, the future course of events will depend on the interaction between the wage and price determination hypotheses on the one hand and monetary policy on the other. Unfortunately, the dilemma model fails to provide any clear guidance at this juncture.

Let us assume that for a few periods at least (or, more specifically, throughout the remainder of Stage II) the change in atmosphere brought about by the addition of unemployment and reduced real incomes to the inflationary process does not alter the wage and price determination processes at all. The same wage and price determina-

---

[14] At this point it is appropriate to anticipate our later discussion of the monetary policy assertion to the extent of noting the rather artificial way in which the impact of a restrictive monetary policy on the spending decisions of the firm is being handled here. In actuality, it is quite likely that monetary restraint impinges most directly on the investment spending of firms rather than on the size of wage bills. However, at the start of our "closer look at the dilemma model," we made the simplifying assumption that the economy contains but a single, fully-integrated firm, which purchases only labor services from the rest of the economy. Consequently, the impact of a restrictive monetary policy must (temporarily) be assumed to fall on the wage bill.

tion formulae continue to grind out inflation at the same steady rate. And, if the monetary authorities persist in their resolve to fight the continuing inflation by maintaining a tight ceiling on the loan potential of the commercial bank, unemployment will continue to grow so long as money wages and prices continue to rise.

Perhaps the most significant observation to be made about this "unyielding" stage of the dilemma model is that what we have here is a model of unemployment *and* inflation rather than either unemployment or inflation without the other. This need not contradict the dilemma conclusion that free collective bargaining will lead to unemployment or inflation—provided that the word "or" does not imply that the two alternatives are mutually exclusive. And, it is certainly true that many discussions of the wage-price issue accept the possibility that inflation and some unemployment can coexist. However, it is also generally agreed that this will not be a peaceful coexistence and that when unemployment reaches some figure, inflation will come to a halt.

Hence, Stage II cannot be regarded as the denouement of the dilemma model since thus far there is no mechanism which either reduces the rate of inflation as unemployment increases or halts price increases altogether when the "critical" amount of unemployment is reached. What the above discussion does do is reiterate the intuitively obvious point that the central bank cannot halt inflation by creating unemployment except insofar as the unemployment itself affects the wage or price determination mechanisms. Thus it is necessary to add a third stage to the dilemma model, in which inflation is halted via the impact of increasing unemployment on wage-price behavior.

The Dilemma Model: Stage III

A detailed consideration of the many ways in which the appearance of unemployment may affect wage and price determination would be inappropriate here, and so is postponed to succeeding chapters. For the present, it is sufficient to make a single, somewhat arbitrary, assumption which is sufficient (though certainly not necessary) to ensure at least a temporary halt to the inflationary process. Suppose that after employment falls to the "critical" level that marks the end of Stage II, wage adjustments cease to exceed productivity gains but advance at the same rate instead.

Unit costs will level off, and—assuming that prices are still set on a cost-plus basis—the steady increase in prices will finally have come to an end. However, if the monetary authorities continue to pursue the tight money policy enunciated in Stage II, joy at the achievement of price stability will be marred by the continuing existence of unemployment. In fact, so long as the money wage increases at all—even though the rate of increase is consonant with the improvement in output per man-hour so that unit labor costs are steady—a fixed amount of employment would require the financing of an ever-higher wage bill. Consequently, if the monetary authorities continue to prevent the financing of a wage bill larger than the one financed at the end of Stage I (that is, if they impose a rigid ceiling on the size of the wage bill), unemployment will not only fail to disappear, but will continue to increase.

Thus the most important thing to note about Stage III is that while the moderation in the magnitude of wage adjustments brought about by unemployment reaching the "critical" point was sufficient to halt inflation and bring stable prices, it was insufficient to prevent the employment situation from worsening. And, since few if any economists have envisioned the dilemma model as culminating in an ever-increasing volume of unemployment, Stage III—like Stage II—must be a transient stage in the development of the over-all dilemma process.

The Dilemma Model: Stage IV

It is easy to conceive of a number of ways in which the dilemma model might develop from the end of Stage III onward. However, since our discussion has already fulfilled its main objective of suggesting sufficient conditions for the emergence of each horn of the dilemma conclusion (namely, inflation, inflation and unemployment, and unemployment alone), and, furthermore, since the instructions supplied by the dilemma model have become increasingly vague and incomplete, it is probably best to be content with a brief general discussion of two of the more obvious routes which the dilemma process might take.

The first, and perhaps simplest, possibility is that after a few periods of price stability the monetary authorities become convinced that they no longer need to keep such a strict reign on the supply of credit and that they should relax credit conditions in an effort to improve the employment situation. Thus it now becomes possible to finance a higher wage bill, and if the monetary authorities permit the commercial bank to increase loans more rapidly than wages are now increasing, the unemployment situation can improve. Of course, when the level of employment falls back below the critical level at which wage increases were modified, wage adjustments may again exceed productivity gains. The course of events from this point on will depend on many considerations, possibly the most important being the relative allegiance of the monetary authorities toward the competing objectives of high-level employment and price stability.

A second possibility, less simple but possibly more intuitively plausible, combines the above monetary policy hypothesis with a different wage determination assumption. After all, it is not unreasonable to suppose that the rate at which wages increase may be reduced still further as unemployment increases. That is, it is likely that wage determination is a more continuous function of the level of employment than implied above, and that wages will not continue to increase even as fast as productivity if unemployment also continues to go up. And, if wages increase at a decreasing rate—or perhaps fail to increase at all or even decline somewhat—the monetary authorities will be able to permit a given volume of employment to be financed with a smaller expansion of commercial bank reserves. Furthermore, prices may even decline somewhat in response to the appearance of idle capacity and reductions in unit labor costs—depending on the rigidity of the cost-plus pricing formula and whether it works in the downward as well as in the upward direction. To the extent that prices do decline, fears of inflation will be lessened and there will be a still greater incentive for an expansionary credit policy.

Of course, if the volume of unemployment declines as the commercial bank increases its loans, relatively higher wages and prices are likely to result; also, as the volume of unemployment declines the central bank may reduce the rate at which it permits the commercial bank to expand credit. And, both of these developments are apt to impede the march to a higher level of employment—in fact, the resurgence of inflationary pressures may prevent the re-attainment of the level of employment enjoyed at the start of the dilemma process.

What we have here is a situation in which the wage rate, the price level, the level of employment, and the volume of bank loans are being mutually determined. And, while it is difficult to say very much about this phase of the dilemma process without a more careful examination of wage, price, and monetary behavior, it can be observed that when (if) the level of unemployment falls back to the initial level the economy will have completed the full dilemma cycle and will be back at the start of Stage I. From here events may again be expected to follow the general path laid out in the preceding discussion of the dilemma model.

Comments and Questions Inspired by the Dilemma Model

Since the ultimate objective of this chapter is not to describe the dilemma model for the sake of description but rather for the sake of evaluation, it is appropriate to conclude this discussion with some comments and questions. The main purpose of the comments is to make some modest contribution toward our over-all understanding of the nature and characteristics of the dilemma approach to the problem of inflation. The purpose of the questions is to provide a focus for the rest of the study.

Organizationally, it is convenient to begin by making a few general observations on the dilemma model. Then, the more specific comments and questions are grouped under the three main assertions which comprise the model —wage determination, cost and price determination, and monetary policy. The main issues falling within each of these categories are in turn explored in Parts II, III, and IV of this book.

A Few General Observations

1. The dilemma model is exceedingly macro-economic in its methodological orientation. In fact, it is every bit as macro-economic as most Keynesian and quantity-theory analyses. The assumptions of a single wage and a single price are indicative of the high level of aggregation which characterizes this model. Discussions of the significance of this macro-economic orientation will occupy much of the remainder of this study.

2. The dilemma model is very loosely formulated. It cannot be over-emphasized that many of the conditions outlined in the preceding discussion are sufficient but not necessary to arrive at the dilemma conclusion. Any number of alternative assumptions would have produced the

same general order of results, although the specific trend of events might have varied considerably. To illustrate, the assumption that the firm maintains a fixed percentage profit margin led to the conclusion that the distribution of income between workers and profit-recipients is unaltered during the dilemma process. If instead it had been assumed that business maintains a constant dollar profit margin, the distribution of income would have moved steadily in favor of labor as the inflation progressed—and yet, the general order of events would not have been radically affected.

3. A rather similar observation is that the dilemma model is incomplete as well as vague. In the preceding discussion it was not only necessary to state more precisely the explicit assumptions of the model, it was also necessary to add a number of new assumptions. The problem of the existence of idle balances in the bank accounts of the firm and consumers, or both, is one illustration. By far the most important example, however, is the matter of the spending or consumption side of the economy. This omission is sufficiently important to merit designation as a separate point.

4. The general statement of the dilemma model concentrates solely on the production side of the economy and completely neglects the income or spending side. While it may be perfectly proper to minimize the separate importance of income and spending considerations, they cannot be ignored altogether and must be handled in some way; consequently, in the preceding discussion, two assumptions were manufactured to do the job. The significance of these assumptions will be discussed subsequently—the important point here is that the wage-price approach can no more neglect the income side of the economic process than the income analysts can neglect wage-price relations.

5. Turning to the wage determination, cost and price determination, and monetary policy assertions proper, it

is significant that all these assertions (and especially the wage and price determination assertions) are of an almost empirical sort. That is, there is little discussion of *why* wages tend to rise faster than productivity or *why* prices are set on a cost-plus basis. This lack of consideration of the factors behind wage and price determination becomes a real problem when we leave Stage I of the dilemma process. As was noted above, the development of later stages depends to a very great degree on the extent to which the appearance of unemployment alters the wage and price determination processes.

6. A closely related point is that the dilemma model contains very little discussion of the inter-relation of the three main assertions. While it is true that there is some consideration of the effect of wage and price determination on monetary policy insofar as these processes determine price level movements, there is almost no consideration of the impact of *forms* of wage and price determination proper on monetary policy. Monetary policy is envisioned as being concerned only with price level changes and not at all with the way these changes happen to come about. Similarly, price and wage determination are treated as independent of the form of one another. Perhaps most significant of all, the impact of monetary policy—both directly and via its effects on the level of employment—receives little or no attention, and yet it is of central importance for the development of the entire dilemma process.

7. In addition to these primarily methodological comments, a single comment on the economic implications of the preceding discussion of the dilemma model seems in order. In contrast to the simple or basic dilemma model, which is couched primarily in terms of the danger of unemployment *or* inflation, the more detailed discussion of this model was much concerned with the problem of unemployment *and* inflation. It is easy to make the tacit assumption that there exists some monotonically falling function

which relates degrees of unemployment and degrees of inflation—and yet the possible existence of a period (Stage II in the preceding discussion) during which inflation continues to increase at the same time unemployment grows suggests that this may be a rather dangerous and misleading assumption.

The Wage Determination Assertion

1. The dilemma model asserts that wages will increase faster than productivity. The central importance of this assertion for the development of the entire inflationary process is evident from the preceding discussion. The basic question to be investigated in the wage determination part of this study is, of course, the validity of this strong and unequivocal assertion. Actually, the word "validity" is not well chosen. It is better to say that the central problem consists of explaining the factors behind the wage determination process and under what circumstances these factors are apt to generate a movement of the general wage level such as to result in an increase in unit labor costs. Of particular interest is the impact of unemployment (or the threat of unemployment) on the magnitude of wage adjustments.

2. The nature of the relationship between wage adjustments and productivity changes also needs to be clarified. It is not clear from the dilemma assertion whether it is assumed that wages will always increase more rapidly than productivity, or whether wages are expected to increase at a relatively constant rate and that this rate is apt to be greater than the rate of increase in productivity. In short, the dilemma model raises, but does not even discuss—much less solve—the issue of whether the wage determination and productivity functions are to be treated as completely independent, or whether wage determination depends on the rate of productivity growth. The importance of this

issue is self-evident. If wage determination is independent of productivity, the course of productivity over time may have a very significant autonomous effect on the entire inflationary process.

3. The dilemma model posits but a single wage and a single method of wage determination. This highly aggregative assumption raises a number of interesting questions. The most basic issue is whether or not the conclusions of the dilemma model need to be modified in the light of: (a) the existence of a number of classes of workers being paid different rates; (b) the possibility that wages are set by different institutional arrangements in various sectors of the economy; and (c) the existence of a number of independent unions negotiating for their own members rather than a single, national union.

The Cost and Price Determination Assertions

1. The first question here is the impact of wage adjustments on unit labor costs and unit total costs. The existence of a less-than-fully-integrated economy, in which firms incur non-labor costs as well as labor costs in the process of producing and distributing a product, threatens the rigid link between wage adjustments and unit costs which characterizes the dilemma model.

2. Turning to price determination, the basic assertion of the dilemma model is that prices are mainly, if not solely, cost determined. In the preceding discussion this assertion was made a bit more precise by the assumption that a fixed percentage profit margin is always maintained. The important questions suggested by this treatment are: (a) Does this cost-plus pricing hypothesis constitute a useful picture of price behavior? (b) Does the cost-plus pricing convention work in the downward as well as the upward direction? (c) What factors might

persuade the firm to alter its profit margin? and (d) What effect will unemployment or excess capacity have on price formation?

3. The dilemma model deals with but a single price and a single method of price determination. Once the existence of more than a single firm is admitted, the possibility of diverse price policies arises, and this potential diversity must be appraised.

The Monetary Policy Assertion

1. As noted above, the monetary policy assertion is the least specific and least clear of the three main assertions which make up the dilemma model. The main source of this imprecision is the tendency of the dilemma model to skip over important intervening steps by describing only the source of the central bank's power (control over the money supply) and the consequences which flow from the exercise of this power (inflation or unemployment depending on the wishes of the monetary authorities). Little or no attention is devoted to the vital subject of the links which transmute the initial monetary policy decision into an alteration in the level of prices and employment.

2. One obvious point highlighted by the preceding discussion of the separate stages which comprise the dilemma process is that the monetary authorities possess no magic wand, and can halt the inflationary process only by affecting the wage and price determination processes. Monetary manipulations clearly cannot halt an inflationary process if there is some wage and price determination mechanism which continues to grind out inflation irrespective of conditions in the labor and product markets. This is the moral conveyed by Stage II of the dilemma process.

3. A more subtle point implicit in the preceding discussion, though not mentioned until now, is that not only must the monetary authorities exercise their influence *via*

the mechanism of wage-price determination, they must influence this mechanism *before* they themselves become discouraged and alter the basic monetary policy. To illustrate, it was assumed in Stage II that the monetary authorities stick to the tight money policy in spite of increasing unemployment so long as inflation continued. In the light of our society's strong desire to maintain high-level employment, this is certainly an assumption of doubtful validity. Suppose that the monetary authorities base their policies on the degree of unemployment as well as on the degree of inflation and that preventing unemployment is adjudged more important than halting a relatively slowly moving inflation. Then it is quite likely that if the wage and price determining mechanisms are not readjusted very soon after the tight money policy is applied (that is, if Stage II lasts very long), the monetary authorities may decide that a tight money policy is not the way to fight this particular inflation since the only effect of such a policy thus far has been to increase the amount of unemployment. Consequently, they may elect to fight this growing unemployment by a policy of monetary ease, and so the economy may move directly from Stage II back to Stage I again—and, in this case, unabated inflation would be the result. The significant point is that this outcome depends not only on the direction of the impact exerted by unemployment on the wage-price determining institutions and on the monetary authorities, but also on the *time* it takes for this impact to be reflected in specific decisions. It is not enough to know, for example, that the rate at which wages move upward will be moderated by a certain amount of unemployment. It is also necessary to know how quickly it will be moderated—for, if the moderation process is too slow, moderation itself may never occur.

4. The question of *how* monetary policy exerts an impact on price and employment decisions still remains to be considered. More specifically, it is necessary to ask: (a)

59

How closely can the monetary authorities control price level movements and the volume of employment by the simple expedient of imposing a ceiling on commercial bank reserves? (b) To what extent are increases in velocity apt to offset the restrictive actions of the central bank? (c) Is it reasonable to think of employment decisions as being governed by the firm's inability to finance a higher wage bill? (d) What difference does it make if credit is rationed by rising interest rates rather than by non-price means? and (e) Is it reasonable to suppose that unemployment can be quickly eliminated by increasing the expansionary potential of the banking system?

5. Closely related to the question of the *modus operandi* of monetary policy is the question of the significance of the special assumptions made about the spending or consumption side of the economy in the preceding discussion. It is certainly necessary to ask if elimination of the assumption that all income is immediately spent on a single composite consumer commodity would alter both the way in which monetary policy works and the development of the inflationary process in general. The course of events might well be altered by the introduction of: (a) a private investment component of spending; (b) the possible existence of a money illusion; and (c) a real-balance effect.

6. Finally, it is necessary to note that the dilemma model conceives of the monetary authorities as the sole representatives of government economic policy. The addition of a broader type of government—complete with expenditure programs, a budget, and a tax system—might have a significant effect on the development of the inflationary process. In particular, it is necessary to appraise the possibility and potential consequences of a "full employment guarantee" supported by a willingness on the part of the government to use an expansionary fiscal policy to achieve its ends.

PART II
The Wage Determination Assertion

4. INTRODUCTION AND GENERAL APPROACH TO WAGE THEORY

The discussion of the dilemma model contained in the preceding chapter provides the organizational framework for the remainder of this study. It is now time to start filling in this framework by examining the sets of assertions which comprise the dilemma model. And, it is convenient to begin with the wage determination assertion—namely, that wages will increase faster than productivity for the economy as a whole. More specifically, the task of the next few chapters is to suggest answers to the questions in this wage determination area which were raised by our brief inquiry into the characteristics of the dilemma model. Thus, our main objective is to explain the factors behind the wage determination process and circumstances under which these factors are apt to generate a movement of the general wage level such as to result in an increase in unit labor costs.

It is, of course, obvious that we cannot reach a final conclusion as to the likelihood of wage increases in excess of productivity gains without extensive empirical analysis. However, a necessary preliminary to efficient statistical work on this assertion is an appreciation of the significant variables and the manner of their interaction. It is to this limited but essential task that Part II of this study is addressed. Thus, our present objective is *not* quantitative conclusions. It is rather the theoretical understanding which constitutes the essential first step toward meaningful empirical analysis.

Organizationally, it is useful to begin by describing the general approach to wage theory used throughout Part II. Then, in subsequent chapters, an attempt is made to apply this approach to the questions involved in the wage determination assertion of the dilemma model.

In searching for a useful approach to the theory of money wages the first thing to be decided is the appropriate degree of aggregation. The general point of view adopted here is that it is best to begin with an analysis of individual wage-setting units, and then to see what additional factors must be considered in moving to an analysis of the general wage level. This preference for starting with small building blocks is most certainly not based on the view that a macro-economic theory of money wages is in some sense "impossible."[1] It is based instead on the conviction that trying to start from a macro-economic vantage point has three rather severe disadvantages.

First of all, it is not clear that in all circumstances we should be interested in the movements of some general wage index to the exclusion of the components of the index. Consequently, there are advantages in building up an aggregate wage theory from smaller parts which can themselves be used if the occasion arises. Secondly, any macro-economic theory of money wages must be based on some conception of micro-economic wage theory. Consequently, it would seem reasonable to commence work at the macro-economic level if and only if a generally accepted micro-economic theory of wage determination already exists— and, as is well known, such is not the case. A third, closely-related, disadvantage of starting at the macro level is that, given the present nebulous state of micro-economic wage theory, the resultant macro-economic formulations are not likely to be "rigid" or "tight" enough to supply answers to questions such as the likely effect of changes in productivity, profitability, and employment on wage behavior.[2]

[1] A paper by Sidney Weintraub ("A Macroeconomic Approach to the Theory of Wages," *American Economic Review*, XLVI, December 1956, pp. 835-856) provides a good illustration of how one can surmount certain difficulties involved in deriving determinate labor demand and supply functions.

[2] J. Pen ("Wage Determination Revisited," *Kyklos*, Vol. XI, Fasc. 1, 1958, p. 5) makes much the same point when he sug-

If the advisability of starting at the micro-economic level be granted, the next question is the most profitable mode of attack at this level. The approach adopted in this study is admittedly and unashamedly declared to be eclectic. And, perhaps the best way of describing the general outlines of this approach is to indicate very briefly its kinship to three prevalent ways of looking at the wage determination problem: (1) the marginal productivity theory; (2) the informal bargaining theories; and (3) the formal bargaining theories.[3]

The present approach borrows from the marginal productivity theory in that an attempt is made to incorporate

---

gests that the neoclassical attempts to rehabilitate the money wage level via the impact of rising wages and prices on the interest rate and on real balances suffer not so much from logical difficulties as from an inability to say very much about the elasticities involved. This article by Pen contains a very good review of recent developments in wage theory, with special emphasis on the reasons for the lack of consensus.

[3] Space does not permit either a full description or a full evaluation of these alternative approaches to wage theory. The marginal productivity theory and the main objections to the use of this theory in the labor field are sufficiently well known to render additional comment unnecessary. For a good analysis of the marginal productivity theory, see Allan M. Cartter, *Theory of Wages and Employment* (Homewood, Illinois: Richard D. Irwin, 1959), Part I. The category labeled "informal bargaining theories" is meant to include those wage theories which proceed by appraising the factors affecting union and company "bargaining power" without recourse to mathematical exposition. For a review of the use made of the bargaining power concept by various authors, see Neil W. Chamberlain, *Collective Bargaining* (New York: McGraw-Hill, 1951), pp. 213-238. The "formal bargaining theories" group is meant to include writings which do make use of mathematics to develop a rather precise framework within which to explain the outcome of negotiations. For a synthesis of certain formal bargaining theories, see Harvey M. Wagner, "A Unified Treatment of Bargaining Theory," *Southern Economic Journal*, XXIII (April 1957), pp. 380-397.

the factors behind the marginal revenue productivity curve into the analysis; it borrows from the informal bargaining theories in that it deals with collective bargaining as well as with unilateral employer wage-setting and tries to appraise the impact of various economic factors on the wage policies and bargaining positions of the employer and the workers; and, finally, it borrows from the formal bargaining theories in that an attempt is made to organize the factors affecting wage decisions into a fairly systematic framework.

The approach adopted here also differs to some extent from each of the three prevalent approaches: it is based on a broader concept of management aims than is the marginal productivity theory; it is more concerned with the weighting of factors and the interactions among various wage-determining factors than are many informal bargaining theories; and, the present approach is considerably less "complete," less "universal," and less abstract than the formal bargaining theories.

In somewhat more specific terms, the approach employed throughout Part II is based on the following reasoning. First of all, it seems reasonable to start out by examining the significance of changes in certain rather "identifiable" economic factors such as productivity, the excess demand for labor, the cost of living, profitability, and "other" wages. The main justification for taking this tact is that many of the most important questions germane to the wage determination aspects of the dilemma model concern the likely impact of changes in these factors. Secondly, the fact that in our economy there is more than a single mode of wage determination requires that we also appraise the effect of various institutional considerations (such as the nature of organization on the supplier side of the market) on the magnitude of wage adjustments. Finally, it is necessary to recognize that we dare not content ourselves with an appraisal of each of the above factors on a partial differentiation or once-at-a-time basis. This is because wage-determining factors interact in diverse ways—and, this interaction reduces the usefulness of simply listing the change in the wage rate between two points of time as an unspecified function of these factors and requires instead that we examine the significance of the factors *in combination*.

As a consequence of this methodological orientation, Part II is organized as follows. Chapters 5-7 contain an appraisal of the role of certain specific economic factors in the wage-setting process. Chapters 8 and 9 discuss the significance of certain institutional considerations, including unionization. Then, in Chapter 10, an attempt is made to draw together our analysis of wage determination in the individual firm by considering the way in which these various wage-determining factors interact. Finally, in Chapter 11, we turn our attention to the problem of changes in the general wage level and see to what extent our analysis of wage determination in the individual firm must be modified when applied to this broader question.

5. Economic Factors in the Wage Determination Process: Productivity

Since the over-all objective of this part is to examine the validity of the dilemma assertion that wages will increase more rapidly than productivity, it is fitting that we commence our discussion of the factors affecting the wage determination process with an analysis of the role that the rate of productivity growth per se plays in determining the magnitude of wage adjustments.[1]

As was emphasized in Chapter 3, the wage determination assertion of the dilemma model is extremely vague as to the nature of the relationship between wage adjustments and productivity movements. It is not clear whether it is assumed that wages will always increase more rapidly than productivity, or whether wages are expected to increase at a relatively constant percentage rate, and that this rate is apt to be greater than the rate of increase in productivity. In short, the dilemma model implicitly raises the important issue of whether the wage determination and productivity functions are to be treated as largely

[1] The over-all topic of wage-productivity relations encompasses a number of questions, including: (a) What is "productivity"? (b) What is the optimum wage-productivity relationship? (c) How significant a determinant of the magnitude of actual wage adjustments is the rate of productivity growth? (d) What factors determine the actual relationship between wage adjustments and productivity growth during any given period? and, (e) What are the consequences of various wage-productivity relationships for the level of prices and employment throughout the economy? In this chapter our primary concern is with question (c). However, questions (a) and (b)—the problems of defining productivity and selecting a normative or optimum wage-productivity relationship—must also receive some attention insofar as they themselves are relevant to the basic question of the significance of productivity in the wage-setting process. Question (d) is the subject of this entire wage determination part of the study. Question (e) forms the subject matter of Part III.

independent, or whether the magnitude of money wage adjustments depends in some way on the rate of productivity growth. The importance of this issue is almost self-evident. To the extent that wage determination is independent of changes in output per man-hour, the course of productivity over time may have a very significant autonomous effect on the entire dilemma process.

Definition and Determinants of "Productivity"

Before the question of the significance of productivity movements for the wage adjustment process can be discussed properly, it is necessary to examine carefully the meaning of this word "productivity" and the various factors which can affect its rate of growth. Unfortunately, "productivity" seems to be a charter member of that class of words in the English language which mean all things to all people—and this semantic difficulty has been an important contributor to the general failure of communication which has characterized much of the wage-price discussion.

In our earlier examination of the dilemma model, "productivity" was defined as the number of units of output produced during a period divided by the number of man-hours worked during the period—that is, "productivity" equalled output per man-hour.[2] To appreciate the difference between this definition and other definitions as well as to appraise the significance of these differences for the wage determination process, it is convenient to divide our discussion into two parts and to consider labor productivity first from the standpoint of the individual firm and

[2] The word "productivity," when unmodified, usually refers to some relationship between an index of output and an index of input. Labor services are generally used as the index of input and, when this is done, the resulting measure is sometimes named "labor productivity." Whenever, throughout this study, the word "productivity" appears unmodified, it should be assumed that we are talking about output in relation to the labor input.

69

then from the standpoint of the economy as a whole.

In their expositions of the factor-purchase aspect of the theory of the firm, economic theorists have often distinguished four productivity concepts: average gross productivity, marginal gross productivity, average net productivity, and marginal net productivity. These four productivity functions for the labor service factor of production are illustrated below.

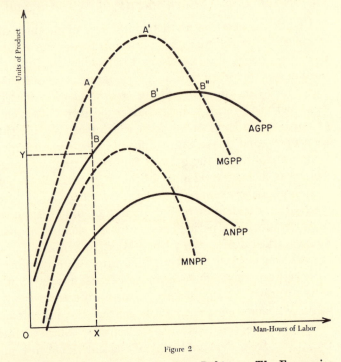

Figure 2

Figure 2 has been copied from: Joan Robinson, *The Economics of Imperfect Competition* (London: Macmillan & Co., Ltd., 1954 printing of 1933 edition), p. 246. However, a few modifications have been added to her original figure.

The *average gross physical productivity* curve (*AGPP*) represents the average amount of output per man-hour per period. It is the total output divided by the number of man-hours worked. *Marginal gross physical productivity* (*MGPP*) is the increment of output which results from combining an additional man-hour of labor with the optimal additions to other factors and bears to average gross physical productivity the ordinary relationship of marginal to average value. *Average net physical productivity* (*ANPP*) is average output per man-hour less the average cost (in terms of units of product) of other factors employed per man-hour. *Marginal net physical productivity* (*MNPP*) is the net increment of output which results from employing an additional man-hour of labor; it is the marginal gross physical productivity resulting from combining an additional man-hour with the optimal addition to other factors, less the addition to the cost (in terms of units of product) of the other factors.[3]

It is now obvious that the productivity ratio employed in the formalized dilemma model represents *one point* on the *AGPP* curve. In short, what we have thus far loosely called "productivity" is really the average gross physical productivity of labor. For example, in Figure 2, *OY* is the average gross physical productivity of labor when *OX* man-hours are worked.

Now that we have a more precise definition of productivity, it is time to consider the various ways in which the productivity increases which were discussed throughout our exposition of the dilemma model can come about and to consider the significance of these alternative sources of

[3] This description is adapted from Joan Robinson, *Economics of Imperfect Competition*, 1933, p. 239. It differs from Mrs. Robinson's terminology in that we are talking in terms of physical units of output while she is talking in terms of dollars of revenue. This general treatment differs from the usual discussion of marginal physical product found in introductory economic textbooks (for example, Samuelson, *Economics*, 1958, pp. 501-521) in that it permits the firm to vary other factors along with the labor input.

growth in the productivity ratio. It is essential to distinguish at the outset between the two general ways in which an increase in the output per man-hour ratio can come about: first, an increase in the productivity ratio can result from a movement *along* the average gross physical productivity curve towards its maximum (that is, a rightwards movement from B towards B'') ; second, an increase in the productivity ratio can be brought about by an upward shift in the entire $AGPP$ curve.

A change in the productivity ratio resulting from a movement *along* the $AGPP$ curve is attributable to a change in the scale of operation of the firm. The importance of volume as a determinant of short-term changes in output per man-hour cannot be disputed.[4] The reluctance of many managements to lay off workers in response to cut-backs in orders that are expected to be mild or temporary may well serve as an important source of upward pressure on the unit labor cost ratio whenever output declines.

An increase in the productivity ratio resulting from an upward shift of the entire $AGPP$ curve may be attributable to any number of factors including: (1) an improvement in the skill and effort of the workers themselves; (2) an increase in the number of machines or an improvement in the quality of the machines; (3) an improvement in the quality of raw material; (4) an increase in the quantity or improvement in the quality of the managerial input; and (5) other general improvements in technology, such as the discovery of a more efficient way to organize production. In short, as has been emphasized by many people, improvements in "labor productivity" (in the sense of output per man-hour of labor) cannot be attributed solely to the labor input itself, but may be due to any one of a whole complex of factors.

[4] See Jules Backman, *Steel Prices, Profits, Productivity, and Wages* (New York: Public Relations Department, United States Steel Corporation, 1957), p. 2.

The importance of distinguishing among the above sources of an increase in output per man-hour is that for many purposes we are not interested in output per man-hour per se, but are more interested in one of the other three productivity functions—and the relationship between an increase in the output per man-hour ratio and these other productivity measures depends on the source of the initial increase as well as on the shape of the curves.

Dealing first with the relationship between the average gross physical productivity curve and its marginal, it can be seen from Figure 1 that an increase in output per man-hour need not mean that marginal gross physical productivity has also increased. For example, as we move from B' towards B'', $AGPP$ is increasing but $MGPP$ is decreasing.[5] Thus, even if an increase in volume increases $AGPP$, we cannot be sure $MGPP$ has also increased.

[5] For a rigorous demonstration of this proposition, see Karl Menger, "The Laws of Return, A Study in Meta-Economics," *Economic Activity Analysis*, ed., Oskar Morgenstern (New York: Wiley, 1954), pp. 419-481. Menger has proven that an increase or decrease in either an average or marginal value need not imply that the other value is also increasing or decreasing. Albert Rees, in his doctoral dissertation, "The Effect of Collective Bargaining on Wage and Price Levels in the Basic Steel and Bituminous Coal Industries, 1945-1948" (unpublished Ph.D. dissertation, Dept. of Economics, University of Chicago, 1950, p. 52, cited hereafter as Rees, thesis, 1950), also recognized that marginal productivity could be falling while average productivity is rising. However, his discussion of the relationships seems unclear. Rees writes: "Average productivity is affected by all the factors which affect output, of which the skill and effort of workers is only one. Hence the marginal productivity of labor could be falling while output per man-hour was rising. In practice, this is probably not typical. Increases in the quantity of capital per worker and improvements in technology usually require increased skill and responsibility on the part of workers, so that in general, average and marginal productivity would be expected to move in the same direction." The basic difficulty with Rees' discussion is that it fails to distinguish between net and gross pro-

The relationship between the average gross physical productivity curve and the average *net* physical productivity curve is even more uncertain since here we have no marginal-average relationship to fall back on. Considering first an increase in the output per man-hour ratio as a consequence of .an increase in the volume of operations, average net physical productivity can either increase, decrease, or stay the same as the result of such a movement along the *AGPP* curve. As the number of man-hours of labor employed increases, it is likely that the expenditure on other factors (especially raw materials) will also increase—however, it does *not* follow from this that the increase in the average net productivity of labor must be less than the increase in the average gross productivity, since the expenditure on other factors *per man-hour* may have fallen even though total expenditures on other factors have risen. It is quite likely that a given increase in employment will result in a greater proportionate increase in the average net productivity of labor than in the average gross productivity, since the cost of the fixed co-operating factors such as plant and machinery can be spread over more units of labor service, while the amount of other variable factors required (such as raw materials) is not likely to increase more rapidly than the labor input.

When the increase in *AGPP* is the result of an upward shift in the entire *AGPP* schedule with the number of man-hours worked unchanged, it is still more difficult to predict the change in average net productivity that will accompany such an increase. It is possible that the *ANPP* schedule would rise only slightly (or conceivably not at all) in response to an upward shift in the *AGPP* curve. For example, a significant increase in expenditure on raw materials and machinery per man-hour might raise the output per man-hour ratio considerably but have almost no

ductivity *and* between the average and marginal values of each of these concepts.

effect on the average net physical productivity schedule. On the other hand, an upward shift in the gross physical productivity schedules could result in a greater proportionate shift in the net physical productivity schedules if the initial increase in output per man-hour were the result of an organizational insight that was costless to the company. In short, the various factors listed above that can lead to an upward shift in the *AGPP* schedule differ considerably in their cost to the firm, and the less the non-labor cost of the particular productivity improvement, the greater will be the rise of the net productivity schedules relative to the gross productivity curves.

Finally, for the sake of completeness, it should be pointed out that the marginal net physical productivity of labor need not increase just because the average net physical productivity has risen. Thus we can see that it is exceedingly difficult to translate any given change in the output per man-hour ratio into a change in marginal net physical productivity—a priori we cannot even be sure of the direction of the change, much less of the magnitude.

Thus far our analysis has run solely in terms of the productivity concepts relevant to the individual firm. However, much of the discussion of wage-productivity relationships has also been carried on in terms of a "national" or economy-wide productivity figure and so we must now turn our attention to the characteristics of this over-all productivity ratio. Our formal definition of the unmodified word "productivity" need not be altered as we move from the realm of the firm to the economy as a whole: "productivity" still is the ratio of output to units of labor input or, more simply, output per man-hour. However, it is no longer possible to identify this definition with a point on a familiar curve of economic theory. As Steiner has emphasized vehemently, an aggregate statistical measure of productivity should be thought of as a simple arithmetic *ratio* of two variables—output and employment—rather than as a single autonomous variable in its own right.[6]

The problems involved in constructing an economy-wide index of productivity are almost legendary, and need not be recapitulated here.[7] For our present purposes it is sufficient to note that, as in the case of the productivity ratio for the individual firm, there are a number of ways in which this national output per man-hour figure might be increased: (1) we could import more raw materials and machines and thus produce more with the same number of men; (2) if the denominator of the productivity index includes just hours of manual labor, we could increase the number of non-manual employees and get an increase in output via this route; (3) output can increase as a result of our having more or better machinery at our disposal in this period than in previous periods, and this in turn might be the result of a distribution of labor in the previous periods such that more machinery was produced than wore out—that is, net investment took place; (4) output might increase because of technological improvements which do not require additional net investment; (5) output per man-hour might increase as a result of over-all changes in the economy's level of operation comparable to the movement along the $AGPP$ curve by the individual firm towards a higher point; and (6) productivity can increase simply as a consequence of changes in the general product mix.

While it is not possible to analyze all these various sources of an increase in the productivity ratio in terms of

[6] Peter O. Steiner, "The Productivity Ratio: Some Analytical Limitations on Its Use," *Review of Economics and Statistics*, xxxii (November 1950), p. 328.

[7] A lengthy discussion of the statistical problems involved in constructing an economy-wide productivity index is to be found in: U.S. Congress, Joint Economic Committee, *Productivity, Prices and Incomes*, 85th Cong., 1st Sess., 1957, pp. 5ff.

their effect on specific productivity functions, as was done in the case of the individual firm, it should be noted that these sources of productivity increase do differ among themselves as to cost for the economy as a whole. An increase in output per man-hour attributable to a single brilliant insight may be tantamount to an almost equivalent increase in goods and services available for distribution to the populace, whereas an increase in the productivity ratio achieved by importing more raw materials may mean little if any increase in the real disposable income of the community. Thus, in the case of changes in the productivity ratio for the economy as a whole, there does seem to be a distinction to be made that is roughly analogous to the distinction between gross and net productivity for the individual firm.

Productivity as a Determinant of the Magnitude of Wage Adjustments

Now that we have examined alternative productivity concepts and the various sources of productivity increases, it is time to turn our attention to the basic question of the significance of productivity increases for wage-setting. More specifically, the central problem here is the extent to which wage adjustments in a particular firm are functionally dependent on the trend of: (1) average gross physical productivity in the particular firm; and (2) output per man-hour in the economy as a whole.

The Likelihood of a Direct Link Between Productivity and Wage Determination

It seems appropriate to begin this discussion with a brief analysis of the likelihood that productivity improvements will have a *direct* effect on the magnitude of wage adjustments. At the outset it is necessary to reiterate that while there has been considerable discussion of productivity as a wage determination "principle," much of this discussion is not directly relevant to our present problem because it deals with normative rather than descriptive aspects of the wage-productivity relationship. The question of the *desirability* of gearing wages to changes in some productivity index is, of course, quite distinct from the question of the *de facto* impact of productivity changes on the wage-setting process.

In an examination of the actual relationship between productivity and wage adjustments, perhaps the first point to be made is that there is little or no likelihood that the negotiators themselves will agree to accept productivity changes as a binding governor of wage adjustments. There are a number of good reasons why neither the union nor the company is likely to agree to this kind of arrangement. The most obvious reason is simply that both institutions want to do as well for themselves in the wage determination area as they can and that there are times when adherence to a productivity formula would not satisfy this institutional imperative.

A second good reason is that neither unions nor employers are in agreement with the general principle that wages should vary precisely with changes in output per man-hour. The unions cannot accept this principle without accepting the existing distribution of income as equitable, and this they are not willing to do.[8] Also, there is the

[8] For example, the United Steelworkers of America (*Facts on Steel: Profits, Productivity, Prices and Wages,* 1956 [reprinted as an exhibit in: U.S. Congress, Joint Economic Committee, *January 1957 Economic Report of the President; Hearings,* 85th Cong., 1st Sess., 1957, p. 211]) assert: "It is now commonly accepted that, over long periods, wage gains and rising living standards must come largely from increased productivity, i.e., rising output per man-hour. With this concept the Union has no quarrel as long as one prior condition is met—namely, that the

argument that there are still many workers whose wages are below the decency level and that this situation must be rectified regardless of productivity movements.[9]

Employers are also reluctant to accept the productivity principle since they feel that the workers have no inherent right to productivity increases that have been brought about by such factors as better management or increased capital investment. Rees noted in his study of the steel and coal industries that companies like to stress the concept of "employee performance rates," which supposedly measures changes in output per man-hour due only to changes in employee skill and effort.[10]

Thirdly, Professor Kerr has argued rather convincingly that productivity increases in general do not directly generate strong pressures on either party. This is especially true in the case of the union. The essence of his argument is that statistics are hard to get, not available quickly, and difficult to interpret when available. The fact that productivity changes irregularly from plant to plant and from industry to industry makes it difficult for the union to argue for uniform wage adjustments in line with productivity advances. And, perhaps most important of all, "union members and unorganized workers alike do not press overly much for quick matching of wages to productivity when the latter is moving up, since this movement has little effect on their daily lives."[11] However, it is necessary to amend Professor Kerr's argument to take account

income shares as between management and investors on the one hand and labor on the other at the beginning of any period of computation of productivity changes are fair and equitable. There is no such equitable sharing in the Steel Industry today."

[9] See "Sharing the Gains of Productivity," *Labor's Economic Review*, ii (June-July 1957), p. 47.

[10] Rees, thesis, 1950, pp. 55-58.

[11] Clark Kerr, "The Short-run Behavior of Physical Productivity and Average Hourly Earnings," *Review of Economics and Statistics*, xxxi (November 1949), p. 304.

of situations in which workers are paid by the piece rather than by the hour. Where piece-rate systems of pay are used, productivity changes are exceedingly important in the daily lives of individual workers, unions, managements, and arbitrators. Payment by the piece may well result in a fairly tight link between productivity and wages so long as the changes in output per man-hour are the result of relatively minor technological innovations that do not necessitate a re-setting of piece rates.

The above considerations suggest that, except where piece-rate systems are in effect, we would not expect a rigid link between productivity and the magnitude of individual wage adjustments. However, it certainly does not follow that the behavior of productivity is of no consequence for the behavior of wages. The important and rather obvious point is that the impact of productivity on the wage determination process may take place indirectly via induced changes in other variables such as the excess demand for labor, the cost of living, and profitability. Consequently, it is now necessary to analyze the likely effect of variations in productivity on these other wage-determining factors.

Effect of Productivity Changes on Other Wage-Determining Factors

The demand for labor. Let us begin by considering the impact of a change in output per man-hour within the individual firm on the firm's demand for labor. We shall follow the usual practice of identifying the demand curve for a factor of production with the marginal net revenue productivity curve for the factor ($MNRP$)—that is, the curve showing the net addition to the income of the firm expected as a consequence of continually employing more units of the factor. Unfortunately for us, the path between the output per man-hour ratio of the firm and the

MNRP of labor curve is tortuous indeed. It will soon be apparent that there is no simple, undirectional connection between increases in the output per man-hour ratio and changes in the demand for labor.

In our above general discussion of the productivity concept, we emphasized the need to distinguish between increases in the output per man-hour ratio that occur as a consequence of movements *along* the *AGPP* curve and increases that occur as a consequence of alterations in the production function itself—that is, via an upward shift in the entire *AGPP* function. In accord with this distinction, it is convenient to abstract initially from volume changes and to concentrate instead on the class of productivity increases attributable to alterations in the production function itself.

There are two main links connecting an upward shift in the *AGPP* schedule and an alteration in the demand curve for labor. The first of these links is the marginal net physical productivity of labor schedule (*MNPP*), and the second is the demand curve for the final product of the firm, or alternatively, the marginal revenue curve (*MR*).

The problem of translating shifts in the *AGPP* curve into shifts in the *MNPP* curve has already been discussed, and so this job need not detain us here. It is sufficient to recall that this relationship depends primarily on the *source* of the upward shift in the productivity schedule,[12] and that it is thus impossible to predict the effect on the net productivity schedule without detailed knowledge of the happenings which brought about the particular productivity increase. A given increase in *AGPP* could have any number of consequences for the *ANPP* function ranging from no shift at all to a more than proportionate upward movement.

---

[12] The supply curves of the factors of production are also relevant. See Joan Robinson, *Economics of Imperfect Competition*, 1933, pp. 235ff.

The second link—the demand curve for the product—can be almost as troublesome. If the firm we are investigating happens to sell its output in a perfectly competitive market, there is no difficulty since changes in the *MNPP* curve can be quickly translated into changes in the *MNRP* curve by simply multiplying the change in *MNPP* associated with each number of man-hours by the given product price and then adding this result to the previous *MNRP* curve. In this case of perfectly elastic demand, the increase in net physical productivity associated with each number of man-hours will result in a proportionate increase in net revenue productivity, with the price of the product as the factor of proportionality.

However, if the demand curve for the final product of the firm happens to be less than perfectly elastic it is impossible to translate alterations in the net physical productivity schedule into changes in the net revenue productivity schedule unless the precise elasticity of the demand curve is known. However, if we assume the demand curve is downward sloping throughout, we can be sure that a given increase in the marginal net physical productivity of a certain number of man-hours will be associated with a *less* than proportionate increase in the corresponding marginal net revenue productivity since the firm will have to subtract the loss of revenue on preceding units attributable to the fact that a lower price is associated with the greater output. It follows that the less elastic the demand curve in the region under consideration, the smaller will be the increase in the demand for labor associated with any given increase in the marginal physical productivity of labor. In fact, if the elasticity of demand is sufficiently near unitary elasticity, an increase in the marginal physical productivity of labor will actually result in a *decrease* in the demand for labor.

The intuitive sense of this at first somewhat surprising conclusion is that if demand is not very elastic it will not pay the firm to expand production much as a consequence of lower costs; and, as a consequence of increased output per man-hour, it may be possible to turn out the desired volume of production with fewer man-hours of labor than before. More precisely, if the decrease in the marginal revenue associated with the given amount of labor is greater than the increase in the marginal net physical productivity of this amount of labor, the demand for labor will have decreased rather than increased.

It is interesting to note here that the change in the demand for labor depends not only on the elasticity of demand for the product of the firm, but also on the average gross physical productivity of labor associated with the given marginal net physical productivity. This is because it is the average gross productivity that determines the total output that would be produced if the specified number of man-hours of labor were employed, and marginal revenue is a function of total output, not of total labor input. Thus we can assert that the larger the increase in the average gross productivity of labor relative to the increase in the marginal net productivity, the smaller the increase in the demand for labor as a consequence of this increase in marginal net productivity—and, if the differential rate of increase between gross and net productivity is sufficiently great, the demand for labor will *decrease* as a consequence of an increase in marginal net physical productivity.

So far we have abstracted from productivity changes attributable to increases in the scale of operation of the plant. Increases in output per man-hour solely attributable to a change in the volume of output do not, of course, have any effect on the marginal net physical productivity *schedule*, but rather cause movements along the existing schedule. However, such changes in the productivity ratio normally *signal* the prior occurrence of an increase in the demand for labor, since the increase in output is presumably the result of a shift to the right in the demand curve for the product that in turn shifts the demand curves for the factors to the right. It is probably better to say that this kind of increase in the productivity ratio is itself the result of a prior increase in the demand for labor rather than the initiator of the rightward shift in the demand curve for labor.

This completes our analysis of the effect of improvements in output per man-hour within a particular firm on the demand for labor of this firm. It has been argued that there are a number of factors that influence the outcome and that without knowledge of these factors it is very hazardous to predict the impact of any given change in the productivity ratio on the firm's demand for labor. In fact, on a priori grounds, we cannot even be certain of the direction of impact, much less of the magnitude. That is, it is not even safe to say that increases in productivity always shift the demand curve for labor to the right.[13]

Let us now shift our attention to the question of what effect a change in a national output per man-hour index (unaccompanied by any change in intra-firm productivity) is likely to have on the individual firm's demand for labor. Since in this case the production function of the firm is unchanged, the national productivity index can exert an influence on the firm's demand curve for labor only by altering the demand curve for the product of the firm. The demand for the product of the firm will be altered if the increase in national output per man-hour is accompanied by a change in relative prices, in the distribution of disposable income, or in the total real disposable income of the country. Since it is very difficult to say anything defi-

---

[13] Rees (thesis, 1950, pp. 52-58), one of the few labor economists to even consider this question, has asserted that increases in productivity shift the demand curve for labor to the right and so would have increased wages in the absence of unions. Our analysis suggests that this is an extremely dubious proposition.

nite about the distribution of income or the alteration in the relative prices of the goods that are either competitive or complementary with the product of the specific firm we are examining, it is necessary to concentrate our attention on the possible change in total real disposable income.

Again, there are two links between the initial change in output per man-hour and the change in the demand for labor. First, there is the link between the increase in output per man-hour and the potential increase in real disposable income. We have already examined the various potential sources of improvement in the output per man-hour ratio and have emphasized that the magnitude of the increase in real disposable income associated with any given change in output per man-hour will vary with the source of the initial increase. The change in total real disposable income will also depend, of course, on the total number of man-hours worked. If the populace wishes to take its increased productivity primarily in the form of leisure, total disposable income might increase only slightly or not at all in response to an increase in output per man-hour.[14]

Secondly, there is the link between whatever increase in real disposable income results from the initial increase in output per man-hour and the individual firm's demand curve. If the product of the firm is not an inferior good we can expect some rightward shift in the demand curve, with the exact dimensions of the shift dependent on the income elasticity of demand for the product. Of course, if the national increase in output per man-hour was moderate and if the firm is a relatively small component of the economy, the magnitude of the rightward shift would probably be very slight.

[14] Actually, total real disposable income may decrease if the output per man-hour ratio increases as a consequence of a greater decrease in man-hours worked than in output produced. Steiner (*Review of Economics and Statistics*, November 1950, pp. 323-324) classes this sort of an increase in productivity as "undesirable."

"Ability-to-pay" and the cost of living. It is convenient to discuss at the same time the impact of increases in output per man-hour on two other factors whose significance for the wage determination process will be examined a bit later—namely, the "ability-to-pay"[15] of the firm and the cost of living. One reason why joint consideration of these two wage-determining factors is convenient is that the effect of productivity increases on both the profitability of the firm and the cost of living depends not just on the rate of productivity growth but also on the rate at which wages increase. It is perhaps best to think of the ability-to-pay and cost-of-living links between productivity and wage determination as affecting wage adjustments on the second "go-round." That is, the initial increase in productivity has a certain effect on the wage negotiations immediately following the productivity increase. Then the combined change in productivity and wages affects the cost of living and the profitability of the firm, which in turn may affect the next wage negotiation.

To measure the impact of an increase in the output per man-hour of the individual firm on the profitability of the firm and the price of the product, it is first necessary to ascertain the effect of such an increase on the average cost curve of the firm.[16] The extent to which we may expect a downward shift in the average cost curve to result from an increase in intra-firm gross productivity varies: (1) inversely with the immediate increase in wages that follows the productivity improvement; and (2) directly with the upward shift in the net physical productivity schedule that accompanies the increase in gross productivity.

[15] For the purposes of this section, "ability-to-pay" is provisionally identified with the total dollar profits of the firm. The whole concept of "ability-to-pay" is discussed much more fully in Ch. 7.

[16] The impact of changes in both productivity and wages on the cost schedules of the individual firm is discussed in considerably more detail in Part III.

As we observed earlier, the relationship between the increase in gross productivity and the attendant change in net productivity depends mainly on the source of the initial increase in output per man-hour. If this productivity increase is the result of an increase in capital or raw material costs equal to the reduction in labor costs per unit of product, there will be no upward shift of the net productivity curves; and, consequently, no downward shift in the average cost curve at all. On the other hand, if the productivity increase is the result of a relatively costless discovery or reorganization of the method of production, there will be a significant increase in net productivity as well as gross productivity; and, consequently, a significant downward shift in the average cost curve.

To predict the magnitude of the change in profits and product price associated with any given change in intra-firm productivity, it is necessary to know not only the shift in the average cost curve induced by the productivity improvement, but also the characteristics of the demand curve for the final product. For example, if the elasticity of demand is very high, a reduction in average costs will have little immediate effect on prices; whereas if the marginal revenue curve is more steeply inclined, the effect on price will be more significant. However, we can be reasonably sure of the *direction* of impact if we know only that the demand curve is negatively sloped. Any given decrease in average costs will, of course, tend to *increase* profits and to *decrease* price.[17]

Before turning to the question of the impact of econ-

---

[17] The pricing practices of the firm are, of course, also significant. Some would argue that many prices are inflexible downward so that a reduction in costs will not result in lower prices. While this may be true to some extent, in general we may expect an increase in net productivity unmatched by a wage increase to exert some downward pressure on prices and to act, at the least, as a partial offset to other pressures for price increases that might be present.

omy-wide increases in productivity, it is necessary to note that the impact of intra-firm productivity increases on ability-to-pay and the cost of living is dissimilar, not only with respect to direction of impact, but also as far as general magnitude of impact is concerned. While an increase in the net productivity of a single firm not offset by an increase in wages may result in a substantial increase in the profitability of this firm, it is unlikely to have any significant effect on the cost of living of the workers in this firm since the price of the firm's product is presumably a small component of the over-all price index.

Whereas the intra-firm increases in productivity discussed above affect both the firm's profitability and the workers' cost of living by shifting the average cost function, economy-wide increases in productivity exert their influence on profitability mainly from the demand side. As was pointed out above, nation-wide increases in productivity are likely to increase the demand for the product of the firm if there is an increase in the total disposable income of the community. And, any such rightward shift in the demand curve could be expected to increase the short-run profitability of the firm. Increases in the national output per man-hour ratio affect the cost of living in much the same way as an increase in the productivity of a single firm affects its price. However, in the case of a nation-wide productivity increase, the potential quantitative impact on the cost of living is much greater, whereas the probable magnitude of impact on the profitability of the individual firm is much less, than in the intra-firm productivity situation.

Thus it appears that an increase in either intra-firm or economy-wide productivity not offset by an increase in wages will probably lead to some increase in the total short-run profits of the firm and to some decrease in the cost of living. The magnitude of the changes depends, in the main, on the cost of the productivity improvements and on the shapes of the relevant cost and demand functions. The longer-run profit picture will, of course, depend on such factors as the possibilities of entry to the industry.

Conclusions

Our discussion of productivity as a factor in the wage determination process is now as complete as it can be at this stage of our inquiry. The main conclusions can be summarized as follows:

1. The question of the *desirability* and *practicality* of any normative assertion about wage-productivity relationships is logically quite distinct from the question of the functional dependence of wage adjustments on productivity movements, and the two must not be confused.

2. The parties to collective bargaining are unlikely to agree to alter wages automatically in accord with productivity changes because: (a) there are times when it is not in the economic or institutional interest of the parties to follow such an arrangement; and (b) there is lack of agreement as to the basic equity of increasing wages in accord with productivity growth.

3. This lack of agreement on productivity as a "principle" of wage determination does not imply, however, that there is no functional relationship between productivity and wage changes, since productivity movements may exert an indirect influence via other wage-determining factors.

4. In examining the influence of productivity changes on these other factors, it is essential to distinguish between intra-firm productivity increases and economy-wide productivity movements. It is also essential to know the source of the initial productivity increase so that it is possible to distinguish movements along a given productivity function from shifts in the entire function and the *net*

productivity increases from *gross* changes in output per man-hour.

5. An intra-firm increase in gross productivity attributable to an upward shift in the average gross physical productivity function may be expected to have the following indirect effects:

(a) It may shift the demand curve for labor to either the left or the right. An increase in output per man-hour cannot be depended upon to lead to an increase in the demand for labor, as has sometimes been thought. Any given increase in gross productivity will have a greater positive effect (or less of a negative effect) on the demand for labor: (i) the greater the corresponding increase in average *net* productivity; and (ii) the more elastic the demand curve for the product.

(b) It will increase the profitability of the firm if accompanied by an increase in net productivity not offset by an equivalent increase in wages. The magnitude of the short-run increase in profits will depend on the elasticity of demand for the product as well as on the increase in net productivity and the induced change in wages.

(c) Also, if accompanied by an increase in net productivity not offset by an equivalent increase in wages, it will exert a very slight downward pressure on the cost-of-living index by tending to reduce the selling price of the product of the firm. The magnitude of this downward pressure on the cost-of-living index will vary inversely with the elasticity of demand for the product and directly with the importance of the product in the index.

6. An intra-firm increase in gross productivity attributable to an increase in the volume of operations will have no effect of its own on the demand for labor but may increase profits and exert some slight downward pressure on the cost of living.

7. An economy-wide increase in output per man-hour

may also have certain indirect effects on wage determination:

(a) To the extent it results in an increase in real disposable income, it may increase the demand for labor and the profitability of the firm.

(b) To the extent it is not offset by higher labor and non-labor costs, it will exert downward pressure on the cost of living.

8. Since productivity increases have indirect effects on other factors, a final evaluation of the significance of productivity increases cannot be given now but must await our discussion of the importance of these other factors in the wage determination process.

9. However, on the basis of the evidence presented in this chapter, there are numerous grounds for doubting the likelihood of a one-to-one relationship between changes in either intra-firm gross productivity or economy-wide increases in output per man-hour and the wage level of the firm. It has been argued that there is not likely to be a direct tie between these factors, and we are entitled to suspect strongly that the indirect connections will also be loose. This suspicion stems from our discussion of numerous, rather elastic links between gross productivity changes, and other wage-determining factors.

6. ECONOMIC FACTORS IN THE WAGE DETERMINATION PROCESS: EXCESS DEMAND FOR LABOR

The second economic factor whose role in the wage determination process must be appraised is the excess demand for labor. For the purposes of the present chapter, this phrase "excess demand for labor" is probably best defined in a rather loose sense to mean the difference between the quantity of labor employers would like to hire and the quantity of labor available at a given wage.[1]

Excess demand for labor differs from productivity as a factor in the wage determination process in at least one important respect: there is much more agreement that the demand and supply conditions in the labor market are a significant determinant of wage movements. It has already been pointed out that the dilemma model implicitly assumes that when unemployment reaches some level there will be an abatement in the magnitude of wage adjustments—in fact, if prices are set on a cost-plus basis, some sort of functional dependence between the level of unemployment and wage adjustments is absolutely essential if inflation is ever to be halted.

As a consequence of this general acceptance of the dependence of wage and price movements on the level of unemployment, much work has been invested in attempting to find the "critical" level of unemployment at which the

[1] It is the mode by which the terms relating to the purchase of labor services are decided as well as the whole host of problems involved in the construction of a labor supply schedule that necessitate the admission that the excess demand terminology is being used in a very loose sense. It is quite difficult to apply the more precise Hicksian excess demand concept (see J. R. Hicks, *Value and Capital; An Inquiry into Some Fundamental Principles of Economic Theory* [2d ed., Oxford: Clarendon Press, 1946], p. 63) to most contemporary labor markets.

wage or price level will cease to rise.[2] These interesting studies are not evaluated here, however, because our immediate concern is wage-setting within the context of the individual firm[3] rather than the behavior of some aggregate wage index. We shall return to this question of the "critical" level of unemployment when we consider the fusing of specific wage bargains into an over-all wage level. Organizationally, the following discussion is divided into two main sections. The first and lengthier section discusses in some detail the impact of local labor market conditions, whereas the second section is concerned with the significance of the nation-wide employment situation.

Local Labor Market Pressures and Wage Determination

It is convenient to proceed by considering in turn the impact of a change in the local labor market situation on: (a) wage decisions arrived at by the employer without the direct participation of a union, and (b) wage decisions reached via the mechanism of collective bargaining.

Impact of Local Labor Market Pressures on Wages Set by the Unilateral Action of the Employer

In the case of unilateral employer wage-setting, a formal analysis couched in supply and demand terms yields

[2] See, for example: Joseph W. Garbarino, "Unionism and the General Wage Level," *American Economic Review*, XL (December 1950), pp. 893-896; Sumner H. Slichter, "How Bad Is Inflation?" *Harper's Magazine*, CCV (August 1952), p. 55; and A. J. Brown, *The Great Inflation, 1939-1951* (London: Oxford University Press, 1955), pp. 90ff. This last source contains the most thorough attempt to find the "critical" level of unemployment.

[3] Throughout this discussion the word "firm" is used in a rather loose sense to mean any wage-determining unit.

a simple, unequivocal answer: The appearance of a positive excess demand (that is, a rightward shift in the excess demand curve) will raise the price of labor, whereas the appearance of negative excess demand (that is, a leftward shift in the excess demand curve) will lower the wage; the magnitude of the increase or decrease in wages will depend on the magnitude of the initial shift in the demand or supply curve and on the relevant slopes of the demand and supply functions.

While the direction of impact suggested by this simple analysis seems to be beyond question (that is, no one argues that an increase in the demand for labor would ever, in and of itself, reduce the wage), numerous difficulties arise when we try to modify this analysis to take account of some of the especially significant peculiarities and imperfections of the labor market.

At this juncture it is necessary to turn for assistance to some empirical studies of labor markets, which, while failing to answer adequately many of the basic questions here, do provide some leads and are helpful in forming general impressions.[4]

Perhaps the most dominant theme of these studies directly relevant for our present problem is their emphasis on the diversity of ways in which individual firms react to

[4] The labor market studies that have proven most useful are: R. A. Lester, *Hiring Practices and Labor Competition* (Princeton, N.J.: Industrial Relations Section, Princeton University, 1954); R. A. Lester, *Adjustments to Labor Shortages; Management Practices and Institutional Controls in an Area of Expanding Employment* (Princeton, N.J.: Industrial Relations Section, Princeton University, 1955); Charles A. Myers and George P. Shultz, *The Dynamics of a Labor Market* (New York: Prentice-Hall, Inc., 1951); and Lloyd G. Reynolds, *The Structure of Labor Markets; Wages and Labor Mobility in Theory and Practice* (New York: Harper, 1951). A good brief review of this literature may be found in: Charles A. Myers, "Labour Market Theory and Empirical Research," *Theory of Wage Determination*, ed. Dunlop, 1957, pp. 317-326.

changes in the "scarcity" of labor. A reading of these empirical studies might even lead one to despair of ever finding any kind of meaningful relationship between the employment situation and the wage adjustment process. This is certainly too pessimistic an attitude. While the case studies do suggest a more complex relationship than is envisioned in the formal analysis, it still seems possible to set forth in a rather systematic manner the factors impinging on this relationship.

In general, it can be asserted that an increase in the firm's demand for labor or a reduction in the supply of labor available to the firm will tend to increase wages in this firm and that the magnitude of this increase will be greater: (a) the greater the impact of this "labor scarcity" on the firm's operation and thus the greater the pressure on the firm to make some kind of adjustment; and (b) the less desirable are forms of adjustment "competitive" to a wage increase. Let us now look briefly at the determinants of each of these considerations.

The extent of the pressure on the firm to make some kind of adjustment will, first and most obviously, depend on the absolute increase in the firm's demand for labor or the absolute decrease in the supply of labor available to the firm. A less obvious, but not necessarily less important, consideration is the quantity and quality of applicants who have recently been seeking employment at the firm. The smaller the quantity and the poorer the quality of this pool of applicants, the greater will be the pressure exerted on the firm by any given increase in its demand for labor.

The empirical labor market studies have made an important contribution by demonstrating that almost all firms have a certain number of men of varying qualities applying for jobs regularly. Even the poorer-paying and less "desirable" places to work have some applicants because of the imperfect mobility of the labor force, which is in turn a result of lack of knowledge and the psychology of the unemployed worker. This imperfect mobility manifests itself in random job applications and a tendency for workers not to "shop around" very much for jobs. The important implication of this characteristic of the labor market is that if the new manpower needs of a firm are very slight (say, for example, it is not expanding and needs only to replace retiring workers), a general tightening of the labor market triggered by the expansion of some other firm may have almost no impact on this firm since random job applicants and relatives of existing workers may be adequate for its limited manpower needs.

It would, of course, be incorrect to assume that such pools of applicants afford all firms equal protection from labor market pressures. The firm that is already paying relatively high wages and is generally regarded as a "good place to work" will normally receive more and higher quality job applications—and thus face less immediate pressure to make some kind of wage adjustment in the face of a tightening labor market—than the firm that is less favorably situated.

So much for the pressure imposed on a firm by the appearance of a positive excess demand for labor. Let us now examine the various types of adjustment that the firm may make in response to such local labor market pressures and the considerations affecting the firm's choice among these alternatives. The main point to be developed here is that it will often be possible for a firm to counter labor market pressures more cheaply by adopting some technique such as increasing the work week, diluting the quality of the work force, or increasing recruiting expenditures, rather than by raising the base wage. The basic economic appeal of these non-wage forms of adjustment is that they may permit a rather subtle yet profitable form of wage discrimination.

In analyzing the modes of adjustment open to a firm

faced with a labor shortage, it is convenient to begin by examining the factors that determine the desirability of the most obvious alternative—namely, an increase in the base wage. In this connection, the first factor to be considered is the extent of wage-oriented labor mobility in the area. An increase in the base wage is clearly less desirable: (a) the greater the extent to which workers already employed in other companies are "tied" to their present employer and are thus insulated from the inducements of a slight wage increase elsewhere, and (b) the greater the extent to which the new entrants to the labor force and the unemployed are unaware of the hypothetical wage increase.

The oligopsonistic nature of wage policy is also quite important. If local employers adhere to a "no-pirating" code of recruiting, a plant industrial relations manager may be very reluctant to try to bid labor away from his fellow personnel executives. Furthermore, if the firm believes that any increase it makes in its own wage scale will be quickly matched by other firms in the area, there is little point in this firm raising its base wage. A "wage-war" will usually not be to the advantage of anyone.

Finally, the cost of meeting a labor shortage by raising the base wage depends on how many members of the firm's present labor force will also have to be given a wage increase. For a firm with a large number of current employees, the over-all marginal cost of raising the base wage is likely to be significantly greater than the wage bill of the new men.

Against the costs of raising the base wage, it is, of course, necessary to weigh the costs of alternative modes of adjustment. Certainly one obvious alternative is an increase in the length of the work-day or work-week. The desirability of meeting a labor shortage in this way will depend not only on the attitudes of the workers towards such a proposal, but also on the technical feasibility and

97

cost of such a move. The cost will, in turn, depend on the overtime pay schedule and on the proximity of the present work-week to the point at which overtime rates go into effect. To the extent that the men in the plant are working less than "full" schedules, it is possible to envision an internal pool of labor-hours on which the firm can draw without increasing the base wage.

Another very important option is a reduction in the quality of the work force. According to some of the labor market studies referred to earlier, one of the most common reactions to an alteration in the "tightness" of the labor market is an adjustment in hiring standards.[5] The willingness of a firm to lower its quality requirements depends partly on the nature of the firm's operation (that is, the extent to which certain kinds or qualities of men are indispensable), partly on the general attitude of management on this subject, and partly on the economic benefits to be attained by this form of adjustment.

The most obvious advantages of reducing the quality of the work force rather than raising the wage rate stem from the fact that—assuming the work force is not paid on an incentive basis—such a procedure is really a form of wage discrimination that is much less overt than the alternative of raising wages for the new men alone. To the extent that a reduction in hiring standards results in lower output per man-hour, this policy will increase the efficiency wages of the new men just as surely as an increase in the base wage with hiring standards unchanged. And, since the higher efficiency wage is paid only to the new workers, the firm is able to expand its work force without the added cost of higher wages for existing em-

[5] For example, Lester observed in his Trenton study (*Adjustments to Labor Shortages*, 1955, p. 52) that half of the firms interviewed lowered their hiring standards in response to the growing "tightness" of the labor market occasioned by the expansion in the work forces of several large firms.

ployees. The beauty of the less overt form of discrimination is the very fact that it is less overt and less visible. Present employees are not likely to get very excited about a diminution in the quality of new additions to the plant work force, but they are apt to be very excited if a new man is paid a higher wage than they are getting. And, other employers are not nearly so aware of a decrease in their neighbor's hiring standards as they are of an increase in his base wage; hence the danger of a "wage-war" is much less.

Another advantage of quality deterioration as opposed to a wage increase is that the former is more likely to result in at least a temporary respite from labor market pressures. Since the applicants who come under consideration by the personnel manager normally vary greatly in quality, it is a relatively easy matter to be less particular. Also, to the extent that there is a certain amount of random movement into the employment office, it will almost always be possible to get someone if the employer is willing to reduce his hiring standards far enough. On the other hand, a wage increase policy will be successful only if a sufficient number of properly qualified men respond to the incentive of a higher wage—and this is more problematical. Still another advantage of the quality dilution procedure is that if the number of applicants appearing at a given employment office depends mainly on the number of men hired by the particular employer, then a policy of hiring more men by lowering quality standards may increase the flow of applicants almost as much as an increase in employment accompanied by a wage increase—and at a much lower cost. Finally, it is easier to reverse an easing of hiring standards than it is to eliminate an increase in wages.

However, the above arguments suggesting the advantages of quality dilution should not be pushed too far. There are also several rather significant disadvantages to the lowering of hiring standards. Apart from the possibility that lower-quality employees will simply be unable to do the work expected of them, there is the longer-run danger that quality dilution will be self-perpetuating—that is, management may have trouble attracting higher quality employees when the labor market is not so "tight." Perhaps even more important, managements are reticent to lower hiring standards because they like to hire "good" workers and fear that quality dilution may impair the "reputation" of the firm. For these reasons, a lowering of hiring standards is apt to be employed mainly as a short-run solution to labor shortages.

Two other possible responses to a labor shortage also deserve at least brief mention. A firm may choose (1) to increase its recruiting expenditures and (2) to improve the "net advantages" of working in its plants. Attempts to get new employees by such aggressive recruiting methods as paying cash bonuses to existing employees for bringing in new recruits and hiring busses to go into the hinterlands in search of willing workers have some of the same advantages as quality dilution. The recruiting cost technique can be a rather profitable form of wage discrimination in that higher employment costs are associated with the procurement of new workers than were associated with the procurement of the existing work force. Furthermore, this technique has the same reversibility advantage as quality dilution in that it is certainly no problem to cease putting advertisements into the newspapers.

Attempts to improve the "net advantages" of working for a firm may take any of a variety of forms ranging from greater generosity with merit increases, more rapid promotion, upgrading, and less strict regulation of piece rates, to non-pecuniary improvements such as more desirable working conditions. This sort of adjustment is apt to be most successful in holding present employees at the firm and preventing a drain of longer-service employees to other employers. It is not likely to be very successful in inducing new workers to join the fold because such improvements are difficult to publicize and are apt to have even less effect on worker movements than a simple increase in the base wage. This technique is also very useful if increases in wage rates are either prohibited by government edict or are frowned on for any other reason. That is, the fact that this adjustment is really a *disguised* form of wage may, in certain circumstances, be highly desirable.[6]

This completes our discussion of the impact of a positive excess demand for labor on the wage policy of a non-union firm. Before moving on, it may be useful to summarize briefly the two main implications of this all-too-hurried excursion into alternative ways of adjusting to a labor shortage. The first implication is that in many circumstances (and particularly when the labor shortage is relatively mild) we would *not* expect a tightening of the labor market to be accompanied by much of an increase in base rates. The second, equally significant, implication is that since most of the non-wage adjustments also involve costs, there will normally be an increase in unit labor costs and that this increase in labor costs may often be somewhat understated and hidden by pure wage data.

Let us now consider very briefly the impact of an excess *supply* of labor on the wage policy of a non-union firm. While much of what has been said above in discussing a positive excess demand is applicable here in reverse, the

[6] The popularity of this type of adjustment under conditions of a tight labor market and attempts to restrain wages from increasing has been demonstrated by the Swedish experience with the phenomenon known as "wage-drift" or "wage-slide" (loosely defined as the tendency for earnings to increase more rapidly than wage rates). See Bent Hansen and Gösta Rehn, "On Wage-Drift: A Problem of Money-Wage Dynamics," *Twenty-Five Economic Essays, in English, German and Scandinavian Languages, in Honour of Erik Lindahl* (Stockholm: Ekonomisk Tidskrift, 1956), pp. 89ff.

two cases are not perfectly symmetrical. The sudden appearance of an excess supply of labor is not apt to exert as much direct pressure on the firm as the appearance of excess demand. The extent of the pressure exerted will depend to a large extent on the situation of the firm at the time the excess supply appears. If the firm is relatively prosperous and has a qualified work force, a sudden increase in the number of applicants is not likely to have much of a direct impact on the firm's operation. On the other hand, if the firm has not been doing well, or is in some way dissatisfied with its present labor policies or labor force, it may jump at the chance to alter the situation.

What type of adjustment is the appearance of excess supply likely to occasion? Again, there are a number of possibilities, the most obvious of which is a reduction in the wage rate. While the study by Myers and Shultz referred to earlier does suggest that some firms may actually lower their hiring rates when faced with an expansion in the supply of labor,[7] wages in general seem to be less flexible downward than upward. Even in the absence of unions, managements hesitate to reduce the money wages of men already employed.[8] The reasons for this tendency to accept the present wage as a "floor" vary from humanitarian concern for the employee's well-being to the fear that employee morale and productivity would be adversely affected by a wage reduction. However, this does not mean that the appearance of an excess supply of labor will have no effect on wage-setting. The existence of a larger pool

[7] Myers and Shultz, *Dynamics of a Labor Market*, 1951, pp. 152-153.

[8] W. Rupert Maclaurin's study of the paper industry during the depression of the 1930's ("Wages and Profits in the Paper Industry," *Quarterly Journal of Economics*, LVII [February 1944], pp. 196-228) still serves as good documentation of this point. See also Albert Rees, "Wage Determination and Involuntary Unemployment," *Journal of Political Economy*, LIX (April 1951), pp. 143-153.

of labor may not entice management to cut the wages of its own work force, but it certainly acts as a brake on any other pressures to raise wages.

Whether or not the excess supply of labor affects wage rates directly, it is very likely to result in many of the other forms of adjustment discussed in detail for the case of a positive excess demand. If the appearance of an excess supply of labor to a particular firm stems from a reduction in its demand for units of labor input rather than from an increase in the supply of labor available to it, a reduction in the hours of work is highly probable. Such a reduction may manifest itself simply in a shorter work-week for all members of the labor force, or it may be translated into layoffs of some workers. If the excess supply of labor has arisen on the supply side in the form of an increase in the number of job applicants, the firm is quite likely to respond by raising its hiring specifications. Also, the firm may attempt to increase plant discipline, tighten work standards, and adopt a tougher policy concerning promotions. In short, almost all of the adjustments discussed for the case of an excess demand may be instituted in reverse. The extent of such adjustments will depend, of course, on the initial situation within the firm. If the firm already had high selection standards and good plant discipline, an increase in the number of job applicants is not likely to result in significant non-wage adjustments.

Impact of Local Labor Market Pressures on
Wages Set by Collective Bargaining

Turning now to the question of the significance of the local labor market situation for wages set via the mechanism of collective bargaining, it is heartening to note that there is general agreement on three main points: (1) the demand and supply conditions in the labor market are an important determinant of the "bargaining power"[9] of both the union and the management; (2) the greater the demand for labor relative to the supply, the greater will be the relative bargaining power of the union; and (3) the greater the relative bargaining power of the union, the larger will be the wage adjustment agreed on. However, this three-pronged generalization, while generally valid, does not seem to provide a sufficiently detailed explanation of the behavioral implications of changes in the excess demand for labor. Consequently, in this section, we shall look into the ways in which the demand and supply conditions in the labor market influence: (a) the wage policy of the union, and (b) the resistance to the union's wage demands by the company. Throughout we shall emphasize the necessity of distinguishing very carefully between: first, an excess demand for labor in the local labor market area as a whole and an excess demand for labor in a particular firm; second, an excess demand for labor induced from the *demand* side and an excess demand for labor induced from the *supply* side; and third, *realized* excess demand and *potential* excess demand.

The labor market situation and union wage policy. There are several reasons why the union's bargaining power is likely to be greater the "tighter" the area labor market in general and the more favorable the employment situation at the particular firm with which it happens to be negotiating. First of all, the financial resources of the members of the union and of the union itself are likely to be greater if area-wide employment has been high than if it has been low.

A second and possibly more important reason is that

[9] While many authors making this kind of assertion do not define "bargaining power," by this phrase, they seem to mean nothing more than "the ability to gain concessions in bargaining." This is the definition proposed by Alfred Kuhn (*Labor; Institutions and Economics,* New York: Rinehart, 1956), p. 127.

the greater the positive excess demand for labor within the individual firm, the lower the probability that the imposition of higher costs on management will put workers out of jobs. While no one denies the direction of impact suggested by this reasoning, it is necessary to note that the key question of the extent to which union wage policy is actually influenced by the *possible* effects of wage decisions on employment opportunities has been very hotly debated.[10]

From the standpoint of our present problem, there are three significant points to be noted about this debate. (1) It is concerned with the effects of *potential* unemployment rather than already *realized* unemployment on union wage policy; consequently, complete acceptance of the Ross proposition that union policy makers cannot consider potential employment problems in no way implies that union wage demands are formulated without reference to existing levels of employment and economic activity.[11] (2) There is certainly a connection between "potential" unemployment and "realized" unemployment. That is, while the prospects of unemployment may not initially moderate

[10] On the one hand, Arthur M. Ross has argued that ". . . the union is not automatically or continuously concerned with the quantity of labor sold; and further that the typical wage bargain (with certain significant exceptions) is necessarily made without consideration of its employment effect." (*Trade Union Wage Policy* [Berkeley: University of California Press, 1948], p. 79.) The fullest account of the pro-employment effect position has been presented by George P. Shultz and Charles A. Myers ("Union Wage Decisions and Employment," *American Economic Review*, XL [June 1950], pp. 362-380).

[11] Ross himself is fully cognizant of the importance of what he calls "underlying economic influences" as determinants of the ability of the union to win concessions from employers (*Trade Union Wage Policy*, 1948, p. 13). However, he does not go out of his way to distinguish actual from potential unemployment; nor does he note that potential unemployment may be transformed into actual unemployment.

union wage demands, if these prospects are realized as a consequence of this lack of moderation, the union may then be forced to accept a lower wage adjustment in a subsequent negotiation. (3) The evidence presented by Myers and Shultz, as well as a priori reasoning, suggests that fears of potential unemployment are more likely to modify union wage demands at a time when there is an excess supply of labor than when there is a labor shortage. Hence we can conclude that whatever the strength of the employment effect under given employment conditions, it is likely to be less of a deterrent to union wage demands the greater the demand for labor relative to the supply.

A third and final reason why we should expect union wage demands to be responsive to the local labor market situation is that employers are likely to put up less resistance to union proposals the greater their own excess demand for labor. The determinants of company wage policy are discussed in some detail below. The important point to be noted here is that union wage policy and employer wage policy cannot be thought of as independent variables; what the union presses for certainly depends to some extent on what it expects it can get.

Thus far it has been argued that union bargaining power is likely to vary directly with the "tightness" of the local labor market and the need of the specific employer for labor. It must now be noted that there is no automatic tie between union bargaining power and the size of wage demands. After all, unions have goals other than higher wages and may seek to invest their bargaining advantage in the pursuit of one of these other objectives. However, we would normally expect a positive correlation between union bargaining strength and the wage expectations of the union. This is likely to be especially true the more "secure" the union feels and the more satisfied it is with the non-wage terms of its contract.

ECONOMIC FACTORS: EXCESS DEMAND FOR LABOR

The labor market situation
and employer wage policy.

Employer wage policy influences wage adjustments in two ways: first, it helps shape union wage policy; and, second, it affects the translation of union wage demands into new wage agreements. In general, it seems reasonable to suppose that the employer will be more willing to make concessions the greater his own excess demand for labor. This generalization is based on the following reasoning.

If the employer has a positive excess demand for labor, it may be to his own advantage to increase wages, regardless of union demands. A generally "tight" labor market will reduce an employer's resistance by making it more difficult for him to find replacements for his present work force if there is a strike. The union can make a strike more effective at a time of high employment.

In addition, the cost of an interruption of work to the employer will normally be greatest when he is faced with a positive excess demand for labor. Under such circumstances the "opportunity cost" of a stoppage to the employer in the form of foregone profits will be particularly heavy. On the other hand, in poor times, a strike may impose little loss on the employer and may actually give him an excuse for shutting down while his inventories are depleted. In addition to these direct costs in the form of foregone profits, a strike may impose certain indirect costs on the employer as a consequence of his inability to fulfill his contracts and the possible disappointment of customers. If the firm has no reserve of goods and is engaged in a hotly competitive race to maintain the favor of important customers dependent on it for essential supplies, it will be very reticent to suffer a strike. A reputation as a dependable supplier is of extreme importance to many firms.[12]

[12] J. R. Hicks, in his *The Theory of Wages* (London: Macmillan, 1935), pp. 154-158, presents the classic discussion of many of these points. For a more recent exposition of the importance to management of such considerations, see Leland Haz-

Finally, employers will put up less resistance to wage claims if they think they can pass these higher costs forward in the form of higher prices or backward in the form of lower costs. And, while the extent to which such a "shifting" adjustment is profitable depends mainly on conditions in the product market rather than in the labor market, it is reasonable to expect that a positive excess demand for labor will usually "signal" a positive excess demand in the product market as well.

Significance of the Nation-wide Employment Situation

Thus far our discussion has been restricted to the impact of local labor market conditions on wage-setting in the individual firm. And, while local labor market conditions are certainly of paramount importance, it is also necessary to comment briefly on the significance of the employment situation throughout the country as a whole.

A change in the national unemployment index will influence an individual wage adjustment insofar as it either sets off or represents a significant change in the local labor market situation. However, there are several good reasons why we should not expect a close correlation between the magnitude of changes in this unemployment index and wage adjustments in the individual firm.

First of all, the unemployment index does not measure the national "excess demand for labor" in the sense of the difference between the number of man-hours demanded and supplied at the going wage level. While this index gives us some idea of the number of people unsuccessfully seeking jobs, it tells us little about the number of vacant jobs. The number of unemployed is especially inaccurate as an index of the excess demand for labor at a time of low em-

---

ard, "Wage Theory: A Management View," *New Concepts in Wage Determination*, ed. George W. Taylor and Frank C. Pierson (New York: McGraw-Hill, 1957), pp. 32-50.

ployment, for then it is possible to have a substantial increase in the demand for labor with little or no change in the number of "frictionally" unemployed.[13] Consequently, even if all local labor markets were small replicas of the economy as a whole, there could be a striking change in the excess demand for labor in each of these markets with little or no change in the national unemployment index.

In the second place, there is no "national labor market" in the sense that we can expect workers to move with any degree of rapidity between two points in the market. While over a fairly long period of time people may move from low-paying and depressed areas, in the short run workers are very unwilling to move. Reynolds has suggested that: "It is approximately correct to identify 'a labor market' with a locality small enough so that people can readily travel from homes in any part of the area to jobs in any other part."[14] The important implication of this characteristic of the American labor scene is that in the short run all localities need not experience the same degree of excess demand. Not only may excess demand be increasing more rapidly in one market than in another, but excess demand and excess supply might even coexist. Consequently, even if we could translate movements of the national unemployment index into changes in excess demand, it would still be hazardous to assume that any specific labor market (much less any specific firm within the local market) would be experiencing the same change in its employment situation.

[13] It is for these reasons that Bent Hansen suggests we use "gap" analysis and not mere unemployment analysis in the study of changes in the wage level. (*Theory of Wage Determination*, ed. Dunlop, 1957, p. 72.) An interesting attempt to measure the *excess* demand for labor in Great Britain has been made by J.C.R. Dow and L. A. Dicks-Mireaux ("The Excess Demand for Labour: A Study of Conditions in Great Britain, 1946-56," *Oxford Economic Papers*, x [February 1958], pp. 1-33).

[14] Reynolds, *Structure of Labor Markets*, 1951, p. 41.

Conclusions

1. The most general statement we can make about the relation between the excess demand for labor and the magnitude of wage adjustments is the following negatively-worded assertion: whether the wage is determined by the unilateral decision of the employer or by negotiation between a union and the employer, we would not expect an increase in the firm's excess demand for labor to lead to a reduction in the wage; nor would we expect an increase in excess supply to lead (in and of itself) to a wage increase.

2. In the case of unilateral employer wage-setting, it is much more difficult to make a positive statement because of the nature of the local labor market and the variety of adjustments open to the employer.

3. However, we can say that an increase in the firm's demand for labor or a reduction in the supply of labor available to the firm will tend to increase wages and that this tendency will be stronger: (a) the greater the impact of this "labor scarcity" on the firm's operations and thus the greater the pressure on the firm to make some kind of adjustment, and (b) the less desirable are forms of adjustment "competitive" to a wage increase.

4. A systematic analysis of the determinants of these two factors suggests that there are sound economic reasons why management may choose to make *no* adjustment in its base rate in response to a change in the excess demand for labor. A zero response is most likely if: (a) the initial change in excess demand is not too large in magnitude, (b) the source of the change in excess demand is the supply side rather than the demand side of the labor market, (c) the firm in question is near the top of the hierarchy of "good" places to work in the area, (d) the local labor has not been overly "tight," and (e) alternative adjustments such as changes in work schedules and hiring specifications are more profitable than a wage increase.

5. However, the absence of a change in base rates in

response to a given change in the excess demand for labor does not imply that there has been no change in either unit labor costs or in average hourly earnings. In fact, since most of the more popular forms of adjustment (such as quality dilution) are far from costless, there will normally be some increase in unit labor costs, even though such increases are not reflected in pure wage data. The use in the dilemma model of a single wage as the indicator of both costs and earnings can be very misleading.

6. In the case of wages set by collective bargaining, there are a number of good reasons for thinking that an increase in the demand for labor will increase union strength and union demands at the same time it is reducing employer resistance. And we would expect a higher wage adjustment to result from this enhancement of the relative bargaining power of the union—unless the negotiators were especially concerned with some other aspect of union-management relations, such as union security.

7. Without attempting at this point to pass final judgment on the question of the impact of the union on wage negotiations, we can say that the replacement of unilateral wage-setting by bilateral negotiations may well increase the probability that the firm will grant a wage increase rather than attempt to meet a labor shortage by some other form of adjustment. This is because (a) an out-and-out wage increase will be more desirable to the members of the union and to the union as an institution than other forms of adjustment such as quality dilution, and (b) the introduction of the union on the scene increases the potential costs to the employer of refusing to grant a wage increase.

8. It must be emphasized that the substitution of an increase in the base wage for non-wage forms of adjustment does not necessarily imply a proportionate increase in either the costs of the firm or the incomes of the workers. As we mentioned above, the non-base wage forms of adjustment also involve costs and revenues, though these are

less obvious. Consequently, a part of the impact of the union may be spent on altering the *form* of the adjustment without an equivalent change in the magnitude.

9. Both the magnitude and the form of the adjustment may depend to a considerable extent on the precise characteristics of what we have loosely called a change in the "excess demand for labor." First, while conditions in the local labor market as a whole are certainly important, the circumstances of the individual firm are of greater significance. Second, the union is apt to be more successful in securing a large wage adjustment if the increase in the excess demand for labor of the firm has been induced from the demand side than if its source has been a shrinkage in the supply of applicants.

10. It is very hazardous to draw any inferences for specific wage negotiations from movements in the national unemployment indices. The main reasons for this are that (a) unemployment indices are not a satisfactory measure of the excess demand for labor, and (b) local labor markets may be quite unconnected so that excess demand and excess supply can coexist.

11. Finally, we should at least mention one question raised by the dilemma model that we have not answered directly. This is the question of the *time* it takes for an alteration in demand and supply conditions to exert an influence on wage determination. While we cannot be very definite on this point, there is some evidence to suggest that, apart from a major change in labor market conditions, the response will not be very rapid: (a) the imperfections in the labor market and the variety of relatively costless adjustments open to the employer suggest that a decision to change the wage rate can be postponed for a considerable period, and (b) possibly the main conclusion to be drawn from the Ross "employment-effect" argument is that potential unemployment is not nearly as significant a deterrent to wage increases as the real thing.

7. Other Economic Factors in the Wage Determination Process

While productivity and the excess demand for labor are the two wage-determining factors discussed most prominently in conjunction with the dilemma model of the inflationary process, they most certainly are not the only economic factors of significance. This chapter is devoted to exploring the potential impact of three other economic factors: "ability-to-pay," the cost of living, and wage comparisons. Organizationally, it is convenient to discuss each of these wage-determining factors in a separate section and to summarize the main conclusions germane to each at the end of the individual sections.

Ability-to-pay

As in the case of the "productivity principle," there has been some tendency to dismiss "ability-to-pay" as unimportant because it is not the sole principle of wage determination, because it is sometimes used by one party and sometimes by the other, and because there has been so much controversy as to the ethical and economic desirability of varying wages with the "ability-to-pay" of the firm. For example, one labor economist has written: "Since arbitrators seem to reject it [ability-to-pay] about as often as they use it, its actual net effect on wages is probably negligible."[1] It is difficult to understand statements such as this since none of these objections to the ability-to-pay principle necessarily implies anything about the functional relationship (or lack of such relationship) between the ability-to-pay of the firm and the magnitude of wage adjustments. And it is this latter question that is relevant here.

[1] Kuhn, *Labor: Institutions and Economics,* 1956, p. 440.

Definition, Determinants, and
Indices of Ability-to-pay

Before going any further, it is necessary to specify more precisely just what is meant by "ability-to-pay." As in the case of the productivity concept, the problem of definition is of overriding importance. Once the phrase "ability-to-pay" has been invested with some substance, the problem of its significance in the wage determination process becomes manageable. Any number of possible definitions suggest themselves, including, as a first possibility, the difference between actual profits and the return necessary to keep the firm in operation. This is tantamount to defining ability-to-pay as the amount of economic rent being received by the firm. This definition, while possessing a certain theoretical appeal, suffers from serious measurement difficulties in that, among other things, the time-horizon of the firm must be specified. A second conceivable definition is the difference between actual profits and "fair" profits—only no one knows what "fair" profits means. As a third alternative, ability-to-pay might be defined simply as the historic profitability of the firm. The difficulty with this suggestion is that it is *expected* profits that are relevant for decision-making, and there is no assurance that past profits can be projected.

Probably the most satisfactory procedure is to start out by identifying ability-to-pay with *prospective profitability*, a phrase that at least has the merit of emphasizing the importance of expectations.[2] Next, it is necessary to invest this new phrase with the economic content most relevant to the wage determination process. For wage-setting purposes, it is best to think of a *family* of pro-

---

[2] The main qualification to this identification is that it is dangerous to compare the ability-to-pay of firms in different industries by examining their profit and loss statements since higher profits may be necessary to keep a firm in a risky field than in a more secure and stable industry.

spective profitability estimates, each of which corresponds to some hypothetical wage adjustment. Then it is useful to think of each member of this family of prospective profitability estimates as the algebraic sum of two parts: (1) a basic or "unadjusted" estimate of the level of future profits based on the assumption that there is no new wage adjustment at all, and (2) a "wage adjustment" that represents the amount of the revision in the basic profit estimate necessitated by the particular wage change under consideration.

The basic or "unadjusted" estimate will probably be higher, (1) the higher the level of historic profits with more recent years weighted most heavily, (2) the more favorable the *trend* of profits in recent years, and (3) the more favorable are underlying factors such as (a) the trend of demand for the firm's product and the immediate sales outlook, and (b) the trend of net productivity and the prospects for future cost-reducing innovations.

The wage adjustment associated with any hypothetical wage change can normally be expected to reduce this unadjusted profit estimate more, (1) the less advantageous a wage increase is to the firm for labor market reasons,[3] and (2) the poorer is the possibility of "passing-on" these higher costs in the form of higher prices. While a full discussion of this latter factor must await a later chapter, we can surmise that a firm is likely to be less successful in recouping higher wage costs through higher prices, (a) the greater the excess capacity throughout the industry in general, (b) the more elastic the demand for the product

[3] See our discussion in the preceding chapter. It is, of course, possible that a wage increase might increase the firm's profits if the "morale" and labor supply effects were strong enough. But it is doubtful that such a wage increase would raise the estimate of future profitability (unless the situation was really desperate) because these effects are so uncertain compared to the higher costs.

115

of the industry as a whole, (c) the easier it is for new firms to enter the industry, (d) the greater the price competition within the industry itself, and (e) the poorer the possibility that a similar wage change will take place in the plants of the firm's competitors.[4]

Influence of Prospective Profitability on Wages Set by the Unilateral Action of Management

In the formal theory of the firm, the volume of profits is the residual result of a number of decisions and would not be expected to exert an *independent* influence on wage adjustments. It is true, of course, that many of the underlying determinants of prospective profitability are also underlying determinants of the demand for labor. For example, a steady increase in the demand for the firm's product would presumably shift the demand curve for labor to the right, and this increase in the demand for labor may stimulate the firm to increase wages. However, this sort of wage increase should not be attributed to the higher profits which may also result from the higher demand for the firm's product, but to the basic alteration in the supply and demand conditions in the labor market.[5]

However, when we take into account the complexity of management objectives and the possibility that short-run profit maximization may not be paramount among these

[4] Points (c), (d), and (e) are discussed more fully later, when the significance of various institutional arrangements for the wage determination process is discussed (Ch. 9). At this juncture, it is also worth noting that a wage adjustment might actually raise the prospective profitability estimate if circumstances were such that the firm needed an "excuse" to institute a potentially profitable price increase.

[5] The one obvious case in which the absolute level of profits can affect wages within the framework of formal theory is if profits fall sufficiently to induce the firm to cease operations altogether. In this case, the wage will be zero.

116

objectives, prospective profitability can exert some independent influence on wage decisions. It may be helpful to think of the firm as having a preference structure that relates the values it attaches to various objectives of company policy to the amounts of these objectives attained. That is, the firm can be imagined to have a series of indifference curves which portray the amount of one "good" (for example, dollar profits for the coming quarter or year) that it may be willing to sacrifice to obtain an additional unit of some other "good" (for example, a high ranking in the hierarchy of good places to work in the community).

To extend our analogy to the theory of consumer behavior, the firm's choice of the optimum combination of these various objectives will depend not only on this preference structure (the "tastes" of the firm), but also on (a) the absolute level of the firm's profits (the income of the firm), and (b) the cost of substituting a small amount of one of these objectives for a small amount of some other objective (the relative prices faced by the firm). Thus the firm's willingness to increase the wages of its workers would be expected to be greater, (a) the more the firm covets a high wage scale,[6] (b) the more the firm can "afford" to pay high wages, and (c) the "cheaper" it is for the firm to increase wages a certain amount.

[6] Why would a firm covet a high wage scale? There seem to be two interrelated groups of reasons: first, a high wage scale has certain positive advantages in that it facilitates recruitment and permits higher hiring standards and more rigid discipline of the labor force; second, management may simply enjoy the prestige of being a high-paying firm. As Reynolds has suggested (*Structure of Labor Markets*, 1951, p. 162): "It is much more satisfying to be running 'the best place in town,' than to be known as the manager of 'a cheap shop.'" For a much more detailed discussion of the forces that encourage employers to prefer high wages, see Alfred Kuhn, "Market Structures and Wage-Push Inflation," *Industrial and Labor Relations Review*, XII (January 1959), pp. 244-246.

To understand the relevance of prospective profitability to this schema, it is necessary to recall that estimates of prospective profitability are the algebraic sum of two parts, each of which has its role to play. The basic or unadjusted estimate of future profits (which assumes no wage increase) can be considered an index of the "wealthiness" of the firm. The larger this basic estimate, the more the firm may feel that it can afford the higher wage scale it has been coveting. That is, if a higher wage level is not an "inferior good," the higher the income of the firm, the more of this good we would expect it to consume. The wage adjustment part of the prospective profitability estimate is an index of the opportunity cost of any hypothetical wage increase in terms of profits foregone. The smaller the magnitude of this adjustment, the cheaper it is for the firm to move up a notch in the hierarchy of good places to work. And we would expect the firm to enjoy more of a good (a higher wage scale in this case) the smaller the price that must be paid to procure it.

The empirical study of the New Haven area by Reynolds provides some evidence in support of this interpretation of the influence of prospective profitability on unilateral wage-setting.[7] However, one must be very careful in interpreting such conclusions since at least a part of the higher wage increases in the more profitable firms may have been due to an increase in the demand for labor "signaled" by the higher profit prospects.

The Influence of Prospective Profitability on Wages Set by Collective Bargaining

In the case of wages set by collective bargaining, there is general agreement that the greater the prospective profitability of the firm, the larger will be the wage ad-

[7] Reynolds, *Structure of Labor Markets,* 1951, pp. 162-166.

justment agreed to by the negotiators. However, armed with our earlier distinction between the two parts of a prospective profitability estimate, it is possible to say a bit more than this. It is first necessary to observe that in general we would expect the firm to put up less resistance to a union wage demand the greater the costs of disagreeing with the union and the smaller the costs of agreeing.

The significance of distinguishing between the two components of the prospective profitability estimate is that the costs of agreeing and disagreeing depend on the ratio of these two parts as well as on their algebraic total. The over-all estimate of prospective profitability is a rough index of the cost of *disagreeing* since it provides some guide to the amount of profits that would be lost by the firm if it were forced to take a strike. However, the cost of *agreeing* depends not on this total estimate, but just on the amount of the downward adjustment in the basic estimate necessitated by the proposed wage increase. Thus, the net opportunity cost of the wage increase exerts an independent influence. In sum, we would expect the firm to offer less resistance the greater the total prospective profitability associated with the given wage demand *and* the smaller the net opportunity cost to the firm of agreeing to the wage demand. Why should employers risk a strike by being especially stubborn at a time when the cost of a strike in terms of foregone profits is high *and* the net cost of agreeing to a higher wage may be relatively low?[8]

---

[8] The distinction between the two parts of the prospective profitability estimates also explains why one representative of management has suggested that the level of profits is even more significant in the down-swing of the business cycle than in the up-swing. (Hazard, *New Concepts in Wage Determination*, ed. Taylor and Pierson, 1957, p. 48.) The main argument offered in support of this hypothesis is that in bad times it is harder to pass on higher costs in the form of higher prices. This is perfectly consistent with our analysis since we would expect the

So far, no direct mention has been made of the significance of the union for the influence of prospective profitability. As was implied in the preceding paragraph, the appearance of a union on the scene alters the influence of prospective profitability in two closely-related ways: first, the union brings with it the possibility of an organized withdrawal of the labor force and may thus increase the cost to the employer of not agreeing to any hypothetical wage increase—especially if the over-all estimate of prospective profitability is high; second, the union may serve as an independent source of pressure for a wage increase. That is, the union will formulate wage demands of its own, and, as we have already argued, these demands will be based to a considerable extent on the union's anticipation of employer resistance.[9] Consequently, the greater the prospective profitability of the firm, the greater will be the union demands and the weaker will be the incentive of management to offer substantial resistance. This combination would certainly suggest a positive correlation between the magnitude of wage adjustments and the prospective profitability of the firm.

Not only may the union influence the impact of any given estimate of prospective profitability on wage de-

same total level of prospective profitability to generate more employer opposition under such circumstances than at times when it is easy to raise prices.

[9] Arthur Smithies ("The Control of Inflation," *Review of Economics and Statistics*, xxxix [August 1957], p. 276) has suggested that another reason why greater ability-to-pay will lead to higher union wage demands is that the union will seem stronger in the court of public opinion if firms have high profits. While this may or may not be true, Smithies' further statement that "But for this political factor it is hard to see how either the cost-of-living or profits is relevant [for wage determination]. . . ." is most difficult to understand. We have seen that there are several very plausible other reasons why wages will tend to vary with the profitability of the firm.

termination, but it may also alter the prospective profit-ability estimate itself. There are at least two reasons why this may be the case. First, it is necessary to recognize that expectations of any sort are, by their very nature, uncertain. Management naturally prefers to underestimate future profits than to overstate them, since actions based on an over-optimistic estimate would endanger the very life of the firm. When management alone is making wage decisions, it is free to estimate profits in any way it wishes, and can be as conservative as it desires; however, when the union also has a hand in negotiations, it too forms some estimate of future profits—and it does not have quite as conservative a bent as does management. As Reynolds has emphasized, the union "does not allow as large a discount for uncertainty as management would like."[10] Thus, what might be termed the "mean expectation" of profitability will be greater when there is collective bargaining than when the employer alone has the responsibility for formulating wage policy. Consequently, the existence of unions may force managers to assume a greater degree of risk than they would be willing to assume voluntarily.

The introduction of a second party to the wage-setting process changes things in yet another way. Whereas under unilateral wage-setting management is free to adjust wages whenever it desires, under collective bargaining wages are normally negotiated for a set period of time, and this period of time has been lengthening in recent years.[11] The unilateral wage-setter, of course, does not want to be continually tampering with wage rates, and so there is some minimum amount of time during which he would expect any wage adjustment to stay in effect. How-

[10] Reynolds, *Structure of Labor Markets,* 1951, p. 165.

[11] For statistics on the growth of long-term contracts see the references cited in Ch. 9. The significance of the length of agreements for wage determination is examined more fully in this later chapter.

121

ever, this minimum period is not apt to be as long as the period between wage negotiations under collective bargaining. The significance of this difference in the time horizon involved in the wage-setting process is that the longer the period for which wages are being determined, the more uncertain is the prospective profitability, the less significant are current data such as recent profits and the number of unfilled orders, and the more important are vague feelings about the course of business in general.

Before concluding this section it is necessary to say a brief word about the hoary problem of measuring "profits." It has already been argued that past profits are in no way synonymous with what we have argued is the most useful definition of "ability-to-pay." Be this as it may, recent profits are one element involved in the estimation of prospective profitability for which figures are published. It is not surprising, therefore, that there has been a terrific controversy between management and labor over the conceptual definition of "profits" and the reliability of published figures.[12] This controversy has centered on the problem of how to estimate depreciation in a time of rising prices. The central point that needs to be made here is that most of the public controversy on this subject is designed to justify in the eyes of the public, the government, or some arbitrator, a position already taken by the parties or an agreement already reached. This debate is of little relevance for the problem of the functional dependence of wages on prospective profitability except insofar as it actually influences what the parties themselves regard as

[12] Rees, in his study of post World War II bargaining in the steel and coal industries (thesis, 1950, pp. 58-66) emphasized the controversy at this time on the subject of profit measurement. This controversy has continued right up to the present and has been especially pronounced in the steel industry. The study by Backman (*Steel Prices, Profits, Productivity, and Wages,* 1957) contains a thorough discussion of this issue and many references to other literature, including the union point of view.

the relevant measure. However, the controversy does emphasize, in a slightly different way, a point made earlier—namely, that both the union and management make some estimate of prospective profitability, and these two estimates need not coincide.

Conclusions

1. In some ways the most difficult aspect of assessing the significance of ability-to-pay for the wage determination process is investing this concept with the appropriate economic meaning.

2. The most appropriate definition of ability-to-pay seems to be the *prospective profitability* of the firm. However, this definition by itself is not sufficient for our purposes and it is necessary to "fill it out" by (a) envisioning a family of prospective profitability estimates, each of which corresponds to a specific hypothetical wage adjustment; and (b) conceiving of each member of this family of estimates as the algebraic sum of two parts: (i) a basic or unadjusted estimate of future profits that assumes no wage increase at all, and (ii) a wage adjustment that represents the opportunity cost to the firm (in terms of foregone profits) of agreeing to the hypothetical wage change.

3. The basic estimate will depend on such things as the trend of profits, sales, and productivity for the firm, while the magnitude of the wage adjustment will depend mainly on the ease with which the firm can pass on higher wages in the form of higher prices.

4. When we recognize that the firm may have a complex combination of objectives, there are good reasons for expecting the magnitude of wage adjustments to vary directly with the over-all prospective profitability of the firm and inversely with the opportunity cost of the wage increases, even where management has sole responsibility for wage-setting.

5. In the case of collective bargaining, prospective profitability will probably exert a considerably stronger influence. This is so primarily because a union can increase the costs to the firm of *not* translating a high prospective profitability into substantial wage increases.

6. The appearance of the union on the scene may also increase the mean expectation of prospective profitability and lengthen the time period over which estimates are made.

7. The extensive public discussions of the proper way to measure "profits" are probably of very limited significance for the present problem.

Cost of Living

The next economic factor whose significance for the wage determination process must be appraised is the "cost of living." By this phrase we mean simply some index of the retail prices of goods and services purchased by the "average" wage earner. It is indeed fortunate that the Bureau of Labor Statistics compiles the Consumer Price Index (*CPI*) which, while far from perfect, does provide us with a reasonably good measure of the cost of living. The *CPI* is certainly more reliable than any statistic we have for the other wage-determining factors examined thus far.

The cost of living differs from the wage-determining factors discussed earlier not only with respect to ease of measurability, but also with respect to point of impact in the inflationary process. In brief, wage adjustments inspired by changes in the cost of living can reinforce and magnify initial increases in the price level, but cannot themselves initiate an inflationary spiral.

As a final preliminary, it is necessary to emphasize the dangers involved in using comparative wage-price data to arrive at generalizations concerning the impact of the cost of living on wage movements. The important point is simply that the discovery of a close parallel between the behavior of wage and price data tells us very little about the dependence of wages on the cost of living. An equi-proportionate increase in wages and the cost of living is compatible with any one of three hypotheses: (1) that wages are determined in some unknown manner and that prices are then raised in the same proportion as wages, (2) that wages and prices are both determined by some third factor or factors, or (3) that wages are always increased in proportion to the increase in prices during the previous period. Without other information, there is no justification for singling out any particular one of these alternatives.[13]

Influence of Changes in the Cost of Living on Wages Set by the Unilateral Action of Management

An increase in the Consumer's Price Index is likely to exert some upward pressure on wages even in the absence of a union. The main reason is that higher living costs create dissatisfaction and discontent among both workers and their wives. This common-sense observation is supported by Reynolds' study of the New Haven area, in which he found that workers regarded the cost of living as an important determinant of the "fairness" or "unfair-ness" of their wage.[14] This dissatisfaction can manifest itself in one of two ways. It could result in a reduction of labor supply as a consequence of the fall in the real wage; or, it could simply result in lower morale within the plant. The first alternative seems rather unlikely since we are not even certain that the supply curve of labor has a posi-

[13] A. J. Brown's study (Great Inflation, 1955, pp. 96ff.) affords an excellent illustration of how easy it is to commit this dangerous methodological fallacy.

[14] Reynolds, Structure of Labor Markets, 1951, pp. 99-100.

tive slope throughout. It is quite plausible that the income effect of a fall in the real wage would outweigh the substitution effect, and thus we might have an increase in the quantity of labor supplied rather than a reduction. The possibility that rising prices will produce a less satisfied work force is more convincing.

If poorer plant morale does accompany rising prices, employers may elect to increase wages. Both Reynolds and Lester found that for economic and non-economic reasons employers are anxious to keep a contented work force and are willing to pay something to avoid discontent.[15] Of course, the extent to which management is willing to make wage adjustments for morale reasons will depend on the economic position of the company as well as on its labor policies.

Influence of Changes in the Cost of Living on Wages Set by Collective Bargaining[16]

The introduction of the union as a party to wage-setting probably increases the likelihood that an increase in the cost of living will be translated into a wage increase. In the first place, the union as an institution provides a focus for the worker dissatisfactions discussed above. The

[15] *Ibid.*, pp. 167-168, and Lester, *Adjustments to Labor Shortages*, 1955, p. 81.

[16] Although in this section we are concerned only with "private" wage determination, we should at least mention that the cost of living is of great significance in the event of government wage-setting. It is an especially attractive guide to the government wage-setter because of its "definiteness" and "equity." Escalator agreements can be used in many ways as instruments of government wage policy. See the account of wage escalation in France by François Perroux and Edmond A. Lisle ("Structural Inflation and the Economic Function of Wages: The French Example," *Theory of Wage Determination*, ed. Dunlop, 1957, pp. 257-259).

126

workers now have an outlet for what may otherwise have been repressed "grumblings." Also, the union can keep the workers informed of upward movements in the cost-of-living index and thus encourage worker dissatisfacton with a falling real wage. Movements of the cost-of-living index are an important determinant of union wage policy.[17] And, in addition to increasing the pressures generated by a rising cost-of-living index, the existence of a union also provides the workers with an instrument to apply these pressures—namely, the organized strike.

As for employer resistance to the increased pressures generated by an increase in the cost of living, we would expect it to depend on the same factors that determine employer resistance to any proposed increase in labor costs. And, changes in the cost of living probably do not alter employer resistance significantly, except insofar as these changes "signal" changes in other variables, such as the prospective profitability of the firm or the firm's demand for labor.

Thus, since increases in the cost of living heighten significantly union pressure for wage increases and probably do not increase employer resistance, we would expect a rising *CPI* to be translated into rising wages.[18] It would

[17] The importance to unions of the cost-of-living index is illustrated by their continued scrutiny of the construction of this index and by the terrific controversy over the reliability of the *CPI* in the post World War II period. During a time of relatively rapid inflation, the cost of living comes close to dominating union wage policy. W. S. Woytinsky (*Labor and Management Look at Collective Bargaining* [New York: Twentieth Century Fund, 1949], p. 73) found, during the 1947-1948 negotiations, that cost-of-living changes were mentioned by 84.2 per cent of the respondent unions as the most important wage criterion.

[18] It has also been argued that increases in the cost of living are likely to be translated into wage increases because the pub-

be hazardous, however, to carry over this conclusion to the case of a fall in the cost of living, since workers are prone to resist very strongly any reduction in their money wages, and as was mentioned earlier, employers are not apt to push for wage reductions unless they themselves are extremely hard-pressed. Hence, it would appear that the cost of living is a more significant determinant of wages when it is moving upward than when it is falling.

In addition to these general arguments, there is a more definite reason for expecting at least some wages to respond to changes in the cost of living. This is, of course, the existence of the so-called "escalator" agreements in some labor contracts. Where these clauses exist, we can be quite sure that there will be a connection between changes in the cost of living and wages. Furthermore, these clauses are evidence that some unions and employers are willing to translate the cost-of-living principle into formula terms. It is worth noting that no other wage determination principle has been written into union contracts in such rigid form.[19] However, this point must not be pushed too far. After all, the fact that the cost of living is more "measurable" than other wage-determining principles is an important reason for the adoption of the escalator agreements. Also, it must be remembered that the presence of an escalator agreement in some contracts but not in others does not imply that changes in the cost of

lic is more convinced of the "reasonableness" of wage claims justified in this manner. (Smithies, *Review of Economics and Statistics*, August 1957, p. 276.)

[19] The so-called "annual improvement factor" might be regarded as the translation of the productivity principle into formula form. But there is a most significant difference. The amount of the "productivity" increase to be received by the workers is spelled out in advance and has no necessary relation to any actual productivity changes, whereas cost-of-living increases depend on the change that actually occurs in the *CPI*.

living are relevant for wage determination in the first case only. As has been emphasized repeatedly, absence of overt acceptance of any "principle" does not imply it is of no significance.

Conclusions

1. The cost of living differs from other wage-determining factors in at least two important respects: (a) it is more "measurable"; and (b) it cannot instigate an inflationary spiral but can only reinforce a given price rise.

2. It is very important to recognize that the observation of parallel movements in wage and price indices does not permit one to conclude that wages are determined solely by the cost of living. Such an unwarranted deduction can suggest very misleading conclusions.

3. Increases in the cost of living can be expected to lead to dissatisfaction on the part of workers and their wives, and this discontent is likely to exert a strong upward pressure on the wage level, especially if the workers are organized.

4. The cost of living is not symmetrical in its impact. A decrease in the price level will exert less downward pressure on the price level than an increase will exert in the upward direction.

5. The existence of escalator clauses in contracts is *prima facie* evidence of the significance of cost-of-living changes for wage determination. However, the absence of such clauses carries no necessary implications.

Wage Comparisons

An evaluation of the probable significance of wage comparisons as a factor in the wage-setting process is especially critical for our analysis of the wage determination assertion of the dilemma model. The special importance of wage comparisons stems from the fact that, unlike the other wage-determining factors examined thus far, this consideration is significant at two levels of our analysis: first, as a factor in determining the magnitude of specific wage adjustments, and second, as an important element in the transmission of specific wage adjustments throughout the economy. That is, the relevance of the wage comparison factor extends beyond our present concern with specific wage adjustments over into the area of the fusing of these individual adjustments into changes in the general wage level.

Wage comparisons differ from the other wage-determining factors in another obvious respect. The very notion of wage comparisons has implicit within it the concept of a wage structure and wage differentials. That is, when we examine the significance of wage comparisons we are forced to deal with more than the single, all-embracing "wage" which was so convenient in our exposition of the dilemma model.

As a final preliminary, it might seem advisable to define "wage comparisons" more carefully, in the sense of specifying just what wages are to be compared with one another. Unfortunately, this is not so easy as it might seem; and, it is convenient to postpone consideration of this question of the locus of wage comparisons until some of the pressures exerted by various comparisons have been examined. However, it is appropriate to point out here that comparisons of the *rate* of wage increase are usually more significant than comparisons of absolute wage levels, although the latter are, of course, also important at times. The main reason for the greater relative importance of rates of change seems to be that differences in absolute level that have existed for some time come to be recognized as customary. Also, wage adjustments are usually agreed to and announced in terms of the magnitude of change rather than in terms of the new absolute level.

Influence of Wage Comparisons on Wages Set by the Unilateral Action of the Employer

Although the significance of wage comparisons in the wage-setting process has been discussed primarily in the context of collective bargaining, it is possible to suggest a number of ways in which the movement of another firm's wage level may influence unilateral wage-setting. As was the case with the other wage-determining factors we have already considered, many of the pressures that are mediated through the institutions of the union and the corporation in collective bargaining also condition the decisions of the manager with sole responsibility for wage-setting.[20]

One way in which wage comparisons influence unilateral wage adjustments is through their effect on worker attitudes. Wage earners are not solely interested in their own wages per se, but are also interested in the relationship between their own rate of pay and the wages of others. Of course, this "propensity for invidious comparison" is certainly not restricted to the production worker, but seems to be a more general phenomenon. It is easy for all of us to understand the feelings of Ross' hypothetical stenographer "who celebrated jubilantly when she received an increase of $10.00 a month [but was] disillusioned upon finding that an office mate received $15.00."[21] Such worker dissatisfaction can manifest itself in lower plant morale, lower efficiency, and a generally unpleasant work atmos-

---

[20] Arthur Ross, the veritable fountainhead of the relatively recent emphasis on the importance of wage comparisons, presented the classic statement of the pressures generated by "coercive comparisons" in his *Trade Union Wage Policy* (1948). Thus it is not hard to see how the discussions of this factor tended to concentrate on collective bargaining as the wage-setting mechanism. Nonetheless, many of Ross' vivid word pictures of the significance of wage comparisons are very helpful in dealing with the case of unilateral wage-setting, and are used below.

[21] Ross, *Trade Union Wage Policy*, 1948, p. 51.

phere. And, as has already been mentioned, both a priori reasoning and empirical labor market studies suggest that an employer may be willing to make a wage adjustment to obviate this undesirable possibility.

A second reason why an employer might choose to at least meet a wage increase announced by another firm involves the recruitment policies and position of the firm. The employer might feel that any deterioration of his present position in the local wage hierarchy would eventually make labor recruiting difficult and might force him to reduce his hiring standards. Thirdly, a well-paying firm might choose to "keep up with the area" simply because management either enjoys the firm's reputation as a "good place to work" or would regard a failure to keep up with the area as an admission of managerial failure. There is also the possibility that management may feel a "moral" responsibility to pay prevailing wages. A fourth possibility is that management may be anxious to "keep up with the area" as part of a program to lessen the possibility of union penetration of its work force.

While these reasons help explain the pressures wage comparisons exert on the management of a firm to raise its wage level, they clearly do not provide the basis for explaining management's response to these pressures. The final decision of management will depend, of course, not just on the advantages of raising wages in response to an increase in other wages, but also on the impact of the potentially higher labor costs on the firm's profitability and market position. However, these latter considerations have already been discussed rather fully in the first part of this chapter (in the "ability-to-pay" section), and so it is unnecessary to recapitulate that discussion here.

We come finally to the problem of specifying more precisely just what wages are being compared. It is apparent that there is a multitude of "other wages" that the unilateral wage-setter could contrast with his own pay scales, and so the question here is which of these "other wages" are especially significant and why. The main boundaries of the unilateral wage-setter's "orbit of comparison" seem to be delineated by the product market in which he sells and the labor market in which he hires. While there is general agreement in the literature that these are the significant boundaries, it has not always been clear that these two boundaries may affect the final wage decision in significantly different ways.

The important point is that, in the majority of cases, wage adjustments elsewhere in the local labor market serve as the comparison most relevant for determining the pressures exerted on the firm, whereas the wages being paid by the firm's competitors in the product market serve as the relevant comparison for determining the feasibility or opportunity cost of a comparable wage increase. On the one hand, worker dissatisfaction and the adjustment needed by management to maintain its reputation as a good place to work depend mainly (though not exclusively) on the wage adjustments made at other plants in the same area, and especially on wage agreements at those firms with which management competes most directly for labor or with which there has grown up a "customary" wage relationship.[22] On the other hand, the firm's reaction to this

[22] It is, of course, impossible to be perfectly precise as to which firms and which wage rates within these firms are "the" significant points of comparison. In general, it is perhaps most satisfactory to think of an index of the area wage level, with wage changes in immediately neighboring firms, in firms in the same product market, and in other firms which compete actively for the same source of labor weighted more heavily. The inherent ambiguity of this concept of an "area wage level" should warn us not to expect a wage change in any single plant to have perfectly predictable results throughout the area. As Reynolds (*Structure of Labor Markets*, 1951, p. 157) has emphasized, the complexity of this area wage level concept makes it possible for

pressure will depend to some extent on wage adjustments at the plants of its principal competitors, since it is these adjustments that are relevant for determining the prospective profitability associated with any hypothetical wage adjustment.

However, it must be noted that the above generalizations are subject to an important qualification. In the case of large firms that are members of rather clearly defined industries (such as steel, glass, and oil), industry comparisons may be much more important as a source of pressure on management wage-setters than local labor market comparisons. While it is true that these same industries are in general rather strongly unionized, it must also be noted that in some of these industries (and most notably steel) uniform industry-wide wage adjustments antedate effective unionization. Hence, the strength of intra-industry wage comparisons cannot be attributed solely to unions but must also be explained in terms of such factors as the location and size of firms, management aims, and the nature of competition in the product market.[23]

Influence of Wage Comparisons on Wages Set by Collective Bargaining

The appearance of the union on the scene requires that the above analysis be modified to take account of the significance of wage comparisons for union wage policy.

"any management to convince itself that it is 'keeping up with the area' *in one sense or another*."

[23] For a brief discussion of the situation in the steel industry, see John T. Dunlop, "Allocation of the Labor Force," *Proceedings of the Conference on Industry-wide Collective Bargaining, May 14, 1948* [sponsored by the Labor Relations Council of the Wharton School of Finance and Commerce], ed. George W. Taylor (Philadelphia: University of Pennsylvania Press, 1949), pp. 38-40.

Wage comparisons may affect union wage policy in two ways: (1) via their effect on worker attitudes, which was discussed in the previous section; and (2) via their influence on the union officers and the union as an institution. It is this latter aspect that must be examined here.

There have been numerous statements to the effect that the political nature of the union and the "competition" among the leaders of various unions is an important factor linking various wage agreements together.

In brief, the prestige of union leaders, the security of their present job, and their prospects for advancement are dependent to some extent on how they do vis-à-vis other union leaders. And, wage comparisons are a readily available index of performance.

Thus, to the extent that the union's wage policy is influenced by wage comparisons and to the extent that the union is willing to fight for demands based on such comparisons, the employer will be faced with stronger pressure for "comparable" wage increases than he encountered when setting wages on his own initiative. On the other hand, he is no longer tempted to give a wage increase to keep the union out and may even fight harder against proposals for wage increases in the hope of discrediting the existing union. In the "usual" case, however, it seems reasonable to expect the former consideration to be more important than the latter.

The extent to which this increased pressure for comparable wage increases is translated into actual wage adjustments will again depend, of course, on the prospective profitability of the firm and on the union's ability to shut down the firm and impose financial hardships upon it. *If* the firm is relatively prosperous or expects to be able to convert a higher wage into a higher price, a wage settlement based on some other agreement has certain advantages from the standpoint of the firm as well as from that of the union. First of all, there are the advantages listed

135

in the previous section that might tempt the firm to "keep up with the area" even in the absence of the union. In addition, the ready-made settlement may be attractive to the company negotiator because it supplies a definite answer, is face-saving to both the management and the union, and can be most readily defended by both sides.[24]

Not only may the appearance of unionism on the scene increase the importance of wage comparisons in general, but it may also alter the *locus* of comparison. Where collective bargaining is the mode of wage determination, comparisons extending beyond the local labor market are of much greater relative importance. In the case of non-union wage determination, it is the wage adjustments in neighboring firms that are usually of primary significance. Industry-wide comparisons serve mainly as an ultimate check on the local equalizing tendencies—and they perform this function only if competition in the product market is fairly strong. In the case of collective bargaining, industry-wide comparisons acquire additional significance in that such comparisons not only help determine management's reaction to wage pressures arising from other sources, but they themselves contribute to these very pressures.

In an economy where collective bargaining is widespread, comparisons may extend even beyond the confines of a single industry, though they generally lose some of their force in the process. Broader wage comparisons may be expected to be of some relevance in situations such as the following: (1) a single union has organized the workers in more than a single industry and formulates its wage policy at the national level; (2) there are active organizational or political rivalries within the labor movement.

Before making a few comments on "wage leadership" in general, it may be helpful to say just a word about the

[24] See Ross, *Trade Union Wage Policy*, 1948, p. 52.

significance of wage comparisons for wages set by arbitration or government edict. It is quite likely that any significance that wage comparisons may have for collective bargaining negotiations is multiplied many fold when some "impartial" body enters the wage-setting picture. The "impartial" authority needs a reasonably definite basis for settlement that has some appearance of equity and that may satisfy both parties. Wage comparisons and the cost of living are the criteria that best satisfy these requirements.

Problems Involved in Evaluating the Significance of "Wage-Leadership"

In our discussion of each of the wage-determining factors examined up to this point it has been necessary to appraise some "methodological" problem. In the cases of productivity, the excess demand for labor, and ability-to-pay, the problem of defining the significant economic concept was paramount. In the case of the cost of living, it was a question of the validity of deductions from statistical evidence. Evaluating the role of wage comparisons as a factor in the wage-setting process unfortunately involves all of these difficulties. First of all, there is the problem of the unit of measurement to be used in measuring the "comparability" of wage adjustments; secondly, there is the problem of defining the locus of wage comparisons; and, thirdly and most important of all, there is the problem of the conclusions that can legitimately be drawn from available statistical studies.

Subsumed within the broad problem of defining the appropriate unit with which to measure wage comparisons are such specific questions as the advisability of using percentage *vs.* absolute changes in wage rates and the choice of a particular wage figure to serve as the index of changes in the over-all plant wage level. The relatively broad focus of this study precludes our going into these problems here—however, we can at least recognize their existence. It is also unnecessary to add to our above discussion of the locus within which wage comparisons may be expected to be significant.

However, it is necessary to say a bit more about the third and most important problem involved in evaluating the role of wage comparisons—namely, the question of the significance of statistical studies that recognize the measurement problems discussed above. Here it seems absolutely essential to distinguish conceptually between two types of "wage leadership."[25] The essence of the distinction is that exactly equivalent changes in wage rates among a number of firms or industries may signify one of two things: (1) that all the firms have been subject to the same wage pressures and have responded in a uniform way; or (2) that a wage change was agreed to in a "key" firm or industry and that this wage change then spread through the remaining firms or industries even though wage pressures in these other plants were different.

The first possibility may be referred to as "barometric" wage leadership since the instigating wage change commands adherence only because and to the extent that it reflects general wage pressures with tolerable promptness. Two influences that do affect many firms in essentially the same way and may thus be especially conducive to "barometric" wage leadership are rapid changes in the cost of living and the introduction of government wage control. Hence, it is not surprising that during a war and postwar period there is a striking similarity in the magnitude of

[25] The following discussion has been inspired by discussions of price-leadership models, and especially by the work of Professors Stigler and Markham. See G. J. Stigler, "The Kinky Oligopoly Demand Curve and Rigid Prices," *Journal of Political Economy*, LV (October 1947), pp. 444-446; and Jesse W. Markham, "The Nature and Significance of Price Leadership," *American Economic Review*, XLI (December 1951), pp. 891-905.

138

wage adjustments.[26] The second form of wage leadership may be referred to as "coercive" wage leadership since in this case the wage adjustment negotiated in a given firm or industry is followed in other firms or industries regardless of whether the same exogenous wage pressures are present.

The important point is that wage comparisons are a significant *independent* factor in the wage-adjustment process only to the extent that "coercive" wage leadership exists. Wage adjustments explainable in terms of the "barometric" wage leadership model are also explainable in terms of other wage-determining factors, such as changes in the cost of living or in the general profit position of an industry. Our discussion leaves unanswered the difficult question of how in a specific situation one disentangles "barometric" and "coercive" wage leadership since both may be present to some extent. However, it does warn us to be very careful not to overestimate the independent significance of wage comparisons—especially if our assessment of the significance of wage comparisons is based on data for firms subject to very strong and very similar exogenous wage pressures.

Conclusions

1. An appraisal of the significance of wage comparisons in the wage-setting process is especially critical because this factor is important not only as a determinant of individual wage bargains, but also as a part of the transmission

[26] See the data collected by Arthur M. Ross ("The External Wage Structure," *New Concepts in Wage Determination*, ed. Taylor and Pierson, 1957, p. 193). To be fair to Ross, it must be pointed out that he explicitly recognizes the importance of these pervasive influences on wage comparisons (see his conclusion on p. 202). The difficulty, however, is that he does not go on to draw out the implications of this for the *independent* significance of wage comparisons.

process by which individual wage adjustments are transmuted into changes in the over-all wage level.

2. Wage comparisons create pressures for wage adjustments in both union and non-union environments. In the case of unilateral wage-setting by management, wage comparisons exert their influence by making workers dissatisfied (the phenomenon of "invidious comparison") and by threatening the position of the firm in the local wage hierarchy.

3. The appearance of the union on the scene adds another avenue through which wage comparisons exert pressure on wage decisions—the avenue of political rivalry. The union is a political organization, and the prestige of its leaders as well as the security of their present jobs and their prospects for advancement depend partly on how successful the union is in negotiating wage adjustments that are at least as good as those obtained by other unions and other leaderships.

4. Actual wage adjustments depend, of course, not just on pressures for wage increases but also on pressures to resist. In both the union and non-union case, the likelihood that upward pressures based on wage comparisons will be turned into actual increases varies directly with the prospective profitability associated with the hypothetical wage increase and inversely with the reduction in prospective profitability attributable to the wage demand.

5. The orbits within which wage comparisons are significant differ depending on the wage-setting institutions. In the case of unilateral employer wage-setting, the local labor market is the most important boundary of this orbit while the product market is generally of lesser significance. In the case of collective bargaining, the local labor market is of relatively less importance while industry and even inter-industry comparisons gain in significance.

6. In attempting to evaluate the significance of wage comparisons on the basis of statistical evidence, it is essen-

tial to determine carefully the most satisfactory method of measurement for the problem at hand. There are two main problems: (a) some index of "the wage" in a firm or firms must be selected; and (b) the relative usefulness of percentage and absolute comparisons must be decided.

7. In appraising the implications of statistical wage comparisons, it is also essential to distinguish carefully between at least two forms of wage leadership. "Barometric" wage leadership characterizes a situation in which uniformity of wage adjustments results from uniform wage pressures such as changes in the cost of living. "Coercive" wage leadership exists when wage adjustments are transmitted from one firm to another even though exogenous wage pressures are not the same in the two cases. Only the latter form of wage leadership is evidence of the *independent* influence of wage comparisons in the wage adjustment process.

8. Institutional Factors in the Wage Determination Process: the Union

Thus far, our discussion of the forces affecting wage determination in the individual firm has been concentrated on the significance of rather broad economic factors. The "institutional"[1] aspects of the wage-setting process have been considered only insofar as they provide the channels through which these broad economic factors exert their influence. It now seems appropriate to redress this balance somewhat by devoting the next two chapters to a more direct examination of certain institutional considerations. From the standpoint of organization, the present chapter is confined to an analysis of the impact of a single wage-setting institution—namely, the union. Chapter 9 contains a discussion of the importance of certain other institutional factors, such as the length of contract, the scope of bargaining, and the "public" nature of collective bargaining.

Probably no other aspect of the wage-price issue has received more attention than this question of the impact of the union on price movements. It is very easy to list a number of reasons that account for this emphasis: (1) The union is an important economic institution and it is natural that there would be considerable intrinsic interest in the question of the general impact of this institution on our economy. (2) The union is a "dramatic" institution whose activities are interesting to the public and thus to the men of the press and other authors. (3) Both the supporters and the opponents of unions tend to "play-up" the importance of the institution. Union leadership has a

[1] Here the word "institutional" is being used in a rather loose sense to mean both the characteristics of organizations such as the corporation and the union and the wage-setting practices of these organizations.

142

natural pride (as well as vested interest) in expounding the effectiveness of its organization; and the opponents of unions have an understandable inclination to stress the magnitude of the harm being done the economy by this institution.

However, the "naturalness" of this special interest in the union does not justify the over-emphasis on the significance of this institution for the wage-price issue that seems to have occurred. It is well to remember that: (1) There may be many slips betwixt a wage increase attributable to any source and an upward movement of the entire price level; (2) Not all wages in our economy are set with the direct participation of a union, and even where collective bargaining exists the union is but one party to the wage-setting process; and (3) The union does not operate independently of its environment, and thus to some extent it may simply mediate wage pressures that would have taken their toll under non-union circumstances.

In sum, unionism as a form of organization on the supplier side of the labor market is simply one more factor whose significance for the wage determination process must be appraised; and, we must be especially careful if we are to avoid exaggerating its influence unduly. With this warning before us, let us now proceed to examine in turn the impact of the union on (1) the wages of its own membership, and (2) the wages of other workers.

The Impact of the Union on the Wages of its Own Membership

It seems logical to begin an evaluation of the impact of an institution by inquiring briefly into its aims—what it would like to do if it could. The union is similar to most institutions (and individuals) in that it has multiple objectives. These objectives include not only a steady improvement in the economic position of its members, but

143

also such things as the security and growth of the institution itself, better working conditions, shorter hours of work, and the protection of the individual worker's job and his rights on this job. In short, higher wages for the membership is only one of many union aspirations, and even the instrument of wage policy itself can be used to pursue non-income objectives. Consequently, it is not surprising that many economists question the usefulness of treating the union as an institution that seeks to maximize any particular wage variable.

However, as Chamberlin has emphasized, this conclusion does not carry any necessary implications for the question of whether unions raise wages: "Certainly it is not shown that unions cannot raise wages by establishing that the concept of maximization is inappropriate in the labor market!"[2] All that is needed for the possibility of union impact on wages is a desire by the union to raise the remuneration of its members above the level that management would unilaterally select. And there is every reason to believe that union views on this subject are essentially the same as they were when Gompers defined the objective of his union in one word: "More."

Professor Charles Lindblom has painted essentially the same picture of union wage aims by suggesting that the income goal of the union is "All we can get!"[3] The danger with this sort of characterization is that we may forget that the goal of higher wages may conflict with other union objectives, including some of the ones mentioned above. In brief, "All we can get" is an elliptical statement of union wage policy. A more complete statement would be "all we can get *without A, B, and C occurring.*"

[2] E. H. Chamberlin, *The Economic Analysis of Labor Union Power* (Washington: American Enterprise Association, January 1958), p. 28.

[3] Charles E. Lindblom, *Unions and Capitalism* (New Haven, Conn.: Yale University Press, 1949), p. 35.

The extent to which the two most likely deterrents to union wage claims—possible unemployment and heavy strike losses—may lessen union wage pressure have already been discussed. At this point it is necessary to consider one other possible mitigator of union wage demands which is especially relevant for the wage-price issue—namely, inflation itself.

The papers have been filled with pious pronouncements calling for unions and management to exercise "restraint" in their wage and price demands in order to lessen the danger of inflation.[4] Without being unduly cynical, it is possible to suggest a number of reasons for expecting such calls for restraint to fall on rocky soil: (1) there is no agreement as to the role played by wage increases in the inflationary process; unions do not feel that they can be sure any wage sacrifices they make will be translated into lower prices;[5] (2) the union as an institution will not appear to be doing as much for its members if their real wages go up by the route of falling prices rather than by means of rising wages; (3) no single union can expect a reduction in its wage demands to have much influence on the prices of the products its members buy, whereas a reduction in its own wage demands will have a strong and direct adverse effect; and (4) even if higher wages are translated into higher prices, workers are likely to gain

[4] See, for example, a call for restraint by President Eisenhower as reported in *The New York Times,* January 10, 1959, p. 6.

[5] Unions argue that it is the pricing policies of corporations that have forced recent price rises and that the companies could easily have afforded to pay the higher wages agreed to without raising prices. (See, for example, Weinberg's testimony before the Joint Economic Committee [*Hearings on the 1957 Economic Report of the President,* pp. 306-313].) Also, it has been argued that higher wages make the economy grow more rapidly and may thus actually encourage lower rather than higher prices. (See *Consumption—Key to Full Prosperity* [Washington: Conference on Economic Progress, 1957].)

145

more in their capacity as workers through the higher wages than they will lose in their capacity as consumers through higher prices.[6]

In short, we should not expect unions to reduce their wage demands very much (if at all) out of fear of inflation. Unions should be expected to push for higher wages so long as (1) the danger of these demands being translated into either direct unemployment for the membership or extensive strike losses is not too high; and (2) these wage demands do not interfere seriously with the attainment of other important union objectives, such as the maintenance of a satisfactory or workable relationship with the employer.

Given this desire of unions for higher wages than management would choose to offer in the absence of the union, the next question is: What devices or instruments can be used by the union to effectuate this policy—how can the union translate its desires into actualities? There seem to be two main routes available: First, there is the indirect method of restricting the supply of labor; and second, there is the direct method of persuading employers to agree to pay a higher wage than they would normally elect. The fundamental reason why, a priori, we would expect a union to be able to secure a higher wage settlement than unorganized workers is that a union can put much stronger economic pressures on the employer. As we have had occasion to mention in earlier sections, employer resistance to any hypothetical wage increase can be expected to vary inversely with the cost of refusing to agree

[6] Points (3) and (4) really amount to arguing that there are external economies involved in the pursuit of stable prices and that for this reason we cannot expect private economic groups (wage earners or corporation leaders) to assume responsibility for this objective of national economic policy. For a discussion of this point from a broader perspective, see William J. Baumol, *Welfare Economics and the Theory of the State* (Cambridge, Mass.: Harvard University Press, 1952), pp. 100-101.

to the increase—and the strength of the union is based to a large extent on its ability to increase this cost over what it would be in the union's absence. A non-union employer would normally not be faced with the alternative of having his entire plant shut down if he increased wages 5¢ an hour rather than 10¢ an hour, while this costly possibility might be very real in the case of a unionized firm.

Whatever the reasons (theoretical or empirical), it seems fair to say that today there is no real disagreement with the basic proposition that unions may have the power to raise the wages of their members, and that at times they exercise this power.[7] However, this apparent agreement should not delude us into thinking that all theoretical questions concerning the impact of the union on the money wages of its own membership have been settled. One very important topic remains to be discussed—namely, the question of the extent to which the impact of the union may be expected to vary as environmental conditions change.

The central point to be made in the following pages is that the *independent* influence of a given union on the wages of its membership should not be expected to be the same in all situations, but should be expected to vary in a fairly systematic manner with the general economic climate of the nation and with the economic circumstances of the specific firm with which it negotiates. Before going any further, it is essential that there be no doubt about what this proposition means and what it does *not* mean. By the phrase "independent influence of a given union" we mean the difference between the size of the wage settle-

---

[7] Thus Friedman, one of the main spokesmen for the school of thought that would "play down" the impact of unions on wages, has recently argued that the real issue is the *magnitude* of the impact exerted by unions on wages, not the existence of the impact itself. See Milton Friedman, "Comment" [on paper by Lloyd Ulman], *Review of Economics and Statistics*, xxxvii (November 1955), p. 401.

ment reached through the media of collective bargaining and the settlement that would have been reached in the same circumstances had there been no union. We are *not* arguing here that the absolute size of the wage settlement will vary as economic conditions alter (although this is rather obvious and has been argued elsewhere). What we are arguing is that this critical "difference"—the measure of the independent influence of the union—will vary as the economic environment changes.

Let us first consider the significance of the product market conditions facing the individual firm with which the union negotiates. It has already been suggested (in our discussion of ability-to-pay) that in general the more sheltered the competitive position of the firm and the easier it is for the firm to pass on higher wages in the form of higher prices, the greater will be the success of the union in raising the wages of its members.[8] This earlier, and rather general, analysis can (hopefully) be improved by distinguishing three aspects of competition in the product market: (1) the *intensity* of competition from present members of the industry, (2) the *nature* of competition within the industry, and (3) the *potential* competition from new firms.

As far as the intensity of competition is concerned, little needs to be added to our earlier discussion. It is apparent that in a highly competitive product market characterized by many firms, each eagerly seeking to expand its share of the market, any single firm would have to resist union

[8] This broad proposition enjoys general acceptance, and one economist has gone so far as to argue that, "For the most part, it is unionization that gives to oligopoly its significance for the wage structure, and the converse is also true—that it is oligopoly that gives to unionism its significance for the wage structure." (James R. Schlesinger, "Market Structure, Union Power, and Inflation," *Southern Economic Journal*, xxiv [January 1958], p. 304.)

148

wage demands doggedly since higher costs might put it right out of business. Hence, it is easy to see why a labor organization might prefer to deal with an oligopolist.

The nature or form of competition in the industry is at least as important for the union as the intensity of competition. An executive of a large glass firm has emphasized that big business management is often unwilling to take a strike even when the wage increase it has to grant to assure labor peace is substantial. This is due to the long-run necessity of maintaining production in order to hold important customers.[9] While it is possible that Hazard generalizes too much on the basis of the rather special situation in the glass industry, it is undoubtedly true that there are situations in which the customers of a firm are more interested in continuity of supply than in maintenance of prices, and that where competition takes this form there is likely to be less resistance to union wage pressures than where price is of relatively greater significance.

The extent of potential competition in the product market also has its role to play in determining the degree of success enjoyed by the union's wage-raising efforts. Several economists have argued that if there are no restrictions on entry, new firms will be attracted to an industry in which there are high product prices (due to high union wages) and a supply of non-union labor. These new firms would then presumably compete away at least a part of the pool of profits the union was feeding on.[10] While it is no doubt true that some kind of barrier to entry is needed to permit "monopoly" profits in the first place and that limitations on entry may enhance to some extent the size of the wage adjustment that a union will be able to obtain

[9] Leland Hazard, "Management Action on Wage Inflation," *Management Record*, xix (August 1957), p. 287.

[10] See, for example, Lloyd Ulman, "Marshall and Friedman on Union Strength," *Review of Economics and Statistics*, xxxvii (November 1955), p. 394; and Friedman, *Review of Economics and Statistics*, November 1955, p. 403.

149

from a firm, the significance of potential competition can easily be overemphasized—and probably has been.

In general, it is difficult to see why higher wages forced on an industry by a strong union would encourage other producers to enter the industry. Presumably these higher wages in and of themselves have not resulted in higher profits for the industry—we would expect just the converse. Thus, new firms would be tempted to enter the industry only if they thought the higher wages would make it possible for them to produce at lower labor cost than established producers. However, it is by no means obvious that new firms could avoid paying the same wage as the existing members of the industry. Unless new firms are able to locate in "traditionally" non-union areas (such as the South or rural communities), it seems reasonable to expect the new entrants to be subject to the same organizing pressures that resulted in the unionization of the established firms, and then the same wage pressures that resulted in the "high" wage scale throughout the industry. In many cases, it would seem that the only way in which the new firm would have any real hope of staving off unionization would be to offer at least as high a wage level as existing firms—and this alternative of course eliminates the labor-cost advantage that was supposed to entice the new firms into the industry. Consequently, it is important to avoid exaggerating the special contribution that restrictions on entry make to the wage successes of the union.

Let us now shift our attention from the nature of competition in the product market to the broader and more perplexing question of how the vagaries of the business cycle affect the ability of the union to exert an independent influence on money wages. Do unions have a stronger impact in periods of boom or in times of economic contraction?

We may as well admit without further ado that this

question belongs to that infamous category that can only be labeled "unresolved." A basic difficulty is that economists have not yet been able to agree on the subsidiary issue of how unions affect wages at a time of general excess demand, such as characterized the American economy during the immediate post World War II years.

The "popular" view that during such periods of widespread shortage unions play a far from passive role in the propagation of a wage-price or price-wage spiral has been challenged by certain "skeptics." These "skeptics" (under the leadership of Professors Morton, Friedman, and Rees) have suggested that in such circumstances unions do not raise the wages of their members very much and may even retard wage increases. A number of by-now-familiar arguments concerning the nature of trade union leadership, the psychology of workers and employers, the significance of fixed-term contracts, and the effect of public opinion have been marshalled in support of this position.[11] The views of the "skeptics" have in turn been subject to criticism, and so the debate has continued.[12]

The major stumbling block to a resolution of this controversy is that the evidence offered in support of both positions is beset by a great number of minor and major methodological difficulties. While it is convenient to postpone a full discussion of these difficulties until later, this forthcoming discussion can be anticipated to the extent of

[11] See Walter A. Morton, "Trade Unionism, Full Employment and Inflation," *American Economic Review*, XL (March 1950), pp. 13-39; Milton Friedman, "Some Comments on the Significance of Labor Unions for Economic Policy," *The Impact of the Union*, ed. David McCord Wright (New York: Harcourt, Brace, 1951), pp. 204-234; and Rees, thesis, 1950.

[12] See Sumner H. Slichter, "Do the Wage-Fixing Arrangements in the American Labor Market Have an Inflationary Bias?" *American Economic Review*, XLIV (May 1954), pp. 322-346; and Lloyd Ulman, "The Union and Wages in Basic Steel: A Comment," *American Economic Review*, XLVIII (June 1958), pp. 408-426.

noting that there are two main problems here. Thus far, no one has succeeded in discovering a way of separating out the *independent* influence of unionism from the impact of other wage-determining factors. There has been an important difference of approach in that some authors have concentrated their attention on the impact of unions on the general wage level while others have been more interested in the question of the impact of unions on relative wages or the wage structure.

The problem of estimating the independent influence of unions on the wages of their members during a general recession or period of rapidly declining demand is, of course, beset by these same methodological difficulties. However, there does seem to be more agreement here as to the direction of impact. Those economists who have expressed an opinion as to the impact of the union in the downswing of the business cycle seem to agree that union organization is better able to fight wage cuts than non-unionized workers and that therefore wages in an organized establishment are less likely to fall during periods of declining demand.

Returning to the original question of whether unions exert more influence on the upswing or downswing of the business cycle, it seems reasonable to conclude this brief excursion into the present-day status of this topic with the following observation: The position of economists in general seems to be that the union is more important in putting a floor under wages than it is in pushing wages up in times of general excess demand. Professor Slichter is the main dissenter from this view.[13]

[13] Economists who seem to feel that the impact of the union is greater during business contractions include (in addition to Friedman, Rees, and Morton) Kenyon E. Poole, "Full Employment, Wage Flexibility, and Inflation," *American Economic Review*, XLV (May 1955), pp. 583-597 and Frank C. Pierson, "Discussion" [of paper by Kenyon E. Poole], *American Economic Review*, XLV (May 1955), pp. 601-604.

However, extreme care must be exercised in applying this conclusion, at least as it is worded above. We shall now argue that a considerable part of the disagreement between Professor Slichter and these other economists (and possibly also a part of the agreement among the economists listed in the preceding footnote) is attributable to a semantical problem, and that, when this is cleared up, it is possible to set forth a somewhat more useful set of propositions.

The key question is what is meant by "more important." Does this mean that the independent influence of the union on the wages of its membership is greater in absolute cents-per-hour terms during a depression, or does it mean that the independent influence of the union on the wages of its membership is a greater proportion of the total adjustment that occurs? While there is no explicit evidence to suggest that the economists who have made general statements about the cyclical nature of union impact have thought about this distinction, we can hazard the guess that at least some of them mean to suggest that the union exerts a greater *relative* influence in times of extensive unemployment. The important point, of course, is that the union could exert a greater relative influence on wages in times of severe unemployment and still exert a smaller absolute effect than in times of increasing demand. And, it is absolute cents-per-hour changes in wages that are relevant for computing changes in the dollar costs of firms and changes in the dollar incomes of workers.

Armed with this distinction, we can now conjure up a set of broad hypotheses of our own. It does not seem unreasonable to suggest that the independent influence of the union on the wages of its membership is related to movements of the economic environment in the following way:

1. The existence of a union will result in a greater cents-per-hour increase in the money wages of its members: (a) the more favorable are employment and profit trends

throughout the economy as a whole, but especially in its own firm, occupation, or industry; and (b) the more sheltered is the competitive position of the firm with which it negotiates.

2. These positive correlations may break down if the nation is caught up in an extremely rapid inflation, especially if the union has not had to deal with such a situation before. It is conceivable that an inexperienced union faced with a relatively rapid inflation may negotiate a smaller wage increase than would have occurred in the absence of the union.

3. The proportion of the total wage adjustment attributable to the independent influence of the union will probably be greatest when the economy in general, and especially the firm with which the union deals, is faced with declining demand and widespread unemployment; and this proportion will probably be smallest when large wage increases were "in the cards" anyway.[14]

The first hypothesis is based primarily on a point developed earlier—namely, that the ability of the union to win concessions in excess of those that management would agree to in the absence of the union depends mainly on the ability of the union to increase the opportunity costs to the firm of refusing to grant a hypothetical wage increase. And, these union-induced increases in opportunity cost probably vary roughly with the two sets of factors listed in the proposition.

The second proposition is based partly on the argu-

---

[14] This proposition is deliberately worded in terms of the two cyclical extremes. It is very difficult to estimate the relative impact of the union over the wide band of conditions between these extremes. It might either decline continuously as economic conditions improve or it might drop off suddenly when unemployment or profits reach some key figure and remain approximately constant until some critical statistic is reached near the apex of the up-swing, at which point the relative impact would again fall off sharply.

ments of Morton-Friedman-Rees noted above, and partly on an unwillingness to do much projecting of the 1945-48 American experience. It is conceivable that the plausibility of the Morton-Friedman-Rees reasoning depends on the existence of a union inexperienced in dealing with inflations. It is not at all apparent that if another war were to break out now, union wage demands would be as restrained during the war and postwar period as they were during the World War II period. With World War II happenings as background, union leaders might well try to anticipate continued rising prices by demanding higher wages, and management might accede to such demands. Finally, it must not be forgotten that union leaders read what we economists say about their ineffectiveness in inflationary situations—and even if they do not believe what we write, they may resolve to dispel any doubts in our minds next time.

The third and last proposition is primarily a concession to prevailing opinion on the impact of the union, the arithmetic fact that any union impact in times of low employment is likely to be a large percentage of the change that would have occurred in the absence of the union, and to the psychological propensity of union leaders to think in terms of cents-per-hour and to be less difficult to satisfy when negotiations are already running in terms of a large absolute settlement.

In addition to these broad economic trends, the impact of a union on the wages of its members will depend on another set of factors—namely, the characteristics of the union itself. As every labor economics textbook tells us, "there are unions and there are unions"; and it would be surprising indeed if all unions had the same influence on the wages of their members. Thus the impact of a particular union will probably depend partly on such characteristics as its own internal strength,[15] its broad economic policies,[16] and its age and rate of growth. While we cannot dwell on the more fundamental factors that determine these characteristics, it is possible to add a fourth hypothesis to our list by noting that:

4. New unionism or expanding unionism is likely to be a greater source of wage increases than continuing or stable unionism.

The basic explanation for this phenomenon is simply that a new or rapidly expanding union will be very anxious to demonstrate to its newly acquired membership (as well as to its potential members) that it can "deliver the goods." Also, it is not unlikely that the same forces or conditions that spawned the formation or expansion of the union will also be conducive to fairly sizeable wage increases. So far as empirical evidence is concerned, the impact of unionization is generally credited with playing a fairly significant role in some of the substantial wage increases granted in the latter half of the 1930's.[17]

[15] The phrase "its own internal strength" is used to stand for the whole complex of factors which include: the cohesiveness of the union membership; their willingness (and ability) to endure strikes; the attitudes, ability, and militance of the union leadership; and the nature of the political struggles for power (if any) within the union. Internal strength can be contrasted with bargaining strength (or ability to wrest concessions from the employer), which also depends on the economic environment and the characteristics of the firm with which the union is negotiating.

[16] The significance of union policies or the general philosophy of the union for its impact on wages is emphasized by Clark Kerr ("Labor's Income Share and the Labor Movement," *New Concepts in Wage Determination*, ed. Taylor and Pierson, 1957, pp. 260-298, but especially pp. 266ff.). Professor Kerr distinguishes six possible economic programs of unions.

[17] See, for example, Arthur M. Ross and William Goldner, "Forces Affecting the Interindustry Wage Structure," *Quarterly Journal of Economics*, LXIV (May 1950), p. 267.

The Impact of a Union on the Wages of Non-Members

The discussion thus far has been confined to the impact of a given union on the wages of its own membership. Let us now look briefly at the impact of this same union (Union X operating in Firm X) on wage determination in some other firm (Firm Y). This question of the impact of Union X on wages outside its own jurisdiction is important not only for our understanding of wage determination in the individual firm, but also for a methodological problem—the suitability of measuring the impact of the union via wage comparisons—to which we shall turn shortly.

A union can influence the wages of workers in some other plant in at least four ways: The first possibility is that an increase in the wages of Union X members will impel the management of Firm Y to raise the wages of its workers in order to forestall the possibility that these workers will be so impressed with the accomplishments of Union X that they too will decide to be represented by a non-company union. "Anticipatory" wage increases have long been recognized as a useful implement in an employer's anti-union kit of tools. Slichter has supplied us with an extensive list of "cases" in which unions appear to have had a significant effect on non-union wages.[18] Outstanding examples include the 1914-1920 period of "welfare capitalism," during which non-union employers raised wages and adopted employee representation plans to keep unions out, and the New Deal days of 1933-1941, when the steel and auto companies apparently attempted to forestall unionization by liberal pay increases.

While there seems to be no disagreement that "anticipatory" wage increases may occur in Firm Y if it is presently non-union and hopes to remain so, the likelihood of

[18] Slichter, *American Economic Review*, XLIV (May 1954), pp. 334-337.

this possibility is open to question. Slichter himself has suggested that anticipatory wage increases are much less likely during severe recessions and much more likely "in periods of strong sellers' markets, when unions are gaining members rapidly and winning large wage increases."[19] As far as Firm Y in particular is concerned, an even more important consideration may be the extent to which unionization is feared. After all, it is difficult to understand why "anticipatory" wage increases would be given by a firm or employer who either had no strong desire to avoid dealing with a union or who thought the likelihood of unionization of the workers with whom he dealt was extremely slight. As Rees has argued, it does not seem likely that fear of unionization has impelled employers to raise the wages of such groups as domestic servants or agricultural workers in response to an increase in the wages of a certain manufacturing union. Anticipatory wage increases seem much more likely in situations where an employer is trying to operate non-union in a predominantly unionized industry or area.[20]

One final point should be made in connection with this anticipatory wage increase argument. For a union to influence non-union wages in this manner, it may *not* be necessary for the union to exert much of an independent influence on wages in Firm X. This is because the employees (and possibly also the management) of Firm Y may tend to credit the union with the entirety of any wage increase granted at Firm X. And this is one situation in which it is the *apparent* success of Union X rather than its *actual* success which is relevant.

The second way in which Union X may influence the wages of workers in Firm Y is through the mechanism of

[19] Slichter, *American Economic Review*, XLIV (May 1954), pp. 334-335.

[20] Albert Rees, "Discussion" [of papers by Slichter and Christenson], *American Economic Review*, XLIV (May 1954), p. 364.

wage comparisons, which we described earlier. As pointed out in this earlier discussion, there are a number of reasons other than fear of unionization that might motivate a non-union firm to meet a wage increase agreed to elsewhere. Of course, Union X can influence the wages of workers in Firm Y by this route only to the extent that: (1) Union X has an *independent* influence on wages in Firm X;[21] and (2) that Firm X is within Firm Y's orbit of comparison. The recognition of this "coercive comparison" avenue of impact is especially important for the methodological measurement problem, since it implies that a union can influence non-union wages even in cases where there is no fear of unionization.[22] As a final point, it should be noted that this second avenue of impact differs from the anticipatory wage possibility not only by requiring that Union X exert an actual impact on wages in its own firm, but also by applying to unionized as well as non-unionized firms. That is, by this "coercive comparison" route, Union X can affect wages in Firm Y even if Firm Y is also unionized. In fact, it has been argued earlier that the pressure of wage comparisons may be even stronger in cases of inter-union comparisons.

The third way that a union can influence wages in another firm is by affecting the supply of labor. The argu-

[21] This is because in this case (in contrast to the anticipatory wage increase case) it is only the *magnitude* and not the *source* of the wage increase at Firm X that matters.

[22] For some reason this point seems to have been overlooked in the union-impact literature. Thus Rees' reply (*American Economic Review*, May 1954, p. 364) to the assertion that unions may raise non-union wages is couched entirely in terms of the lack of fear of unionization in some sectors. This is understandable in the light of Slichter's emphasis on this route of impact, but it is nonetheless true that Rees' argument does not dispose of the wage-comparison possibility. Rees has repeated this line of reasoning in his more recent reply to Ulman ("Reply," *American Economic Review*, xlviii [June 1958], p. 428).

ment here is that an increase in the wages of Union X members[23] will exert a *downward* pressure on the wages at Firm Y by increasing its supply of labor. The likelihood of this possibility would seem to depend on three factors: (1) the direct effect of a wage increase in Firm X on the *excess* supply of workers to Firm Y; (2) the indirect effects of the wage increase on the *excess* supply of workers to Y via price and income elasticities as well as via government response to the consequences of the wage increase; and (3) the extent to which wages are determined in Firm Y with reference to the excess supply of labor facing the firm.

Considering first the direct effects of a wage increase secured by Union X on the supply of labor to Firm Y, there will be little or no exodus from Firm X if its demand curve for labor is relatively inelastic or if the wage increase is accompanied by some work-sharing arrangement such as shorter hours. And, in the light of our earlier analysis of wage determination in general and our more recent examination of the conditions under which union impact on the wages of its own members is most likely, it does not seem very probable that the union would be responsible for a wage increase that would bring about a direct reduction in the number of men employed by Firm X. Even if there was an exodus of workers from Firm X, this would have the effect of raising the supply of labor to Firm Y only if the displaced workers were willing and able to be active candidates for job openings in the latter firm. And this would appear likely only if the firms were located fairly close together and hired essentially the same type of person.

The indirect effects of a union-inspired increase in the

---

[23] Throughout the remainder of this section, whenever we speak of an increase in the wage of Union X members or at Firm X what we mean is that part of the total wage increase which is attributable to the independent influence of the union.

wages at Firm X are much more complex and difficult to predict. Three sets of indirect effects can be distinguished: (1) The price of the product produced in Firm X may be increased because of the higher wages, and customers of Firm Y may be tempted to increase their purchases because the product of Y has fallen in price relative to the product of X (the substitution effect); on the other hand, the increase in the price of X may force people to spend more dollars on X and thus result in a decrease in their demand for Y (the income effect). It is impossible to predict a priori which of these effects will outweigh the others. (2) The income of the workers in Firm X has presumably increased and so we would expect them to demand more of Firm Y's produce since for this group of people the income and substitution effect will work in the same direction. (3) The ultimate consequences of the higher wages in Firm X may be unemployment (either in Firm X or elsewhere), and the government may respond to such unemployment by steps designed to increase aggregate demand. Such government policies might be expected to increase the demand for labor in Firm Y to some extent.

While we must recognize the theoretical possibility of these indirect avenues of impact, it seems safe to suggest that the magnitude of any such effects is likely to be quite small. Leaving effect (3) to be discussed separately below, there are several reasons for thinking that the indirect price and income effects of that part of the wage increase in Firm X attributable to Union X will not have much impact on the labor market conditions facing Firm Y. First of all, the initial contribution of the union to the wage hike in Firm X was probably not extraordinarily large. Secondly, there are a number of links between this increment to the wage and higher prices—for example, labor cost may be a small proportion of total cost for this firm. Thirdly, it is improbable that the products of X and Y are either sufficiently important in the consumer's budget or sufficiently competitive or complementary to make the substitution and income effects quantitatively important. Finally, we should remember that the probable ultimate effect on wages in Firm Y is further minimized by the possibility that this firm will either choose to make no adjustment to whatever shift in its excess demand curve for labor does occur, or that it will elect a non-wage form of adjustment. In sum, it seems considerably less likely that Union X will affect wages in Firm Y via this supply of labor effect than via the first two possibilities discussed above.

A fourth way in which Union X might affect wages in Firm Y is through the economy-wide repercussions set off by the initial union-inspired wage increase. Effect (3) mentioned above is just one of a number of possibilities of this sort. Analysis of this family of possibilities cannot, of course, be undertaken at this stage of our inquiry since it involves price policy and monetary policy questions that constitute the subject matter of subsequent chapters. However, we can be fairly sure that this temporary postponement will not distort significantly our present examination of wage determination in the individual firm. After all, it is rather unlikely that any single firm or union could, through its own efforts, alter government economic policy.[24]

[24] Many unions acting simultaneously (either independently or together) could, of course, have a significant effect on important national economic variables such as the level of employment and could thus exert a strong indirect influence on government economic policy and ultimately back on wage and price determination. It was recognition of this possibility that inspired the construction of aggregate dilemma models similar to the one outlined in Chapter 3. Thus, in a sense, this entire study is an inquiry into an economy-wide version of this fourth possibility.

Appraising the Impact of the Union: Some Methodological Problems

A number of references to the problems involved in the quantitative evaluation of union impact are scattered throughout the above discussion. Consequently, it seems appropriate to devote the last substantive section of this chapter to some brief comments on the two most basic methodological difficulties. It is hoped that this discussion will serve both to warn against drawing improper conclusions from certain types of evidence and to enhance our understanding of the measurement problem in general.

The first, most obvious, and most basic methodological problem is that there are a number of factors at work in the wage-setting process, and it is extremely difficult to know how much of any given wage adjustment to impute to any specific factor. Unfortunately, the tremendous difficulties involved in overcoming this problem do not in any way diminish its importance. The important point is that we are obliged to at least attempt to separate out the *independent* influence of the union as an institution from the influence of other wage-determining factors. Without evidence to suggest that a given wage increase would not have occurred in the absence of the union it is certainly improper to attribute the wage increase to union influence.

This point is so obvious and elementary that it would be quite surprising if it were not recognized by those seeking to measure the impact of the union. And, even a cursory examination of some of the literature shows that the problem has indeed been recognized.[25] However, recog-

[25] Lloyd Ulman has provided the most detailed explicit discussion of the way this methodological difficulty can hamper the assessment of union impact within the confines of a single industry (*American Economic Review*, June 1958, pp. 408-426). For a more general discussion of this problem, see Robert Ozanne, "Im-

nition of the problem does not, in and of itself, increase the usefulness of the data. As a result, almost all of the more common measurement techniques are handicapped by this problem to some extent. In particular, both inter-temporal and inter-industry comparisons are plagued by the possibility that the use of the *ceteris paribus* assumption may produce some quite misleading results.

This methodological problem is not, of course, peculiar to the measurement of union impact. However, it is particularly troublesome here because many of the significant wage-determining factors seem to have a way of appearing together. The sectors of the economy in which unions are strong are the same sectors in which employment has been increasing, the most profitable firms are to be found, and oligopolistic market structures are most common. Consequently, it is very difficult to know what changes in the ratio of union to non-union wages imply as to the significance of any one of these factors.

The second methodological problem that has impeded analysis of the impact of the union concerns the question of what it is that unions are supposed to influence. The main alternatives seem to be: the structure of relative wages, the level of money wages, the level of real income, and the division of this real income. Now it seems fairly apparent that unions might influence any of these economic variables, and that which of these concepts is significant for measuring the impact of the union depends primarily on the reason one is interested in measuring this impact. Since the ultimate concern of this study is the inflationary impact of the union, it is the influence of the union on absolute changes in money wages that is of primary relevance here. In assessing the relevance of various studies of union impact for this specific question, there are two important points to be kept in mind.

---

pact of Unions on Wage Levels and Income Distribution," *Quarterly Journal of Economics,* LXXIII (May 1959), pp. 177-196.

We must first be perfectly clear as to which wage variable is being examined in any particular study.[26] We must then be very careful to avoid a casual carrying over of conclusions relating to the impact of the union on some wage variable such as wage structure to the question of the impact of the union on changes in cents-per-hour wages. These two precautions are absolutely essential because of the possibility that a union or unions might influence wage structure without affecting wage levels, or *vice versa*. That is, a demonstration that unions have not had a significant impact on wage structure does not imply that unions have failed to exert a significant influence on the movements of money wages. Thus, comparisons of wage movements between union and non-union industries as well as the Chicago studies of the "relative" advantage gained by strong unions in specific industries are relevant mainly for the question of the impact of the union on wage structure and carry no necessary implications for the question of the impact of the union on the general level of wages or on the absolute money wages of its members. Similarly, studies of the trend of labor's share in the national income are of limited usefulness when we are interested in appraising the impact of the union on absolute money wages.

It is equally important that we avoid going to the other extreme of treating the impact of the union on wage structure and wage level as separate questions. That is, while it is dangerous to confuse the impact of the union on wage structure and wage levels, this distinction should not be pushed so far that it appears as though wage structure studies are of absolutely no use for wage level prob-

[26] Friedman has suggested that some of the appearance of contradiction between his own estimates of union impact and Ulman's observations results from a failure to distinguish properly between movements of real, relative, and money wages (*Review of Economics and Statistics*, November 1955, p. 404). In Ulman's defense, it must be said that Friedman's original article (*Impact of the Union*, ed. Wright, 1951) was also not entirely clear on this point.

lems. As has already been pointed out, an increase in the wages of a certain group of union workers vis-à-vis other workers (either union or non-union) can lead to a general upward adjustment in money wages via either direct "coercive comparisons" or through the less visible chain of higher prices, unemployment, and government fiscal-monetary policy. The main point here is simply that it may be possible to learn a good bit about the forces that impinge on absolute wage changes by examining pressures (union or other) on the wage structure.

There is no denying the complexity of the analytical problems involved in the interrelatedness of wage structure and wage levels. Friedman and Rees seem to be quite right in arguing that the total impact of the union on the general wage level cannot be appraised without going into questions of price and monetary policy, and in criticizing economists such as Ulman and Slichter for putting undue reliance on partial equilibrium tools in dealing with this problem.[27] However, there is also a serious danger in the Friedman-Rees approach. This danger is that such excessive reliance can be placed on the significance of monetary-fiscal policy that the importance of the behavior of wage- and price-setters is ignored. In brief, an evaluation of the impact of the union on the general wage level must be based on an integrated application of both partial equilibrium analysis and monetary or income theory. Any compartmentalization of the wage-price problem must be avoided—and the Friedman-Rees position can involve just as much compartmentalization as the ignoring of the fiscal-monetary authorities altogether.

[27] See Friedman's "Comment" on Ulman's paper (*Review of Economics and Statistics*, November 1955, p. 404); and Rees' "Comment" on Slichter's paper (*American Economic Review*, May 1954, p. 365).

Conclusions

1. The magnitude of specific wage adjustments depends not just on the broad economic factors examined thus far, but also on the characteristics of the institutions through which these pressures are transmitted.

2. The union has received considerably more attention than any other institutional characteristic of the wage-setting process. While it is easy to understand why so much attention has been lavished on the impact of this particular institution, great care must be exercised to keep the significance of the union for the wage-price issue in proper perspective.

3. Recognition that the union has multiple objectives and cannot usefully be treated as a maximizer of any simple wage variable is perfectly compatible with a conception of the union as a source of strong upward pressure on the wage level. While there are factors that will restrain union wage demands (for example, considerable unemployment or the fear of high strike losses), it is doubtful if the union will lessen its demands in the hope of holding prices down.

4. The union has numerous instruments to translate its desire for higher wages into actuality—the most important is the organized strike. Since by threatening to strike the union can exert economic pressure on the employer, it is natural to suppose, a priori, that the existence of a union could increase the wages of its members.

5. However, there are reasons for believing that the independent influence of a union on the wages of its membership should not be thought of as some universal constant, but should be expected to vary with general economic conditions and especially with the circumstances of the firm with which it negotiates.

6. It was suggested that variations in the impact of the union can be understood at least partly with the aid of the following hypotheses:

(a) The existence of a union will result in a greater cents-per-hour increase in the wages of its members: (i) the more favorable are employment and profit trends throughout the economy as a whole but especially in its own firm, occupation, or industry; (ii) the more sheltered is the competitive position of the employer with which it negotiates; and (iii) the more important are non-price forms of competition in the industry.

(b) These positive correlations may break down in time of very rapid inflation, especially if the union lacks experience in dealing with such situations.

(c) The *proportion* of the total wage adjustment attributable to the *independent* influence of the union will probably be greatest when the economy in general, and especially the firm with which the union deals, is faced with declining demand and widespread unemployment; and this proportion will probably be smallest when large wage increases were "in the cards" anyway.

7. An important methodological consequence of this variability in the impact of the union is that we cannot predict the consequences of a given level of unionism for wage determination on an "other things being equal" basis unless we know *the level at which these other things are equal.*

8. It was also noted that new unionism or expanding unionism is likely to be a greater source of wage increases than continuing or stable unionism.

9. The union may affect not only the wages of its own membership but the wages of non-members as well. Union-induced wage increases in a given firm may increase the wages of workers in certain other firms via two main routes: (a) "anticipatory" wage increases granted in an effort to forestall unionism; and (b) the mechanism of "coercive comparison" discussed earlier. It has also been argued that unions influence the wages of non-members by increasing the supply of labor to other firms and by im-

pelling the fiscal-monetary authorities to alter national economic policies. However, neither of these two latter possibilities seems likely to be of much quantitative significance for wage-setting in the individual firm.

10. Efforts to investigate the magnitude of union impact on wages have been hampered by a number of methodological difficulties, two of which are of paramount importance.

(a) There are a number of factors involved in the wage-setting process, and it is very difficult to know how much of any given wage adjustment to impute to a specific factor such as unionism.

(b) The union may influence a number of wage variables such as wage structure and wage level, and it is essential: (i) to know what specific variable is being scrutinized in any given inquiry and to avoid casually carrying over conclusions to other variables; and (ii) to avoid going to the other extreme of treating the impact of the union on the wage structure and the wage level as completely separate problems.

9. OTHER INSTITUTIONAL FACTORS IN THE WAGE DETERMINATION PROCESS

Whereas the main focus of the preceding chapter was on the direct impact of the union on wages, the focus of this chapter is on certain institutional attributes of the collective bargaining *process*. The general conviction underlying the present chapter is that the wage-price literature has not paid sufficient attention to these less dramatic aspects of the wage-setting process. Consequently, we shall now examine in turn: (a) the nature of the relationship between the parties, (b) the scope of bargaining, (c) the duration of the collective bargaining agreement, (d) the "habitual" nature of wage increments, and (e) the "public" nature of collective bargaining.

Nature of the Relationship Between the Parties

It is convenient to begin our analysis of the institutional aspects of the wage-setting process with a brief discussion of the significance of the general tenor of the relationship between the union and the corporation. In any specific bargaining situation, the nature of this relationship between the parties may influence the magnitude of the wage adjustment in two ways. First, the company may be more concerned about the impact of various hypothetical wage increases on the status of the parties than on its own short-run costs. It must not be forgotten that the size of a wage increase serves as a very handy index of the success or failure of the union. Consequently, if a company is anxious to discredit the union with which it deals, it may fight especially hard to avoid giving a large wage increase for which the union could take credit. The company may even be willing to go so far as to take a sizeable economic loss (in the form of a long and costly strike) in its effort to embarrass the union or certain union leaders. At the other extreme, a firm may grant an extremely generous wage increase in order to strengthen the hand of union leaders that it hopes will be able to remain in office.

In the second place, the amount of the wage increase may depend on the preferences of one or both of the parties for non-wage concessions. That is, the wage is usually but one among many items up for negotiation, and it is often possible to trade a wage concession for some other advantage. For example, a union seeking to consolidate its position may be willing to reduce its wage demands if the company will grant some sort of union security clause. Conversely, management may be willing to increase its wage offer in order to protect "management prerogatives."

It is, of course, difficult to generalize about the impact on wages of these non-income objectives of the union and corporation since individual attitudes can differ markedly. However, it does seem safe to suggest that managements today are not so anxious to discredit the union as they once were, and that the union security issue has been settled at or near the union's terms. Consequently, we would not expect institutional rivalry between the union and the company to exert downward pressure on wage adjustments.

The Scope of Bargaining

One of the most widely discussed institutional progeny of the union and the modern corporation is multi-employer or industry-wide bargaining. The nature, purposes, and economic implications of the area of bargaining have been the subject of an extensive and unresolved debate. One school of thought has argued that broadening the area of bargaining to encompass the entire industry is inflationary (that is, it will lead to larger wage increases than would occur in its absence). The main argument in support of this position is that competition among firms in the product market will be less of a limitation on union wage demands in the case of industry-wide negotiations because the demand curve for an individual firm is almost always more elastic than the demand schedule for the industry as a whole. That is, it will be easier to pass on higher wages in the form of higher prices when all firms in the industry are faced with the same increase in their costs; and, consequently, employers will have less incentive to resist union wage demands.[1]

There are a number of difficulties with this position. In the first place, the elasticity of demand argument is not so convincing as it at first appears. While it is true that a single firm selling in a competitive product market would rightfully be more concerned about a wage increase restricted to its own operations than it would be about an industry-wide increase in costs, these are often not the relevant alternatives. Even in the absence of industry-wide bargaining, a firm may be relatively confident that its competitors will be faced with the same wage demands and the same pressures to grant these wage demands. If this is the case, the competitive position of the firm need not be injured any more by agreeing to the wage increase demanded of it than if the industry as a whole had done the negotiating. Thus the fundamental difficulty with the argument that the single firm faces a more elastic demand schedule than the industry as a whole is that it is necessarily valid only for a demand schedule drawn up on the assumption that wages and prices in other firms in the industry are constant—and there are good reasons for thinking this sort of partial equilibrium assumption may not be helpful in many cases.

[1] Among the exponents of this argument are: W. G. Broehl, "Trade Unions and Full Employment," *Southern Economic Journal*, xx (July 1953), pp. 69-70; and Lindblom, *Unions and Capitalism*, 1949, pp. 89-92.

A less technical but more fundamental objection to the general proposition that industry-wide bargaining will result in larger wage increases than other alternative forms of wage-setting is that the cost to an individual employer of taking a strike is likely to be much higher if he alone is faced with this unpleasant prospect than if the entire industry would be shut down. It is apparent that an individual employer will be very loathe to take a strike while his competitors are still operating, since to do so might mean a significant diversion of his business to these other firms. This is apt to be an especially important consideration in an industry in which competition for "share of the market" is especially keen and under conditions of generally expanding demand. Thus one reason employers may favor "master" agreements is that in this way they are better able to prevent themselves from being "whip-sawed" by a union or unions.

Two other reasons why industry-wide bargaining may result in smaller rather than larger wage increases are: (1) Local union leaders are under less political pressure to get a settlement as good as the best increase obtained from any single member of the industry; and (2) The bargaining program of an association of employers may reflect the needs of the "poorer" employers to a greater extent than a bargain between the union and a single prosperous employer which the union may then attempt to apply "across-the-board."

In sum, there are a number of general theoretical considerations that lead us to suspect that in many instances industry-wide bargaining, in and of itself, will not lead to higher wage increases than would have occurred in its absence.[2] This is especially probable where the alternative

[2] Two relatively old empirical studies have also come to this conclusion. See Clark Kerr and Lloyd H. Fisher, "Multiple-Employer Bargaining: The San Francisco Experience," *Insights into Labor Issues*, ed. Richard A. Lester and Joseph Shister (New

is a form of pattern bargaining. If the alternative were completely atomized and independent bargaining or unilateral employer wage-setting, it would appear that industry-wide bargaining might well increase wages. However, in most situations, the choice is apt to be between industry-wide negotiations and pattern bargaining.[3] In such situations, broadening the *formal* scope of bargaining is not apt to exert upward pressure on wages and may even bring about *smaller* wage adjustments.

Length of Contract

A number of statistical studies have shown that there is an unmistakable trend in American industrial relations toward longer-term contracts.[4] While there has been considerable discussion of the factors responsible for this empirical phenomenon and of the attitudes of management and labor toward duration of agreements, the potential

---

York: Macmillan, 1948); and Richard A. Lester and Edward A. Robie, *Wages Under National and Regional Collective Bargaining: Experience in Seven Industries* (Princeton, N.J.: Industrial Relations Section, Princeton University, 1946).

[3] One is reminded of rather similar comparisons between the effects of monopoly and perfect competition in the product markets. As Joan Robinson (*Economics of Imperfect Competition,* 1933, p. 169) has pointed out, it is hard to think of practical situations in which these would be the alternatives. Comparisons of monopoly and oligopoly might be more relevant.

[4] See, for example: James J. Bambrick, Jr. and Marie P. Dorbandt, "The Trend to Longer-Term Union Contracts," *Management Record,* XVIII (June 1956), pp. 206-208; and U.S. Department of Labor, Bureau of Labor Statistics, "Major Agreement Expirations or Reopenings in 1957," comp. Cordelia T. Ward, *Monthly Labor Review,* LXXX (January 1957). For a brief listing of general literature on this subject as well as other statistical sources, see "The Trend Toward Longer-Term Contracts," *Selected References,* No. 73 (Princeton, N.J.: Industrial Relations Section, Princeton University, 1957).

significance of longer-term contracts for the secular behavior of wages and prices has not really been explored. When economists have considered this subject, they have often concluded that longer-term contracts are a "friend of fiscal policy" and act to stabilize wage rates.[5]

While this proposition may be true in certain circumstances, it is of dubious validity as a broad generalization. In the first place, "there are long-term contracts and there are long-term contracts"—and the significance for secular wage movements of any given contract of a certain length will depend to a considerable extent on its accoutrements or specific provisions. It is certainly improper to assume that a five year contract means that there will be no wage adjustments during this period. Contracts exceeding a year in length are generally accompanied by either provisions for wage reopenings during the life of the contract or automatic wage increases of the annual improvement or escalator clause variety. And where the long-term contract includes either a wage reopener or a combination of an annual improvement clause and an escalator, the duration of the contract will not be marked by wage "stability" either in the sense of no wage increases at all or even in the more restricted sense of definite advance knowledge of the course of wage rates throughout the life of the contract.

The inflationary impact of contract length depends not only on the "trappings" of the contract, but also on a second factor of greater theoretical interest—namely, the economic environment in which the long-term contract is

[5] Economists who have suggested that long-term contracts serve an anti-cyclical function include: Kenneth E. Boulding, "Collective Bargaining and Fiscal Policy," *American Economic Review*, XL (May 1950), pp. 314-315; Rees, thesis, 1950, pp. 66-67; John T. Dunlop, "Wage-Price Relations at High Level Employment," *American Economic Review*, XXXVII (May 1947), p. 251; and Friedman, *Impact of the Union*, ed. Wright, 1951, p. 226.

175

negotiated and observed. In fairness to the authors cited above as supporters of the view that long-term contracts tend to stabilize wages, it should be pointed out that they were probably thinking mainly of the 1945-1948 experience in the United States. And it is quite likely that longer-term agreements were a stabilizing influence on wages during this period. In the first place, escalator clauses and annual improvement factors had not yet been "discovered"; and, secondly, in a time of rapidly expanding demand unions may well undercompensate in the basic settlement for the wage increases they could probably win if they negotiated more often during the life of the contract.

However, in times of less steady economic advance and of cyclical fluctuations in the prosperity of the economy, long-term contracts may well increase the upward tilt of the wage trend. For one thing, workers may not be forced to negotiate at all during temporary slumps in economic activity and may receive an "automatic" or "deferred" wage increase even though the firm's demand for labor and short-run prospective profitability have declined significantly.

Furthermore, long-term agreements can exert significant upward pressure on the wages of other workers currently engaged in negotiating new wage agreements. Leaders of these other unions may feel an obligation (either to their members or to themselves) to get at least as large a wage increment as "automatic" increases are giving their brethren. Thus, invidious comparisons of this sort may inspire these other union leaders to put an extra measure of pressure on their own employers—and, this increased pressure may be rewarded with some measure of success. Schlesinger has suggested that the 1950 GM-UAW five-year contract with its 5¢ an hour annual improvement factor made it difficult for other major industries to offer less than this amount without causing trouble for union leadership, and that this was one of the considerations which caused steel management in 1952 to give a 5¢ an hour increase when the industry was operating at 70 per cent of capacity and a third of the union members were partially unemployed.[6]

These comments suggest that the *timing* of negotiations in general (and especially of· "key" negotiations) with respect to general economic conditions may be of considerable importance for the secular movement of wage rates. The arguments in the preceding paragraph tacitly assumed that the long-term agreement was negotiated *prior* to a temporary slump in economic activity. If the negotiation occurred *during* a temporary slump, one might argue on parallel grounds that a long-term agreement would depress wages below what they would otherwise be over the life of the contract.

However, we must be careful not to let this altogether proper recognition of the importance of the timing of negotiations lead to the conclusion that the trend toward longer-term agreements has no inherent bias toward either higher or lower wages and that the direction of impact depends solely on the somewhat fortuitous relationship between the chronological date of important negotiations and the swings of the business cycle. It seems more plausible to argue that while long-term contracts may smooth out the path of wage movements by retarding wage increases in times of rapid expansion and increasing wages in more troubled times, they may also impart at least a slight upward bias to the broad secular trend of wages.

One reason for this conclusion is that the duration and form of the collective bargaining agreement cannot be thought of as independent of the economic environment,

---

[6] James Rodney Schlesinger, "Wage- Cost- Price-Relationships and Economic Progress" (unpublished Ph.D. dissertation, Dept. of Economics, Harvard University, 1955), pp. 301-303. (Cited hereafter as Schlesinger, thesis, 1955.)

and that *rigid*[7] long-term agreements are more apt to be negotiated when they will encourage rather than retard upward movements of the wage level. While a long-term contract may be advantageous to either the employer or the union from the standpoint of its effect on the magnitude of wage adjustments, management may have an additional, more compelling reason for desiring a long-term agreement—namely, the prospects of labor peace over a comparatively long period of time. Consequently, it seems likely that the employer would be more willing to negotiate a long-term contract when such an arrangement is to his own disadvantage from the standpoint of its impact on wage rates than would a union.

A second, closely-related consideration is that the union is likely to exercise somewhat greater control over the time at which new negotiations take place. As the 1958 negotiations between the auto companies and the UAW illustrate, there are circumstances in which a union can choose to work without a contract rather than sign a new agreement at a time when economic conditions are unfavorable. It is, of course, the unwillingness of companies to "lockout" employees that enables a union to adopt this strategy.

A third reason why the instrument of the long-term contract is more apt to increase than retard the upward bent of the secular wage trend is that unions seem more willing and able to take steps to prevent the existence of a long-term agreement from harming their position than do managements. For one thing, the union may be able to protect the real standard of living of its members by securing the inclusion of an escalator clause in the contract; management, on the other hand, does not have available any comparable sort of clause to protect its own profit position. An equally important possibility is that if, dur-

[7] By this we mean long-term agreements without wage reopeners.

ing the life of an agreement, the union feels that conditions are such that it would be to its advantage to renegotiate, it is more likely to press for and succeed in obtaining a new contract (or at least a wage adjustment) than the company would be in opposite circumstances.[8] While the terms of the contract may prohibit the union from striking to enforce its desire for a higher wage, it may still enforce its wishes for an upward wage adjustment by either striking over some other issue (for example, work standards) or by simply working less effectively while staying on the job. By way of contrast, it is difficult to imagine management even trying to set aside the provisions of a long-term agreement, much less attempting to enforce such aspirations by parallel devices such as the lockout.[9]

The "Habitual" Nature of Wage Increases

Whereas it is fairly easy to measure the trend toward longer-term contracts, it is more difficult to describe in quantitative terms another trend in wage negotiations that may be of even greater significance. This is the tendency for wage earners to expect a significant increase in money

[8] Note, for example, Reuther's "living document" interpretation of long-term contracts that was proposed when it became apparent the long-term auto contracts were not advantageous to the UAW as a consequence of the outbreak of the Korean War. At its 1953 convention the UAW announced a resolution on this subject ("Resolution on Long-Term Contracts," *Ammunition*, xi [April 1953], pp. 28-29) which said in part: "Such living documents must not, during their lifetime, foreclose the working out of . . . practical problems that may arise which the parties could not anticipate at the time such agreements were negotiated."

[9] The theoretical argument presented in this section receives at least general support from an empirical study made by Benson Soffer ("The Effects of Recent Long-Term Agreements on General Wage Level Movements; 1950-1956," *Quarterly Journal of Economics*, lxxiii [February 1959], pp. 36-60).

wages each year as the "normal" thing. While the existence of this attitude cannot be documented by reference to statistical evidence, it is possible to cite the observations of a number of American and British economists.

Professor Samuelson, for example, has suggested that in present-day America: "Labor and management accept it as axiomatic that money wages will rise each year."[10] Hawtrey has commented in a similar fashion on British experience: "Since the end of the war work-people in all industries have become used to periodic rises of wages at moderate intervals, and many are likely to regard an apparently arbitrary cessation of the series as a grievance."[11]

The existence of this tendency to expect steadily rising money wages is certainly not hard to understand in the light of (1) the strong upward pressures on money wages generated by World War II and its aftermath, which got workers used to "rounds" of wage increases; (2) the natural desire of wage earners for what many salaried employees have enjoyed for a long time—a periodic increase in pay; and (3) the "discovery" of the annual improvement factor, which has translated into formal terms this expectation of periodic wage increases.

The real question is not the source of this "habit" of higher wages but the strength of its grip on wage-setters. That is, if this habit should prove strong enough to persist in the face of temporary declines in productivity or

[10] Paul A. Samuelson, "Wages and Prices in the United States," Paper prepared at the request of the financial editor of the *Sydney Morning Herald* for its annual Financial Supplement (1957), pp. 6-7.

[11] R. G. Hawtrey, *Cross Purposes in Wage Policy* (London: Longmans, Green, 1955), p. 123. See also: H. A. Turner, "Inflation and Wage Differentials in Great Britain," *Theory of Wage Determination*, ed. Dunlop, 1957, pp. 130-131; and Guy Farmer, "What's Ahead in Collective Bargaining?" *Management Review*, XLV (June 1956), p. 510.

mild business contractions, we may face yet another source of upward pressure on the secular course of money wages.

The "Public" Nature of Collective Bargaining

As we have already had occasion to point out, the development of our present-day wage-setting institutions has been accompanied by an impressive increase in public interest in collective bargaining. Both the dramatic nature of bargaining (especially when such colorful men as David McDonald and Walter Reuther are involved) and the importance of the results of the larger negotiations imply that this is no passing fancy and that widespread attention will continue to be lavished on collective bargaining.

The significant question here is: What is apt to be the probable impact of this public attention and interest on specific wage negotiations? In seeking to answer this question, it is useful to distinguish between two broad ways in which public interest can affect wage determination: first, public interest may be translated into formal, governmental measures that directly affect the wage determination process; second, the concern of the public may motivate the parties themselves to modify voluntarily their wage-setting behavior.

There would seem to be almost no limit to the potential impact of public interest when channeled into direct government controls. There is no denying the potential significance of such measures as direct wage controls or government seizure of industries. However, public opinion traditionally has manifested itself in such directly potent ways only on rare occasions such as "hot wars," and so, since our interest is more general, we shall concentrate our attention on three less overt ways in which public opinion may be reflected in the size of specific wage agreements.

One possibility is that wage-setters will be tempted to adjust their behavior "voluntarily" to the norms of the public out of fear of what the public will do if the parties do not "voluntarily" behave in such a high-minded manner. The essence of this argument is that the ghost of Senator Sherman graces wage-negotiations as well as meetings of boards of directors. Senator Sherman's ghost presumably derives its strength from the awesome nature of the modifications that Congress might introduce into wage determination or the wage-setting institutions themselves. However, the awesome nature of the ultimate sanction here may impart more weakness than strength to public opinion. After all, it is unlikely that the government would adopt extreme measures in response to a 10¢ an hour wage increase in a situation in which it had hoped for only 5¢ an hour. Strong measures altering long-standing, highly-regarded and respectable (as well as politically potent) institutions are apt to be taken only under the severest sort of pressure—and this sort of pressure is not likely to be generated by a slow but steady increase in unit labor costs.

A second general possibility that has inspired hope in the breasts of those who have faith in the basic altruism of Americans and American institutions is that the public's desire for price stability will percolate back down to the parties and exert a moderating influence on individual wage settlements. One need not class himself as a cynic to suggest reasons for doubting the likelihood of this possibility.

1. It is difficult to estimate how intensely the public desires price stability or to what extent the public desires to pursue a price stability policy by holding wages down. The public may be convinced that higher wages are a necessary source of purchasing power and economic growth and that untoward price increases are the result of corporate greed; or, the public may simply feel that indirect techniques such as monetary policy should be used to fight inflation.

2. The public's other desires in the collective bargaining area may not always be consistent with the non-inflationary wage objective. In fact, the public's conception of how the parties ought to behave may encourage higher rather than lower wage adjustments. More specifically, the demands of the press and the populace for labor peace weaken rather than strengthen the main impediment to higher wage agreements—the incentive of the employer to resist. The employer is encouraged *not* to fight rather than supported in his effort to resist wage demands—and at the same time the union is strengthened in its resolve for higher wages by the hope that the public will not wish to witness a lengthy strike. In his recent testimony before a congressional committee, Mr. Blough argued that in the past eleven years U. S. Steel has taken five costly strikes in an effort to hold the line against inflation, but that:

> . . . Hardly has one of these strikes begun before there is a nationwide demand that we settle it. Our customers must have steel or close their plants. Their employees face layoffs and loss of pay. The Government, too, must have steel; and daily the pressures upon us keep building up. And ultimately—if we do not settle—we may face the threat of government intervention. . . .[12]

3. Even if we grant that the public's standard of "reasonableness" influences wage demands, it appears that the public's view of what is reasonable is not apt to put much of a check on wage settlements.[13] After all, wage changes based on: (a) increases in the cost of living; (b) productivity increases; (c) increases in "comparable" wages;

[12] Roger M. Blough, *The Great Myth* (New York: Public Relations Dept., United States Steel Corporation, 1957), p. 22.

[13] This point has been emphasized by Peter O. Steiner ("Collective Bargaining and the Public Interest," *Labor Law Journal*, IV [June 1953], pp. 414-415).

and (d) high or increasing profits are usually accepted as "reasonable." Consequently, it is fairly easy to justify most any wage settlement which economic considerations permit.

4. Finally, even if the public did have an unequivocal desire for smaller wage settlements which it made perfectly clear, there is some question as to whether the parties to collective bargaining would be persuaded—unless, of course, statements of the public's preferences were accompanied by threats to the parties, a possibility discussed earlier. After all, both the union and the corporation have an understandable inclination to act in the manner best calculated to further their own interests. They may even feel that in a free enterprise economy their social responsibility is to do as well for their constituents as possible. It is, of course, possible that behavior based on such "selfish" aspirations may conform to the public's conception of the national interest. To the extent that this happens, fine and good, but we certainly cannot ascribe this happy congruence to the effectiveness of public opinion.

A third way in which public opinion may affect wage determination without directly altering the mechanics of wage formation is via the channels of fiscal-monetary policy and the general economic environment in which wage decisions are made. It has frequently been suggested that if employers are confident the government will permit them to pass on in higher prices whatever wage increases they grant, employer opposition will dwindle.[14]

While anything resembling a full discussion of the in-

[14] For example, Kerr has argued that one way in which the employers of the fifties differ from their counterparts of World War II times is that they have a "certain kind of faith in the government"; and that "their faith in government is a faith that moves wage levels." (Clark Kerr, "Governmental Wage Restraints: Their Limits and Uses in a Mobilized Economy," *American Economic Review*, XLII [May 1952], pp. 369-370.)

terdependence between wage determination, public opinion, and fiscal-monetary policies cannot be attempted here, it is possible to make a few general comments. First of all, it is clear that both the potential impact of public opinion on fiscal-monetary policy and the return impact of fiscal-monetary policy on wage determination may be quite significant. And, to the extent that public opinion does influence wage adjustments via this channel, it is more likely to encourage than retard wage increases.

At the same time, it is necessary to be very careful to avoid overestimating the extent to which government concern with the level of employment will reduce employer resistance and thus exert upward pressures on money wages. For one thing, the government is not committed to "full employment at whatever cost" but also has some interest in other goals, including price stability. Furthermore, it has yet to be demonstrated that the government is sufficiently skilled to prevent all vestiges of unemployment, even if this were its ambition. Finally, it is important to remember that even if the economy as a whole is shorn up by government policies, individual industries and certainly individual firms may still suffer declines—in both absolute and relative terms—and it is the expectations of individual negotiators that are significant for wage determination.

Conclusions

1. Apart from the independent significance of the union and the corporation, various attributes of the wage-setting process that result from the joint existence and interaction of these two institutions may also affect the magnitude of wage adjustments.

2. The general tenor of the relationship between the parties may either encourage or retard high wage increases, depending on the preferences of the parties for

non-wage concessions and the interest of the company in discrediting the union.

3. Much general speculation to the contrary, it does not appear that industry-wide bargaining, in and of itself, is apt to lead to higher wage increases than would have occurred in its absence. This is especially likely if the alternative is a form of pattern bargaining.

4. There has been a perceptible trend in American industrial relations toward longer-term contracts. This trend seems to carry with it two implications: (a) the troughs and hills of cyclical wage movements may be smoothed out somewhat, and (b) a slight additional upward bias may have been imparted to the secular wage level. It should also be noted that the introduction of longer contracts increases the significance of the *timing* of negotiations in general, and especially of key negotiations.

5. Another characteristic of present-day wage-setting is the existence of an apparent tendency for wage earners to expect a significant wage increase each year as the "normal" thing. Annual increments seem to have achieved an habitual status.

6. Finally, the wage-setting process has come in for increasing public attention. While there is little doubt about the potential impact of direct government intervention in the wage-setting process, a generally cynical attitude is not necessary to opine that wage increases are not apt to be "restrained" by the voluntary deference of the parties to the wishes of the public.

10. THE FACTORS IN COMBINATION

In the preceding chapters an effort has been made to analyze the impact of a number of specific factors on the magnitude of wage adjustments. The purpose of the present chapter is to tie together these individual threads and thus to form an over-all picture of the wage determination process within the individual firm.

It is just as well to admit at the outset that the wage determination process is an exceedingly complex animal. The basic reason for this complexity is that the individual factors which influence wage decisions are not independent but interact in diverse ways. It is this interaction that reduces the usefulness of simply listing the change in the wage rate between two points of time as an unspecified function of the factors already considered, and requires us to examine the significance of the factors *in combination*.

Consequently, rather than contenting ourselves with a simple enumeration of the specific factors that influence the magnitude of wage adjustments—such as productivity, the excess demand for labor, ability-to-pay, the cost of living, wage comparisons, and the institutional characteristics of the wage-setting parties—we must try to develop a simple schema that will bring out: (1) the role or roles played by each of these factors; (2) the circumstances under which each is of paramount importance; and (3) the combinations of these factors that are especially potent.

In order to investigate the interaction of the individual wage-determining factors, it will be helpful to make use of a very simple conceptual schema. It is convenient to think of the magnitude of the total wage adjustment (Δw) as the algebraic product of two components: the maximum cents per hour wage adjustment ($max \ \Delta \ w$) needed to alleviate—at least temporarily—all pressures on the firm to raise wages; and a reaction coefficient (r) rep-

187

resenting the proportion of the maximum wage adjustment put into effect by the wage-setting parties. Thus, in formal terms:[1]

$$\Delta w = r \cdot max \, \Delta w, \text{ where } 0 \leqq r \leqq 1.$$

An attempt will now be made to explain the determinants of both $max \, \Delta w$ and r given two differing modes of wage determination. We shall first investigate that class of cases in which wages are set by the unilateral action of the employer and shall then turn our attention to situations in which collective bargaining is the mode of wage determination.

Unilateral Wage-Setting by the Employer

An employer enjoying sole responsibility for wage fixing may encounter three closely related sorts of pressure to raise the wage level of his plant: (1) at the wage currently offered, he may be experiencing difficulty either in holding onto his present work force or in meeting his recruitment needs; (2) discontent on the part of his work force may be growing, with a concomitant diminution in plant morale and efficiency as well as an increased susceptibility of his employees to unionization; (3) the ranking of his establishment in the local hierarchy of good places to work may be threatened.

How large a wage increase will be necessary to obviate each of these pressures? The magnitude of the wage adjustment needed to solve labor supply problems will depend on the extent of the individual firm's excess demand for labor, the "tightness" of the whole local labor market, and the degree of "perfection" or the extent of wage-oriented labor mobility in the local labor market area.

[1] The sole justification for using this notation is expositional convenience. This treatment is certainly not intended to imply that these parameters can actually be calculated with any degree of precision.

Growing discontent on the part of the work force is probably attributable to either an increase in the cost of living or an increase in the wages of "comparable" workers. And, since a threat to the firm's position in the wage-hierarchy is probably also a consequence of increases in the wage paid by other firms, these latter two sources of pressure can presumably be countered by the employer raising his wage in line with the increase in the cost of living and wage increases being granted elsewhere.

Consequently, it seems that the maximum cents-per-hour adjustment necessary to satisfy the pressure on the firm to raise wages is a function of the firm's excess demand for labor, changes in the cost-of-living index, and movements of "comparable" wages. However, it would certainly be a grave mistake to view *max* Δ *w* as the *sum* of these three indices. Suppose that the employer thinks a wage increase of 5¢ an hour would solve his labor supply problems, that the cost of living has gone up the equivalent of 4¢ an hour, and that other firms in the area have been granting 6¢ an hour wage increases. Surely the employer need not consider raising his own wage rate 15¢ an hour to counter these pressures. A 6¢ an hour hike would not only meet the "going increase" but would also be more than sufficient to offset the increase in the cost of living and to eliminate (at least temporarily) the firm's excess demand for labor. The obvious point is that the same increase can relieve pressures on a number of fronts. Thus we can conclude that *max* Δ *w* equals the *largest* wage increase needed to counter an excess demand for labor *or* an increase in the cost of living, *or* an adverse wage comparison, rather than the sum of the wage increases necessary to offset each of these factors taken individually.

Hence, the necessity of considering the wage-determining factors in combination as well as separately is already apparent. Without knowledge of the present state of other wage-determining variables, it is impossible to predict the significance of a change in any one factor. For example, an increase in the cost-of-living index equivalent to a 4¢ an hour wage hike may increase the maximum cents-per-hour adjustment necessary to satisfy the pressures on the firm to raise wages any amount ranging from zero (the case in which other pressures were already at least equal to 4¢ an hour as in our example) to the full 4¢ an hour (the case in which *no* other wage pressures were already present).

Let us now turn our attention to the roles played by the various wage-determining factors in shaping the firm's reaction to *max* Δ *w*. Most generally, the value of the reaction coefficient *r* can be thought of as a function of: (1) the relative profitability of acquiescing to *max* Δ *w*; (2) the absolute profitability of the firm; and (3) the firm's preference structure.

The relative profitability[2] of acquiescing to the wage pressures embodied in *max* Δ *w* is at the same time both the most complex and the most significant of these three variables. It is, of course, possible that raising wages sufficiently to alleviate the pressures discussed earlier may be the most profitable alternative open to the firm, and where this is the case we would naturally expect the firm to offer no resistance at all to *max* Δ *w*—that is, *r* would equal

---

[2] Before proceeding further, it is absolutely essential that there be no doubt as to the meaning of the phrase "relative profitability." By the relative profitability of acquiescing to *max* Δ *w* we mean simply the *difference* in the profits of the firm which will result from increasing wages the prescribed amount rather than keeping wages the same but making the most favorable alternative adjustment possible. There is, of course, a clear distinction between the relative profitability of *max* Δ *w* and the absolute level of profits enjoyed by the firm. The relative profitability measures the *impact on or change in* the firm's profits as a consequence of raising wages, whereas the absolute level of profits represents the *end results* of *all* aspects of the firm's operations.

unity. On the other hand, it is also possible that the firm would lose money by raising wages. To determine whether, in any specific situation, acquiescence to the wage pressures will reduce or increase profits and by how much, we must examine *and compare* the impact on the firm's profit position of: (a) yielding to the pressures by raising wages; and (b) resisting.

The profitability of yielding to the wage pressures depends on the relative strength of the positive advantages of removing the pressures and the more visible disadvantages of a higher wage bill. The positive advantages of removing the wage pressures will, of course, vary with the specific origin and intensity of the pressures themselves. However, one generalization is possible: the nature of the firm's operations and work force will be an important consideration in determining the profitability of yielding to these wage pressures. For example, in the case of a firm that must be very selective in hiring and that is forced to invest considerable sums of money in training its employees, maintaining a high wage level may be absolutely essential to profitable operation. On the other hand, a firm with less demanding labor requirements, which is able to fill replacement needs from its pool of casual applicants, and which is not greatly bothered by high labor turnover or low employee morale may see very little positive advantage in matching a wage increase granted by some other company.

Against these positive advantages must be weighed the cost of the higher wage. It is tempting to suggest that the first determinant of the magnitude of these costs will be the relationship between $max \, \Delta \, w$ and the rate of change in average net labor productivity within the firm, since if the increase in productivity is equal to $max \, \Delta \, w$ there will be no increase in unit total costs as a consequence of relieving the wage pressure. However, to argue in this fashion would be to misinterpret the meaning of the word "costs."

191

By the "costs of the higher wage" we mean the profits *foregone* by raising wages, and a wage increase that matches an increase in productivity represents foregone profits just as surely as a wage increase unaccompanied by any productivity gain.[3] The magnitude of these opportunity costs is better thought of as dependent primarily on: (1) the proportion of labor costs to total cost; and (2) the nature of competition in the product market. The cost of raising wages by the full amount of $max\ \Delta\ w$ will, of course, be much less for a firm in which labor costs are a relatively small element in total costs and which competes in a product market in which it is relatively easy to recoup higher costs via higher prices.

The final step needed to calculate the relative profitability of acquiescing to $max\ \Delta\ w$ is to examine the costs or profitability of the main alternative to acquiescence— namely, resistance. It might seem that the disadvantages to the firm of failing to raise wages the prescribed amount are simply the obverse side of the positive advantages of raising wages—which have already been said to depend

---

[3] Actually, this opportunity-cost argument also represents a simplification and slight distortion of the significance of productivity changes. First of all, the rate of productivity change may affect the opportunity costs of raising wages by shifting the whole cost function to a new point of intersection with the demand function. That is, demand conditions in the industry may be such that maintaining the going price may not harm the competitive position of the firm, whereas raising the price in response to higher labor costs might result in a serious loss of customers. Secondly, firms may not view potential profits eliminated by an increase in wages commensurate with rising productivity in the same way as an actual reduction in profits brought about by rising labor costs. The latter may be regarded as much more unfortunate. For both of these reasons, there will probably be some correlation between the rate of productivity increase and the magnitude of the reaction coefficient. The firm is likely to offer less resistance (i.e., r will be nearer unity), the more rapid the increase in intra-firm productivity.

192

on the nature of the firm's operations and work force. This would be true if the only way in which the firm could adjust to labor market pressures was by altering the wage. However, it was pointed out earlier that there are a number of non-wage forms of adjustment available to the firm and that there are very, very good reasons for suspecting that a firm can relieve pressures emanating from a relatively small excess demand for labor more cheaply by reducing its hiring standards, pursuing more vigorous recruitment policies, or possibly lengthening the work week, than by raising wages.[4] To the extent this is the case, we would *not* expect the firm to raise wages (that is, r would equal 0) even though it might be more profitable to raise wages than to do nothing. Of course, we must recognize that these non-wage forms of adjustment are not very suitable for dealing with wage pressures that did not originate in an excess demand for labor. Consequently, where movements in the cost of living or a firm's desire to maintain its rank in the local wage hierarchy account for a large part of *max* Δ *w*, the realistic alternative to a wage increase is the *status quo* since these sources of pressure cannot be eliminated by non-wage adjustments. However, the possibility of non-wage adjustments may reduce the value of r significantly if the firm is concerned mainly about a labor shortage—and especially if the shortage is not serious or is regarded as temporary.

Although the relative profitability of acquiescing to the pressures for a wage increase is certainly a major determinant of the firm's response, it does not appear to be the sole determinant. Whereas we would normally expect the firm to make upward wage adjustments where acquiescence is the most profitable available alternative, we can

[4] See the arguments in Chapter 6. The economic rationale for the attractiveness of many of these alternative forms of wage adjustment is that they may permit a rather subtle yet profitable form of wage discrimination.

not be confident that the firm will refuse to grant all wage increases that do not promise to increase the firm's dollar profits. It is at this point that the nature of the firm's preferences and its over-all profitability enter the picture.

While it is very difficult to generalize about management objectives, it seems reasonable to suggest that a firm may sometimes yield to wage pressures in situations where acquiescence is unprofitable if: (1) the firm is strongly motivated by non-profit considerations such as ethical compulsions to meet the "going increase," a desire to be known as a high-wage firm, or a strong aversion (on per se grounds) to the prospects of unionization; and (2) the firm's overall level of profits (or, more correctly, the total prospective profitability of the firm) is sufficiently high to enable it to "afford" such motivations.

The firm's prospective profitability and its preference structure may also interact to increase its resistance to wage pressures. Firms may not only resist wage pressures whose elimination would be unprofitable, but may also refuse to grant a wage increase that *might* (on an actuarial basis) increase the firm's profits. This is because of the greater uncertainty attached to the potential dollar advantage of raising wages compared with the more visible disadvantages of higher wages. A firm that is not very inclined to take risks may elect to stick with the relative certainty of the level of profits associated with its present wage level rather than to gamble on increasing its profits by raising wages. And, the level of profits may be a significant determinant of a firm's willingness to risk a wage hike in the hope of improving its long-run profit position. The firm without much of a financial reserve may feel that it cannot afford to make such a long-run investment— especially when the size of the ultimate payoff is so uncertain.[5]

[5] On the other hand, it should be noted that in some cases it is the person (or institution) in really dire straits that is willing

It may be helpful to conclude this discussion of the determinants of a unilateral wage-setter's reaction to wage pressures with a few general observations.

1. A firm is almost certain to acquiesce fully to the wage pressures (that is, $r = 1$) if it appears as though such a course of action will ultimately be profitable and if the firm is financially able to take whatever gamble is involved.

2. At the other end of the spectrum, the combination of wage pressures which it is not profitable to remove and a generally unprofitable firm are quite likely to result in no positive response (that is, $r = 0$). And, if a firm is either unwilling or unable (because of low prospective profitability) to take the long view, it is unlikely that wages will be increased unless removal of the wage pressures promises to increase the firm's profits in the very near future.

3. Between these extremes, r can be expected to be nearer unity: (a) the greater the relative profitability of removing the wage pressures compared with the other available alternatives; (b) the higher the level of the firm's over-all prospective profitability estimates; and (c) the greater the extent to which the firm is motivated by the non-pecuniary incentives which encourage elimination of the wage pressures.

Collective Bargaining

Let us now see in what ways the appearance of a union on the scene alters the significance of the various wage-determining factors and forces us to modify our analysis of the determinants of $max \Delta w$ and r.

(forced?) to gamble. However, it does not seem terribly likely that a hard-pressed firm would elect to gamble its very limited resources on something as unspectacular as a wage increase. It seems more likely that the company fighting to keep its head above water would gamble on something carrying a larger potential reward (such as a new production process or merchandising technique).

195

The existence of collective bargaining may affect the maximum cents-per-hour adjustment necessary to alleviate the pressures on the firm to raise wages in two general ways: first, the old pressures for higher wages are now transmitted through the union and thus become more formal and more visible; second, and more important, new pressures for wage increases appear and thus the very magnitude of $max\ \Delta\ w$ may be altered.

Where collective bargaining is the method of wage determination, we can generally identify $max\ \Delta\ w$ with the wage expectations of the union.[6] The employer will rarely consider raising wages more than the union requests, and will normally regard acceptance of the union wage demand as complete compliance with the pressures for higher wages.[7] The question of the determinants of $max\ \Delta\ w$ thus becomes identical with the question of the determinants of union wage expectations.

Changes in the cost of living and movements of wages

[6] There is a troublesome problem of terminology here. The phrase "wage expectations of the union" is used here in place of "union wage demands" because the total cents-per-hour wage increase announced by the union as its official demand will often contain not only the real wage expectations of the union but also a certain number of cents per hour designed either to satisfy certain elements within the union or to provide bargaining room. And, for the purposes of this analysis, it is not the total announced union wage demand that is relevant, but only that part which the union actually thinks it can get and is willing to fight for.

[7] An exception to this generalization is provided by the experience in Britain and Sweden during the postwar period when employers on occasion unilaterally raised wages above the level agreed to in national negotiations in order to combat the widespread excess demand for labor. However, we must remember that the unions in these two countries were pursuing a policy of "wage restraint" when such happenings were most prevalent. Thus, the circumstances surrounding this "exception" were indeed "exceptional."

in neighboring establishments play essentially the same role in the formation of union wage demands that they did in the case of unilateral employer wage-setting: they are potential sources of worker discontent. The rank and file will usually expect the union leadership to demand that wages be increased at least sufficiently to compensate for changes in the cost of living and probably sufficiently to match "going increases" as well.

In addition to these "old" pressures, union wage demands will probably be subject to two "new" sources of pressure: (1) the size of wage increases won by other unions in the same industry or by other union leaders regarded as "rivals" will encourage the leadership of the union to try to get as large a wage increase here; and (2) the economic position of the employer and his probable reaction to various hypothetical wage demands will now be taken into account in shaping demands. The influence of political rivalries within the labor movement on wage demands has already been discussed at some length and need not be elaborated here.

The influence of the employer's position on wage pressures as well as on the response to these pressures is particularly significant in that it implies that $max \; \Delta \; w$ is not independent of the value of r where collective bargaining is the mode of wage determination. It certainly seems reasonable to expect the union to take the employer's general economic situation into account in formulating its wage demands. Thus, even in the absence of pressures from the cost of living or wage comparisons, unions are likely to demand sizeable wage increases if it is thought that the employer is likely to accede to the union demands. Demands for wage increases based on arguments that the firm's productivity has increased, that profits are "excessive," or that the economy needs more "purchasing power" can more realistically be viewed as the result of this source of pressure. In sum, the prospective profitability of the firm can serve either as an independent source of pressure for higher wage demands or as a check on wage pressures emanating from changes in the cost of living or wage comparisons. Whether the result will be an increase or decrease in *max* Δ *w* depends primarily on whether prospective profitability is high or low and on the strength of other pressures for a wage increase.

So far we have not mentioned one other wage-determining factor which was said to be a significant determinant of *max* Δ *w* in the case of unilateral employer wage-setting: the firm's excess demand for labor. This factor plays quite a different role in the case of collective bargaining. No longer does a positive excess demand for labor serve as a direct source of upward pressure on wages, since the union is not particularly concerned about the employer's recruitment problems. However, a positive excess demand for labor may exert an indirect influence on wage demands by suggesting that the employer may have an interest in raising wages a certain amount and so would not resist a moderate wage demand. An excess supply of labor may have a more direct influence on union wage demands in that workers are much less likely to push for a wage increase that might result in a strike if there is widespread unemployment in the area. Thus a general labor surplus can also restrain union wage demands emanating from other sources.

It is much more difficult to assemble the determinants of *max* Δ *w* in a meaningful whole under collective bargaining than under unilateral wage-setting. Nonetheless, a few general observations do seem in order. First of all, it may be useful to envision a first approximation to *max* Δ *w*, which is equal to the larger of the wage increases necessary either to offset a rise in the cost of living or to match an increase negotiated elsewhere. This first approximation may then be adjusted either upward or downward. Widespread unemployment or poor profit prospects within the individual firm (or a combination of both) may well force the union to modify the approximate *max* Δ *w* downward. However, this tendency towards a downward readjustment is likely to encounter a "floor" below which wage pressures are not likely to be reduced. The level of this floor will be set either by movements of the cost of living or, if the *CPI* has been approximately constant, by the minimum annual wage increment that the workers have come to regard as normal.[8]

The first approximation may be adjusted upward if the union feels that the firm is in a position where it will be more willing to negotiate a significantly larger wage increase than that indicated by approximate *max* Δ *w* than it would be to take a strike. An upward adjustment is especially likely if the cost of living and wage comparisons are not exerting significant pressure and if the union regards itself as a pattern-setter. The interesting, important, and unresolved question is whether the union will take full advantage of the employer's position or will behave as a "sleepy" bilateral-monopolist. It is entirely plausible that most unions will not push for wage increases significantly larger than are necessary to placate the membership or to demonstrate the bargaining skill of the union leadership. That is, there may be a somewhat pliable ceiling to union wage demands at that level of wage increase generally regarded as a significant achievement for the union. Of course, this conventionally-set ceiling may be revised upward over time.

Turning now to the question of the determination of *r* under collective bargaining, it is again useful to think of the value of the reaction coefficient as a function of the same three general variables described in the case of uni-

---

[8] In most cases we would expect a situation conducive to a downward adjustment of the first approximation to *max* Δ *w* to be characterized by a relatively stable cost of living so that the floor may be more frequently set by the "habitual" level of wage increases.

lateral wage-setting: namely, the relative profitability of acquiescing to *max* Δ *w*, the absolute level of the firm's profits, and the firm's preference structure.

While the significance of each of these variables may be altered by the introduction of collective bargaining, the appearance of a union on the scene will exert its strongest influence on the relative profitability of acquiescence. Remembering that the relative profitability of acquiescence is determined by comparing the impact on the firm's profit position of (a) granting the wage increase and (b) resisting, it is obvious that a strong union can alter the relative profitability of acquiescence by increasing the costs of resisting—after all, this is the main route by which the union seeks to secure its objectives. However, before exploring this possibility more thoroughly, it is necessary to recognize two less dramatic ways in which the union may also influence the profitability of granting a wage increase.

The immediate costs of establishing a higher wage will probably be essentially the same regardless of the institutional mode by which the wage decision is reached. After all, we argued above that the negative impact of a higher wage on the firm's profits depends mainly on the proportion of labor costs to total costs and on the nature of competition in the product market—and the existence or non-existence of a union would not be expected to affect either of these factors significantly. However, a firm may feel that the longer-run costs of agreeing readily to a wage increase demanded by a union are higher than the costs of a unilaterally elected wage hike. The rationale behind such thinking might be that the size of future union demands will depend on how hard management resists *this* demand, and that if the firm gives in too easily the union will think that it can take advantage of the firm in the future. Thus the firm may have a strong long-run interest in persuading the union that it is no "soft touch."

200

There is also a second reason why the profitability of agreeing to a given $max \, \Delta \, w$ may be less under collective bargaining. As noted earlier, the adverse effects of higher wages on the firm's costs may be offset at least partially by positive advantages of higher wages such as better worker morale and fewer recruitment problems. However, we would expect, a priori, that such advantages would be less of an offset under collective bargaining for the simple reason that the union wage demand may be based on pressures that are not significant to the firm. That is, under unilateral wage-setting the firm itself determines $max \, \Delta \, w$ on the basis of pressures that it would like to see removed, whereas under collective bargaining the union determines $max \, \Delta \, w$; and it would be surprising indeed if the removal of the pressures that generated the union demands (such as matching the wage increase won by a political rival of the local union leader) offered the same positive advantages to the firm as the removal of pressures that the firm itself identified.

In spite of the existence of these two ways in which the costs of agreeing to $max \, \Delta \, w$ may be increased under collective bargaining, the total effect of the injection of the union into the wage-setting picture is probably to *increase* rather than reduce the relative profitability of acquiescence. The basis for this conclusion is simply that the costs of resisting are apt to be increased much more significantly than the costs of agreeing. Consequently, the tendency of higher agreement costs to reduce the relative profitability of acquiescence will be swamped by the much stronger tendency of the higher resistance costs to increase the relative profitability of acquiescence.

As hinted earlier, the main source of the potentially significant increase in the costs of resisting wage pressures under collective bargaining is the threat of the organized strike. Whereas under unilateral wage-setting, the costs of resisting depend mainly on (a) the effect of a refusal to raise wages on the firm's ability to recruit and to maintain a contented work force, and on (b) the utility and relative costs of alternative non-wage forms of adjustment, under collective bargaining there is the additional danger of a complete shutdown of the firm's operations. The probable costs of such a shutdown will vary primarily with: (a) the union's ability to make the strike effective, (b) the cost of the strike in terms of customers disappointed and profits foregone (which in turn will depend largely on the over-all level of the firm's profits, the current state of demand for the firm's product, and the probable length of the strike), and (c) the probable outcome of the strike.

A secondary source of higher resistance costs under collective bargaining is the concomitant reduction in the usefulness of non-wage forms of adjustment that might have served as cheaper alternatives to a wage increase. The existence of collective bargaining renders these non-wage forms of adjustment less useful primarily because such techniques as the lowering of hiring standards or the lengthening of the work week are not apt to assuage the union and thus will not reduce the main source of pressure on the company negotiator—namely, the possibility of a strike.

The determinants of the relative profitability of acquiescence are not the only set of factors altered when we shift our attention from unilateral wage-setting to collective bargaining. The other two variables involved in the determination of r—the absolute level of the firm's profits and the firm's preference structure—also undergo several mild changes in character. It has already been noted that under collective bargaining the absolute level of the firm's profits (the total estimate of prospective profitability) is one of the underlying determinants of the costs of resisting union wage demands and thus of the relative profitability of acquiescence.

Secondly, the combination of the firm's preferences and

the over-all level of profits enjoyed by the firm influence r in a slightly different way. It is possible to suggest two reasons for thinking that under collective bargaining a fairly profitable firm is less likely to agree to a wage increase when the relative profitability of acquiescence is negative: (a) the existence of a union may lessen the employer's ethical or egotistical interests in raising the wages of his workers since the union will now be the primary recipient of either the "blame" or the "credit" for the economic well-being of the workers; and (b) the employer may now take pride in resisting the "unwarranted" demands of the union and may seek to discredit the union or certain union leaders. This latter consideration may even lead the employer to offer resistance to a union wage demand when it may appear that such a course of action will reduce his profits. On the other hand, we must not forget the public's desire for labor peace, which may persuade the employer not to resist as strongly as his economic interests might dictate.

While it is both difficult and dangerous to condense our analysis of the determinants of r any further, it may be useful to conclude this part of our discussion with three general comments:

1. Under collective bargaining the value of r is very dependent on the relative profitability of acquiescence. If it is considerably cheaper for the firm to meet the union's wage demand than to fight, r would be expected to equal unity. On the other hand, if it is far less costly to fight, we might expect r to equal zero. However, we shall now argue that this latter possibility is rather unrealistic.

2. In any randomly selected situation where collective bargaining is the mode of wage determination, the probability is strong that the value of r will be considerably nearer unity than zero. On first glance, this may sound like an extraordinarily strange assertion. However, the aura of mystery is quickly removed when we recall: (a)

that in collective bargaining not only does the value of *r* depend on the value of *max* Δ *w* (which was also true in the case of unilateral wage-setting), but the value of *max* Δ *w* in turn depends to a significant degree on the expected value of *r*; and (b) that the union is not likely to select a value of *max* Δ *w* which is so high that the employer will be better off taking a strike than meeting the union's demand. In short, in the case of collective bargaining, the value of *max* Δ *w* will frequently adjust itself so that *r* will be fairly near unity.

3. The important implication of this observation is that there is little point in exerting much effort searching for the value of *r* per se. The coefficient *r* is a significant independent determinant of the magnitude of wage adjustment only when *max* Δ *w* is determined autonomously (as in the case of unilateral wage-setting). Where there is a strong interdependence between *max* Δ *w* and *r*, the real reason for analyzing in detail the determinants of *r* is that such an analysis is absolutely essential if we wish to explain the magnitude of the over-all wage adjustment —and this, of course, is our major interest.

A Restatement

As a consequence of this interdependence between *max* Δ *w* and *r* (which, as we have just seen, is especially acute in the case of collective bargaining), it may be helpful to restate the essence of our analysis in a way that will focus attention on the determinants of the over-all wage adjustment.

1. *In the case of unilateral wage-setting—*

a. There are two *necessary* conditions for a wage increase:

i. First of all, there must be some source of wage pressure. *Either* the existence of an excess demand for labor *or* an increase in the cost of living, *or* an increase in "comparable" wages is sufficient to satisfy this first condition.

ii. The second necessary condition is that the firm elect to respond affirmatively to this wage pressure. This condition will be fulfilled *either* if it is more profitable for the firm to eliminate the wage pressures than to do anything else *or* if the firm has a strong preference for the wage adjustment even though it is not profitable and if the firm is wealthy enough to afford this sort of preference.

b. While both of these conditions are necessary, neither is sufficient by itself. That is, the existence of a high level of profitability and a sheltered position in the product market will exert no influence on wage determination in the absence of some source of pressure for a wage increase; conversely, strong pressures for a wage increase will come to naught without the concomitant presence of factors which both encourage and permit the firm to meet these pressures. On the other hand, the *joint* existence of the two conditions is sufficient as well as necessary for a wage increase.

c. The magnitude of the adjustment that will occur when the necessary and sufficient conditions exist will not exceed *max* Δw, and may fall short of this figure if financial considerations neither encourage nor permit the firm to make the full adjustment.

2. *In the case of collective bargaining*—

a. An increase in *either* the cost of living *or* "comparable" wages *or* the firm's excess demand for labor is no longer a necessary condition for a wage increase.

b. The relative profitability of acquiescence to a hypothetical wage increase is sufficient in and of itself for a wage increase since it will stimulate the union to put pressure on the firm for a higher wage at the same time it dictates that the firm yield to this pressure.

c. In general, we would expect the magnitude of the wage adjustment to be determined largely by the size of the wage increase the firm can be persuaded to grant without the unpleasantries of a strike. However, the magnitude of the wage adjustment can still not be thought of solely as a well-behaved function of even this conglomerate variable.[9]

i. The most basic reason for this lack of a simple and clear functional relationship is that unions do not "normally" push their wage demands right up to the point at which it is barely more profitable for the firm to acquiesce than to resist. This characteristic of union wage policy permits other variables to exert influence too. Thus, the existence of such other pressures for a higher wage increase as rapid increases in the cost-of-living index, a large wage increment won by other union leaders, or even the tendency of rank and file workers to regard a certain wage increase as "usual" may arouse the union to exploit more fully the profitability and market position of the firm with which it deals.

ii. Secondly, we must not expect every wage negotiation to be decided with reference to the *immediate* profitability of resistance and acquiescence. As noted earlier, an employer may resist more doggedly than economic conditions seem to justify either to "discredit" the union or to protect himself from "exorbitant" union demands in future negotiations.

[9] The word "conglomerate" is used here as a reminder that many of our individual wage-determining factors interact to determine the "relative profitability of acquiescence." Consequently, this composite concept cannot be regarded as an independent variable whose movements are described by any single statistical series or even by any simple combination of series.

11. THE GENERAL WAGE LEVEL

Preliminaries

Thus far our discussion of the wage determination assertion of the dilemma model has been couched solely in terms of the factors influencing individual wage decisions. It is now time to shift our attention to the fusion of individual wage adjustments into movements of the over-all wage level. However, before plunging into an examination of the factors responsible for increases in the general wage level, it is necessary to retreat a step and examine the meaning of this phrase "the general wage level," the reasons why we should be interested in studying its laws of motion, and how we should go about such a study.

In the United States today there is no nation-wide wage that is set by a single negotiation or wage decision. Consequently, the concept of a general wage level is an abstraction. What we mean when we speak of an increase in the general level of wages is that some index of the multiplicity of real-life wages has gone up a notch or two. However, the arresting characteristic of the general wage level is not merely that it is an abstraction (after all, economics requires the frequent use of abstraction), but that it is an especially vague and poorly defined abstraction. By way of contrast, the general price level is also an abstraction, but it is at least a bit better defined since we have two generally accepted indices of price movements (the Consumer Price Index and the wholesale price index), whereas there is no index of wage changes that enjoys a comparable degree of acceptability.

Why should we be interested in discussing the behavior of this amorphous index of wage movements? Perhaps the first response that should be made to this query is that it is important *not* to exaggerate the significance of changes in the general wage level, since price and employment decisions are made in individual firms on the basis of wage adjustments (and, of course, variations in other factors) peculiar to this firm. That is, it is necessary to be very careful not to let concern with some broad index of economy-wide wage changes obscure the importance of the individual components of this index.

Nonetheless, there are a number of reasons why it is useful to investigate changes in the general wage level: (1) We would expect movements of the general wage level to be at least roughly typical of wage adjustments that are occurring in individual decision-making units; and, to the extent that this is the case, concentration on the determinants of over-all wage movements may be a great time saver. After all, no one can possibly investigate every wage decision individually. (2) Even if there is a considerable dispersion of individual wage adjustments around the "mean" wage change, this dispersion may be of minimal significance for the present problem. (3) Changes in the general level of wages may be especially significant for studying the effects of wage adjustments on consumer spending. (4) Analysis of the general wage level both forces and permits consideration of the implications of broad factors (such as labor mobility and national economic policies) which may be of limited significance for individual wage decisions but whose composite effect may be quite important. (5) Still another reason for examining the determinants of the general wage level is that such an examination is essential if the existent wage-price literature is to be appraised, since so much of it is couched in terms of economy-wide wage changes.

As a last preliminary, it is necessary to say a word about appropriate and inappropriate approaches to this problem of explaining changes in the general wage level. In general, it seems inappropriate to: (1) regard changes in the wage level as a datum determined by exogenous forces; (2) analyze changes in the general wage level by analogy with wage determination in the individual firm; and (3) treat changes in the general wage level as almost entirely a monetary question not susceptible to any kind of partial equilibrium approach. The first possibility represents an unduly pessimistic orientation. Wage movements are so crucial that we are obligated to attempt to discover their rationale—and it does seem possible to make some progress in this endeavor. The second and third alternatives are both too extreme and represent unhealthy compartmentalizations of the wage-setting process.[1]

Rather than adopt any of these approaches, it seems more fruitful to proceed by taking the analysis of the wage determination process developed thus far as a starting point and making whatever modifications are necessary to allow for the existence of a number of partially interdependent wage decisions.

Factors Determining Movements of the General Wage Level

In a rather general and schematic sense, movements of the general wage level can be regarded as dependent on four main sets of considerations:

1. the same wage-determining factors that explain the magnitude of wage adjustments within the individual firm;
2. the *distribution* of these factors;
3. the price, output, and employment reactions of firms to wage adjustments as well as the reaction of the government and the monetary authorities to the resultant changes in price and employment indices; and

[1] The compartmentalization of the wage determination process that is involved in each of these two polar approaches has already been discussed. See the last section of Chapter 8.

4. such other factors as the characteristics of labor mobility and price and income elasticities of demand.

The first two sets of factors constitute the *proximate* determinants of broad movements in the wage level, whereas the latter two groups influence these proximate determinants at a deeper and less perceptible level. At this stage in our analysis it is necessary to concentrate on the proximate determinants, leaving a discussion of the more underlying factors until later.

The importance of the factors that influence wage decisions within the individual firm is self-evident. Our old stand-bys such as productivity, the cost of living, ability-to-pay, and the excess demand for labor will, of course, influence the index of economy-wide wage movements at the same time they are determining wage decisions. And, if our contemporary economy actually consisted of but a single firm and a single union (as pictured in our discussion of the dilemma model), or if there were a single auction-type labor market throughout the land, then movements of the general wage level could be explained with sole reference to these factors and to our earlier discussion of their interaction.

However, when we recognize the fact that we live in a *sectored economy* characterized by a plethora of wage-setting institutions and a whole complex of loosely connected labor markets and sub-markets, it becomes necessary to know more than that the level of unemployment has risen or that there has been a productivity increase. Knowledge of the aggregate movements of these factors needs to be supplemented by *distributional information*. That is, to appraise the impact on the wage level of a given change in, say, aggregate unemployment, it is necessary to know how this change in unemployment is distributed with respect to such other wage-setting factors as: (a) the location of strong unions, (b) the location of oligopolistic product markets, and (c) the general economic position (for example, profitability, amount of excess capacity, productivity) of various firms and industries. The central point is simply that the same set of average or aggregate conditions can lead to significantly different movements in the general wage level, depending on the dispersion of the conditions.

In order to deal more systematically with such distributional considerations, it is helpful to recognize that in our sectored economy an upward movement of the general wage level is not likely to be brought about by a single, all-embracing wage increase. Rather, a general wage movement is likely to begin in certain sectors, industries, or firms within the economy and then be transmitted with various degrees of success and at varying rates of speed to other parts of the economy. The total magnitude of the change in the general wage level will thus depend on the size of the wage increase agreed to in the "growth points"[2] of the wage structure and on the extent to which this instigating wage increase is transmitted throughout the economy.

In recent years, this conception of changes in the general wage level has become increasingly popular among economists, and the importance of distributional considerations has been acknowledged either explicitly or implicitly in several discussions of the wage-price issue. Possibly the best-known case in point is the "high-low" productivity model of wage-price movements popularized by Edwin L. Dale, Jr., in the *New York Times*.[3]

[2] This phrase is used by Reynolds (*New Concepts in Wage Determination*, ed. Taylor and Pierson, 1957, p. 240) when he explains movements of the general wage level in essentially these terms.

[3] See, in particular, the two main articles by Mr. Dale ("Living Cost Rise Laid to Services, Rent, and Transit," *New York Times*, March 10, 1957, Sec. 1, pp. 1, 54; and "Inflation Linked to Pay Increases in New U.S. Study," *New York Times*, May 19,

The essence of the wage determination aspect of Mr. Dale's model can be summarized in three propositions: (1) The economy can be divided roughly into two sectors: sector A is inhabited by strong unions and is also characterized by above-average increases in productivity; sector B consists of those areas of the economy such as the service trades in which productivity advances are minimal. (2) Wages in sector A rise at least as rapidly as productivity *in this sector*—that is, at a more rapid rate than the average increase in productivity throughout the whole economy. (3) The wage increases in A then spread to sector B, in spite of the fact that the productivity of such folk as barbers and teachers has not risen nearly so rapidly as the productivity of auto and steel workers.

For our present purposes, this high-low productivity model is most usefully thought of as an example or specific instance of the way in which movements of the general wage level are generated in a sectored economy. The best use we can make of this model is as a starting point for a more general analysis of the factors affecting: (1) the size of the initiating wage increases; and (2) the extent of transmission.

Concentrating first on the size of the instigating wage increases, it should be noted that Dale puts great stress on the distribution of a particular wage-determining variable—namely, economy-wide productivity changes. In his model, the size of the initiating wage increase is determined solely by the rate of productivity growth in the more progressive sector of the economy; consequently, the size of the instigating wage increase varies directly with the extent of dispersion of individual productivity increases around the mean increase in output per man-hour.

1957, Sec. 1, pp. 1, 48) as well as the critique of Dale's position by William Fellner (Letter to the Editor concerning the article of March 10, *New York Times*, March 25, 1957, p. 24).

The main a priori difficulty with this aspect of Dale's wage determination assertion is simply that his basic stress on the importance of distributional considerations is not carried far enough. Our earlier analysis of wage determination in the individual firm provides a strong warning against the placing of too much emphasis on the behavior of any factor in *isolation*—what is important is the *combination* of factors present in various situations. That is, the size of the initiating wage increase will depend on the *composite distribution* of all the wage-determining factors rather than on the distribution of productivity increases alone. An extreme dispersion in rates of productivity growth among various sectors of the economy might reduce rather than increase the size of the instigating wage increase—for example, suppose that the most rapid productivity increases occurred in areas where the absence of cooperating factors such as strong unions and imperfectly competitive product markets resulted in a translation of the high productivity gain into higher profits or lower prices rather than sizeable wage increases.

The important point is that the real source of significantly large instigating wage increases is the existence in our economy of certain especially "potent" or "deadly" combinations of wage-determining factors. Large productivity increases by themselves may not be overly significant, but when they are combined with an aggressive union, a high capital-to-labor ratio, and little price competition in the product market but sufficient non-price competition to encourage the maintenance of production at almost any cost, large wage increases are very likely to result. And from the standpoint of those who decry sizeable wage increases, the disturbing corollary to this analytical point is that such a "potent" or "deadly" combination seems to occur frequently in real life. Several studies have found rather close correlations between increasing productivity, rapid expansions in output, unionization, and a high de-

213

gree of concentration in the industry.[4] And we are entitled to suspect on a priori grounds that the profitability of the industry is also positively correlated with the above factors, although the empirical studies cited above do not investigate this possibility.

Let us now turn our attention to the more widely (and hotly) debated problem of the extent to which these instigating wage increases are transmitted throughout the economy. There seems to be some tendency for the exponents of the high-low productivity model simply to assert, without much if any argumentation, that wage increases negotiated in the more "progressive" sector will in fact be transmitted to other sectors. It is thus not surprising that other economists have asked *why* we should expect wages in the low-productivity sector to rise commensurately with wages in the high-productivity industries.[5] Probably the main reason we might expect at least some transmission is that "invidious" or "coercive" comparisons exert a very compelling pressure on the wages of workers whose relative position has worsened.[6] The postwar experiences of Britain and Sweden afford especially clear and impressive examples of the chain reaction which can be set off by an increase in the wages of certain workers and of the strength of the tendency for coercive

[4] See, for example: John T. Dunlop, "Productivity and the Wage Structure," *Income, Employment and Public Policy; Essays in Honor of Alvin H. Hansen* (New York: W. W. Norton, 1948), pp. 346ff.; Solomon Fabricant, *Employment in Manufacturing, 1899-1939* (New York: National Bureau of Economic Research, 1942) [cited by Dunlop, *ibid.*]; and Ross and Goldner, *Quarterly Journal of Economics*, May 1950, pp. 254-281.

[5] See the comments by Fellner (*New York Times*, March 25, 1957, p. 24).

[6] See our earlier analysis of wage comparisons as a factor in the wage adjustment process (Chapter 7). Many of the following points are discussed in considerably more detail in this earlier chapter.

comparisons to cause an upward spiral of the entire wage structure.[7]

In any sectored economy characterized by free wage-setting (of either the collective bargaining or unilateral employer action variety), the existence of this sort of transmission cannot be denied. The more significant and difficult question is the *independent strength* of this coercive comparison mechanism. There is, of course, no universal answer to this question since the impact of wage increases in the progressive industries on wages of other workers will vary with the combination of factors present in any given situation. It is, however, possible to list six *proximate* determinants of the extent of transmission.

First of all, there is the nature of organization on the supplier side of the labor market. In general, wage comparisons seem to exert more pressure on wages where there are unions than where the employer has sole responsibility for wage decisions. The main exception to this generalization would seem to be a situation in which a non-union employer was attempting to forestall unionization by quickly agreeing to a wage increase won by the feared union. And even in this case the existence of a union in the firm that granted the instigating wage increase is crucial to the transmission.

Secondly, there is the "political" situation within the labor movement. Assuming the existence of unionism in general, the extent of transmission is apt to be greatest if there is strong rivalry between the union that won the instigating wage increase and union leaders in other industries. Dunlop has emphasized at some length the importance of the location of wage leadership within the economy, and has suggested that: "If leadership in set-

[7] See, for example: Gösta Rehn, "Swedish Wages and Wage Policies," *The Annals*, cccx (March 1957), p. 106; Flanders, *The Annals*, March 1957, p. 98; and Turner, *Theory of Wage Determination*, ed. Dunlop, 1957, pp. 129-130.

ting the pattern of wage adjustments is held by unions and firms in the expanding sector, where increases in productivity are high, the rounds of wage increases will no doubt be larger than in case the pace is set in contracting industries."[8] While this statement would certainly seem to be valid, it is possible that Dunlop somewhat overstates the independent significance of the location of "key" unions by failing to emphasize that there is a natural tendency for wage leadership to be located in those industries in which the largest wage increases are negotiated. Consequently, it may well be that the degree of compulsion of the leaders of unions in the less prosperous industries to match the wage increases won by their more favorably situated colleagues is a more crucial determinant of the total movement of the wage level than the location of the wage leader—which, after all, is preordained to a considerable extent.

The "sleepiness" of union leaders constitutes a third factor. A wage increase won by a particular union may exert an especially strong independent influence on other wage adjustments if the union leadership in other industries has been "drowsing" and can be roused to take fuller advantage of whatever bargaining strength it happens to enjoy. On the other hand, if unions in the less progressive industries have already been getting all from the employer that they possibly can, larger wage increases won elsewhere may raise only envy and not wages.

Fourth, there is the dedication of workers and employers to "historical differentials." No matter whether wages are set by collective bargaining or unilateral employer action, the instigating wage increase will be more completely transmitted the more nearly historical differentials have achieved the status of natural law.

[8] Dunlop, "Productivity and the Wage Structure," *Income, Employment and Public Policy; Essays in Honor of Alvin H. Hansen*, 1948, pp. 354-356.

A fifth consideration is the "tightness" of the labor market. Wage increases in certain sectors will be spread especially rapidly if there is a general shortage of labor. This consideration is particularly important for wages set by unilateral employer action, since a wage increase granted by another firm that draws from the same labor market may not only make the existing employees of the first firm dissatisfied, but may also impair the employer's ability to hire the type of men that he desires. Consequently, there is a strong incentive to match the wage increase granted elsewhere.

Finally, there is the general profitability of the economy to be considered. The factors listed thus far determine, in the main, the pressures on employers to raise wages; and, as has been emphasized repeatedly, these pressures may come to naught in firms or industries that simply cannot afford to raise wages.

This whole discussion of the proximate determinants of wage transmission can be summarized most readily by re-emphasizing that wage comparisons run in limited orbits and that we should not expect a wage increase in any particular firm or group of firms to exert a direct influence on the wages of every other group of workers throughout the economy. The workers whose wages are most likely to be influenced will be those employed by firms that either: (a) compete for labor with the wage-setting units responsible for the instigating wage increase; or (b) traditionally have their wage scales compared (either by the units involved, the workers themselves, or the managements) with the wage scales of the "pattern-setting" firms. Even within this loosely defined and pliable orbit of influence we would not expect complete transmission of the instigating wage increase in all circumstances. The extent of compliance with the wage comparison pressures will depend on all the factors determining the relative profitability of acquiescence and resistance that were discussed earlier.

If the transmission of wage increases from one firm or sector to some other specified firm were the only significant question here, this general analysis of the proximate determinants combined with our earlier and more detailed discussion of wage comparisons as a factor in the wage adjustment process would be sufficient. However, our present aim is to explain movements in the general wage level, and this broader perspective requires at least some mention of certain more underlying determinants of the extent of wage transmission.

The reactions of the firms at which the instigating wage increase occurred (the high-productivity sector of the economy in our illustrative model) to this basic wage increase constitutes one important underlying determinant. The negotiation of the wage increase may reduce the firm's demand for labor, it may result in a price increase, or it may affect profits and investment decisions of the firm. Each of these alternatives may, of course, affect the proximate determinants of the extent to which the wage increase is transmitted to other firms.

A second underlying determinant is the price and income elasticities of demand of the workers at the firms that receive the higher wage increase and of consumers generally. These variables will influence the demand for labor and the profitability of other industries.

The extent of labor mobility is another underlying factor whose influence on movements of the general wage level has not as yet been investigated sufficiently. Authors who have considered this factor at all (either explicitly or implicitly) have tended to assume that the extent of increase in the general wage level will be less the greater the extent of labor mobility.[9] The reasoning behind this view seems

[9] See, for example, Joan Robinson, *Essays in the Theory of Employment* (London: Macmillan, Ltd., 1937), pp. 40-60, but

to rest on the twin assumptions that: (a) wages are fairly responsive to shifts in the supply of labor; and (b) firms in which wages were raised initially will either lay off workers or not hire as many new workers as they otherwise would because of the wage increase. To the extent that these assumptions hold, we would expect movements of the general wage level to vary inversely with the mobility of labor. However, suppose that higher wages in the prosperous firms result in no perceptible layoffs in these firms—in this case high labor mobility in the sense of workers in other industries or occupations desiring or attempting to secure jobs in the better paying firms may *increase* the over-all wage level by putting more pressure on other firms to raise wages. To the extent that labor mobility is low, firms whose relative positions have been worsened by the wage increase in the high-productivity firms may not feel under any pressure to raise their own wage level. Finally, it should be noted that a lack of labor mobility may affect the wage level by increasing the number of men unemployed. However, the ultimate direction of this impact is not clear. Whereas the existence of unemployment normally retards wage increases to some extent, it may also provoke government economic action that may have the reverse effect.

Finally, it is necessary to recognize explicitly that government economic policy is an important determinant of the extent to which "initial" wage increases are transmitted throughout the economy. The government may be impelled to take various actions in response to the composite result of: (1) the initial price and employment response to the higher wage; (2) the secondary effects via price and income elasticities; and (3) the tertiary effects de-

---

especially pp. 43, 48. For a discussion of the role of mobility in the general context of anti-inflationary policy, see Bent Hansen, *Economic Theory of Fiscal Policy*, 1958, p. 350.

pendent on the extent of labor mobility and employer reaction to a change in the labor supply situation. Stated most simply, the extent of transmission depends to a considerable extent on the level of aggregate demand,[10] and this is a magnitude in which the government is presumably interested. The important question here is the extent to which unemployment provoked by the instigating wage increase and the attempts of others to emulate this increase will in turn provoke the government to increase the level of aggregate demand, thereby permitting a fuller transmission of the initial wage increase as well as another instigating wage hike—and so on, and so on. This important question (as well as the problem of the direct impact of higher wages on aggregate demand) will be discussed in Part IV. All we can do now is indicate where the answer to this query "plugs" into the present discussion.

Our discussion of the mechanism by which movements in the general wage level are generated and effectuated is now almost complete. We have only to make two final points. First, instigating wage increases may be transmitted throughout the economy not only via the wage comparison route but also as a consequence of changes in the cost of living that result from the initial wage hike. An appraisal of the magnification of the initial change in the general wage level that will result from this avenue of impact must, of course, await our discussion of price determination and the impact of wage increases on costs and prices. However, it can be noted here that it is very dangerous to rely solely on input-output techniques to pre-

[10] This point has been emphasized repeatedly by Rees. See, for example, Rees' statement before the Conference Board Economic Forum (National Industrial Conference Board, *Wage Inflation: A Discussion by the Conference Board Economic Forum and Guests*, "Studies in Business Economics Number fifty-six," New York: National Industrial Conference Board, 1957), pp. 26-27.

dict the ultimate increase in the general wage level that will result from the translation of initial wage increases into movements of the cost-of-living index. This is because, as was emphasized earlier, increases in the cost-of-living index may impart no extra upward push to wages if a larger wage increase was already being considered to obviate some other source of pressure. Sources of wage pressure are not additive.

Secondly, it must be admitted that the preceding analysis of the determinants of the instigating wage increase and of its transmission throughout the economy does not supply a complete picture of movements of the over-all wage level. An important source of difficulty is that wages simply do not move upward in neat discontinuous jumps as is assumed in the above discussion. Rather, what we have is an ongoing process in which the tail and the head of the ascending serpent are not easily distinguished. That is, the size of wage adjustments in the instigating sector of the economy cannot really be thought of as independent of the extent of their transmission. An initial wage increase in a prosperous firm or industry that is matched by a wage increase elsewhere may in turn be followed by another wage increase in the first firm, another wage increase in the second group of firms, and so on.

Final Comments on the Wage Determination Assertion of the Dilemma Model

Our detailed inquiry into the specific determinants of wage adjustments within the individual firm, the ways in which these factors are combined in the wage-setting process, and the generation of movements in the over-all wage level is now complete. However, before shifting our attention to the price determination aspects of the dilemma model, it is appropriate that we return briefly to the original questions that inspired this quest into the realm of

221

wage theory. Consequently, this final section is devoted to enumerating some of the more general implications of the above analysis for certain key wage determination questions involved in the dilemma model. It is convenient to begin with a few general comments and then to turn to the two most basic issues raised by the dilemma model—namely, the relation of wage adjustments to: (a) the level of unemployment, and (b) productivity movements.

Some General Comments

The broadest—and yet at the same time the most important—implication of the preceding analysis can be summarized as follows: the empirical sort of assertion about wage determination employed in the dilemma model is both unsatisfactory and unnecessary. It is *unsatisfactory* because: (1) it conveys an unrealistic picture of wage determination—wage adjustments are not an island unto themselves, but both depend on and shape the over-all economic and political environment; and (2) because it is absolutely essential for us to understand the underlying determinants of wage movements if we are to appraise intelligently the nature of the economic problem confronting us and if we are to select wise policies for dealing with whatever problems are unearthed. The empirical-type assertion is *unnecessary* because, although extraordinarily complex, the wage determination process is not totally undecipherable. The entirety of Part II has been designed to demonstrate that it is possible to suggest key factors and combinations of factors that are especially significant in determining the magnitude of both specific and general wage adjustments.

A second general shortcoming of the wage determination aspect of the dilemma model is that it posits but a single wage and a single mode of wage determination—collective bargaining. In analyzing aggregate wage behavior it is necessary to remember (1) that changes in wage structure can themselves influence the general wage level, and (2) that more than half of the wage earners in our economy have their wages set by methods other than collective bargaining.

Finally, the preceding inquiry has revealed clearly that the wage determination assertion cannot be so neatly distinguished from the price and monetary policy assertions as implied in our earlier discussion of the dilemma model. The price and employment policies of manufacturers, the fiscal and monetary policies of the government, and the broader factors such as labor mobility that influence these policies—all these have a role to play in the wage determination process. Consequently, any final evaluation of the wage determination assertion must be postponed until after we have had an opportunity to consider these other assertions as well.

The Level of Unemployment and Wage Determination

Turning now to more specific problems, one of the most urgent questions raised by the dilemma model has to do with the likely effect of various levels of unemployment on wage behavior. In particular, the dilemma discussion has inspired many quests for the "critical" level of unemployment at which wages will cease rising more rapidly than productivity. Perhaps the first salient comment to be made in this connection is that the potential usefulness of such a "critical" value must not be overestimated. What we really need is a nice, well-defined, *continuous* function relating levels of unemployment to movements of aggregate wages. This more general function would be of considerably more use in the formation of wise policies than the single "critical level" statistic, which, after all, may do no more than convince us that a high level of employment and price stability are incompatible given our present wage-setting mores.

As far as the possibility of deriving such a continuous function is concerned, the foregoing analysis of the wage determination process suggests that the discovery of a close relationship between unemployment and money wages is quite unlikely. This pessimistic conclusion is based on the following reasoning. First of all, the extent of unemployment is *not* synonymous with the excess demand for labor since unemployment data tell us nothing about the number of unfilled jobs. In the second place, even if the level of unemployment were an accurate index of the excess demand for labor, we would not expect to find a close correlation between changes in labor market pressures facing an individual firm and the magnitude of wage adjustments. The existence of a number of other wage-determining factors as well as the attractiveness of many non-wage forms of adjustment make this link quite elastic. Finally, the prospects for a predictable aggregative relationship between money wages and unemployment for the economy as a whole are rendered still dimmer by the important distributional considerations discussed in the earlier part of this chapter.[11]

However, the probable absence of a simple and precise relationship between the level of employment and wage movements should not be permitted to obscure the basic fact that high levels of employment are certainly more

[11] Professor A. W. Phillips of the London School of Economics has made a noteworthy attempt to discover such an aggregative relationship in the United Kingdom ("The Relation Between Unemployment and the Rate of Change of Money Wage Rates in the United Kingdom, 1861-1957," *Economica*, xxv [November 1958], pp. 283-299). But, Phillips presents no formal analysis of the closeness of his fit. For a criticism of Phillips' efforts, see K. J. G. Knowles and C. B. Winsten, "Can the Level of Unemployment Explain Changes in Wages?" *Bulletin of the Oxford University Institute of Statistics*, xxi (May 1959), pp. 113-120.

conducive to large wage increases than are low levels. No one has ever suggested that increasing *un*employment will lead to larger wage increases. Thus the basic assertion of the dilemma model to the effect that "sufficient" unemployment will moderate the magnitude of wage adjustments still seems valid. And yet, it should also be noted here that this may be because of the *associated effects* of a high level of employment rather than as a direct consequence of the alteration in labor market pressures. More precisely, wage adjustments may be expected to vary inversely with the level of unemployment because: (a) a high level of employment is likely to be accompanied by high profits and lessened price competition in the product market; and (b) a high level of employment may itself contribute to prosperity by supplying workers with the wherewithal to purchase the fruits of their own efforts. In brief, the level of employment is at the same time both an index and a determinant of employer profitability and resistance to wage pressures.

Our final conclusion on this subject is that the significance of the level of unemployment as a determinant of wage movements has probably been *overemphasized*. It is easy to understand the extreme stress on the level of unemployment as a wage-determining factor in the light of the importance of high employment as an objective of public policy. And it is certainly altogether proper that policy formulators and economists seek to find the rate of exchange or "terms of trade" between unemployment and inflation. However, the formulation of sound public policy also requires that we do not move inadvertently from commendable concern with the twin problems of unemployment and inflation and their interrelation to an unwarranted emphasis on unemployment as a *determinant* of wage and price movements. We dare not confuse the objectives of public policy with the determinants of these objectives.

Productivity and Wage Determination

The final question that merits attention here is in some ways the most basic issue raised by the wage determination assertion of the dilemma model: Are productivity changes and wage adjustments to be regarded as independent or interrelated? The answer, of course, is that these two variables are partly independent and partly interrelated. Wage and productivity movements are partly independent because wage adjustments are affected by many factors other than changes in output per man-hour (the level of employment, for example); consequently, productivity improvements will lead to higher wages only if the *total combination* of circumstances is favorable. Wage and productivity movements are partly interrelated because productivity changes certainly exert an important influence on wages.[12]

The nature of the relationship between productivity changes and wage behavior that emerges from the foregoing analysis can be summarized in somewhat more specific terms, as follows. Changes in productivity (appropriately defined) can be envisioned as exerting a potential influence on wages at a number of points: first, there may be a direct effect via piece-rate systems of pay; second, productivity improvements may increase the firm's demand for labor; third, the profitability of firms and their "ability-to-pay" may be influenced; finally, the profitability of other firms may be affected.

As far as the relative importance of these various avenues of impact is concerned, the prevalence of time-rates of pay suggests that most frequently productivity changes will not be directly and instantaneously translated into

[12] It is also likely that wage adjustments influence productivity; however, discussion of this possibility must be postponed to Chapter 12.

wage increases, but instead will exert their main influence in more indirect and less perceptible ways by influencing the behavior of other wage-determining factors. Furthermore, while productivity has usually been thought to affect wages mainly by altering the demand for labor, our earlier analysis has suggested several reasons for questioning the supreme importance of this avenue of impact. Consequently, it seems reasonable to suspect that the main link between productivity movements and wage adjustments is the profit position of firms.

In short, wage earners get a number of opportunities to participate in productivity gains, and while they are not especially likely to "cash in" on the first two chances, the profitability channel offers much more hope. Our analysis of the wage determination process leads us to conclude that increases in productivity are most likely to result in higher wages by reducing the firm's resistance to wage pressures generated elsewhere. The probability of some increase in the general wage level via this avenue of impact is quite high. Even if wages in the firm that enjoyed the productivity improvement do not increase at all—either because the firm was forced by competitive pressures to lower prices or because the firm was able to raise its profits by the full amount of the cost reduction—there is still the chance that wages elsewhere in the economy will rise. This is because the higher real income of either the owners of the innovating firm or the customers of this firm will probably be translated into increased demand and increased profits for some other firm or firms. And these second-stage beneficiaries may be less successful in resisting wage pressures. Even if they are successful in resisting, there will be third stage beneficiaries, and so on. In the absence of a perfectly competitive economy, an eventual wage increase for some group of workers is highly probable.

Thus the final conclusion that emerges from this analysis is that productivity movements exert *some* independent influence on price movements. A speed-up in the national rate of productivity increase may well reduce the rate at which labor costs rise, and, conversely, a fall in the national rate of productivity increase is even more likely to lead to higher costs. However, we must be careful not to overestimate the impact of productivity changes on labor costs. To take the case of an increase in productivity, it must be remembered that a more rapid rate of technological progress is likely to steepen the upward tilt of the money wage level at the same time output per man-hour is going up. Consequently, while we are entitled to expect that spectacular increases in output per man-hour will reduce the pressure of wages on prices somewhat, too much hope should not be pinned on this possibility.

PART III
The Cost and Price Determination Assertions

12. THE IMPACT OF WAGE ADJUSTMENTS ON COSTS

Before plunging directly into the main business of the present chapter, it may be helpful to say just a word about the aims and structure of Part III as a whole. The basic purpose of Part III is to provide an appraisal of the second pillar of the dilemma model—namely, the cost and price determination assertion. The essence of this assertion is that prices are mainly, if not solely, cost-determined, and that any wage increment that exceeds the rate of productivity increase will be rapidly translated into an "equivalent" price increase.

Among the many questions raised by this assertion, the two most fundamental are: (1) what factors influence price movements? and (2) in what ways do wage adjustments affect these factors? In short, what are the consequences of wage adjustments for product prices? At the outset, it is necessary to emphasize that wage adjustments may affect product prices in *two* general ways: (a) by affecting the *costs* of firms; and (b) by altering the *demand* for goods and services. However, there is a serious organizational problem involved in trying to evaluate both these routes of impact at this time. The difficulty is that to analyze the demand-side aspects of wage adjustments it is necessary to consider many of the questions raised in the monetary and fiscal policy area of the dilemma model. Consequently, it is necessary to postpone examination of this latter avenue of impact until later and to confine ourselves in Part III to a discussion of the influence wage adjustments exert on prices via the cost-side route.

The vast array of questions involved in appraising the price determination hypothesis of the dilemma model and the way in which variations in costs impinge on the price determination process are discussed in Chapters 13-16. The purpose of the present chapter is to prepare the way for this analysis of price behavior by considering the logically prior issue of the impact of wage adjustments on costs. And, it is convenient to proceed by first saying a few words about the impact of wage adjustments on unit labor costs and then examining in somewhat more detail the link connecting unit labor costs and unit total costs.

Wage Adjustments and Unit Labor Costs

The impact of a wage change on unit labor costs constitutes the first link in the chain of logic used to explain (and thus to predict) the price-employment reaction of the firm to an initial wage adjustment. The connecting rod between a wage adjustment and an alteration in the firm's unit labor costs is, of course, the production function of the firm—and, unless one has some knowledge of the behavior of this production function it is very hazardous to predict the significance of a new wage agreement for the firm's labor costs per unit.

While there can be no doubt about the importance of productivity movements as a determinant of unit labor costs, it is equally true that many discussions of the wage-price issue have explicitly recognized this point. In our own discussion of both the general dilemma model and the wage determination assertion, the rate of productivity increase has been assigned a prominent place. And, once the importance of productivity has been recognized, it would certainly seem that the wage→unit labor cost link is rigid indeed, and that nothing more needs to be said. If we are given the wage and the rate of productivity increase, the question of the impact of wage adjustments on unit labor costs is certainly settled *ipso facto*.

However, this treatment is not entirely adequate for our purposes since there are still two groups of problems that must at least be mentioned: (1) the eternally trouble-some problems of choice of concept or definition; and (2) the issue of the impact of a "given" wage adjustment on the future course of productivity.

As far as the definitional problems are concerned, the most interesting and important questions all revolve around the selection of the appropriate meaning for the numerator of the unit labor cost index—namely, "the wage."[1] More specifically, the three main conceptual difficulties concern: (a) the treatment of "salaries"; (b) the treatment of "fringes"; and (c) the selection of the most appropriate index of "the" wage from among the multitude of real-life wages found within the confines of the typical firm.

A detailed inquiry into matters of this sort would, of course, take us too far afield and cannot be attempted. However, in addition to recognizing the existence of these conceptual difficulties, we do have an obligation to state explicitly the conventions adopted here. For the purposes of this study, it seems useful to: (a) exclude salaried workers from the labor cost category; (b) include fringe benefit expenses in labor costs; and (c) use average hourly earnings as the index of "the" wage.

Of these three definitional conventions, the choice of average hourly earnings is the most obvious and the most easily defended. The inadequacy of picking out any single quoted wage (such as the base rate) is readily apparent. The basic difficulty here is that unit labor costs are not just a function of productivity and any single quoted wage, but also depend on (a) the behavior of the entire galaxy of quoted wages, and (b) the quantitative importance of the various labor grades. That is, there can be a significant change in the unit labor costs of a firm with

---

[1] The definitional aspects of the denominator of this ratio—output per man-hour—have already been discussed in considerable detail (see Chapter 5).

absolutely no change in any quoted wage if there is an intra-firm shift in the number of man-hours which different classes of grades of labor must contribute in order to turn out a single unit of product. The average hourly earnings concept has the advantage of reflecting in a precise manner all the forces that render the connection between quoted wages and unit labor costs so tenuous.

The case for excluding salaries and including fringes is not nearly so unequivocal. The decision to avoid lumping wages and salaries together is based, first of all, on the fact that hourly wages in general are determined under somewhat different institutional arrangements than are salaries. Consequently, it may be very helpful to identify trends in the composition of aggregate employee remuneration—and this can be accomplished only if the wage and salary categories are distinguishable. Furthermore, it may also be helpful to separate wages and salaries from the standpoint of cost-price relationships. This is because cost accountants tend to make this distinction and to treat wages as a more variable cost than salaries, which are customarily regarded as semi-variable manufacturing expenses.[2]

Fringe benefits are included in "the wage" because, in general, they are determined via the same institutional arrangements as base wages and, in addition, the two forms of employee compensation have essentially the same effect on the costs of the employer.

Let us now shift our attention from the conceptual difficulties surrounding the definition of unit labor costs to a more substantive difficulty—namely, the possibility that a given wage adjustment will itself alter output per man-hour and thus interfere with the rigidity of the wage→ unit labor cost link. So far in our discussion, productivity

[2] See Theodore Lang (ed.), *Cost Accountant's Handbook* (New York: The Ronald Press, 1952), pp. 124-126, 839-840, and 908-915.

(or output per man-hour) has been taken as a datum, presumably determined by a number of exogenous forces. The time has now come to relax this procedure to the extent of noting three broad ways in which a wage adjustment might have a direct effect on output per man-hour.

First of all, a change in the wage is quite likely to encourage some movement *along* the firm's production function, and this may well change the unit labor cost *ratio* even though the production function itself is unaffected.[3] Secondly, a wage adjustment may alter output per man-hour by making it profitable for the firm to make minor or major changes in the production process. Thirdly, a wage adjustment may alter the entire production possibility map by rousing management from a state of semi-lethargy, inspiring a "drive on costs," and thus bringing about productivity improvements that would have been profitable even prior to the wage increase.[4]

It is difficult to find an adequate way of incorporating these considerations into our conceptual schema. Perhaps all that can be done is: (a) recognize that the numerator and denominator of the unit labor cost ratio are truly interdependent; and (b) consider the wage-productivity ratio as the resultant of the general trend in the output

[3] Ross (*Trade Union Wage Policy*, 1948, pp. 81ff.) and Lester (*New Concepts in Wage Determination*, ed. Taylor and Pierson, 1957, pp. 221-222) emphasize the possibility that changes in the volume of the firm's operation may affect output per man-hour. Unfortunately, however, neither of these men point out that changes in volume result only in movements *along* a given curve. Consequently, economists accustomed to think of unit labor costs or productivity as a schedule rather than as a ratio may not see how this "volume effect" loosens the wage-unit labor cost link.

[4] While the debate concerning the significance of this so-called "shock effect" has not led to any terribly conclusive results, the weight of the evidence does seem to suggest that there is something to this view. Schlesinger (thesis, 1955, pp. 58-62) reviews most of the literature and comes to this conclusion.

per man-hour of the firm, the magnitude of the wage adjustment itself, and the "kick-back" of the wage adjustment on output per man-hour.

Unit Labor Costs and Total Costs

Now that the content of the unit labor cost index has been explored somewhat more fully, let us turn our attention to the second link in the wage-price chain—namely, the impact of a "given" change in the unit labor cost ratio (ulc) on the total costs of the firm.[5]

A systematic analysis of this relationship for the case of an individual firm would involve the following steps. First, it would be necessary to know the nature of the production possibilities open to the firm (the isoquant map), the relevant factor prices, and thus the cost schedules faced by the firm prior to the given change in unit labor costs. Second, one would have to construct new isoquants and equal-cost lines on the basis of whatever changes in relative factor prices and production possibilities were responsible for the given change in unit labor costs. The third step would involve the construction of a new set of cost curves from the above data. And, the fourth and final step would then consist of combining the "old" and "new" sets of cost schedules with demand considerations in order to calculate the actual change in unit variable costs (uvc) and unit total costs (utc) that have resulted from the initial change in ulc.

This type of analysis is not presented here, however, both because of space considerations and because of the difficulties involved in trying to generalize about the nature

---

[5] At this point it is necessary to avoid defining "total costs" any more precisely because the problem of deciding which definition is most appropriate has not as yet been discussed. Consequently, it is necessary to appraise the impact of a change in unit labor costs on the *schedules* of both average variable cost and average total cost.

236

of the production possibilities open to the "typical" firm.[6] For our present purposes, it is sufficient to discuss in somewhat more general terms three specific aspects of the unit labor cost→unit total cost link that are of especial significance for wage-price relationships.

"Tightness" of the Unit Labor Cost→Total Cost Link

Certainly one of the most basic questions of interest is the "tightness" of the link in the over-all wage-price chain, which connects unit labor costs and total costs. That is, the basic question here is whether the dilemma model assertion that in the "normal" case uvc and utc can be expected to change by the same dollar amount as ulc seems plausible. In general terms, the answer to this question is that while a one-to-one correspondence is certainly possible, it does not seem very likely. This point can best be illustrated by enumerating some of the major considerations that mediate or influence the translation of a given increase in unit labor costs into an alteration in unit variable costs or unit total costs. Confidence that labor costs and total costs will change by the same amount can be justified only if there is good reason to rule out each of the following possibilities.

1. The firm may be able to substitute other factors for

---

[6] Unfortunately, there does not seem to be any formal treatment of the unit labor cost→ total cost link available in existent literature. However, there are, of course, numerous textbook treatments of those aspects of the traditional theory of the firm that are relevant here (see, for example, Tibor Scitovsky, *Welfare and Competition: The Economics of a Fully Employed Economy* [Chicago: Richard D. Irwin, 1951, Chaps. VI-VII]). For an extremely well written presentation of the rudimentary linear programming approach to similar problems, see Robert Dorfman, "Mathematical or 'Linear' Programming: A Nonmathematical Exposition," *American Economic Review*, XLIII (December 1953), pp. 797-825.

labor in response to a wage increase. The possibility of factor substitution in turn depends on: (a) the technological considerations, which are summed up in the firm's production possibility map; and (b) the shift in relative factor prices brought about by the change in wages. In the event some factor substitution is to the advantage of the firm, the alteration in the firm's non-labor costs will depend on: (i) the quantity of non-labor factors needed to replace a unit of labor; and (ii) the prices of the non-labor factors.

2. There is the possibility of a change in the costs of non-labor factors even if we assume that there is no alteration in the proportion of factors employed in the production process. A good illustration of this possibility is afforded by the assertions of the steel producers in the 1945-1948 period that higher unit labor costs by themselves were not the sole effect of higher wages but that their material costs as well were markedly increased by the general wage pattern.[7] And, it is not just materials costs that may be influenced by wage adjustments. The firm may also choose (or be compelled) to increase the salaries of clerical and supervisory employees *pari passu* with an

[7] The validity of this assertion by the steel producers is examined in considerable detail by Rees (thesis, 1950, pp. 104-112). Rees disagrees with the steel producers and argues, in effect, that movements in raw material prices cannot be explained by wage data. However, there are several technical objections that can be raised against the methodology employed by Rees to arrive at this conclusion. Without going into this issue in detail here, it seems reasonable to suggest that while movements of raw material prices most certainly cannot be explained entirely by reference to wage changes, it would be nothing short of astonishing if the raw materials employed by many industries (the auto industry's use of steel, for example) were not influenced by wage movements. The real methodological issue here is how far back in the production process wage costs should be traced and in what way wage costs are transmitted throughout the economy.

increase in the wages of hourly-paid workers.[8] In short, a wage increase may be transmitted into higher costs for non-labor cooperating factors and thus alter unit variable and unit total costs in a manner not predictable on the basis of unit labor cost data alone.

3. The capital costs of the firm may be altered as a consequence of the introduction of a productivity improvement. This is, of course, not a terribly unlikely possibility. Friedrich Lutz (among others) has suggested that "increases in productivity per man-hour are, as a rule, accompanied and made possible by an increase in the amount of capital per unit of labor."[9] And, such capital-intensification of the productivity process may increase the capital costs of the firm.[10]

4. An alteration in output per man-hour may also affect the costs of production in a less direct way by changing the optimal factor proportions. That is, an increase in output per man-hour attributable to the introduction of a new process may alter either the quantity of certain raw materials required per unit of product or the number of salaried personnel needed, and thus affect the non-labor variable costs of production as well as overhead costs.

5. There is also the possibility of an alteration in the firm's rate of output as a consequence of the change in unit labor costs. The extent of such a change in output will depend on (a) the price policies of the firm, and (b) the

[8] It should be recalled that salary-recipients are to be distinguished from wage-earners (see the first part of this chapter). Consequently, the services of salaried personnel are included in the "non-labor" category.

[9] Friedrich A. Lutz, "Inflation in Europe," *South African Journal of Economics,* xxv (December 1957), p. 235.

[10] However, capital-intensification of the production process does not necessarily raise the capital costs per unit of output. It is possible that an increase in capital per unit of labor can be accompanied by a *reduction* in capital per unit of output.

nature of the demand conditions facing the firm. Shifts in the level of output must, of course, affect unit total costs so long as the firm has any fixed costs at all.

6. If there is a change in the firm's rate of output, there is the further possibility that unit variable costs will be affected. This will, of course, depend on whether or not the average variable cost schedule is horizontal, which in turn depends on both (a) the nature of the firm's production function, and (b) the nature of the various factor supply schedules.

Unit Labor Cost as an "Index" of Total Costs

The above discussion has answered the first broad question about the connection between unit labor costs and the total costs of the firm by suggesting that there is likely to be considerable "free play" in this link. The next logical question would seem to be to what extent the "looseness" or flexibility of this link impairs our ability to predict changes in unit variable cost and unit total cost on the basis of unit labor cost data alone.

The answer to this question suggested at once by the above discussion is that it would be very hazardous to attempt to predict the change in the total costs of a randomly selected firm solely on the basis of labor cost data. The existence of so many intervening variables between the initial change in *ulc* and the final changes in *uvc* and *utc* certainly supports this conclusion.[11] While this ob-

[11] If the prediction problem we are discussing involves the actual magnitude of total costs at two chronological dates, then there is an additional consideration which may make prediction on the basis of *ulc* data alone even more hazardous. This is the possibility that there may be an autonomous change in non-labor costs completely unrelated to the increase in unit labor costs. For example, a sudden world-wide reduction in the supply of raw materials might raise variable costs apart from any wage change. This class of possibilities has not been discussed in

vious answer appears both valid and somewhat helpful—helpful in both the negative sense of warning us against casually assuming a one-to-one correspondence between unit labor costs and total costs and in the positive sense of suggesting the additional data or information needed for more accurate estimates—can we not say a bit more about this prediction problem?

Certainly one other avenue worth exploring is the question of the bias (or lack of bias) involved in using the *ulc* ratio as an index of *uvc* and *utc*. That is, suppose we need an estimate of the change in the firm's variable and total costs between two periods and have no information other than unit labor cost data. Can we offer any guidance to an investigator in such circumstances other than "be careful"? On the basis of the above discussion, it does seem possible to make several general observations, the most important of which is that in most cases *we should expect the change in unit labor costs to underestimate the absolute change in both unit variable and unit total costs*. This observation is based on the hypothesis that relaxing the assumptions needed to insure *equal* absolute increases in *ulc, uvc,* and *utc* should be expected, in most cases, to increase both *uvc* and *utc* (while, of course, leaving *ulc* unchanged).

Dealing first with the relationship between changes in *ulc* and the average variable cost *schedule*, it should be noted that a given increase in unit labor costs will shift the entire average variable cost schedule upwards by the same absolute amount only if non-labor variable costs are left

---

our above analysis because we have been making use of the usual *ceteris paribus* assumption in our investigation of the impact of changes in unit labor costs. However, in spite of the analytical convenience of this assumption, it may be very dangerous if used to predict real-life magnitudes in situations in which it is not a good approximation of the facts.

unchanged by the increase in unit labor costs. Thus the extent of the upward shift in the variable cost schedule will be *over*estimated only if non-labor variable costs fall. And, this could, of course, come about only as a result of either (a) a *fall* in the index of non-labor prices as a result of a *rise* in unit labor costs, or (b) a reduction in the quantity of non-labor factors needed to turn out a unit of product. However, neither of these alternatives seems particularly likely. In fact, it seems more plausible to suppose that in most cases a rise in unit labor costs attributable to a wage increase alone or to a wage increase accompanied by a partially-offsetting productivity hike would, if anything, raise the prices of non-labor factors[12] and increase the use of such cooperating factors as salaried personnel.[13] Consequently, there are some grounds for thinking that *ulc* data will often understate the upward shift in the average variable cost curve.

Turning now to the total cost schedule, we encounter the additional question of the plausibility of assuming that higher unit labor costs will have no effect at all on the fixed costs of the firm. In the case of an increase in unit labor costs attributable to a wage hike alone, this assumption seems fairly satisfactory. However, if there

[12] However, it is possible to cite cases in which a wage increase exerted such strong pressure on a firm that it was able to secure a *reduction* in its materials prices. Lester (*New Concepts in Wage Determination,* ed. Taylor and Pierson, 1957, p. 222) has described a shoe manufacturing firm in which this appears to have happened.

[13] This conclusion is strongly supported by the results of a recent study by Samuel E. Hill and Frederick Harbison (*Manpower and Innovation in American Industry* [Princeton, N.J.: Industrial Relations Section, Princeton University, 1959]). This study of trends in the composition of the work force in the post World War II period demonstrates that a high rate of capital investment has been one of the main reasons for the steady increase in the proportion of salaried personnel.

is an improvement in productivity mixed up in the unit labor cost increase, then an increase in capital costs would certainly not be surprising. As was noted earlier, most technological innovations seem to involve capital outlays. Consequently, since the extent of upward shift in the average total cost schedule is the vertical sum of the shifts in the average variable cost and average fixed cost schedules, we have an added reason to expect that the *atc* schedule will move upward at least as much as the amount of the increase in unit labor costs.

Thus far we have talked about predicting shifts in schedules. However, changes in unit variable cost and unit total cost can result from movements *along* schedules as well. Consequently, it is necessary to consider the probable impact of a shift in cost schedules on the firm's rate of output and thus indirectly on movements along these same schedules. Without anticipating our coming discussion of price policies and related matters to any appreciable extent, it seems reasonable to suggest that from the standpoint of the individual firm there is no reason to expect an upward shift in average variable costs to lead to higher sales—and there is some reason to expect the converse. The next question is the likely impact of this tendency toward lower output on *uvc* and *utc*. This, of course, depends on the shapes of the *avc* and *atc* schedules in the neighborhood under consideration. While there is no sense in pretending certainty here, it again does not seem unreasonable to suggest that the *avc* will be approximately horizontal over "normal" ranges of output and, consequently, the *atc* schedule will have something of a negative slope. If this is the case, a reduction in output will not affect *uvc* but will increase *utc*. Hence, we have here an added presumption in favor of the proposition that *ulc* data understate *utc*, but no support for the similar proposition concerning *uvc*.

To sum up: the general conclusion that seems to emerge

from this rather speculative discussion is that changes in unit labor costs put a floor under plausible estimates of the associated changes in both unit variable and unit total costs. That is, we can be fairly confident that a given absolute change in *ulc* will result in *at least* as large an increase in *uvc* and *utc*. Also, it seems that this tendency for absolute changes in unit variable cost and unit total cost to be understated is more acute in the case of the latter than the former.

Significance of the Labor-Cost/Total-Cost Ratio

It would be inappropriate to leave this subject of the unit-labor cost→total-cost link without commenting briefly on the significance of the *ratio* of unit labor costs to total costs. It may seem surprising that this widely-discussed economic variable has thus far never once been mentioned in our analysis. The reason for this lack of attention is that until now we have been talking about *absolute* or *dollar* changes in total costs as a consequence of an increase in unit labor costs—and the height of the labor-cost/total-cost ratio is immaterial in this connection.

However, the labor-cost/total-cost ratio is exceedingly important in determining the *proportionate* change in variable and total costs as a consequence of a specified increase in unit labor costs (measured either in absolute or percentage terms).[14] In short, the larger the proportion of labor costs to total costs, the greater will be the percent-

[14] This is presumably the rationale behind the assertions of labor union spokesmen that, since in many industries wages amounted to only a small per cent of the sales dollar, ". . . even where wage increases resulted in higher labor costs, the effect on total cost was not great." (Katherine Pollak Ellickson, "Labor's Recent Demands," *The Annals*, November 1946, p. 7.) To be correct, this statement must refer to the proportionate effect on total costs.

age change in variable and total costs as a consequence of a given absolute change in labor costs.

It is now apparent that our earlier discussion of the "tightness" of the labor-cost→total-cost link was ambiguous in that we did not specify whether we were interested in comparing absolute or percentage changes. And if we happen to decide, in the course of our inquiry, that for some purposes percentage changes are more relevant, then we shall have to modify our above conclusions about the labor-cost→total-cost link in several ways:

1. An entirely new and different set of assumptions must be conjured up to insure the complete "tightness" of the unit labor-cost→total-cost link in the sense of equal *percentage* changes in *ulc*, *uvc*, and *utc*. So long as labor costs are not the sole element in total costs, equal *absolute* changes will imply smaller percentage changes in *uvc* and *utc* than in *ulc*.

2. The existence of a new and important intervening variable in the person of the unit labor-cost/unit total-cost ratio will have to be admitted. And, it will be even more difficult to predict the *percentage* change in *uvc* and *utc* on the basis of labor cost data alone than it was to predict absolute changes because another piece of information is required.

3. Not only are the over-all difficulties of predicting percentage changes greater, but it is also more difficult to say anything very definite about the bias involved in predicting percentage changes in *uvc* and *utc* on the basis of *ulc* data alone. This is because there are now two offsetting tendencies at work. If we could be sure absolute changes in *uvc* and *utc* were either equal to or less than the absolute change in *ulc*, then we could safely predict that the percentage changes in *uvc* and *utc* would be smaller than the instigating change in *ulc*. However, we have argued above that absolute changes in *uvc* and *utc* are apt to be greater than the increase in *ulc*. Hence, it is very difficult to

245

make any strong assertion about the "normal" direction of bias.

This concludes our discussion of wages and costs within the individual firm. It must be reemphasized that the conclusions and analysis presented here can *not* be casually carried over to discussions of the economy as a whole. Our vantage point has been the individual firm, and the problem of the transmission of wage costs throughout the economy must await our forthcoming discussion of price policies and related matters.

13. THE IMPACT OF COSTS ON PRICES: INTRODUCTION AND THE COST-PLUS PRICING CONTROVERSY

Introductory Remarks

Having analyzed the impact of a wage adjustment on unit labor costs and total costs, we are now ready to embark on the second main leg of our quest for an understanding of the over-all relationship between wage adjustments and product price movements—the question of the probable impact of changes in costs on prices.

This leg of our problem differs from the previous discussion of wages and costs in two respects. First, the question of the impact of costs on prices is less bound-up with technological considerations and more dependent on behavioral assumptions than the problem of the effect of wages on unit labor costs and total costs. Second, the issue of price policy or price theory has received considerably more attention in the wage-price literature than the logically prior issue of wage-cost relationships. Whatever the reason for this greater emphasis, the fact remains that many analyses jump directly from a consideration of wage policy and wage detemination to the question of price policy.

However, we must be very careful not to let this *relatively* greater interest in cost-price over wage-cost relationships delude us into thinking that this obviously important question of price policy has been widely and thoroughly discussed. Far from it. With a few notable exceptions,[1] discussions of the wage-price issue have not

---

[1] The exceptions that come immediately to mind include: Rees, thesis, 1950; John Kenneth Galbraith, "Market Structure and Stabilization Policy," *Review of Economics and Statistics*, xxxix (May 1957), pp. 124-133; Means, Senate Subcommittee on Antitrust and Monopoly of the Committee on the

lavished their attention on price policy. The general tendency has been to handle this aspect of the problem by some fairly simple price policy assertion or assumption and then to proceed to a more detailed consideration of other matters, such as the difficult situation confronting the monetary authorities or the extent to which unions have "caused" the price hikes.

This "assumption approach" to the price policy area has only expediency to commend it. The price policy aspects of the dilemma model are certainly sufficiently important to merit a rather painstaking type of analysis—and, it is to this sort of inquiry that the remainder of Part III is addressed.

From the standpoint of organization, the following discussion of price policy is based on three methodological convictions. First, rather than attempt to evaluate the alternative price policy assumptions used by various authors on a one-at-a-time basis, it seems more useful to undertake a fairly systematic examination of price determination in general, and then to summarize the implications of this analysis for the various individual assumptions. Secondly, although Part III is dedicated primarily to considering the impact of wages on prices via the avenue of costs, it is impossible to exclude demand from our discussion. This is, of course, because an appraisal of the role of costs in pricing simply cannot be made without a simultaneous appraisal of the role played by other price-determining factors. Consequently, the following discussion is of necessity concerned with the price-setting process *in toto*. Finally, rather than attempt to deal with move-

---

Judiciary, *Hearings on Administered Prices*, 1957, pp. 73-125; and Brown, *Great Inflation*, 1955. It should also be pointed out that the various discussions of the charge that corporations have been widening their profit margins involve, though in a somewhat imprecise manner, this question of price policy.

ments of the general price level right off, it seems wiser to begin with an examination of price determination in individual firms, industries, and sectors of the economy and then to see how these pieces can be assembled into some kind of coherent picture of the over-all price level.

More specifically, it is convenient to proceed by devoting the remainder of this chapter to a brief consideration of the so-called cost-plus pricing controversy. Then, in subsequent chapters, we shall consider in turn: the impact on prices of a change in cost or demand according to a narrow version of "traditional" theory (Chapter 14); the ways in which other considerations such as uncertainty and "ethics" may influence the translation of cost and demand adjustments into price changes as well as the over-all picture of price determination in the individual firm which emerges from this analysis (Chapter 15); and the proximate determinants of changes in the general price level (Chapter 16).

The Cost-Plus Pricing Controversy

Perhaps the best way to begin the substantive part of our inquiry into price policy is by discussing the main implications of the cost-plus pricing controversy that has flourished in the United States and Great Britain during the past two decades.[2] This approach can be justified on two grounds: first, the price determination assertion of the dilemma model is generally couched in cost-plus terms, and so a direct examination of the cost-plus doctrine seems

[2] Before going any further it is necessary to note that the present chapter (as well as the next two chapters) is restricted to that class of cases in which the entrepreneur or firm is a *price maker* rather than a *price taker*. This treatment is certainly not intended to imply that prices determined in markets approximating pure or perfect competition are unimportant for the wage-price issue. It is just that it is convenient to postpone consideration of this class of prices until later.

especially appropriate for our particular purposes; second, the cost-plus doctrine was offered as an important challenge to the accepted body of theory, and the debate that has surrounded the enunciation of this doctrine thus provides an excellent starting point for an analysis of contemporary price theory.

The Challenge of the Cost-Plus Doctrine and the Response of Traditional Theory

It is, of course, impossible to enumerate the implications of the cost-plus controversy for the wage-price issue without first sketching (albeit very briefly) the salient features of this controversy. And, in order to appreciate the nature of the challenge to "traditional theory" represented by the "cost-plus doctrine" it is necessary to specify at the outset what is meant by both of these phrases. In order to avoid investing an undue amount of time in semantic problems, let us simply state "convenient" definitions of traditional theory and cost-plus pricing.

For our present purposes, it seems most satisfactory to think of traditional price theory as the simplified, static, apparatus which is based on the assumption of profit maximization and which has been developed in detail by Mrs. Robinson and is presented in popular economics textbooks such as Samuelson and Stonier & Hague.[3] The

[3] Joan Robinson, *Economics of Imperfect Competition*, 1933; Samuelson, *Economics*, 1958; and Alfred W. Stonier and Douglas C. Hague, *A Textbook of Economic Theory* (London: Longmans, Green, 1953). We have deliberately refrained from defining "traditional theory" as "marginal analysis"—this in spite of the fact that much of the cost-plus controversy has generally run in terms of the pros and cons of the marginal technique and is often thought of as the battle between the "marginalists" and the "anti-marginalists." There are two reasons for not using "marginalist" as synonymous with "traditional theory": first,

variety of formulators and versions makes it considerably more difficult to define the cost-plus doctrine. For the purposes of this study, the following rather arbitrary distillation of the cost-plus doctrines will have to suffice: the central tenet of the cost-plus doctrines is that prices are determined primarily, if not exclusively, by the "average costs" of the firm; and, the key phrase "average costs" is most commonly used to mean average total costs at some assumed ("standard") volume rate.[4]

With the above capsule descriptions of "traditional theory" and the "cost-plus doctrine" as background, we must now inquire into the nature of the challenge put to the more traditional approach by the cost-plus theorists. More precisely, we are presently interested in the *intended* challenge of the cost-plus school. It will be argued subsequently that the *real* challenge to traditional theory is

---

the phrase "marginal analysis" can be used to encompass a number of conceptions of the theory of the firm which differ from each other in several respects, the most important of which is the degree of refinement or complexity—and we wish to use "traditional theory" in the sense of a very simplified version of marginal analysis; second, the equation of marginal cost and marginal revenue is not absolutely essential to the application of what we have called "traditional theory"—it is only one way of arriving at the logical consequences of the profit-maximization assumption.

[4] Two basic cost-plus pricing studies are P. W. S. Andrews, *Manufacturing Business* (London: Macmillan, 1949); and R. L. Hall and C. J. Hitch, "Price Theory and Business Behaviour," *Oxford Economic Papers*, II (May 1939), pp. 12-45. For references to much of the remainder of the voluminous cost-plus pricing literature, see Richard B. Heflebower's excellent review article ("Full Costs, Cost Changes, and Prices," *Business Concentration and Price Policy*, National Bureau of Economic Research, Conference of the Universities-National Bureau Committee for Economic Research [Princeton: Princeton University Press, 1955], pp. 361-392).

different from the challenge intended by the early formulators of the full-cost principle and related doctrines.

In brief, the conclusions of the cost-plus school can be interpreted as posing a strong and serious challenge to traditional theory on three closely-related counts: (1) The demand function is either eliminated altogether or drastically reduced in significance as a participant in the price-making process. (2) All "marginal" concepts are eliminated from the micro-economic theorist's tool box, including marginal cost. (3) We are thus left with (a) average cost as the sole governor of price adjustments, and (b) profit maximization as a possible—though fortuitous and by no means necessary—result of the price-making process rather than as the motive force.

Certainly no one would suggest that traditional theory has either passively accepted the above condemnation or has retreated in disorder in the face of the onslaught of the cost-plus doctrine. Far from it. The challenge of the cost-plus doctrine *as summarized above* is too serious to be passively accepted and too easy to attack to be ignored. The basic response of traditional theory can be summarized very simply in what will be referred to as the "consistency argument." The essence of this argument is that the "evidence" or picture of business behavior that serves as the foundation of the cost-plus doctrine most certainly does not disprove the validity of traditional theory and may, in fact, be quite consistent with it.[5]

In general terms, the advocates of the consistency argument have utilized two main lines of defense. First of all, the conception of "traditional theory" being used as the target for the barbs of the cost-plus view has been alleged

---

[5] This seems to be the position of Messrs. E. A. G. Robinson ("The Pricing of Manufactured Products," *Economic Journal*, LX [December 1950], pp. 771-780) and Fritz Machlup ("Marginal Analysis and Empirical Research," *American Economic Review*, XXXVI [September 1946], pp. 519-544).

to involve a misrepresentation of the "real" traditional theory. Secondly, the findings of the cost-plus school have been attacked per se. Since at this point it is the validity of the cost-plus doctrine we are interested in, we shall skip over the question of the alleged misconceptions of traditional price theory and turn directly to the fundamental question of the accuracy of the cost-plus hypothesis.

Apart from certain important methodological questions, the most fundamental criticism raised by the traditional theorists is that the available body of evidence simply does not give unequivocal support to the cost-plus doctrine. More precisely, the available evidence strongly suggests that demand considerations are quite significant in the pricing process and that any attempt to explain price movements solely with reference to cost variables is bound to fail.

Looking just at the pricing data and formulae collected by Hall and Hitch themselves, one is immediately struck by the existence of variations in the margin above average cost "from firm to firm and, within individual firms, from period to period, and from product to product."[6] Without recourse to demand considerations or the nature of competition in the product market (which, after all, is a basic determinant of the demand curve facing the firm), it would seem extremely difficult to explain this empirical phenomenon. Furthermore, the verbal statements contained in the cost-plus literature strongly suggest that product market conditions play an important role.[7] A

[6] Machlup, *American Economic Review*, September 1946, p. 545.

[7] For quotations from businessmen, see columns C and D in the appendix of the Hall-Hitch article (*Oxford Economic Papers*, May 1939, pp. 12-45). In particular, see the responses of firms *d 5*, *e 1*, *a 11*, *a 8*, *e 2*, *b 5*, *a 4*, and *b 3*. For quotations from the cost-plus investigators themselves, see *ibid.*, Table 8; and Andrews, *Manufacturing Business*, 1949, pp. 145ff.

third and final source of evidence for the conclusion that demand cannot be dismissed as a factor in the price determination process is found in supplementary data and comments offered by economists other than those directly responsible for the founding of the cost-plus doctrine.[8]

This concludes our exceedingly scanty sketch of the challenge put to traditional theory by the cost-plus school and the response of traditional theory to this challenge. Let us now attempt a brief evaluation of the implications of this controversy for the price determination assertion of the dilemma model.

Comments

1. The first, and in some ways most basic, implication of the above analysis of the cost-plus controversy is that the cost-plus school's intended challenge to traditional theory has been very neatly repulsed. The "consistency" rebuttal of traditional theory is eminently sound. The findings of the cost-plus investigators themselves are in no way necessarily inconsistent with the profit maximization assumption proper or with the marginal analysis. Furthermore, demand considerations have been shown to undergird much of the cost-plus literature and to occupy a by no means unimportant position in the price-setting process. The most important single reason for this successful first-round defense of traditional theory is that the cost-

---

[8] By far the most suggestive of these "additional" observations or explorations is a seldom-quoted article by Mr. Ronald S. Edwards, an English accountant-turned-economist ("The Pricing of Manufactured Products," *Economica*, New Series, XIX, August 1952, pp. 298-307). A machinery manufacturer interrogated by Mr. Edwards describes a part of the procedure by which he sets his prices in such terms that he would surely receive an "A" on a price theory examination—assuming, of course, that his paper was graded by a "traditional theorist" (see p. 312).

plus theorists have left themselves wide open to attack by (a) stating the positive results of their investigations in a more extreme form than their own data and observations warrant, and (b) criticizing a rather narrow conception of traditional theory without expressly recognizing or defending this procedure. In short, the cost-plus theorists have tried to derive more revolutionary and far-reaching conclusions from their analysis than are in fact there.

2. However, it is equally true that the cost-plus pricing controversy does not validate a narrow conception of traditional theory. That is, while the data and observations that constitute the available evidence do not support the cost-plus pricing hypothesis in its strict form, neither do they demonstrate the applicability of the textbook conception of the theory of the firm. It is one thing to show that a set of data (varying margins between price and cost in this instance) *may be* consistent with an hypothesis (profit maximization or the marginal analysis) and quite another to demonstrate that the data *need be* consistent with the hypothesis. In short, the observed fact that businessmen take account of demand considerations in setting price, while disproving a strict cost-plus interpretation of price-setting, does not therefore prove that the businessman sets his price at the level that he thinks will equate marginal cost and marginal revenue. Much more information would be needed to demonstrate the latter proposition.

3. An even more important observation concerning the "consistency" rebuttal of traditional theory is that it is not enough to show that a certain set of *ex post* data can be "explained" by reference to the profit maximization assumption and its attendant apparatus. The much more significant question is the usefulness of traditional theory as a predictive instrument. And it is at this level of discussion that the *real* challenge of the cost-plus doctrine makes its appearance. The exponents of full-cost pricing and related doctrines have performed an extremely valuable

service by emphasizing the importance of constructing theories capable of yielding useful predictions.[9]

4. The above observation leads directly to a final comment, which is a sort of corollary to the above point. The most unfortunate aspect of the cost-plus controversy is that so much time has been invested in attacking and defending various people's conceptions of "traditional theory." From the standpoint of our immediate concern with price determination in the individual firm, the important issue here is the implications of the entire cost-plus controversy for the impact of a change in costs on the prices charged by a firm. Consequently, we are now obligated to turn our attention to the task of fusing together the insights of both traditional theory and the cost-plus school into an admittedly eclectic picture of the price determination process that will be of maximum usefulness in predicting the impact of cost adjustments on prices. And, viewed in the light of this objective, the difficulty with the above discussion of the cost-plus controversy is not that it is useless—it is an essential first step—but that it stops short of our present objective.

As a first step, the cost-plus discussion has made two major contributions to our quest for a useful analytical framework: (a) it has restored demand to a position of significance in the price-setting process and has thus shown that the simple, textbook model of price theory is still of some use; and (b) it has also implied that there are ways in which this textbook model can be modified, supplemented, or "filled out" to serve as a more useful predictive instrument. An attempt will now be made to draw out the further implications of both these contributions.

[9] Much the same point of view has been expressed by A. G. Papandreou ("Comment" [on paper by R. B. Heflebower], National Bureau of Economic Research, *Business Concentration and Price Policy*, 1955, p. 396).

14. Appraising the Impact on Prices of Changes in Cost and Demand within the Framework of Traditional Theory (Narrowly Conceived)

It is convenient to begin the more detailed part of our inquiry into cost-price relationships by utilizing a highly simplified version of traditional theory in order to appraise the impact of shifts in the cost and demand schedules. The "highly simplified version of traditional theory" used in this chapter amounts to nothing more than the profit maximization assumption coupled with given cost and demand schedules. Thus, we are abstracting from the complications raised by differing management objectives, the presence of uncertainty, varying time horizons, and alternative forms of competition in product markets.

Characteristics of the Cost and Demand Functions

Since within this simple framework, price changes are mediated exclusively through cost and demand functions, it is necessary at the outset to say a few words about the characteristics of these functions.

Dealing first with the cost schedules, little needs to be said by way of definition. We shall follow the customary practice of using an average variable cost schedule (AVC) to depict the dollar amount of variable costs/unit incurred by the firm in producing varying quantities of output, and a marginal cost schedule (MC) to show the increment to total costs as a consequence of a small change in output. However, there is more to be said concerning the likely shapes of these functions.

With respect to the "normal" shape of cost functions, the general consensus among economists seems to be that, in manufacturing at least, the average variable costs of the firm can be expected to be approximately constant over a fairly wide range of output rates. This conclusion is supported, first, by a number of empirical investigations. For example, the National Bureau of Economic Research study of cost behavior, after reviewing a great number of individual empirical investigations, concluded that statistically estimated cost functions, and cost-revenue charts, all indicate with but few exceptions "a linear covariation, that is, a linear cost-output relationship."[1]

The assumption of a horizontal average variable cost schedule has also been defended on the basis of a priori theoretical reasoning. Thus Reynolds has argued that factor prices are not likely to vary significantly with changes in the level of output and that it seems sensible to expect output to be a homogeneous linear function of variable inputs over the normal output range.[2] The best-known and most thorough theoretical investigation of this question of the shape of short-run cost functions is the study made by Stigler, who has emphasized that constant unit variable costs may result from the fact that entrepreneurs often build some "flexibility" or "divisibility" into their plants.[3]

If we are now prepared to grant that average variable costs may be fairly constant over "usual" ranges of output, the next question is what would we expect to be the shape of the cost schedules when unusually high rates of output are reached. This depends, in large measure, on what is meant by "unusually high rates of output." If we

[1] National Bureau of Economic Research, *Cost Behavior and Price Policy*, 1943, p. 109.

[2] Lloyd G. Reynolds, "Toward a Short-run Theory of Wages," *American Economic Review*, xxxviii (June 1948), p. 295.

[3] George J. Stigler, "Production and Distribution in the Short Run," *Journal of Political Economy*, xlvii (June 1939), pp. 305-327.

mean levels of output above those which can be produced during a forty-hour week, then it may be most suitable to think of the average variable cost function as slowly rising over the levels of output which can be most cheaply turned out by working the existing labor force overtime, and then reaching a new and higher horizontal plateau at output levels which would justify the addition of a second shift.[4] However, when we reach the output level at which the fixed factors of production are being utilized as fully as possible and it is no longer possible to increase production by adding variable factors, the average variable cost function would be expected to rise sharply.

For a firm that always operates with a fixed number of shifts (whether it be a one, two or three shift plant), the separate plateaus and kinks would be replaced with a single, horizontal cost schedule that would indicate the existence of constant average variable and marginal costs right up to (or at least near) the maximum output that can be produced with the given plant.

Turning now to the demand and marginal revenue curves, we encounter some rather troublesome problems of definition. For our present purposes, it is probably best to define the individual demand (or sales) curve facing the firm as the schedule of quantities that can be sold by the firm at various alternative prices. The really troublesome question is how to handle situations in which the effect of a price change by one producer on the quantity he can sell depends to a significant extent on the reactions

[4] Reynolds (*American Economic Review*, June 1948, p. 297) has argued that attaining a high rate of output by working overtime or adding shifts involves "not a gradual rise in marginal costs, but a discontinuous shift to a markedly higher level, at which level the marginal cost curve once more runs along horizontally." Actually, it seems more likely that working overtime *would* involve a gradual rise in marginal costs and that Reynolds' conclusion should be reserved for the case in which an entirely new shift is added.

of other firms selling similar products—in short, situations characterized by the existence of "conjectural interdependence."

At the present stage of our inquiry it is best to circumvent this difficulty, and this can be accomplished by making one of two assumptions: (1) we can simply specify that we are presently concerned only with situations in which the number of competitors is sufficiently large to permit the firm under investigation to ignore the reactions of its rivals to any price adjustment it may make;[5] or (2) we can conceive of the demand curve facing the individual firm as showing "the full effect upon the sales of that firm which results from any change in the price which it charges, whether it causes a change in the prices charged by others or not."[6]

For our present purposes, it makes little difference which of these assumptions is embraced, since the net effect of adopting either is: (1) to give us a demand or sales curve that can be handled comparatively easily; and (2) to postpone a consideration of the significance of oligopoly for cost-price relationships until later. Consequently, no choice need be made.[7]

[5] This is the assumption that distinguishes Professor Chamberlin's "large group" case. See E. H. Chamberlin, *The Theory of Monopolistic Competition; A Re-orientation of the Theory of Value* (6th ed., Cambridge, Mass.: Harvard University Press, 1948), Chapter v.

[6] Joan Robinson, *Economics of Imperfect Competition*, 1933, p. 21. This assumption is used throughout Mrs. Robinson's book.

[7] Looked at from a broader standpoint, the two assumptions are not quite on an equal footing. As Robert Triffen (*Monopolistic Competition and General Equilibrium Theory.* [Cambridge, Mass.: Harvard University Press, 1949], pp. 68-70) has emphasized, Mrs. Robinson's assumption (assumption 2 in the text) suffers from certain logical difficulties. If the curve is thought of solely as "subjective," its existence is certainly conceivable; however, if the curve is supposed to be "objective," then to be able to construct A's demand curve we must first know B's demand

As far as the probable shape of the demand (and thus the marginal revenue) curve is concerned, much less can be said than in the case of the cost functions. Individual producers may be faced with such varied conditions in the product market that about all that can safely be said is: (1) the demand curve will normally have a negative slope throughout; and (2) the elasticity of demand at the point on the demand curve corresponding to the "going" price will have an absolute value greater than unity.

Impact of a Change in Costs

Within the narrow framework we have staked out, the problem of appraising the impact of an increase in costs on price would certainly seem to be perfectly straightforward, and we would not expect any disagreement in this area. However, the literature does not fulfill this optimistic expectation. About the only conclusion to which almost all subscribe is that an increase in costs will normally lead to some increase in prices. And even this relatively innocuous conclusion has been disputed by Galbraith. Within the group who agree that higher prices will be the usual result of higher costs, the main difference of opinion centers around the question of whether we should expect prices to increase by the same absolute amount as marginal costs, by the same percentage (and thus a larger absolute amount since price will presumably exceed variable costs by some amount), or by a smaller absolute amount.

Given the mechanistic nature of this problem, there are only three possible sources of different conclusions: (1) different assumptions about the "normal" shape of the cost and demand functions; (2) errors in analysis; or (3) failure to state the qualifications needed to buttress a conclusion. While it would be risky indeed to pretend to be

---

curve—but to know B's demand curve we must first know A's curve.

able to disentangle these sources of disagreement as far as the observations of specific authors are concerned, it can be assumed that the main differences arise from the first and third sources, and that the differences attributable to these sources have in turn been encouraged by the existence of two alternative modes of analysis—geometry and algebra.

Looking first at the question geometrically, the impact of a given dollar increase in costs is seen to depend on the shape of the demand function above the old price and the behavior of marginal costs in the range within which the firm is operating.[8] Starting with the simple case of a linear demand function, it has been proven geometrically that:

a. If the marginal cost function is horizontal over the relevant range, the increase in costs will lead to exactly one-half as great an absolute increase in price, regardless of the slope of the demand function.

b. If marginal costs are a rising function of output, price is raised by less than half the amount of the increase in costs.

c. If marginal costs are a decreasing function of output, the price is raised by more than half the absolute amount of the increase in costs. And, if the slope of the marginal cost curve is: (i) equal to the slope of the demand curve, the increase in price will be exactly equal to the increase in costs; (ii) greater than the slope of the demand curve, the increase in price will exceed the increase in costs.

When we admit the possibility of a demand function with changing slope, it is necessary to modify the above deductions by pointing out that, in general, the more convex from below the demand function (that is, the steeper

[8] By far the most thorough and detailed analysis of the impact of an increase in costs on price is to be found in Joan Robinson, *Economics of Imperfect Competition*, 1933, pp. 76-82. The propositions stated in the next two paragraphs have been deduced in a rigorous manner by Mrs. Robinson.

the slope of the demand curve as output falls), the greater will be the increase in price associated with any given change in costs.

Let us now see how this same problem can be (and has been) attacked algebraically. We start out with the general expression relating marginal revenue (MR), average revenue (AR) or price (P), and the elasticity of demand (E). It can be shown that at a given output:[9]

$$AR = P = MR \cdot \frac{E}{E-1}$$

And, since for continuous functions a necessary condition for profit maximization is that marginal cost (MC) equal marginal revenue, we write the profit-maximizing price (P^*) as:

$$P^* = MC \cdot \frac{E}{E-1}$$

Consequently, the impact on price of a given change in marginal cost is seen to be a non-linear function of the equilibrium elasticity of demand.[10]

[9] This formula is derived geometrically in any number of theory textbooks. See, for example: Stonier and Hague, *Textbook of Economic Theory*, 1953, pp. 97-98. It is important to point out that in this formula E is not the usual, negative elasticity of demand. Rather, it is a positive version. That is, whereas the usual elasticity of demand is taken as a negative number, the E in this formula represents this value multiplied by -1 so as to get a positive number. The important thing to remember is that it is positive elasticity values that are to be substituted in this expression. And, in the text, when we talk about increases in elasticity, we mean increases in absolute value.

[10] This phrase "equilibrium elasticity of demand" is used here to mean the elasticity of demand at the profit-maximizing price. The "E" in the preceding equation stands, of course, for this elasticity concept. It should be noted that any circumstance which inspires the firm to alter either the price at which it sells or the output it produces is also likely to alter the "equilibrium elasticity of demand"; consequently, E cannot be regarded as an inde-

It is apparent from this expression that if the equilibrium elasticity of demand remains constant as marginal cost is altered, then price will go up *in proportion* to the increase in marginal costs. Put another way, a constant elasticity of demand implies that the percentage margin between price and marginal costs will remain unchanged and so the absolute change in price will be greater than the absolute change in marginal costs. However, it must be emphasized that this conclusion rests squarely on the assumption that changes in cost do not bring about any change in the equilibrium elasticity of demand. And, the best argument that can be made for using this assumption is that it simplifies things considerably. It will be argued shortly that not only is it extremely improbable that the equilibrium elasticity of demand will in fact remain constant as costs change, but furthermore that we can say something about the "expected" direction of change. For the moment it is sufficient to note that while there is no simple linear relationship between changes in the elasticity of demand and price, there is a uni-directional relationship: an increase in the elasticity of demand will exert a downward pressure on price and a decrease in elasticity will exert an upward pressure.

Armed with these two modes of analysis, we are now able to draw four conclusions about the probable impact of an increase in costs on price. And, at the same time, we shall try to shed some light on the divergent observations that are found in the literature. The first of these conclusions is of a methodological nature, whereas the latter three are more substantive.

1. An important implication of the above analysis is that without special knowledge about the shapes of the cost and revenue functions, there is no reason to expect

---

pendent variable. When cost conditions change, P^* and E are simultaneously determined.

any specific and unvarying numerical relationship to exist between changes in marginal cost and in price. For example, we have already observed that an increase in price of the same percentage as the increase in costs would occur only if the elasticity of demand at the new equilibrium price happens to be the same as the old price. Similarly, an increase in price equal to exactly one-half the amount of the increase in costs requires that the demand function be linear. We must be wary of all such precise results and recognize that they must depend on some special (and often unstated) assumption about the cost and demand functions. However, this is a rather negative sort of conclusion; and, as long as we do recognize the impossibility of finding any unvarying relationship, it is possible to say a bit more about the *probable* impact of a change in costs on price. The following three observations are directed to this purpose.

2. We can be quite confident that, except in the most unusual situations, an increase in costs will result in some increase in price. There is no need to restate the positive arguments that support this generally accepted conclusion. However, it is necessary to examine critically the contentions of the main dissenter from this conclusion— namely, Galbraith. Galbraith has argued that price increases following wage increases are inconsistent with "accepted economic analysis." This assertion is based on the following reasoning:

> Capacity operations are commonplace, as noted. The meaning of "capacity" is that supply is inelastic because the firm is nearing the output where marginal costs approach infinity. If marginal costs are approaching infinity they are not increased by the wage increase. Thus nothing in the cost situation as it relates to the equilibrium of the firm is changed by the wage increase. Since de-

mand in accordance with usual (and valid) special equilibrium assumptions is also substantially
unaffected, the conclusion is inescapable. If the
increase is profitable after the wage increase, it
would have been just as profitable before.[11]

This reasoning seems to be, at the best, misleading; and,
it can be challenged on several grounds. First, Galbraith's
argument can in no way be considered a "general" treatment; the most generous interpretation that can be made
of his argument is that it *may* apply in the special case in
which the firm is producing the maximum output permitted by its fixed factors prior to the cost increase in
question. Surely no one (including Galbraith) would deny
that many firms operate much of the time at less than 100
per cent of capacity; and when lower levels of output are
being produced, we would expect higher marginal costs to
increase prices in the usual manner. Secondly, even if prior
to the increase in marginal costs Galbraith's "special case"
did apply, there is no guarantee that it would continue to
apply after the increase. That is, the upward shift in the
marginal cost curve may itself move the point of intersection of the MC and MR functions to the left of 100 per
cent capacity, thereby increasing price. There is also a
third criticism that can be made of Galbraith's reasoning,
but since this concerns his treatment of the demand side,
it is convenient to postpone consideration of this point.

3. The finding that higher costs will mean some increase in price is, after all, not a very powerful conclusion,
since it tells us nothing about the probable magnitude of
the price increase. However, it is not necessary to stop
here. Our above analysis suggests that, in general, we can
expect a given increase in marginal costs to result in a
smaller percentage increase in price. The reasoning be-

[11] Galbraith, *Review of Economics and Statistics*, May 1957,
p. 129.

hind this observation can be explained most conveniently by examining the views of a dissenter from this conclusion—namely, Scitovsky, who has argued:

> The simple relation between the market's price elasticity and the price maker's optimum profit margin renders it relatively easy to analyze the latter's pricing policy and response to changes in cost and market conditions if we assume that he aims at maximizing his profit. It is obvious, for example, that a rise in producer's costs—due, let us say, to a rise in wages—will raise prices by the same percentage by which marginal cost has risen, unless there is special reason to suppose that the wage raise has changed the market's price elasticity and hence also the producer's optimum percentage profit margin. In other words, we can generally expect producers not only to shift all changes in costs onto the consumer but to do more than that and change prices in the same proportion in which costs have changed.[12]

The first part of the above statement—dealing with the formal relationship between marginal cost, price, and elasticity of demand—is, as was noted above, quite correct. However, we are certainly entitled to take issue with the conclusion that is drawn from this analysis. The important point to note is that Scitovsky's conclusion (that we may generally expect prices to rise in the same proportion as marginal costs) is completely dependent on a key assumption—that an increase in marginal costs is as likely to lead to a decrease in the equilibrium elasticity of demand as to an increase. And this key assumption appears to be an outgrowth of Scitovsky's use of the algebraic mode of analysis, which, as depicted above, does not emphasize the interdependence of MC and E, and so makes the assump-

[12] Scitovsky, *Welfare and Competition*, 1951, p. 298.

tion of an unchanged equilibrium elasticity of demand comparatively appealing. However, closer inspection (and the use of an at least semigeometrical mode of analysis) suggests that, in general, it may be more reasonable to expect the elasticity of demand to increase as costs rise than to remain constant.

In geometrical terms, the main reason for expecting higher costs to bring about an increase in elasticity is simply that higher costs will almost always move the firm to the left and up along the given demand function. To appreciate the effect of this northwesterly movement on elasticity, it is useful to recall that elasticity of demand (E) can be defined as the proportionate change in quantity (Q) divided by the proportionate change in price. That is:

$$E = \frac{\frac{\Delta Q}{Q}}{\frac{\Delta P}{P}} = \frac{\Delta Q}{\Delta P} \cdot \frac{P}{Q}$$

And, a movement to the left and up the demand curve is certain to increase the ratio $\frac{P}{Q}$ since P is increasing at the same time that Q is falling. Consequently, E will also increase *unless* there is a sufficiently strong offsetting change in the slope of the demand curve. That is, for the elasticity to remain the same at a higher price and lower output, it is necessary for the slope of the demand curve to increase sufficiently to counteract the influence of the predictable change in the $\frac{P}{Q}$ weight. Thus the elasticity of demand will increase as costs rise if we are dealing with a demand curve that is linear, concave from below, or only slightly convex. Consequently, it seems in order to alter Scitovsky's argument to read: an increase in costs will bring about an increase in the elasticity of demand and thus a *less than proportionate* increase in price unless there is some special reason to think that the slope of the demand curve will be sufficiently higher at the new price to outweigh the upward pressure on elasticity brought about by the certain increase in the $\dfrac{P}{Q}$ weight.

4. The above conclusion compares the probable percentage changes in cost and price, and suggests that we would normally expect the percentage change in price to be smaller. However, since price usually exceeds marginal cost in absolute magnitude, this finding does not tell us much about the probable *absolute* change in price as a consequence of an increase in marginal costs. That is, a smaller percentage increase in price than in marginal cost is compatible with a smaller, equal, or even larger absolute increase in price than in cost. However, it is possible to try to strengthen the above conclusion concerning percentage changes by suggesting that the absolute increase in price is also likely to be smaller than the absolute increase in marginal costs. This is the conclusion reached by Mrs. Robinson,[13] and it is supported by the observation that the characteristics of the cost and demand functions necessary to result in an equal or greater absolute increase in price are not likely to occur very often. In less formal terms, it seems unlikely that either the marginal cost curve will decline at a sufficiently rapid rate (it has been argued above that it is apt to be horizontal or rising), or the demand curve will be sufficiently convex to bring about a larger absolute increase in price than in marginal costs. However, it must be remembered that this conclusion is ten-

[13] Joan Robinson, *Economics of Imperfect Competition*, p. 81, says: "We have found that the effect of a tax per unit of output is in general to raise the price by something less than the full amount of the tax."

tative and certainly need not hold for every situation.[14]

This completes our formal analysis of the impact of a change in costs on prices within the narrow framework of the profit-maximization assumption and given cost and demand curves. Before appraising the impact of a change in demand within the same framework, it is necessary to emphasize the limited applicability of the conclusions. The apparatus used above is applicable only to cost changes confined to the particular firm in question. For example, if an industry-wide wage increase were the source of the increase in the firm's costs, the impact of the cost change could not be analyzed on the assumption that the demand curve is a "given." This is because any broad cost change such as an industry-wide wage increase will, of course, shift the firm's demand function, and account must be taken of this change.[15]

Impact of a Change in Demand

The impact of a shift in the demand curve facing the individual firm on the price charged by the firm can be

[14] Thus Heflebower (in *Business Concentration and Price Policy*, 1955, pp. 385-386) goes too far when he says that: "In value theory the price changes by less than the change in marginal cost by an amount determined by the slopes of the marginal cost and marginal revenue curves." While we have argued that this is the most likely outcome, it is certainly not the only possible outcome. The tendency to state this conclusion as to the smaller absolute increase in price too strongly may be an outgrowth of the natural inclination of geometricians to draw the demand curve as a straight line, and is thus similar to the temptation faced by the users of algebra to assume the elasticity of demand to be constant.

[15] This is the other objection to Galbraith's argument which was mentioned earlier. He does not tell us whether the wage increase he has in mind is confined to the particular firm or not, but considering the period in question, it is doubtful that it should be so construed. And, if the wage increase is broader than the individual firm, Galbraith is not correct in suggesting that it is valid to take the demand curve as unaffected by the cost change.

analyzed in comparatively short order. In general terms, the effect on price will depend on (1) the nature of the shift in the demand curve itself, and (2) the shape of the firm's marginal cost function. If more precision is desired, we can say that the price effect of a shift in the demand function depends on the behavior of marginal costs in the neighborhood bounded by the old and new equilibrium outputs, and the elasticity of demand at the old and new rates of output.[16]

It is convenient to distinguish among three cases on the basis of the rate of output at which the firm operates. As case one, let us consider the situation in which the firm is operating at less than 100 per cent capacity output both before and after the shift in demand takes place. If we now make use of our earlier argument that over this interval marginal costs can be expected to be fairly constant, then the effect of a shift in demand on price will depend exclusively on the alteration in the elasticity of demand at the relevant points brought about by the shift. For example, if the elasticity of demand at the old price is the same on the old and new demand curves, there will be no increase in price. On the other hand, if the new demand

[16] This follows from the formula for profit-maximizing price given above. However, as in the case of the analysis of a cost change, this formula can be misleading. The most serious dangers are: (1) that the marginal cost and elasticity variables will be regarded as independent when in fact they are, of course, interdependent—that is, elasticity and marginal cost considerations *jointly* determine the equilibrium output and thus the specific values for MC and E; (2) that we shall make the very similar error of failing to remember that the elasticity of demand is not usually the same at all points on a demand curve, but varies along the curve—throughout the remainder of this discussion whenever we talk about the change in elasticity as a consequence of the increase in demand what we mean in more precise terms is the change in elasticity between the old and new demand curves at specific prices (usually both at the "old" price).

curve is less elastic than the old (at the old price), price will increase; or if the new demand curve is more elastic, price will fall.[17]

So far so good. However, when we attempt to be a bit more precise about the *probable* effect of a shift in demand on price, much rougher terrain is encountered. The main difficulty is simply that we know very little about the whole subject of the impact of shifts in demand on elasticity. In any particular case, the change in elasticity will depend on such factors as the source of the shift in the demand curve (for example, it is important to know whether an increase in demand is the result of a general increase in the wealth of buyers or is attributable to the failure of a competitive firm) and the nature of the product itself.

If we could assume that demand curves always shifted in such a way as to maintain the same slope for each hypothetical price (that is, if the new demand curve were always parallel to the old curve), the problem would be relatively simple. An increase in demand would always decrease elasticity at the old price and thus raise price.[18] However, Mrs. Robinson suggests that in most cases we should expect an increase in demand to be accompanied by a reduction in the slope of the demand curve (at the old price). Hence, it is not so easy to predict the "usual" change in elasticity. All we can do is examine various cases and see what appears to be the most likely possibility. Mrs. Robinson has made such an inquiry and has concluded that in the "common case" an increase in demand will re-

[17] See Joan Robinson, *Economics of Imperfect Competition*, p. 61.

[18] This is easily seen by reference to the elasticity formula presented above. If the slope of the demand curve remains unchanged, the change in elasticity will depend solely on the change in the P/Q weight. And, at the same time P is by definition constant. Hence, a rightward shift of the demand curve will increase Q at each price and thus reduce the elasticity of demand.

sult in some reduction in elasticity at the old price and thus we would normally expect some increase in price as a consequence of an increase in demand.[19] However, it must be emphasized that this is a highly tentative conclusion. Without considerable additional information it is patently impossible, in any particular case, to make any kind of exact prediction of the effect of a shift in demand on elasticity.

Let us now examine briefly a second case, which is characterized by a different assumption concerning the firm's rate of output. Let us now suppose that the firm was producing its maximum output prior to an increase in demand. In this case, we can be much more certain that, if the firm seeks to maximize short-run profits, a price increase will result. This is because the difficulty encountered above— the problem of estimating the impact of the shift in the demand function on elasticity—is no longer troublesome. In fact, the slope of the demand curve is no longer of any consequence for computing the amount of the price adjustment. If it is profitable for the firm to operate at 100 per cent of capacity, the price charged by the firm will be given by the intersection of the demand curve with the vertical portion of the variable cost functions, and the slope of the demand curve at this point of intersection will be immaterial. In short, in this case an increase in demand will surely raise price, and the amount of the price rise will be equal to the magnitude of the vertical shift in the demand function at the maximum output the firm can produce.

A third case intermediate between the "pure capacity" and the "pure less-than-capacity" cases can also be distinguished. Let us now suppose that prior to the increase in demand, the firm was producing at less than 100 per cent of capacity (that is, along the horizontal section of its

[19] Joan Robinson, *Economics of Imperfect Competition*, pp. 70-72.

marginal cost curve), but that the upward shift of the demand curve itself made it profitable for the firm to increase output to the maximum amount allowed by the available plant and equipment. In this case, the new price will be determined, as in the "pure capacity" case, by the intersection of the new demand curve and the vertical portion of the variable cost schedules. However, here we cannot be so sure that the new price will be higher than the old price since the old price was *not* determined by the intersection of the old demand curve and this same vertical line, but was influenced by the slope of the demand function as well. However, the chances of a price increase are certainly greater here than they were in the first case.

Comments

Our formal discussion of cost-price and demand-price relationships is now complete. Three concluding comments seem in order:

1. It is more difficult to say anything useful about the probable change in price as a consequence of a change in demand than in the case of a change in costs. This is primarily because we have a better basis for estimating the change in the shape of the *over-all* cost function that will result from something like a wage hike than we do in the case of a shift in the demand function. In short, the demand function appears to be more capricious in its movements than the cost function.

2. We can be much more confident that an increase in costs will result in a price increase than we can in the case of an increase in demand. Only in rare cases would we *not* expect a price increase to follow an increase in costs. And an increase in costs would almost never lead us to expect a fall in price. On the other hand, while a rightward shift in the demand function is more likely to increase price than to lower it, the degree of confidence with which we

can make this prediction is much less. We should not be terribly surprised if a fall in price did result from an increase in demand. And, it is only in the special case in which the firm is operating at capacity prior to the demand increase that we can be quite confident that higher prices will result from the increase in orders.

3. Finally, it should be remembered that all of the above analysis and commentary is the product of an heroic set of assumptions, some of which we shall now proceed to relax.

15. Broadening the Formal Framework to Include Other Considerations

The foregoing analysis has provided the rough outlines of a picture of the price determination process. The purpose of this chapter is to "fill in" this picture so as to increase its predictive usefulness. To accomplish this "filling in" process, it is necessary to relax some of the very restrictive assumptions that were employed in the above analysis and see in what ways the conclusions arrived at are modified or supplemented by incorporating into our analysis such factors as uncertainty, the passage of time, and more complex motivational assumptions.

It must be emphasized that our central objective here is the construction of a picture of the price determination process that will be of optimal usefulness in appraising the price determination assertion of the dilemma model. Consequently, every effort will be made to avoid becoming embroiled in side controversies that are not essential to the attainment of this objective. More specifically, no direct attempt will be made to separate the contributions of the cost-plus school from the contributions of other economists who have preferred to work more within the framework of traditional theory. Here we are less concerned with the priority of discovery or ownership of ideas than with the implications of the ideas themselves. Similarly, we shall endeavor to avoid the issue of the "real" meaning of the profit-maximization assumption and whether certain behavior is or is not consistent with the "proper" interpretation of this assumption.

Conscience, Social Pressure, and Price Policy

The above analysis of the impact of a change in costs and demand on the price charged by the firm was based on the assumption that the firm is motivated exclusively

276

by the desire for maximum dollar profits. There is no point in belaboring the "unrealistic" nature of this assumption—which, after all, is a dead horse since no one denies that firms are motivated to some extent by considerations other than profit-maximization. Without pretending any special competence in the province of the psychologists, philosophers, sociologists, theologians, and political scientists, it is possible to picture the decision-makers within the firm as having a set of values or a preference structure that guides them in making decisions of all kinds, including price policy questions. And, while one of these values or objectives is certainly the maximization of the short-run profits of the firm, it would be surprising indeed if this were the sole criterion employed in decision-making. However, mere recognition of the existence of "other" objectives is not terribly helpful.

Three much more important and much more interesting questions are: (1) What is the precise nature of these "other" motivations that compete with profit-maximization for the allegiance of the firm? (2) In what circumstances and to what extent will these other objectives override the profit-maximization objective? and (3) What differences in the actual price behavior of the firm result from allegiance to these other objectives?

Much of the remainder of this chapter is devoted to suggesting some very tentative answers to these questions. At present, we shall concentrate on the price policy implications of one particular set of "other" objectives—namely, the desire of entrepreneurs to behave in accord with the standards set by their own consciences and by society at large. There would seem to be little doubt that motives of this sort influence business behavior to some extent.[1] How-

---

[1] Numerous statements by businessmen asserting the moralistic basis of price policy are reported by Hall and Hitch (*Oxford Studies in the Price Mechanism*, ed. T. Wilson and P.W.S. Andrews [Oxford: Clarendon Press, 1951], pp. 107-138) and may

ever, the key question is: Just how much is "to some extent"? It is obvious that this question cannot be answered in an entirely satisfactory manner either by a priori reasoning or by the casual collection of businessmen's comments designed for public consumption.[2] However, we may be able to make some headway by distinguishing three cases. First of all, conformity to social pressure and conscience may coincide with allegiance to other objectives, including profit-maximization. This is, of course, especially likely in the case of behavior designed to avoid punitive reprisals at the hands of the public. Where such a happy congruence occurs, the various motives are self-reinforcing, and there is no particular point in trying to impute behavior to any single motive.

The polar possibility is that yielding to the dictates of conscience or to social pressure may involve a significant financial sacrifice. In situations of this type—which involve conflict among the firm's objectives or values—generalization is exceedingly difficult since so much depends on the specifics of the particular case in question such as the amount of the probable financial loss and how the competing objectives are weighed against one another. About all that can be said here is that we would expect the conscience and social pressure motives to have a better chance of "winning out," (a) the smaller the financial sacrifice involved, and (b) the stronger the over-all financial position of the firm so that it can afford the "luxury" of non-pecuniary motivations in a highly pecuniary society. We would expect a firm that is hard-pressed financially and is

---

also be found in the rest of the full-cost literature. See in particular P.J.D. Wiles, *Price, Cost and Output* (Oxford: Basil Blackwell, 1956).

[2] The difficulties involved in separating rationalizations from "real" reasons have been widely noted and need not be recapitulated here. See, for example, R. F. Kahn, "Oxford Studies in the Price Mechanism," *Economic Journal*, LXII (March 1952), p. 126.

fighting for its very existence to put comparatively little weight on slight deviations from individual or social norms of behavior.

The third case is in some ways the most important. Here we have in mind situations in which it is exceedingly difficult to predict the impact of alternative price decisions on the profitability of the firm. In such circumstances, we would expect the firm to attach considerable weight to other policy objectives, including the "propriety" of the alternatives available. It is certainly difficult to imagine anyone deliberately violating the dictates of his own conscience or of public opinion without some positive incentive. To behave otherwise would be to court hypocrisy and public disfavor for their own sakes. The importance of this case stems not just from the fact that here conscience and social pressure may exert a significant independent influence on price policy, but also from the fact that situations of this sort may be fairly common in the real world. As will be pointed out shortly, once the existence of uncertainty is admitted, situations in which it is extremely difficult for the entrepreneur to estimate the relative profitability of alternative decisions may be fairly common—certainly much more common than the formal analysis of the preceding section would suggest.

To be able to classify any specific decision into one of the above categories, and to be able to suggest the implications of conscience and social pressure for price policy, it is necessary to have some idea of the type of price policy that would result from decisions dictated by these motives. Since the twin objectives of acceptance by society and the avoidance of punitive regulation both impel the businessman to pay some heed to the generally held conception of "proper" entrepreneurial behavior, let us start by considering the public's attitude toward prices and price policy.

Probably the safest generalization that can be made here is that the public prefers low prices to high prices and is disturbed by increases in the prices of any commodity. There is a very important corollary to this general dislike for high prices: price increases that are "visible" and "significant" must be "justified." Society is simply not willing to accept increases in prices as proper entrepreneurial behavior unless the increases are accompanied by some satisfactory explanation. And, most important of all from the standpoint of price policy, changes in the demand conditions facing the firm do not constitute a satisfactory explanation. That is, there is a strong current of opinion that does not consider it proper for a firm to charge "all the market will bear." On the other hand, public resentment against price increases is considerably moderated if the price-raiser can show that he was forced to increase his price because the prices of the things he buys have risen. In short, everyone appreciates the discomforts of higher prices. Consequently, the public can understand and tolerate to some extent price increases that are explainable in terms of prior increases in the firm's cost—but there is much less tolerance for price increases that seem to represent nothing more than the profit "greed" of the firm.

. While it is notoriously difficult to document the existence of anything so nebulous as the climate of opinion concerning price policy, there is some evidence that does seem to support the above interpretation. (1) The President, other government officials, and economists who call on firms to pursue "responsible" pricing practices certainly seem to hold something akin to this view. (2) The public pronouncements, publications, and testimony of businessmen certainly suggest that the business community itself feels the need to justify its price adjustments. And, can anyone either recall or conceivably imagine an industry defending a price increase on the grounds that business was sufficiently good to make such a maneuver profitable? On the other hand, it is common practice to explain price increases by pointing an accusing finger at rising costs. (3) The public's attitude toward price policy is revealed in a less dramatic way by the angry comments that are so familiar when an enterprise such as a local restaurant surreptitiously increases its prices or reduces its portions on the weekends or some other period when demand is particularly high. (4) Finally, we may note that certain Federal legislation supports, in principle at least, price adjustments geared to cost but not price adjustments based on variations in demand. The Robinson-Patman price-discrimination law is the best illustration. Under this law a manufacturer is permitted to charge customers different prices only if price differences reflect differences in his costs.[3]

The above discussion covers the price policy implications of social pressure. There remains the question of the price policy implications involved in adherence to those inner compulsions we have called "conscience." This motive is, of course, much more difficult to translate into a price policy since it is by its very nature extremely personal, and may stem from any number of sources including formal religious systems. In general terms, about all we can say is that "conscience" is likely to tell the businessman not to act dishonestly nor to take unfair advantage of the people with whom he deals. In more specific terms, it does not seem unreasonable to assume that the price policy implications of adherence to conscience would be essentially the same as the views we have attributed to society at large.

[3] However, it has been argued that in practice the courts have interpreted the cost-defense proviso of the Robinson-Patman Act so narrowly that in fact the law has required price discrimination rather than its prohibition. On this point, see M. A. Adelman, "The Consistency of the Robinson-Patman Act," *Stanford Law Review*, VI (December 1953), pp. 3-20. Nonetheless, the intent of Congress in passing the law was clearly to gear prices to costs and not to demand, and this is all that is important here.

Time Horizons and Price Policy

A second consideration that suggests the desirability of supplementing the formal picture of price determination described earlier is the existence of varying time horizons. The possibility that different firms (and, for that matter, the same firm at different points in its history) may base decisions on considerations that extend varying distances into the future carries a number of implications for our analysis of the impact of changes in costs and demand on the price charged by the firm.

For one thing, the existence of differing time horizons implies that two firms faced with the same data may make different price policy decisions. And, it is important to note that this can happen even if both firms are seeking to maximize profits. The hitch is that the time span over which they plan to maximize profits differs, and, consequently, their decisions may also differ.[4] However, it is not

---

[4] More precisely, both entrepreneurs may be seeking to maximize the capitalized value of their respective production plans. The reason different price decisions may result is that the plan based on the more distant time horizon contains *data additional* to that included in the other plan. There is also the question of the discount factor. So long as we set the factor by which future profits are discounted equal to the interest rate, this consideration cannot affect price decisions. However, if for some reason it would be more appropriate to think of different entrepreneurs as attaching different weights to future as opposed to present profits, then the price decisions of the two entrepreneurs could differ even though the cost and revenue data *and* the time horizons of the two firms were identical. The admittance of the possibility of different discount factors into our analysis does not result in serious alterations in the conclusions presented below, since we can treat the entrepreneur with a high discount factor as if he had a shorter planning period than the entrepreneur with a smaller discount factor. For an exposition of the theory of the firm based on the above type of analysis, see William J. Baumol, *Economic Dynamics: An Introduction* (New York: Macmillan, 1951), Chapter v.

terribly helpful to know simply that decisions will vary with the "economic horizons" of entrepreneurs. It would be more useful to know what, if any, general alterations in price behavior we might expect from firms planning for longer periods as compared to firms with nearer horizons.

In general, it does not seem unreasonable to expect firms with more distant economic horizons to be less willing to adjust prices upward in response to an increase in demand than firms who plan less far ahead. There are a number of considerations that support this conclusion. (a) The firm with the more distant horizon is apt to be more concerned about the possibility of new competitors entering his domain; consequently, he may be reluctant to increase his prices in response to an increase in the demand for his product, since this move might encourage rivals by leaving an unsatisfied fringe of customers willing to buy at a slightly lower price and by improving the apparent profitability of the firm. (b) The firm with the more distant horizons may desire to cultivate its long-run market by persuading new customers to buy its product— and this consideration would, of course, argue against raising prices in response to an increase in demand. (c) As argued above, the public may not approve of a firm that takes full advantage of its short-run position, and firms that are planning well into the future must be especially careful to stay respectable. (d) There is the question of the optimal labor policy—it has been argued that firms will have to share higher profits with unions via higher wages and at the same time may incur costs that cannot later be readily reduced; consequently, it may be in the long-run interests of the firm to keep its prices somewhat below the figure suggested by short-run considerations.[5]

To a lesser extent, firms with more distant time horizons may also be particularly reluctant to cut prices in response

[5] See Galbraith, *Review of Economics and Statistics*, May 1957, pp. 127-128.

to a decrease in demand. Among the factors which support this conclusion are the difficulties involved in raising prices when demand again increases (assuming that it will) and the general preference of firms planning way ahead for some measure of price stability.

Finally, it should be noted that perhaps the most important implication of our opening up the whole subject of time horizons is that at the same time the lid has been removed from the Pandora's box that has heretofore confined the problems of uncertainty. While it is difficult to avoid the problems raised by the existence of uncertainty even when dealing with a uniform planning period, such avoidance becomes many times more difficult when we try to deal with firms possessing varying economic horizons. And it is to the implications of uncertainty for price behavior that we now turn.

Uncertainty, Security, and Price Policy

One of the most serious deficiencies of our earlier appraisal of the impact of changes in cost and demand on price is that it did not include any explicit consideration of the problems raised by the existence of uncertainty. In this respect, our earlier analysis certainly does not differ materially from many other treatments of price theory. The fundamental reason for this widespread avoidance of uncertainty is simple enough: uncertainty raises a multitude of exceedingly complex and difficult questions. However, without pretending to do more than scratch rather feebly at some of the less complex aspects of this subject, it is possible to suggest three ways in which the existence of uncertainty modifies our earlier conclusions.

First of all, the existence of uncertainty means that the firm cannot make its decisions on the basis of a single estimate of future conditions, but must take into account a number of alternative possibilities. While it is true that one of these alternative estimates will usually be regarded as most likely to occur, it does not follow that the other estimates will have no influence on the firm's behavior. As Fellner has emphasized:

> ... it is *not* a requirement of rationality to equate the best guess of marginal revenue to the best guess of marginal cost. If this were done, then no allowance would be made for the possibility that the best guesses may turn out to be wrong.[6]

The key question, of course, is the probable effect of more than a single estimate of costs and revenues on the price decisions of the firm. Fellner has answered this question by asserting: (a) that firms are usually especially concerned about the *un*pleasant surprises that may occur and so compromise between maximizing expected profits and maximizing safety margins against the relevant varieties of unfavorable surprise; and (b) that to maximize safety margins, the firm should produce the output for which the gap between the best-guess average revenue and the best-guess average variable cost is at a maximum.[7]

The first part of Fellner's answer is quite appealing. There are a number of reasons for thinking that uncertainty breeds a certain craving for security. It is not unreasonable to suppose that firms are more anxious to avoid either losses or reductions in their existing profits than to make a quantitatively equivalent increase in earnings. For

[6] William J. Fellner, "Average-cost Pricing and the Theory of Uncertainty," *Journal of Political Economy*, LVI (June 1948), p. 249. See also William J. Fellner, *Competition Among the Few* (New York: Knopf, 1949), pp. 148-155.

[7] It must be emphasized that Fellner carefully restricts his conclusion that firms desiring to maximize their safety-margins should maximize the gap between AR and AVC to cases in which the danger being protected against is parallel downward shifts of the demand function and parallel upward shifts of the marginal cost function.

one thing, a reduction in profits is apparent to everyone who reads the firm's financial reports, while a failure to increase profits as much as conditions might have warranted is much less perceptible. A reduction in profits is taken as prima facie evidence of poor management. Consequently, who can blame decision-makers for being reluctant to gamble a "satisfactory" earnings record by a decision that could mean either slightly higher profits or a reduction in earnings?

It has also been argued that "quasi-objective factors justify a greater emphasis on the possibility of unfavorable surprise." This is because moderate losses may have more of a tendency to spiral than equally modest gains; the rating of a firm on the credit market is more likely to deteriorate as a consequence of losses than to climb as a consequence of gains; and, a firm's bargaining power on the commodity markets may be harmed by a reduction in its profits more than it will be helped by an increase.[8] For all these reasons, it is natural to expect unfavorable surprises to be weighted more heavily than favorable surprises of an equal actuarial value.

While Fellner's arguments suggesting that the typical firm will, as *one* of its objectives, seek to maximize something akin to what he has called the "safety margin," his translation of this objective into a price policy is much less persuasive. It is very hard to see why the perfectly understandable quest for some measure of safety or security should impel a firm to produce the output for which the gap between best-guess average revenue and best-guess average variable cost is at a maximum. In the case of a straight-line demand curve and a horizontal average variable cost curve, Fellner's safety-margin rule would suggest that to achieve the security objective the firm cease opera-

---

[8] These quasi-objective factors have been suggested by Fellner (*ibid.*, p. 150).

tions altogether. And while it is undeniable that going out of business affords the entrepreneur the maximum protection against long-run losses, it is hard to see why it would necessarily be the safest course of action in the short-run. The basic difficulty with this type of solution is that, without some notion of the probability that the firm attaches to alternative outcomes, any precise statement as to the "safest" price policy would seem to be unobtainable. Consequently, we are forced to retreat to a more general sort of analysis.

At this less rigorous level of discussion, one fairly important conclusion suggests itself. The firm is not likely to increase its prices in response to pressure from a possibility that is far from certain to materialize. For example, take the case of a firm that is making fairly good profits, and is either advised that there is some probability that the demand for its product will increase in the near future or actually experiences some increase in orders. Unless it were fairly confident that a price increase would not only increase its short-run profits but also offered no very serious threat to the longer-run prospects of the firm, it might well leave its price unchanged. After all, when profits are increasing by dint of higher volume, why rock the boat by raising prices? The incentive of a slight but fairly probable increase in profits might well not be strong enough to offset the more remote possibility that a higher rate of speed will capsize the ship.

This illustration suggests nicely the second main way in which uncertainty may affect price behavior. Thus far we have not differentiated between the effect of uncertainty on the role of demand compared to the role of costs in the pricing process. However, it seems plausible to expect the existence of uncertainty to result in the assignment of a relatively more important role to cost in the price-setting process. This is primarily because the variables which determine the costs of a firm are more under the control of the firm and can be better estimated than the variables which affect the elasticity of demand. For example, it is extremely hard for the firm to predict such important determinants of the demand for its product as the trend in the incomes of customers and the buying opportunities that other firms will make available to these customers. On the other hand, the cost accountant is able to make an estimate of costs which, while far from perfect or exact, is generally more reliable than the available estimates of demand conditions.

Another important reason why costs are particularly significant under conditions of uncertainty is that changes in costs are usually more *permanent* than changes in demand. After all, the demand for a product depends on a whole host of factors, most of which are beyond the control of the individual firm. People's preferences and incomes, as well as the inventiveness of other firms, are not only hard to predict but also dangerous to bet on. Consequently, the firm can seldom be sure that a sudden upturn in the rate of orders will be maintained or that a trickle of orders will not turn into a veritable flood.

Costs, on the other hand, are much less likely to behave in such a capricious manner. The firm cannot expect to wake up many mornings and discover that the wage increase it negotiated last week has suddenly been annulled. Prices of raw materials are apt to be somewhat more variable than labor costs, but still not nearly so subject to change as the demand for the firm's product. The implication of all this is that the firm seeking to avoid frequent price changes and trying to conform to the market's general preference for stability will find variations in costs to be a more useful price policy guide than changes in demand.[9]

[9] The importance to some firms of relative price stability is well illustrated by the way in which the rayon industry has tried to achieve a special status for its product by advertising its sta-

The third way in which uncertainty affects price behavior is bound up with what Scitovsky has called the "turnover lag."[10] A change in price takes time to affect the rate of turnover or the volume of goods sold—and the period of time it takes for the·bulk of customer adjustments to be made is called the "turnover lag." To appreciate the significance of this turnover lag for price behavior, it is necessary to go back a step and note that the effect on the firm's profits of any price change will be the resultant of two forces that usually pull in opposite directions: the change in per-unit profits, and the change in turnover or volume. The important point is that these two forces differ significantly both in their timing and in the certainty attached to them by the price-maker himself. The change in per-unit profit is both more certain and more immediate than the change in turnover, which occurs more slowly and is always very hard to predict. Consequently, the turnover lag exerts an asymmetrical effect on price policy in that it puts an obstacle in the way of lowering prices but not in the way of raising them. From the standpoint of our general picture of price behavior, the main significance of this asymmetrical effect of the turnover lag is that it suggests one reason why we might expect firms to be somewhat biased in favor of price increases and to resist strongly pressures for price reductions.

Interdependence of Firms

Thus far we have largely ignored the important price policy problems that result from the interdependence of firms. That is, we have not expressly incorporated into our picture of price behavior any discussion of the role played

---

bility of quality and price. See Jesse W. Markham, *Competition in the Rayon Industry* (Cambridge, Mass.: Harvard University Press, 1952), especially pp. 143ff.

[10] Scitovsky, *Welfare and Competition*, 1951, pp. 272-281.

in price setting by "conjectural interdependence"—which, in less elegant terminology, means simply a situation in which two or more price setters must take into account the probable reaction of rivals to any price decision they may make. And, while "conjectural interdependence" is most important and has been most widely discussed in conjunction with the price behavior of rather well-defined industries composed of relatively few firms, we must not think its role in price-formation is confined to such a narrow orbit. In a very real sense, no entrepreneur in our economy dares envision his firm as an "island unto itself." To some degree every enterprise competes with other firms for the allegiance of the customer and his dollars; any price-maker who ignores entirely the price policies and behavior of his rivals does so at his own peril.

From the standpoint of formal price theory, the interdependence of firms raises especially perplexing problems in connection with the construction of the demand curve. The draftsman is faced with two fairly unpalatable alternatives. If he constructs the demand curve on the assumption that the prices charged by other firms are "fixed," then he had better be prepared to draw a whole host of demand curves and to recognize that any single curve will not be very useful to the price-setter. After all, any attempt to "play on" the given demand function is likely to result in reactions from other quarters that will shift the initial function and alter the dimensions of the price problem. On the other hand, if he constructs the demand curve to "take into account" the price reactions of the more important rivals of his firm he has: (a) performed a truly Herculean task;[11] and (b) again come up with a function

[11] First of all, a demand curve that includes rivals' reactions cannot be derived from knowledge of consumers' preferences and relative prices. Secondly, there are serious logical difficulties involved in constructing a demand curve on the basis of information about consumers' preferences *and* the demand functions of

that is of rather limited usefulness, since it can give clear advice only in the event of a change in costs confined to the firm in question.[12] As a result of these difficulties, economists have attempted to deal with the problem of price policy under conditions of oligopoly either by starting from an entirely new vantage point (for example, the theory of games) or by constructing a series of special models.

We cannot, of course, stray very far into this complex territory. All we can do here is note certain general characteristics of the existence of interdependence and examine in very broad terms the implications of these characteristics for our picture of price behavior. Probably the most important characteristic of situations in which a few firms are especially strong rivals is that there is likely to be a high premium put on what might be termed "stability of relationships." That is, this sort of situation has within it the seeds of such disturbances as price wars, which do not usually operate to the best advantage of the participants. Consequently, there is a natural inclination to avoid forms

---

competitors. Triffin (*Monopolistic Competition and General Equilibrium Theory*, 1949, pp. 68-70) has emphasized that to be able to draw A's demand curve we first need to know B's, but to know B's we must first know A's, and so on. As a consequence of these difficulties, it is *possible* to draw up this kind of demand curve only on the basis of very special assumptions about the nature of price behavior—the "kinked" oligopoly demand curve represents one example of this type of curve.

[12] To use the "kinked" oligopoly demand curve as an example, the well-known conclusion to which this construction leads is that an increase in the firm's costs will not lead to a price increase so long as the new marginal cost function intersects the marginal revenue curve on its vertical portion. However, it must be emphasized that this conclusion does *not* hold for the case in which the rivals of the firm have also experienced an increase in costs. Consequently, this conclusion must be used with care—it can easily mislead.

of behavior that might precipitate such holocausts. Once any situation that is at all satisfactory has come into being, we can expect the status quo to be maintained so long as there is no fundamental change in the conditions facing the firms. If there is an agreement among the firms involved, the pressures for "stable relationships" are at least equally great since the negotiation of "understandings" is an extremely delicate, arduous, and unpleasant process over which hangs the threat of a mutually unprofitable pitched battle.

The main implication of this quest for stable relationships is that a price adjustment will usually be made only in response to a change in conditions that (a) affects most or all of the firms involved in a fairly *uniform* manner, and (b) is expected to be fairly *permanent*. This is because a fairly uniform change in conditions offers the best chance for a simple, peaceful adjustment, and a fairly permanent change in conditions does not carry with it the disquieting thought that another adjustment—possibly in the reverse direction—will be required in the not too distant future.

Thus the existence of conjectural interdependence would seem to encourage the assignment of a relatively more active role in the pricing process to changes in cost than to changes in demand. That is, changes in costs are more likely to lead to price adjustments than changes in demand, because changes in costs fulfill the criteria listed above much more satisfactorily than do changes in demand. As a rule, cost increments affect most producers in a fairly uniform manner, are expected to be relatively permanent, and in addition provide (thanks to the cost accountant) an available and relatively reliable index of the magnitude of change that has occurred. On the other hand, changes in demand are much less likely to affect all interested firms uniformly, are much more subject to sudden and rather unpredictable change, and are more difficult to measure.

Of especial importance is the relative uniformity and

measurability of broad changes in costs. These characteristics give changes in costs an important advantage over
changes in demand as the prime mover in the price-setting
process: price adjustments in response to fairly broad,
well-documented, and well-understood changes in costs
raise comparatively few questions concerning the touchy
subjects of share of market and intent of rivals, and so are
not terribly likely to be interpreted by other firms as an
"aggressively competitive maneuver."

Price Determination in the Individual Firm: A Synthesis

The preceding part of this chapter has been devoted
to exploring the ways in which considerations such as uncertainty and nonpecuniary motivations modify the rather
formal analysis of price behavior developed earlier. At this
juncture, it' may be helpful to try to pull together the
various threads of our discussion in order to form more
of an over-all picture of the price-setting process within
the individual firm. After this has been done, we shall turn
our attention from the realm of micro-economic price
theory to the more aggregative price determination aspects of the dilemma model.

The main conclusions concerning the roles occupied by
cost and demand in the price-setting process can be presented most conveniently and succinctly in a series of three
propositions.

PROPOSITION ONE: *Prices are particularly "sensitive" to
costs; that is, changes in costs are, in general, more
likely to inspire some sort of price adjustment than
are shifts in demand.*

This assignment of a relatively "active" role in the price-
setting process to the cost variable is based on the following considerations:

a. The "usual" shapes of cost and demand functions suggest that a firm seeking only to maximize short-run profits will receive much clearer and stronger price-adjusting instructions from a shift in costs than from a shift in demand. For instance, the firm can be quite confident that the proper profit-maximizing response to higher costs is a higher price, whereas there is much less probability that an increase in demand will require an upward price adjustment.

b. Costs are more *knowable* and *predictable* than demand conditions. And, the greater availability and reliability of cost data make them the logical starting point for price decisions.

c. Changes in costs are regarded as more *permanent* than changes in demand. Consequently, the appeal of the status quo—due especially to the costs of change and the preference of the market for price stability—is less likely to rule out a price increase suggested by a change in costs than by a shift in demand.

d. Changes in costs are often more *uniform* among the firms competing with one another than are changes in demand. Consequently, adjusting prices to a change in costs is less likely to raise touchy questions of market share. Adjusting prices to shifts in demand might easily be interpreted as a "competitive" or "war-like" act, and thus start a price war.

e. There is some tendency for the public to regard price adjustments based on changes in costs as more "proper" or "socially acceptable" than demand-inspired price adjustments. Hence, firms craving "respectability" have an added incentive to pay particular attention to the cost variable.

PROPOSITION TWO: *It is much more likely that an increase in costs will lead to an upward price adjustment than that a decrease in costs will inspire a price reduction.*

294

This selection of cost increases as an especially crucial factor in the price-setting process is based on the following reasoning:

a. One of the most important considerations involves the nature of the decision-making process and the greater interest of the typical firm in avoiding profit reductions than in earning slightly higher profits. In the present context, the point is that rising costs constitute an "unfavorable" happening and so put pressure on the firm to "do something," whereas cost reductions are "favorable" and thus do not carry a similar mandate for quick action.

b. The existence of uncertainty also encourages different price reactions to cost increases than to cost reductions. The fact that changes in volume are so uncertain and hard to predict leads the firm to pay particular attention to the size of its profit margin. Higher costs are likely to result in an upward price adjustment since failure to increase prices will mean an immediate and certain loss of revenue per unit of sales, whereas the danger that higher prices will result in reduced volume is more distant and problematical. On the other hand, these same uncertainties discourage price reductions in response to declining costs. It is notoriously difficult to estimate the increase in volume a firm may expect from lowering prices, whereas the reduction in per-unit revenue is perfectly apparent and certain.

c. Another consideration that mitigates against cutting prices as costs decline is bound up with longer-run considerations and the firm's desire for security. Instead of cutting prices now, the firm may elect to let its profit margin increase a bit, so as to provide itself with a larger safety-margin in case it is later *forced* to cut prices (for example, in order to counter a rival's aggressive price policy). In short, the firm may store up or stockpile price cuts in preparation for a time when they will be more sorely needed.

295

PROPOSITION THREE: *In the case of shifts in demand, it is much more likely that decreasing demand will provoke a price cut than that increasing demand will lead to a price increase.*

There are three main explanations for this rather important asymmetry:

a. The strong social pressures that discourage the firm from raising price in response to increasing demand do not discourage price reductions in response to decreases in demand. Quite the contrary. The public has an understandable preference for lower prices and is more likely to applaud than to condemn the firm that reduces its prices as orders decline.

b. The desire of the firm to hold the patronage of its customers and to maintain its share of the market discourage a price hike in response to an increase in demand since such action may not only cost the firm customers right now, but may also have longer-run adverse repercussions by encouraging other firms to enter its market. This quest for at least the same (and preferably a larger) share of the market does not, of course, inhibit price reductions in the face of declining demand but instead encourages such price behavior.

c. Perhaps most important of all, a decrease in demand is an "unfavorable" occurrence and may put real pressure on the firm to "do something" and to gamble, whereas an increase in demand is a favorable occurrence and thus constitutes less of a prod to action. That is, the firm can make absolutely no adjustment to an increase in orders and still benefit from such an increase through higher sales volume (assuming it is possible to expand output). Consequently, why should the firm risk upsetting such a favorable trend of events and incurring the wrath of its public by raising prices in the inherently uncertain hope that such a move will increase profits somewhat more? On the other hand, the firm facing what may be a severe challenge to either its very existence or its position in the industry is much more likely to gamble on increasing its volume sufficiently to make a demand-inspired price cut pay.

d. Finally, it is necessary to mention explicitly one specific situation in which a decrease in demand not only penetrates the firm's action-threshold but almost controls price behavior. Here we have in mind the case of a downward shift in the firm's demand curve attributable to a price cut by a rival. Assuming that the price-cutter was an "important" rival, the firm is likely to cut its price also, since the reduction in the price of the rival's product threatens: (i) immediate profits; (ii) the firm's long-run position in the industry—customers weaned away may not return; and (iii) the "pride" of the firm—it may have the attitude that nobody is going to undersell it.

16. The General Price Level

Introduction: the Interdependence of Cost and Demand

Thus far our analysis of price determination aspects of the dilemma model has been kept within the confines of the individual firm. It is now time to broaden our vista and inquire into some of the broader questions relevant to price behavior in the economy as a whole. The word "some" in the above sentence requires both emphasis and elaboration. Before going any further, it must be emphasized that at this stage of our inquiry we are concerned only with the *proximate* determinants of variations in the over-all price level. That is, here we shall discuss price behavior in terms of such familiar concepts as demand, supply, and cost without attempting to go behind these categories and explain the source of any changes that may have occurred. However, while we can put off until Part IV a discussion of the way in which changes in broad economic variables such as the quantity of money are mediated through the cost and demand categories, it is necessary at this juncture to say a few words about the general interdependence of cost and demand.

Although this specific question was not considered in our earlier discussions, it is apparent that even within the narrow orbit of the individual firm cost and demand functions are not strictly independent. As Chamberlin has emphasized, costs influence the demand for the individual firm's product via the institution of advertising and the existence of advertising budgets.[1] In turn, the demand situation confronting the firm influences the costs incurred by the firm in a number of ways. For one thing, a high and increasing level of demand may breed administrative laxity,

[1] Chamberlin, *Theory of Monopolistic Competition*, 1948, Chaps. VI and VII.

whereas a decline in demand may bring pressure on the firm to reduce its costs.[2] Furthermore, the demand situation in the product market may react on the prices paid by the firm for the factors combined in the production process. The demand for certain raw materials is largely derived from the demand for a certain final product, and in this case an increase in the output of the industry may bring about a higher raw material cost per unit of final product. Perhaps most important of all, we have argued earlier that wage determination is strongly influenced by the level of business activity in general, and by the firm's profit position in particular. Consequently, increased demand may lead to higher wages via either the medium of an increasing demand for labor or of increasingly favorable earnings reports.

When we move from the realm of the individual firm to the broader realm of the entire economy, the interdependence of costs and demand is, of course, much more pronounced. Now a shift in the cost functions is almost certain to induce a significant shift in the demand functions as well via the income side of cost adjustments. As Keynes emphasized, some very misleading conclusions can stem from an analysis of the impact of a money wage adjustment that is based on the assumption that aggregate monetary demand is unaffected by variations in the wage rate.

This interdependence of the cost and demand functions does not, of course, imply that there is no purpose to be served by constructing cost and demand functions as an

[2] This point has been emphasized strongly by Reynolds (*American Economic Review*, June 1948, p. 298): "In a business enterprize of any size, efficiency is a matter of organization rather than of correct ratiocination by a single 'entrepreneur.' Costs are administrative decisions, not facts of nature. And since executives usually administer about as well as they have to, the level of costs is by no means independent of the level of demand. Any shelter from the full rigor of competition, or any prolonged period of rising business activity, is likely to breed administrative laxity."

aid to understanding price behavior. What it does mean is that: (a) great care must be exercised in deriving behavioral conclusions from *ex post* cost or output data—for example, an equivalent increase in average cost and average revenue by itself tells us little about the impact of cost adjustments on product price movements; and (b) a shift in either the demand or cost function will often produce a shift in the other function as well. Bearing these important qualifications in mind, we can now proceed to investigate the proximate determinants of changes in the general price level.

Modes of Price Determination in Various Sectors of the Economy

To understand the over-all movements of whatever price index we choose to identify with "the general price level" (say the Consumer Price Index), it is useful to begin by considering briefly the various modes of price determination represented by different components of the index. As will soon be apparent, a certain amount of disaggregation is required by the fact that our picture of the price determination process within the individual firm cannot be applied with equal success to all areas of the economy.

Agriculture is one extremely important segment of the economy in which we find a mode of price determination unique enough to merit special attention. An important characteristic of the agricultural sector of the economy is that the final product is sufficiently homogeneous, the number of independent producers sufficiently large, and the market sufficiently well organized to approximate the perfect competition model. Consequently, in this sector our discussion of the price-maker's behavior is clearly inapplicable, since the individual farmer has little or no control over the price at which he sells his produce.

Furthermore, there are important differences between

price behavior in the agricultural sector of the economy and in those areas where prices are set by conscious policy decision. For one thing, agricultural prices tend to be much more responsive to shifts in demand. This is because (a) agricultural products are sold in open markets of the auction-market variety; (b) outputs cannot be increased significantly in the short-run except at sharply increasing cost; and (c) agricultural prices are strongly influenced by speculative activity.[3] On the other hand, increases in costs incurred by the farmer are not likely to exert any direct influence on the price of agricultural products, and exert an indirect influence only slowly via induced changes in the amount of produce offered for sale.

Another very important characteristic of the agricultural sector is the extent to which it is directly affected by federal legislation and regulations. Without getting into a detailed discussion of federal farm policy, it can be noted that the general effect of the agricultural policy we have known in the past several decades has been to put a floor (albeit, an unsteady one) under certain agricultural prices. From the standpoint of price behavior, the main consequence of this floor is to prevent a downward shift in demand from depressing prices beneath the level at which the floor is set. However, the floor may also prevent an increase in demand from raising prices—this will, of course, happen only so long as the price guaranteed by the government remains above the "market" price. It is also worth noting that, since the floor itself shifts with changes in the costs incurred by farmers, the government farm program serves to increase the potential significance of cost adjustments in the pricing of farm products. Finally, the crop restriction aspects of the government program

[3] For a detailed examination of price-setting in agriculture, see Richard Ruggles, "The Nature of Price Flexibility and the Determinants of Relative Price Changes in the Economy," *Business Concentration and Price Policy*, 1955, pp. 464-470.

301

may affect agricultural prices by altering the supply of agricultural produce.

The second main category of prices that is not explainable in terms of our earlier exposition of the price-maker's behavior contains the prices of what are called "services." Actually, the pricing of services rendered by individuals such as barbers, plumbers, lawyers, domestics, and doctors, is really more a matter of wage determination than of price determination since the individual's remuneration and the price paid by the recipient of the service are almost the same. Consequently, to understand pricing in this sector of the economy it is necessary to return to the realm of wage determination. And, while certain of these services (for example, the labor of domestics) are priced in fairly atomistic markets, others are set by associations or unions of the individuals concerned. In cases of the latter type (for example, the plumbers) we really have a situation in which it is altogether proper to equate union wage policy, wage determination, and price policy. From the standpoint of price behavior, the only significant generalization it is possible to make here is that this class of prices will usually be fairly responsive to increases in demand and (especially in the case of manual workers) to the wages received by other groups of wage earners. A cost-plus pricing theory would not seem to be very useful here.

A more narrow segment of the economy worth distinguishing is the group of firms or industries usually referred to as "public utilities." From the price determination standpoint, the most important common characteristic of this segment of the economy is the existence of government control or regulation of the price-setting process. And, the most important consequence of this mode of price determination is the elevation of costs to a position of unquestioned prominence in the price-setting process. That is, public authorities have an understandable inclination to expect price adjustments to conform to changes in costs.

The distributive trades comprise another sector of the economy that merits a limited amount of individual attention. The most significant characteristics of this group of enterprises are: (1) variable costs are made up primarily of the monies paid to manufacturers in order to acquire goods for resale; (2) these variable costs constitute a high proportion of total costs; (3) variable cost per unit does not vary significantly over the range of outputs available to the typical distributor; (4) changes in the wholesale prices of the goods handled by the individual distributor usually affect his fellow distributors in a rather similar manner; and (5) the distributor usually sells a variety of individual items and so needs some sort of general pricing formula. From the standpoint of price behavior, the main consequence of this set of characteristics is that the distributor is particularly prone to employ some sort of gross margin pricing and to increase his prices in proportion to increases in his variable costs.[4]

The main sector of the economy that remains to be considered is manufacturing or processing in general. Actually, this sector does not really "remain to be considered" since our earlier and rather detailed analysis of the price determination process was expressly designed to apply to the manufacturing segment of the economy. And, since this sector is so broad and heterogeneous, there is little that can be added to our earlier analysis. About the only useful way we can supplement our general discussion of the roles played by cost and demand elements is by emphasizing the variety of price determination models that are applicable to various industries within the manufacturing sector. In addition, one general price behavior conclusion should be noted: changes in costs will be an especially significant determinant of price adjustments where the

[4] Many of the above points have been made by Ruggles (*Business Concentration and Price Policy*, 1955, pp. 485-486) and by Heflebower (*ibid.*, pp. 878-885).

market structure is such that either overt collusive arrangements or an unusually high degree of "conjectural interdependence" exist.

Proximate Determinants of Changes in the General Price Level

Thus far we have been concerned exclusively with the factors that influence price adjustments within individual firms and individual sectors of the economy. However, our ultimate concern is not with individual price movements per se, but with the changes in the general price level that are the product of individual price adjustments. Consequently, it is now necessary to see what contributions our above discussions of price determination in the individual firm and of modes of price determination in various sectors of the economy can make to our understanding of changes in the general price level.

Our initial task is to select an over-all model of price determination in the aggregate from among the galaxy of price determination assertions or hypotheses that have been proposed and employed. The first and most obvious candidate is the rigid cost-plus pricing formula embodied in our earlier exposition of the dilemma model. This extremely straightforward hypothesis tells us that the general price level will vary directly with changes in some economy-wide index of costs—presumably a national unit labor cost index.

The main merit of this model of aggregate price behavior is, of course, its simplicity. However, we shall now argue that in this case the benefits of simplicity come at too high a cost. This is probably the most basic implication of the above analysis of the price determination process. In brief, the difficulty with the cost-plus hypothesis is that it does not constitute a useful *general* description of price behavior in the aggregate—it is a special case that will hold only in certain well-defined circumstances.

For one thing, there are several quite important sectors of the economy (for example, agriculture, the more "competitive" branches of manufacturing, and the service trades) in which prices are not set on anything resembling a cost-plus basis and thus price variations in these sectors cannot be predicted on the basis of *ex ante* changes in costs.[5] Secondly, even within the sectors of the economy in which costs play an especially significant role in the pricing process, there are circumstances in which deviations from cost-plus pricing occur. And, we shall argue subsequently that there are still other reasons (mostly of a distributional sort) why variations in an economy-wide cost index will often provide an inadequate basis for predicting changes in the general price level.

An obvious alternative to the cost-plus model is the Keynes-Bent Hansen assumption that commodity prices are "flexible" in the sense that they move in response to the appearance of excess demand. This micro-economic assumption is easily translated into a macro-economic price determination hypothesis by the simple expedient of summing the excess demand in each individual commodity market. We thus arrive at the well-known inflationary gap model of the general price level. If the excess demand in

[5] The phrase *"ex ante"* is worth emphasizing. As Friedman has pointed out, there are good reasons for defining *ex post* total cost as identical with *ex post* total revenue. (See Milton Friedman, "Comment" [on "Survey of the Empirical Evidence on Economies of Scale" by Caleb A. Smith], National Bureau of Economic Research, *Business Concentration and Price Policy*, 1955, p. 235.) However, this does not, of course, mean that prices will vary with expected changes in what we might (following Friedman) call "contractural costs." Hence, the *ex post* equality between costs and revenue does not support a cost-plus pricing theory.

the composite commodity market is positive, there is a pressure for higher prices and *vice versa.*

Unfortunately, this formulation suffers from the same generic difficulty as the cost-plus hypothesis—it too is a special case, applicable only in certain carefully prescribed circumstances. More specifically, the excess demand model suffers from two rather serious disadvantages, one of which is obvious and the other more subtle. First of all, the excess demand concept in its usual form can only be applied to perfectly competitive markets.[6] And, it is obvious that a model which requires perfect competition in the product markets is inapplicable to an economy containing important sectors in which the mode of price determination differs significantly from the perfect competition model. Secondly, even if all individual prices were perfectly flexible, the summing of the individual excess demands would still not serve as a suitable indicator of the pressure on the general price level unless the shapes of the entire supply and demand functions are the same in each sector.[7] This is because the magnitude of the price increase that will occur within a given industry in response to a given dollar amount of excess demand varies with the shapes of the cost and demand functions. Consequently, if these cost and demand functions do not have essentially the same shapes in all parts of the economy, the change in the over-all price level that will result from a given amount of aggregate excess demand would depend on whether the excess demand were concentrated in markets where price

[6] Bent Hansen has tried to extend the clear concept of excess demand in the perfectly competitive market (as the difference between the quantity demanded and the quantity supplied at a given price) to the case of imperfect markets (*Study in the Theory of Inflation*, 1951, p. 3). However, as noted earlier (see Chapter 2, n. 16), it is difficult to understand Hansen's redefinition.

[7] For a careful elaboration of this point, see Alain C. Enthoven, "Monetary Disequilibria and the Dynamics of Inflation," *Economic Journal*, LXVI (June 1956), pp. 256-270.

fluctuates sharply in response to the appearance of excess demand or in markets that are relatively unresponsive.

If we reject both the cost-plus and the excess demand models, where are we to turn for assistance? In general, the answer is: to a less aggregative and somewhat more complex model of the general price level that recognizes the existence of various modes of price determination and the interaction of cost and demand considerations within the individual sectors. From the standpoint of a formal framework, the publications of Messrs. Enthoven[8] and Pitchford[9] seem the most promising. The "bare bones" of Pitchford's price determination schema can be summarized most simply in the following equation:

$$\Delta P = k_1 (\Delta D_B) + k_2 (\Delta C)$$

This expression can be interpreted, first of all, as a portrayal of the individual firm's price behavior. The total price adjustment (ΔP) is represented as the sum of the

[8] *Ibid.* Actually, Enthoven is less concerned with setting up a model that will permit us to predict actual movements of the price level than he is with determining the initial conditions or "error signal" that will lead to pressure on the price level.

[9] J. D. Pitchford, "Cost and Demand Elements in the Inflationary Process," *Review of Economic Studies*, xxiv (February 1957), pp. 139-148. The following exposition in no way does justice to Pitchford's work. Pitchford's actual price determination model is couched in difference equation form and is combined with two other difference equations (one representing wage determination and one representing aggregate demand) to form an integrated model of the inflationary process. This model is then used to show the various ways in which cost and demand elements interact in determining price movements. All we are interested in here is Pitchford's general conception of the price determination process, and for this purpose our simplified equation is satisfactory. We might also note that Enthoven's general ideas concerning the aggregate price determination process appear to be rather similar to Pitchford's, although quite different terminology and methodology are used by the two authors.

firm's price reaction to whatever change in excess demand (ΔD_E) may have occurred and to the change in costs (ΔC). The coefficients k_1 and k_2 represent the strength of the firm's reactions to changes in demand and cost respectively. While this simple schema permits the firm to respond to changes in both cost and demand conditions, it does not, of course, require such behavior. Thus, if the firm were operating in an industry or situation where only changes in costs could influence price, then k_1 would equal 0. On the other hand, for a firm in a perfectly competitive industry k_2 would equal 0 since its price adjustment would be given to it by the change in the excess demand for its product. If every firm has some function of this general form, we can then obtain an aggregate price determination function by summing all the individual functions. Now, however, the meaning of the coefficients must be reinterpreted. At the economy-wide level, the k's represent not only the sum of the individual reaction coefficients but also the relative importance of the different modes of price determination encompassed in the over-all price index. For example, the impact of a cost increase on the general price level will depend on both the reactions of individual producers to higher costs and the importance of the cost-determined prices in the over-all price index.

This sort of apparatus is all right as far as it goes. Our simple variant of Pitchford's price determination hypothesis has the useful property of warning us not to tie the general price level too closely to any simple variable or "error signal," such as an aggregate index of either unit labor costs or aggregate excess demand. However, by its very nature it cannot supply us with very much positive information about the behavior of the price level. This is mainly because most of the interesting and significant questions are subsumed within the k_1 and k_2 parameters. Consequently, it is now necessary to supplement the broad picture of the price level supplied by this apparatus with a less formal mode of analysis.

For this purpose, it is convenient to state the substance of the above equation in a somewhat different form. In brief, we can envision the *proximate* determinants of changes in the general price level as:

1. The various modes of price determination that exist in different sectors of the economy;
2. Cost conditions;
3. Demand conditions; and
4. Distributional considerations—that is, the way in which certain cost conditions, demand conditions, and modes of price determination are combined or mixed together in our economy.

While we cannot, of course, even begin to discuss individually the vast number of different combinations of these considerations which might lead to various price adjustments, our previous discussions do suggest several additional comments which may help to fill out this extremely general picture of price level movements.

It is appropriate that we start out by considering some of the factors that determine the impact of an increase in an economy-wide index of costs. The first observation suggested by our earlier analysis is that the impact of such an increase on the general price level will depend on the distribution of higher costs among the various modes of price determination that characterize our economy. Assuming for the moment that all sectors of the economy are operating at a relatively high percentage of their capacity, the over-all impact of the cost increase will probably be much greater if the cost increase is concentrated in those sectors characterized by at least a tendency to react to cost increases by raising prices proportionately than if it is concentrated in those sectors closer to the perfect competition pole. Thus a cost increase peculiar to the heavily industrialized part of the economy would probably represent more of an impetus to higher prices than an equivalent increase in the cost of producing farm products.

This conclusion has been deliberately qualified by the use of the word "probably." The main reason for this qualification is that thus far we have not described the composition of the index that represents changes in costs. And, this question of what sort of cost index is involved in cost-price comparisons is sufficiently important and pervasive to merit brief consideration before we go any further. The important point is that even if each individual price is increased proportionately to the cost increase incurred by the particular firm, we still cannot be sure that over-all price index will increase proportionately to the increase in the over-all cost index. This latter result need also come to pass only if the composition of the cost and price indices is the same—that is, when cost and price changes within a given firm are assigned the same weights in the cost and price indices. To take a practical illustration, even if cost-plus pricing were to characterize every sector of the economy, the Consumer Price Index (in which foods and services have been assigned strong weights) might well not vary directly with changes in an index of manufacturing costs.

Of course, if the cost index used represents changes in unit *labor* cost rather than unit total cost, the problem is still more complex. And the added complexity does not arise just from the fact that total costs need not always change in the same proportion as labor costs. It must also be remembered that there are definite differences in the labor-cost/total cost-ratio for different sectors of the economy. Thus the same percentage increase in unit labor costs would mean a much larger proportionate increase in total costs in such high labor cost sectors as the services than it would in the distributive trades or in much of manufacturing.[10]

The impact of the cost increase will depend not only on the distribution of the cost increase among modes of price determination and on the cost index being used, but also on the distribution of the cost increase among the various stages of the production process. This consideration can be ignored (as was done in our earlier exposition of the dilemma model) only by assuming an entirely integrated economy in which inter-firm sales do not occur. The existence of a but partially integrated economy may influence, first of all, the *timing* of the ultimate price increase that will result from a given change in costs. After all, a cost increase centered in a stage of production far removed from the consumer will take much longer to affect the cost-of-living index than will a change in the cost of some industry that sells directly to the public. Furthermore, the *magnitude* of the ultimate effect on the price level may also depend on the location of the cost increase within the production process. If the demand situation is such that firms are able to maintain their profit margins as a percentage of total costs, then the ultimate price increase resulting from a given cost adjustment will be larger the further back in the production process the cost increase initially occurred—that is, costs will be pyramided. On the other hand, if the absolute amount of profit per unit sold is reduced in the face of higher costs, the opposite conclusion will hold—the change in the price index will be *smaller*

[10] It may well be that this difference in labor-cost/total-cost ratios is at least as important as different rates of productivity growth in explaining the tendency of prices in the service sector to increase more rapidly than the prices of goods (see our earlier discussion of this high-low productivity model in Chapter 11). An identical increase in wages in the services and in manufacturing will raise total costs in the service sector much more sharply.

the further back in the production process the initial cost increase occurred.

The above question of the effect of cost increases on profit margins leads directly to a fourth factor influencing the impact of a given cost increase—namely, the distribution of the cost increases among the firms in the economy vis-à-vis the demand situation confronting them. We have argued earlier that a firm that "usually" follows a cost-plus pricing policy may be tempted to depart from this policy if faced with a very adverse situation in the product market. Consequently, it would seem that if a given cost increase were forced on firms in such a predicament the price effect of the higher costs would be less than if the higher costs were incurred by a firm that felt no restrictions on its natural inclination to maintain its profit margin.

A closely related point concerns the distribution of cost increases among firms or industries in which different profit margins are customarily used. Assuming for the present that firms are in fact able to maintain their "usual" percentage profit margins, an increase in the costs of the firms with sizeable profit margins would result in a larger absolute increase in price than an identical cost increase passed on by firms with relatively low profit margins.

A final distributional consideration influencing the impact of an over-all increase in some cost index is the uniformity of the cost increase throughout the economy and over time. Our earlier observation about the asymmetrical impact of cost changes—to wit, that cost increases are more likely to raise prices than lower costs are to reduce prices—leads to the hypothesis that a given increase in the cost index will lead to a greater increase in the general price level if it is made up of a few cost reductions and some fairly substantial cost increases than if it is composed entirely of more moderate cost increases. The same reasoning would suggest that over time a fairly steady but moderate series of cost increases would lead to a smaller total price increase than a more scattered combination of sizeable cost increases and cost reductions.

Thus far, we have restricted ourselves to the factors influencing the impact of a given increase in costs. However, shifts in demand can also serve as the instigator of price level movements. In this connection, perhaps the first point to be made is that the impact of a shift in demand is at least as dependent on distributional considerations as is a shift in cost functions.

To take the case of a general decrease in aggregate demand, our earlier analysis would certainly suggest that the resultant downward pressure on the general price level will be greater the more heavily concentrated is the decrease in demand in the "competitive" sectors of the economy. And, in this connection it is revealing to note that the income elasticity of demand for goods generally considered to be in the "competitive" sector of the economy (food, for example) is relatively low. This consideration certainly portends nothing but ill for those charged with maintaining some degree of over-all price stability while at the same time preventing incomes from falling unduly.

Distributional considerations are also very important in assessing the impact of an increase in demand. Here again demand shifts concentrated in the competitive sector will produce a greater impact on prices than higher orders in the oligopolistic industries. Now, however, the relative inelasticity of the demand for foods and related commodities to rising incomes is a friend rather than a foe of price stabilizers. Furthermore, even within the oligopolistic sector there are important distinctions to be made. We have argued earlier that increasing demand will often be translated into higher profits via higher output rather than via higher profit margins. However, if the industry is already operating at capacity and if the increase in demand appears both significant and reasonably permanent, then the higher price per unit route may be taken. Consequently, the over-all impact of increasing demand on prices will be less the greater the extent to which the rising trend of orders is for the produce of firms presently operating at less than capacity.

This completes our discussion of the proximate determinants of changes in the general price level. It has been argued, in brief, that neither the strict cost-plus pricing assertion of the dilemma model nor the excess demand model provide a useful framework for studying changes in the general price level. Instead, we have advocated a less aggregative approach that recognizes the sectored nature of our economy and emphasizes the importance of both cost and demand conditions in the aggregate as well as the composition or distribution of changes in the aggregate cost and demand indices. It is now necessary to try to go behind these proximate determinants and see what role the monetary and fiscal policy of the government play in shaping the trend of the general price level.

PART IV
The Monetary Policy Assertion

17. THE MONETARY ENVIRONMENT AND THE DILEMMA MODEL: INTRODUCTION AND SOME GENERAL APPROACHES

Thus far in our analysis of the dilemma model we have examined in some detail the factors that influence the magnitude of wage adjustments, the impact of wage adjustments on costs, and the probable impact of changes in cost and demand conditions on price decisions. What we have *not* done is to examine the impact of changes in costs (and especially wage adjustments) on the level and distribution of aggregate money income and aggregate demand. We shall now attempt to fill this gap by examining the questions raised by the third and last assertion comprising the dilemma model—to wit, the monetary policy assertion, which states that the awesome responsibility for affecting the flow of money incomes and thereby deciding whether the wage and price behavior of individual economic units will culminate in inflation or unemployment rests squarely on the shoulders of the monetary authorities. In brief, we are now concerned with the demand side of cost increases and the role played by the monetary authorities in regulating the variations in the flow of money incomes induced by cost adjustments. More specifically, our assignment in Part IV is to try to see what factors or conditions determine the extent to which higher costs are translated into upward shifts of the demand functions facing individual firms and industries.

The relevance of this aspect of our inquiry is readily apparent. Throughout our earlier discussions of wage and price determination we have emphasized repeatedly the significance of both the level and distribution of aggregate monetary demand for wage, price, and output decisions. However, thus far we have scrupulously avoided the problems arising as a consequence of the interdepend-

317

ence of our economic system and have been content to consider the situation in the product market as a datum determined by exogenous forces. That is, our earlier discussions of wage and price determination were admittedly partial analyses in that they dealt only with the *proximate* determinants of wage and price movements. Consequently, we are now faced with the task of going behind these proximate determinants and seeing in what ways wage and price decisions themselves influence the level and distribution of aggregate demand. In this way it is hoped that we shall be able to tie together the loose threads of our earlier discussion and form a more complete, coherent, and better-integrated picture of wage and price behavior within the contemporary American economy.

In emphasizing that the outcome of wage-price pressures depends on the level of aggregate demand we are not, of course, breaking anything remotely resembling new ground. Nothing is more apparent than that a constant volume of output cannot be sold at ever higher prices *unless* total spending increases in step with per unit costs and prices. If for any reason the dollar volume of spending does not rise *pari passu* with prices, there has simply got to be a reduction in either sales, prices charged, or both. Among economists, Rees has been by far the staunchest defender of the role of aggregate demand in determining the course of economy-wide swings in prices and employment. He has argued repeatedly that discussions of the wage-price spiral must specify the level of aggregate demand assumed to exist, and that the on-going wage-price spiral of the editorial page can occur only if aggregate demand is "adequate"; otherwise, higher prices will lead to unemployment and thus to an eventual diminution of the upward pressure on wages and prices.[1]

[1] See Albert Rees, "Collective Bargaining, Full Employment and Inflation," Industrial Relations Centre, *Fifth Annual Conference* (Montreal, Quebec: McGill University, Industrial Rela-

Unfortunately, recognition of the significance of the state of demand for the propagation of price movements is not sufficient for an understanding of the workings of the economy. The more difficult problem of describing the link that connects variations in costs and prices with variations in aggregate demand remains to be solved. One way of approaching this problem is to emphasize that what is cost to one man is income to another and thus that a wage increase in and of itself not only raises the cost of commodities but also tends to raise the money income of potential purchasers as well. And, it may be noted in passing that recognition of the importance of the income side of wage adjustments has not been confined to academic economists, but has long been stressed by union spokesmen as well. The argument that wage increases are needed in time of depression to increase money incomes and stimulate buying is an obvious application of this line of reasoning. The reluctance of unions to carry over this emphasis on the income-creating properties of wage increases to inflationary periods can be charged off to the understandable tendency of any pressure group to use a certain line of argument only when it is in its own advantage to do so.

An extreme form of this wages-as-income approach "solves" the problem of the connection between upward pressure on prices and the level of aggregate demand by suggesting that price increases based on rising costs are self-financing and self-sustaining in that incomes are automatically raised in tune with rising prices. Two illustrations may clarify this argument. In describing inflations attributable to cost-push forces, Due writes:

> Even in a period in which there is no initial excess of aggregate demand, increased strength of union power may produce inflation by pushing up

---

tions Centre, 1953), pp. 93-94 [cited hereafter as Rees, *McGill Industrial Relations Conference*, 1953].

the general wage level. The higher wage incomes raise the aggregate money demand and thus sustain (from the demand standpoint) the higher dollar volume of national income.[2]

And Hart describes the mechanism of "log-rolling inflation" in rather similar terms:

> Once the administered prices become involved in inflation . . . the inflation can gain a momentum independent of the government deficit or other originating cause. A sort of semi-conscious log-rolling among the price-fixers raises farm prices because wages are rising, and wages because farm prices are rising. This process can operate through a price-control mechanism, as we saw during and after World War II. "Log-rolling inflation" is self-financing, since it marks up cost prices but also marks up levels of money income to match.[3]

If this reasoning were valid in all circumstances, the problem of the "adequacy" of aggregate demand could be summarily dismissed, and we could concentrate our attention on the cost side of wage adjustments, content in the knowledge that the demand side will take care of itself. Unfortunately, things are not so simple. A basic difficulty with the above approach to wage-income relationships is that it contains absolutely no mention of the monetary environment within which the wage-price-income-expenditure spiral takes place. It is for this reason that a number of economists (and especially Milton Friedman and Albert

[2] John F. Due, *Government Finance: An Economic Analysis* (Homewood, Ill.: Richard D. Irwin, 1954), pp. 485-486.

[3] A. G. Hart, *Money, Debt and Economic Activity* (New York: Prentice-Hall, 1948), p. 251. A more recent example of this same sort of argument is, W. J. Baumol, "Price Behavior, Stability and Growth," Joint Economic Committee, *Compendium on Prices and Economic Stability*, 1958, pp. 50, 56.

Rees of the University of Chicago)[4] reject the rigid linking of money incomes to wage adjustments.

The basic point is simply that for an increase in money expenditures to occur, there must be an increase in either the stock of money or the rate at which the existing stock is utilized. In terms of the Fisher quantity-theory equation $(MV = PT)$, an increase in the aggregate value of money expenditures can come about only through an increase in either M or V. Consequently, the proponents of the automatically self-financing doctrine are obligated to describe the mechanism whereby wage adjustments affect M or V or both. If there is no increase in either the stock or velocity of money, the higher level of costs and prices cannot be financed without an offsetting reduction in the volume of transactions. If the product of M and V does not increase in proportion to changes in P, there has simply got to be either a reduction in T or a rescinding of the price increases which led to the upward pressure on the price level.[5]

It is at this juncture that the role of the monetary authorities becomes clear. While it is true that the monetary authorities may not be able to exert direct control over the velocity of money, the quantity of money does fall well within their orbit of influence. Consequently, by exerting sufficient pressure on the money supply, the monetary authorities can prevent higher wage adjustments from generating higher money incomes. In short, the self-financing character of a cost-induced inflation is

[4] Friedman, *Review of Economics and Statistics*, November 1955, p. 404; and Rees, *McGill Industrial Relations Conference*, 1953, p. 94.

[5] An especially clear exposition of this same type of analysis may be found in Robert C. Turner, "Relationship of Prices to Economic Stability and Growth: A Statement of the Problem," Joint Economic Committee, *Compendium on Prices and Economic Stability*, 1958, pp. 677-678.

utterly dependent on a particular assumption about the monetary environment—to wit, that the supply of money or credit is sufficiently elastic to permit the expansion in aggregate spending necessary for continued rounds of cost-price increases.

There is no doubt but that the above emphasis on quantity-theory variables performs an important service in discouraging excessive preoccupation with the behavior of unions and firms and in directing our attention to the behavior of monetary institutions. However, this focusing of attention on the monetary institutions can, like most good things, be carried to extremes. Some economists—and most notably Friedman—have placed such great stress on the monetary aspects of the inflationary process as to exclude almost all else from consideration.[6]

This monetary approach is somewhat analogous to the rigid self-financing argument in that its main merit is simplicity. However, it appears that the cost of this brand of simplicity is also so high as to render it unattractive. From the standpoint of one seeking to understand movements of prices and output within the contemporary American economy,[7] this approach seems to suffer from

[6] Milton Friedman, "The Supply of Money and Changes in Prices and Output," Joint Economic Committee, *Compendium on Prices and Economic Stability,* 1958, p. 241; and "Statement" (U.S. Congress, Joint Economic Committee, *Employment, Growth, and Price Levels; Hearings,* "Part 4—The Influence on Prices of Changes in the Effective Supply of Money," 86th Cong., 1st Sess., 1959, pp. 605-669).

[7] At this point it is again necessary to emphasize the sorts of price movements with which we are especially concerned. In this study we are *not* interested in major inflations of the type which frequently accompany world wars and other holocausts. There is little doubt that in studying (and predicting) substantial price movements of this type, a strong emphasis on changes in the quantity of money is entirely justified. However, significant difficulties arise when this monetary emphasis is carried over in un-

several quite serious disadvantages (most of which are expressly recognized, though not stressed, by Friedman himself). In a generic sense, the main difficulty with the purely monetary approach is that it leaves unanswered many of the most important questions.

First of all, there is the question of how variations in price movements that do not happen to coincide with variations in the stock of money are to be explained. As Friedman himself points out, the relationship between changes in the stock of money and the price level is not mechanically rigid even over the long run, much less over shorter intervals of time.[8] An obvious answer to this question is that changes in output or transactions and changes in the ratio of cash balances to income are also significant. However, this answer leads directly to the further question of what factors are responsible for changes in T and V. And, once we have reached this stage, the attractive simplicity of the monetary approach is lost since we are in effect involved in explaining the spending decisions made throughout the entire economy. Whether we choose to attack this problem with the aid of quantity-theory categories or some other schema would seem to be resolvable solely on the grounds of convenience.

A second, and in many ways more serious, difficulty with Friedman's approach is that the crucial question of what determines changes in the quantity of money is left unanswered. Even if there were a perfect correlation between changes in the stock of money and changes in prices, in order to predict the future course of prices it would still be necessary to understand the determinants of the stock of money. The fact that our present-day monetary institu-

---

diluted form to the more "normal" sort of situation with which we are concerned here.

[8] Friedman, Joint Economic Committee, *Compendium on Prices and Economic Stability*, 1958, pp. 243ff.

tions make it possible to control M certainly does not justify treating the stock of money as a completely exogenous or independent variable. The post-World War II episode in which the Federal Reserve was intent on supporting the government bond market at all costs illustrates dramatically that at times the money stock can be quite elastic or "passive."

However, we need not resort to such extreme illustrations to make our central point. While it is certainly true that the size of the money stock is amenable to control by monetary authorities and is not usually the purely passive by-product of economic variables such as the price level, it is no less true that the price and output trends characterizing the economy at a given point of time influence the decisions of the monetary authorities. Without going so far as to accept Hicks' assertion that monetary decisions are dictated solely by happenings in the labor market (that is, that we are now on a Labor Standard rather than a gold standard),[9] one can still stress the significance of wage and price behavior as one element in the conglomeration of forces that shape monetary policy.

In short, what we appear to have in the United States today is a situation in which variations in prices, output, and the money stock are to some extent interdependent and mutually determining. An obvious corollary of this conclusion is that to understand price movements it is necessary to study the behavior of a multitude of institutions and groups including financial and non-financial corporations, unions, banks, and households—in addition to the central banking system itself.

The third and last question left unanswered by the exclusively monetary approach is *how* changes in the money supply exert their influence on the price level. Surely it is not enough to know that sufficient credit stringency *can*

[9] Hicks, *Economic Journal*, September 1955, pp. 389-404.

halt any upward pressure on the price level. We must also know the mechanism by which the impact is exerted, as well as the social and economic costs involved—in short, we must investigate the reactions of the various institutions through which monetary policy is mediated. Only when we possess this kind of information can we decide whether it is best to continue to attempt to control the price level in this manner or whether we should seek some other, possibly less-costly, technique. Certainly it is one thing to say that a given objective can be achieved in a certain manner and quite another to assume without further investigation that this is the optimal way of proceeding. To argue that cost-induced inflation is no problem because price increases *can* be prevented by a *sufficiently* restrictive monetary policy is surely to confuse policy prescription with analysis.[10]

For the above conglomeration of reasons, we are forced to conclude that excessive concentration on the monetary environment is no more satisfactory an approach to the demand side of the inflationary process than is the ignoring of monetary considerations altogether. Both approaches suffer from the same tendency to over-compartmentalize the economic process. To understand the impact of cost adjustments on the level and distribution of aggregate demand it is necessary to emphasize the interdependence of the various institutions in our economy and to examine in some detail: (a) the pressures on the monetary institutions generated by wage-price behavior; (b) the

[10] This methodological point has been emphasized strongly by Joseph Aschheim ("Central Banking and Wage-Induced Inflation" [unpublished Ph.D. dissertation, Dept. of Economics, Harvard University, 1954], p. 201) and James R. Schlesinger ("The Role of the Monetary Environment in Cost-Inflation," *Southern Economic Journal*, xxiv [July 1957], p. 17). Both Aschheim and Schlesinger criticize the tendency of Morton and Warburton to dismiss the significance of wage-induced inflation in this way.

reactions of the monetary-fiscal authorities to these pressures; and (c) the return impact of the monetary policy decisions on wage-price behavior. It is to this sort of analysis that we must now direct our attention.

From an organizational standpoint, it is convenient to divide our discussion into three stages. We shall first discuss the demand side of wage-price adjustments on the assumption that the monetary authorities do *not* seek to interpose any barrier in the way of the inflationary process (Chapter 18). Then we shall assume that the monetary authorities adopt an anti-inflationary policy and shall see in what ways this policy can be made effective (Chapter 19). The third stage will deal with the case in which unemployment exists and the monetary-fiscal authorities are under pressure to alleviate this situation (Chapter 20).

18. Impact of an Elastic Monetary Policy

In our earlier discussion of the dilemma model, we assumed that for the first few periods the monetary authorities followed an "elastic" credit policy in that they did not attempt to interfere with the propagation of the inflationary process, but instead permitted the banking system to supply whatever additional credit was necessary to finance the increased volume of money expenditures needed to support a higher cost structure. The dual observations that (a) at times in the past the government has in fact pursued such an elastic credit policy, and (b) that there exists today a strong body of opinion opposed to the use of a tight money policy in the fight against certain "types" of inflation suggest that this is by no means an utterly unrealistic assumption. However, our immediate concern is with neither the likelihood nor the desirability of such a policy, but rather with its consequences.

At first glance, it might appear that the significance of an elastic monetary policy is simple indeed. Throughout our earlier exposition of the dilemma model—as well as in our introductory remarks to Part IV—it has been assumed that a restrictive monetary policy constitutes the sole impediment to a continuous wage-price inflation. Consequently, the acquiescence of the monetary authorities would seem to remove the only roadblock standing in the way of successive rounds of cost and price increases. So long as the monetary authorities are willing to "ratify" higher costs and prices by permitting a simultaneous increase in money incomes, what is to halt an ongoing cost-price spiral? No answer to this question has as yet been supplied.

A second glance suggests, however, that this conception of the inflationary process and the role of an elastic monetary policy in this process is oversimplified. The most basic difficulty with the above line of reasoning is that it

327

passes much too lightly over one very important link in the inflationary process—namely, the link connecting higher money incomes and increased monetary demand. Only if the higher incomes are automatically translated into an increase in monetary demand sufficient to purchase the "going" rate of output at ever higher prices will there be no downward pressure on costs and prices. And, we shall now enumerate several considerations which suggest that such automaticity may be lacking. In short, the main point to be made here is that there are certain almost "natural" barriers to a cost-price spiral that operate in spite of an "elastic" credit policy.

First of all, there is the much-heralded "built-in flexibility" of our personal income tax system. That is, as money incomes go up more rapidly than real income, the progressive rate structure of the federal income tax will divert an increasing proportion of the country's real income to the government and will thus reduce the real disposable income of the public. As Schouten puts it: "A rise in the money income of workers and entrepreneurs is extremely dangerous in a society where the marginal burden of taxation is very high. The Treasury is then the only beneficiary."[1] Of course, the deflationary effect of the larger tax collections would disappear if the government were to turn around and spend at least as high a proportion of the increased revenues as the people from whom they were obtained.[2] However, given our existing federal budget and appropriation procedures, it does not seem

[1] D.B.J. Schouten, "The Wage Level, Employment, and the Economic Structure," trans. L. Katzen, *International Economic Papers*, II (1952), p. 225.

[2] If the government were to spend the entirety of the increased tax revenues, we would expect total money income to increase rather than decline since presumably part of the higher tax revenues came out of private savings rather than intended consumption expenditures. This is the logic of the so-called "balanced-budget multiplier."

likely that expenditures would respond this rapidly to higher tax revenues.

Secondly, it is necessary to consider the impact of rising prices on the foreign trade component of the gross national product. Since the incomes of our foreign customers are not automatically marked up by an increase in domestic costs, it is reasonable to suppose that higher domestic prices will be accompanied by some reduction in the quantity of goods sold abroad. It is very unlikely that the demand for our exports is completely inelastic. The magnitude of this effect will, of course, depend in part on the significance of foreign trade in the economy of a nation; and, for this reason, the United States is less subject to this particular constraint than are many other countries, such as Great Britain, for example.

Even if we posit a closed economy with no government, there is still the distribution of spending between the consumption and investment categories to be considered. In our earlier exposition of the dilemma model we managed to evade this problem by assuming the absence of all saving and investment—the populace was assumed to spend the entirety of its income on consumption goods. However, once we admit the existence of saving, we must also admit the possibility that *ex ante* saving may—at least temporarily—exceed *ex ante* investment at the full employment level of income. To ignore this possibility is to return to the world of Say's Law. One need not be a secular stagnationist to argue that at times excess capacity—and a concomitant downward pressure on wage and price adjustments—may arise simply from the existence of a disjunction between planned saving and planned investment.

This problem of reconciling saving and investment decisions is, of course, always with us in our type of economy, regardless of the behavior of wage- and price-setters. Consequently, the question arises as to whether an incipient cost-price spiral passively fed by the monetary authorities increases the likelihood that *ex ante* investment will not offset *ex ante* saving without a reduction in the level of aggregate income. There are some grounds for thinking that the answer to this question may be "yes."

For one thing, there is the argument that people are subject to a "money illusion" (act on the basis of changes in money variables rather than real variables) and thus save more in real terms as prices and money incomes rise, since they feel richer. While there may be something to this argument, it is important to note that it is entirely dependent upon a certain assumption concerning the nature of the consumption function. Specifically, the presence of a money illusion will reduce real spending on consumption goods *only* if the average propensity to consume *falls* as money incomes rise. If the average propensity to consume is constant in the relevant neighborhood, it makes absolutely no difference whether people recognize or fail to recognize that higher money incomes need not mean higher real incomes. In either case, an increase in money incomes unaccompanied by a change in real incomes will mean absolutely no change in real consumption.[3] Thus far

[3] Suppose, for example, that people always chose to consume exactly $\frac{4}{5}$ of their income and that suddenly money incomes rise from \$100 to \$200 at the same time that the price index goes up from 1.0 to 2.0. A person not subject to money illusion will, of course, realize that his real income is the same as it was before the doubling of prices and incomes and so will continue to make the same amount of real purchases. However, since prices have doubled, to do this he will now have to spend \$160 rather than \$80. The person subject to money illusion will see only that his money income has risen to \$200 and thus will also decide to spend \$160. However, this person presumably spent \$80 at the previous price level and so his real expenditures are also unchanged. Whether decisions are made in real or money terms is immaterial in such circumstances. This being the case, it is difficult to understand what H. G. Johnson can mean when he criticizes another author for assuming that people spend a fixed proportion of their money incomes regardless of the price level on the grounds

we have talked only about the effect of the money illusion on real consumption expenditures. It is also possible that real investment expenditures will be reduced as money incomes rise while real incomes are held constant. The point here is that some investment programs are fixed in money terms and cannot be revised upward (or simply are not revised upward) as prices rise.

Another way in which rising prices and money incomes might tend to depress the real consumption function is via the mechanism of the so-called "real-balance effect."[4] The argument here is simply that an increase in prices and money incomes that is not matched by an equi-proportionate increase in the nominal money supply will reduce the real value of the community's cash balances and thereby discourage spending. However, we must be careful not to overestimate the restraining impact of this real-balance effect at a time when an elastic credit policy is being pursued. After all, if the nominal monetary stock were to increase proportionately with the price level, then there would be no reason to expect any decrease in real spending as a consequence of this consideration. And, in the absence of a restrictive monetary policy, it is not unlikely that the supply of money will increase significantly as prices and money incomes rise.

However, this is not to say that the real-balance effect is of no significance in this situation. At least a part of increased money spending may be financed without the aid

---

that such an assumption amounts to a "built-in money illusion" (Johnson, as reported by Hague, *Theory of Wage Determination*, ed. Dunlop, 1957, pp. 400-401). Johnson would be correct in making this criticism *only* if we knew either that people's money incomes did not change in proportion to price adjustments or that people's average propensity to consume falls as their money incomes rise.

[4] For a full discussion of the origins and applications of the "real-balance effect," see Don Patinkin, *Money, Interest, and Prices* (Evanston, Ill.: Row, Peterson, 1956).

of an increased supply of money. Furthermore, the potential impact of the real-balance effect carries an important implication for the behavior of the monetary authorities. In order to prevent the real-balance effect from coming into play and dampening the inflationary pressures, it may be necessary for the central bank to do more than act in a purely passive manner. That is, there may well be a limit to the increase in the money supply that can be brought about without strong, positive action on the part of the central bank. Consequently, a "hands-off" policy by the central bank cannot be equated with a thorough-going "elastic" credit policy. A central bank which—while refusing to fight a cost-price spiral by taking directly restrictive actions—also refuses to support the higher cost-price structure by positive actions (such as reducing reserve requirements) will eventually exert a semi-automatic type of restraint on the inflationary process via the real-balance effect.

The money illusion and the real-balance effect both affect the aggregate spending function by shifting the individual spending functions that are subsumed within the aggregate function. However, the aggregate spending function may also be depressed even if there is no shift in any individual's spending plans. This will happen if the upward movement of prices and incomes redistributes the real income of the community in favor of those with a relatively low propensity to consume. Several authors have suggested that this type of redistribution does occur and does exert some restraining influence on the upward course of prices. The argument here is that the reduction in the consumption of the *rentiers* and other fixed income groups necessitated by the decreases that occur in their real incomes may not be fully offset by higher spending on the part of the beneficiaries of the inflationary process.[5] While

[5] Perhaps the clearest statement of this argument is in Joan Robinson, *Essays in the Theory of Employment*, 1937, p. 23.

there may well be some validity in this general position, two rather important qualifications are necessary: (a) it is hard to tell just what income levels will benefit from inflation and in what degree;[6] and (b) it is by no means clear that the propensities to consume of various income groups are as different as economists once thought they were—some evidence has been cited in support of the proposition that the marginal propensity to consume is about the same at all income levels.[7]

The above discussion centers on the distribution of real income among individuals. It is also important to note that rising prices and money incomes may be accompanied by a shift in real income from individuals to corporations. This type of redistribution is encouraged both by the relatively greater ability of the corporation to protect its relative income share in time of inflation and by the tendency of changes in money dividends to lag considerably behind changes in dollar profits.[8] Any such shift in favor of retained earnings must, of course, reduce the aggregate propensity to consume and is therefore likely to exert some downward pressure on wages and prices.

[6] See Slichter's discussion of this point (Sumner H. Slichter, "Thinking Ahead: On the Side of Inflation," *Harvard Business Review*, xxxv [September-October 1957], pp. 15ff.).

[7] See, for example, the references cited by Morton (*American Economic Review*, March 1950, p. 20, n. 9). This whole problem of the shape of the consumption function and the effect of changes in the level and distribution of money income is much too complex to be gone into here. For a detailed analysis, see James Duesenberry, *Income, Saving, and the Theory of Consumer Behavior* (Cambridge, Mass.: Harvard University Press, 1949).

[8] The significance of the distribution of income between individuals and corporations has been emphasized by Walter Morton (*American Economic Review*, March 1950, p. 20, n. 10). The impact of the lag between profit increases and disbursements to owners has been emphasized strongly by Richard Bissell ("Price and Wage Policies and the Theory of Employment," *Econometrica*, viii [July 1940], p. 212).

Thus far we have considered three categories of impediments to an ongoing cost-price spiral: (1) the existence of a federal government that levies a progressive income tax; (2) the existence of a foreign demand for some domestically produced products; and (3) the existence of certain factors that tend to reduce private domestic spending out of a given real disposable income as prices rise. As a fourth and final barrier to a self-perpetuating inflation it is now necessary to consider the impact of shifts in the *direction* of private spending.

The basic point here can be summarized as follows: even if the populace is able and willing to purchase the same aggregate amount of real goods as the general price level rises, there can still be a reduction in over-all output and employment if the composition of the intended volume of aggregate spending does not coincide neatly with the composition of the aggregate supply of real goods. This problem was ignored in our earlier exposition of the dilemma model by means of our assumption that the economy consists of a single firm producing a single, composite product that satisfies all needs. When we admit that the economy in fact consists of a multitude of firms producing a plethora of somewhat dissimilar products, the possibility of what might be termed "structural disequilibria" becomes apparent.

In fact, in the sort of period we are discussing at present it would be remarkable indeed if numerous individual excess supplies and excess demands did not appear. After all, general price movements do not usually consist of equal increases in the price of each and every commodity but more frequently encompass relative price changes within them. Furthermore, aggregate money and aggregate real income are both increasing, and there is a good possibility that income redistributions also occur. Consequently, the increase in the monetary demand for any particular commodity will depend on the trend of consumer preferences for this product, on numerous relative price changes, and on price and income elasticities. Thus it would not be at all surprising if the monetary demand for the produce of one sector of the economy did not increase sufficiently to permit the firms to sell their total output at the higher price, while at the same time another sector was experiencing an excess demand for its output at its new price.

The consequences of this attempt at inter-commodity substitutions will depend, of course, on a whole host of factors, including the price policies and wage-setting characteristics of the sectors involved, as well as the tenacity of the potential purchasers—that is, their willingness to reconsider their purchase preferences. On the one hand, it is conceivable that the simultaneous existence of excess demand and excess supply could be remedied by price flexibility. On the other hand, it is possible that the firm suffering from the excess supply of produce would not choose to cut prices and might be forced to lay off workers instead. The sector with the excess demand might ration its existing supply by either price or non-price means. If the excess demand were not absorbed by additional price increases, and if the disappointed purchasers then decided not to spend the money for anything else, we would have an increase in *ex ante* saving and thus downward pressure on the over-all inflationary process from this source as well as from the appearance of unemployment in the less fortunate sector.

The duration and extent of the unemployment resulting from this kind of structural disequilibria would depend, of course, not just on the magnitude of the initial layoffs but also on the secondary effects of this unemployment as well as on the mobility of labor and the willingness of other firms to expand their work forces. In any case, it is clear that some reductions in employment may stem from a simple lack of congruence between the supplies and demands for individual commodities even if the balance between aggregate demand and aggregate supply is not disrupted by the upward movements of costs, prices, and incomes.

Against these four categories of impediments to the smooth functioning of the cost-price spiral, must be weighed the possibly pro-inflationary impetus of expectations. It is obvious that if people become convinced prices are going to rise continuously they will have an added incentive to increase their present purchases, which will augment the speed of the spiral thereby increasing the incentive to buy now, and so on until a hyper-inflation destroys general confidence in the economy and thus brings on its own elimination. In response to this gloomy prospect about all one can say is that the hyper-inflations of the past do not seem to have slowly grown out of "creeping" inflations but rather to have stemmed from some more dramatic event, such as a war or a sudden influx of money attributable to some other consideration. Furthermore, as Slichter has emphasized, it is not easy for individuals to hedge against a creeping inflation by anticipating future needs.[9] Hence, while we must admit that expectational considerations *may* overbalance the deflationary considerations discussed above, it is by no means clear that this will inevitably occur.

This concludes our very brief sketch of the factors that influence the course of a cost-price spiral fed by an elastic credit supply. Our main emphasis has been on the need to examine the income-demand link in the inflationary process. It is by no means obvious that an elastic monetary policy is sufficient to insure the uninterrupted progression of a series of cost-price increases, and we have described four categories of considerations that may interpose themselves between higher prices and higher money incomes on the one hand and the higher demand needed to sustain

[9] Slichter, *Harvard Business Review*, September-October, 1957, pp. 15ff. It may be somewhat easier for corporations to hedge against inflation.

these increases on the other. This is not, of course, meant to suggest that a country should rely on these "natural" barriers. For one thing, these barriers may be so porous as to slow down the upward course of prices only very slightly; and, there is the possibility that inflationary expectations will take hold and sweep all else before them. All we have tried to do here is indicate that monetary policy is not the only defense against inflationary pressures, and that to understand the course of an inflationary process it is necessary to do more than study the behavior of the monetary authorities.

19. IMPACT OF AN ANTI-INFLATIONARY MONETARY POLICY

In the previous chapter we assigned the monetary authorities a purely passive role, and in this way managed to bypass the tricky and troublesome issue of the manner in which higher costs and prices are financed. While it is plausible that the monetary authorities might passively acquiesce to the financial needs of the community for a time, it is extremely doubtful that such a policy would be followed for long if accompanied by a steady—even though moderate—increase in the cost of living. For one thing, the members of the Federal Reserve Board have made it abundantly clear that they consider the defense of the value of the currency to be perhaps their main *raison d'être*.[1] And, even if the monetary authorities were at first a bit reluctant to assume this duty, we can be confident that irate housewives and Congressmen would not tolerate such a passive policy indefinitely, but would loudly proclaim the necessity of anti-inflationary measures. Consequently, it is altogether proper that we now focus our attention on the impact of a restrictive monetary policy.

It must be emphasized at the outset that our concern here is not with the question of whether or not monetary policy *can* halt an upward movement of wages and prices

[1] See, for example, the statement of William McC. Martin, Jr., Chairman of the Board of Governors of the Federal Reserve System, in response to questions from the Joint Committee on the Economic Report on this subject of the policy objectives of the Federal Reserve System (U.S. Congress, Joint Committee on the Economic Report, *Monetary Policy and the Management of the Public Debt; Their Role in Achieving Price Stability and High-Level Employment; Replies to Questions* . . . , 82d Cong., 2d Sess., 1952, Part I, pp. 212-215). [Cited hereafter as Joint Committee on the Economic Report, *Compendium on Monetary Policy,* 1952.]

—no one denies the ultimate potential effectiveness of monetary policy—but rather with the much more interesting question of *how* various sorts of monetary policy exert their influence. Certainly one of the major limitations of much of the wage-price literature is that discussions of the manner in which a cost-price spiral is financed have often failed to consider this whole issue of the *modus operandi* of monetary policy. And, it is hoped that the following discussion will make a modest contribution towards remedying this deficiency.

In very general terms, the impact of a restrictive monetary policy on prices and employment is easily explained. The monetary authorities simply restrict the quantity of money, force financial institutions to ration credit, curtail aggregate demand, and thus exert downward pressure on prices or employment, or both. Unfortunately, however, this very general sort of portrayal leaves a variety of significant questions unanswered: (1) What differences in impact can we expect from alternative techniques of monetary control? (2) What is the likelihood that increases in velocity will arise to plague the anti-inflationary efforts of the monetary authorities? (3) What difference does it make whether credit is rationed by price or non-price means? (4) In what way is the impact of a restrictive monetary policy likely to be distributed among various types of borrowers? (5) To what extent is a restrictive monetary policy likely to reduce employment rather than prices? Let us now examine each of these questions individually.

General Techniques of Monetary Control and Their Avenues of Impact

In order to appraise the impact of a restrictive monetary policy it is first necessary to recognize explicitly that the monetary authorities possess a number of techniques that may be used to carry out such a policy.

The simplest tack for the monetary authorities to take in fighting an inflation generated by cost increases would be to "do nothing" in the sense of refusing to purchase government securities (often referred to simply as "Governments") and discouraging member banks from increasing their reserves by borrowing at the central bank. The reason that such a "do nothing" attitude can be considered one means of implementing a restrictive monetary policy is that increasing costs and prices will presumably increase the demand for transaction balances and so will eventually result in a shortage of loanable funds at the prevailing interest rates. However, the word "eventually" in the preceding sentence must be emphasized. It may take quite a long time and a considerable amount of inflation to "wear down" the existing liquidity of the economy sufficiently to permit such a tactic to take hold—and, this will be an especially acute problem if the banking system possessed a considerable amount of excess reserves prior to the adoption of the anti-inflationary policy.

Consequently, the Federal Reserve may elect to make use of the more overt or direct weapons at its disposal. More specifically, there are good grounds for presuming that, if the inflationary pressures are at all pronounced, it will be necessary for the monetary authorities to rely primarily on open market operations or variations in reserve requirements.

While an increase in the discount rate may, by increasing the costs of the funds commercial banks obtain by borrowing at the Federal Reserve, exert some downward pressure on the spending stream, too much should not be expected from this line of attack. It must be remembered that in the United States, loans from the Federal Reserve are very "special," in that borrowing from this source is considered a "privilege not to be abused." The strong tradition against "continuous borrowing" from the central bank renders the demand for Federal Reserve credit relatively interest-inelastic, and thus minimizes the direct effect of a change in the discount rate on the quantity of Federal Reserve credit outstanding.

Changes in the discount rate may, however, exert a stronger impact on the spending stream in a rather different way—namely, through the psychological or expectational effects associated with the announcement by the Federal Reserve of a change in this most visible adjunct of monetary policy. In considering this possibility we are, of course, really concerned with the broader question of the effectiveness of "announcement effects" in general.[2] Hence, the basic question here becomes: To what extent can the monetary authorities, by simply announcing to the public their determination to fight inflation, dampen the profit expectations of businessmen and lenders alike and thus reduce the àggregate volume of borrowing and spending?

While it is no doubt true that skillful use of announcement effects may reduce certain spending plans, it is again necessary to warn against expecting too much from this relatively painless technique. First of all, one economist has suggested that, with the passage of time, the announcement of a tight money policy has come to *confirm* rather than dampen the inflationary expectations of some members of the business community.[3] A less controversial and possibly more telling point is that announcement effects cannot be expected to have much of an impact unless ac-

[2] In the present context, the phrase "announcement effects" is being used to include not only those public utterances of the central bank which are explicitly designed to influence the behavior of bankers and others but also the "attitudinal" aspects of the whole complex of anti-inflationary actions (including changes in the discount rate and reserve requirements) taken by the central bank.

[3] See Paul A. Samuelson, "Recent American Monetary Controversy," *Three Banks Review*, xxix (March 1956), p. 11, n. 1.

companied (or quickly followed) by vigorous direct *action* on the part of the monetary authorities.

Consequently, the magic of announcement effects can at best supplement—rather than supplant—the less palatable techniques of adjusting reserve requirements and engaging in open market operations. The immediate implication of this conclusion is that our appraisal of the *modus operandi* of a restrictive monetary policy must center on these latter instruments—and particularly on open market operations.[4]

In general terms, open market operations can be envisioned as affecting spending plans in two closely-related ways. First and most obvious, Federal Reserve sales of Governments tend to reduce the total supply of loanable funds available to the private sector of the economy. However, it is also necessary to remember that, by selling a part of its holdings of government securities in the open market, the Federal Reserve not only absorbs some of the excess reserves of the banking system, but also has a direct impact on the over-all structure of interest rates. And, before considering the effects of open market operations on the aggregate supply of loanable funds, it is convenient to look first at the immediate consequences of this upward pressure on interest rates in general.

From the standpoint of our interest in the problem of financing an ongoing cost-price spiral, the key question now becomes: In what manner and to what extent will this

[4] The reason for singling out open market operations rather than changes in reserve requirements is that, although both of these techniques function by altering the "excess reserves" of the banking system, Federal Reserve officials prefer open market operations on the grounds that changes in reserve requirements are both relatively clumsy and relatively distasteful to member banks. See, for example, Allan Sproul, "Changing Concepts of Central Banking," *Money, Trade, and Economic Growth: Essays in Honor of John Henry Williams* (New York: Macmillan, 1951), p. 317.

increase in interest rates affect the dollar volume of aggregate spending? According to the pre-Keynesian advocates of monetary policy, higher interest rates would reduce spending by increasing people's desire to save (decreasing their willingness to consume) and by diminishing the volume of investment. If savings and investment were as responsive to changes in interest rates as this earlier school of thought seemed to think, a moderate amount of activity in the government securities market would enable the monetary authorities to achieve their objective without further ado. However, within the last three decades the proposition that both saving and investment are quite interest-*in*elastic has become increasingly popular.

To take the interest-rate-saving connection first, it has long been recognized that while an increase in rates may increase desired saving by raising the prospective rate of return (the substitution effect), higher interest rates may also discourage saving by enabling an individual to obtain the same total return by saving less (the income effect). And, on a priori grounds it is hard to see why the substitution effect should necessarily predominate. Furthermore, Keynes has emphasized the importance of other variables—and especially the level of income—as the really significant determinants of the volume of saving, and so it appears that even if interest rate changes did alter intended saving in the "proper direction, this effect might well be swamped by other considerations. For both of these reasons, economists today seem fairly well agreed that we would be unwise to count on much of an increase in savings as a consequence of higher interest rates.[5]

[5] In support of this assertion we have the following statement by Samuelson: "I might add that everybody seems to be agreed—perhaps, there is suspiciously unanimous agreement—that the interest rate has almost no effect upon savings." (U.S. Congress, Joint Committee on the Economic Report, Subcommittee on General Credit Control and Debt Management, *Monetary Policy and*

In the case of the effect of increases in interest rates on investment, there is less unanimity. Here there seems no reason to doubt the *direction* of impact—that is, no one suggests that higher interest rates encourage more borrowing for investment purposes. The real issue is the *magnitude* of the contradictionary effect, and on this question we know far too little. However, it does seem safe to suggest that, in the main, economists today regard investment as less interest-elastic than did their colleagues of the predepression period. This change in the general climate of thinking has been based on a combination of theoretical and empirical work (notably the Oxford studies conducted in the late 1930's and early 1940's).[6] However, it has recently been argued that the numerous empirical investigations of this question suffer from such serious defects as to render many of their findings highly suspect.[7]

Nonetheless, a position of complete agnosticism on this

----

the Management of the Public Debt: Hearings . . . , 82d Cong., 2d Sess., 1952, pp. 694-695.) [Cited hereafter as Joint Committee on the Economic Report, *Hearings on Monetary Policy, 1952.*] A possible exception to the general agreement with Samuelson's proposition is Roosa, who has pointed out that business saving has become an increasing proportion of total saving and has suggested that higher interest rates may increase this segment of total savings by discouraging outside financing and thereby encouraging firms to retain a higher proportion of their earnings for internal use (R. V. Roosa, "Interest Rates and the Central Bank," *Money, Trade, and Economic Growth: Essays in Honor of John Henry Williams*, pp. 281-282). However, even Roosa does not rest much of his case for monetary policy on this argument.

[6] The main body of the Oxford work on the interest rate is reprinted in Wilson and Andrews (eds.), *Oxford Studies in the Price Mechanism*, 1951, pp. 1-74.

[7] W. H. White, "Interest Inelasticity of Investment Demand —The Case From Business Attitude Surveys Re-examined," *American Economic Review*, XLVI (September 1956), pp. 565-587.

question does not seem justified. While the existent studies do have many limitations, no one has yet unearthed evidence to counter their general tenor. Consequently, a healthy skepticism concerning the probable impact of slight increases in the interest rate on the volume of investment seems altogether proper. The available evidence certainly does not encourage resting the case for a counter-cyclical monetary policy on a high interest-elasticity of demand for loanable funds.

Tacit (or explicit) acceptance of the prevalent skepticism concerning the impact of small changes in interest rates on the behavior of savers and borrowers has led, in the last few years, to an exceedingly important (and exceedingly controversial) reconstruction of the theoretical supports for a flexible monetary policy. Many of the proponents of a flexible monetary policy have come to emphasize the impact of open-market operations on the behavior of *lenders* and on the *availability* rather than the cost of credit. In brief, it is now argued that a restrictive monetary policy exerts its impact by inducing lenders to *ration* credit more stringently than before.[8]

Let us suppose that as a result of the Federal Reserve's actions in the government bond markets (a) the volume of aggregate bank reserves is fixed and can expand no more, and (b) the commercial banking system is "loaned

[8] Unfortunately, there is no single source that contains all the elements which make up this new defense of monetary policy. The most frequently cited source of this new doctrine is Roosa, *Money, Trade, and Economic Growth: Essays in Honor of John Henry Williams*, 1951, pp. 270-295. Other "primary" sources include: Howard S. Ellis, "The Rediscovery of Money," *ibid.*, pp. 255ff.; Lester V. Chandler, "The Impact of Low Interest Rates on the Economy," *Journal of Finance*, vi (June 1951), pp. 255ff.; and the replies by Mr. Martin (for the Federal Reserve System) and Mr. Snyder (for the Treasury) to the questions raised by the Joint Committee on the Economic Report (*Compendium on Monetary Policy*, 1952, especially pp. 80ff. and pp. 368ff.).

up" in the sense that aggregate excess reserves are negligible. Given these two conditions, it follows that the money supply (roughly defined as the sum of demand deposits and coin and currency outside the banking system) is approximately fixed. And, since the demand for funds is presumably still increasing as costs and prices go up, it would seem that the lending institutions will simply have to adopt either a price or non-price mode of rationing. Consequently, the cost-price spiral will grind to a halt for lack of monetary fuel, and the monetary authorities will have succeeded in their mission. However, to accept this reasoning as the denouement of our analysis would be to overlook several considerations, including one of the most important links in the long chain of events connecting rising costs and prices with increasing money expenditures—the behavior of the whole complex of factors summed up in the statistical variable called the velocity of money.

Increases in Velocity as an Offset to Credit Rationing

The possibility that a policy aimed at preventing aggregate money expenditure from rising by the simple expedient of controlling bank reserves and the money supply will be frustrated (at least for a time) by an increase in the velocity of the existing money supply must be faced squarely. And, it seems quite likely that the velocity of money will in fact play such a "frustrating" role. The central point here is simply that the commercial banking system, other lending institutions, non-financial corporations, and individuals possess the capacity to offset a considerable amount of pressure by the central bank—and that the incentives to use this capacity are to a large extent inherent in the situation under discussion.

Let us first consider the probable reaction of commercial banks to a situation in which both existing excess reserves and the possibility of obtaining more excess reserves are negligible. There is absolutely no doubt but that banks *could* adjust to such a situation by simply raising their credit standards and refusing requests for new loans. In fact, if the central bank has moved swiftly in putting pressure on reserve positions, commercial banks may initially be forced to ration credit more stringently in order to obey statutory reserve requirements. However, it is equally apparent that such a policy will be quite distasteful to commercial bankers and that they will seek to find some other mode of adjustment within the shortest possible time.

The incentive on the part of the commercial banks to avoid extended credit rationing is easily understood. First of all, commercial bankers are businessmen seeking to make money and so are not likely to take kindly to any situation in which they are forced to turn down profitable transactions—and it must be remembered that loans are, in general, a very remunerative part of a bank's business. Perhaps even more important is the potential effect of credit rationing on the longer-run profit position of a bank. The inherent nature of the commercial banking business renders the maintenance of good customer relations absolutely essential to the long-run prosperity of the bank.[9]

[9] Here we have reference to such characteristics of commercial banking as: the complexity of the loan transaction; the necessity of the bank's undertaking a fairly careful appraisal of the potential borrower's over-all financial circumstances before granting him a "line of credit"; the fact that the initial cost of investigating a customer's "credit worthiness" need not be incurred in equal amount each time he renews a loan or increases his volume of borrowing; the relatively small number of banks in most locales; and, finally, for all the above reasons, the tendency of customers to continue to seek accommodation at the same bank over a period of many years.

Granting the inclination of the commercial banks to meet the "legitimate" needs of their customers, the question of the *capacity* of the banking system to translate this inclination into actuality remains. Since the ability of the central bank to prevent reserves from increasing precludes the possibility of a simultaneous increase in the assets and liabilities of the commercial banks, the dollar volume of loans can be increased only if there is an equal reduction in some other asset. In short, a commercial bank without excess reserves can continue to expand its loans only if it is able and willing to shift the composition of its assets by selling some other asset that it already holds. The obvious candidate for liquidation is the large volume of government securities held by most banks as "secondary reserves."

The possibility that banks might try to expand their loans in the face of fixed reserves by selling Governments has not been overlooked by the credit rationing school. However, they have minimized this possibility by pointing out that a decline in the price of Governments (presumably engendered by the initial open-market operations of the central bank) will discourage the sale of Governments by the simple expedient of imposing the penalty of a capital loss on all who try to unload. Thus holdings of government securities will tend to be "frozen-in."[10] And, it should be noted that the tendency of this capital loss possibility to prevent banks from unloading Governments is at least partly attributable to two institutional characteristics of the commercial banking system—namely, the practice of carrying securities on the balance sheets of banks at "cost" until they are liquidated, and the rela-

[10] See Roosa, *Money, Trade, and Economic Growth; Essays in Honor of John Henry Williams*, 1951, pp. 289ff., and especially n. 29 on p. 290. This consequence of central bank actions has also been referred to in the literature as the "locked-in" and "pinned-in" effect.

tively small capital accounts of many banks. As a consequence of these two characteristics, the capital position of a bank can be rather severely affected by the liquidation of Governments whose price has fallen below purchase cost.

While a fall in the price of Governments may well inhibit some owners of such securities from selling, there are several reasons for thinking that this deterrent effect may not be as strong as has sometimes been implied. First of all, the return on other types of alternative investments may increase concomitantly to such an extent that investors can profitably absorb the immediate capital loss associated with the shifting out of Governments. That is, many investors (including at least some commercial banks) are presumably interested in the *spread* of yields between various types of investment alternatives rather than with the *level* of yields on any particular type of asset.[11] And, at a time when the demand for credit is increasing, it does not seem implausible that those seeking credit accommodation at the commercial banks will be willing to more than compensate the bank for any capital loss it has to incur in the process of obtaining additional loanable funds. Secondly, the "locked-in" effect abstracts from the importance of expectational considerations. As Whittlesey points out: "It is highly unlikely that a decline from 100 to 98 will be effective in preventing sales if it is expected that the price will shortly drop to 96."[12]

In addition to the above theoretical considerations, there is also some recent empirical evidence which suggests that the "locked-in" effect may not be especially potent. Warren Smith has collected statistics which show that during the "tight" money period between December 1954

[11] See Whittlesey's more elaborate discussion of this point (C. R. Whittlesey, "Monetary Policy and Economic Change," *Review of Economics and Statistics*, xxxix [February 1957], pp. 35-36).

[12] *Ibid.*

and September 1957 (when the Federal Reserve was selling almost two billion dollars of its holdings in order to limit bank reserves), the commercial banking system sold about twelve billion dollars of government securities.[13]

Granting that commercial banks are likely to attempt to sell Governments in order to obtain more loanable funds, the next question is: who purchases these securities and what is the final result of the shift in ownership which takes place? First of all, it is apparent that the banking system cannot sell Governments to the central bank, for if the central bank were to purchase the offerings of the commercial banks, the volume of reserves would increase and the central bank would have negated its own efforts at credit restraint. Consequently, the commercial banks must look for other customers. The two most important groups of potential buyers are the Treasury and the non-bank portion of the private sector.

If the Federal Government happens to be running a budget surplus (not an unlikely possibility in the early stages of an inflationary movement), it is quite possible that the Treasury will retire some of the Governments held by private banks. And, if this happens, the restrictive im-

[13] Warren L. Smith, "Monetary Policy and the Structure of Markets," Joint Economic Committee, *Compendium on Prices and Economic Stability*, 1958, p. 497. The $12 billion figure represents the par value of the securities sold, the book value was about $14 billion. An earlier bit of history supporting the proposition that banks will indeed sell Governments when pressed for reserves has been cited by former Secretary of the Treasury Snyder (Joint Committee on the Economic Report, *Compendium on Monetary Policy*, 1952, pp. 107-108). In 1937 the Federal Reserve decided to raise reserve requirements significantly (in fact, requirements were almost doubled). In response to this pressure, the commercial banks reduced their holdings of government securities by $856 million during the first six months of 1937. At the same time that the price of Governments was falling, the banking system expanded its loans by $925 million.

pact of the budgetary surplus is lessened in that a part of the restrictive impact of central bank open-market operations is simultaneously moderated. As evidence that this possibility is not strictly hypothetical, it may be noted that between December 1954 and September 1957 the Treasury purchased over ten billion dollars worth of government securities.[14]

Non-bank investors may also acquire a part of the increased volume of Governments put on the open market by the banks—in fact, the increasing yields on various maturities makes such a possibility quite likely. The initial effect of this type of transaction is, of course, to destroy deposits in the banking system; however, these deposits will presumably be quickly restored as the banks (thanks to the temporary relaxation of the pressure on their reserve positions acquired by selling the Governments) are now able to expand their loans and meet the increasing demands of their borrowers. Thus the total volume of deposits is unchanged by this reshuffling of the asset side of the banks' balance sheets. However, it is quite likely that the average rate of turnover for deposits has increased significantly. This is because the balances created for the recipients of the new loans will be relatively "active" (why would the new borrowers insistently demand credit at higher interest rates unless they planned to use the funds rather quickly?), whereas the balances destroyed by the reduction in the banks' holdings of Governments were presumably relatively "idle" (while it is possible that the funds used to purchase the Governments were diverted from current expenditures, it seems more plausible to assume that the balances eliminated were largely inactive).[15] Conse-

---

[14] This statistic has been taken from Federal Reserve data by Warren Smith (Joint Economic Committee, *Compendium on Prices and Economic Stability*, 1958, p. 497).

[15] As Brown points out (*Great Inflation*, 1955, p. 81), the distinction between active and idle balances is arbitrary in that it

quently, the given money supply now supports a large volume of spending and the restrictive policy of the central bank has been at least partially frustrated by an increase in velocity.

While sales of Governments to the non-banking sector of the economy constitute the most important way in which the banking system can lessen the need for credit rationing, this is not the only avenue of escape available. The banking system *as a whole* can also economize available reserves in at least two other ways. First of all, banks at which the demand for credit is not so intense may purchase additional government securities offered for sale by other banks which are harder pressed for funds. While such inter-bank sales do not, of course, alter the composition of the consolidated balance sheet for commercial banks as a whole, they do serve to concentrate loan-granting capacity in the hands of those banks whose customers are particularly anxious to put it to active use. Secondly, the growth in the Federal Funds market (that is, dealings in reserves at the Federal Reserve by which various banks with excess reserves "loan" or "sell" their excess reserves to other banks) enables a given volume of aggregate reserves to support a larger volume of deposits. That is, a well-functioning Federal Funds market precludes the possibility that some banks will be forced to ration credit while others still have excess reserves, and in this way insures that a given amount of aggregate reserves will be utilized to the maximum possible extent.

The main conclusion to be drawn from the preceding discussion is that it is exceedingly dangerous to assume

---

depends on the "short period under consideration"—that is, active balances are spent during this period and idle balances are not spent. Of course, in the sufficiently long run, all balances are presumably respent. Hence, Brown suggests that the distinction can best be thought of as a distinction between balances with rapid and slow rates of turnover.

the existence of a rigid link between the volume of aggregate member bank reserves and the dollar volume of loans made by the banking system. Our commercial bankers are usually able to satisfy at least some part of an increased demand for loans even if they are unable to secure additional reserves. Consequently, we have a rather sound basis for suspecting that the total volume of spending may increase even if the central bank succeeds in holding the money supply constant.[16] And this is by no means the end of the story. There are also a number of reasons for thinking that the private, non-bank sector of the economy will cooperate with the commercial banks in unearthing ways of increasing velocity at a time when credit is tight and will in this way make an additional contribution to the central bank's miseries.

First of all, what we might term the "initial" liquidity position of the economy is an important determinant of the ability of relatively mild measures of monetary control to prevent increases in the general price level. If at the outset of a cycle of cost and price increases the public possesses unusually large cash balances (as was the case in the aftermath of World War II), then it may be possible to finance a considerably higher level of aggregate spending without much of an increase in the money supply and without the inducement of large increases in interest rates. In such circumstances a decision by the monetary authorities to hold the money supply constant may well

[16] At this juncture it must be reemphasized that by no means all of the funds secured by the banks in order to make new loans can be classed as net additions to the total supply of credit outstanding. After all, some of these funds may have been diverted from other comparable uses—that is, some of the funds may have been obtained from individuals or institutions that would not have let them sit idle in any case but would have made them available to non-bank borrowers or other financial institutions. However, it does seem reasonable to suppose that at least a part of the balances acquired by the banks were relatively "idle."

not exert much of a depressing influence on expenditures.

Even if there is no general legacy of liquidity when costs and prices begin to rise, it is quite possible that the combination of inflationary expectations and rising interest rates (as a consequence of the efforts of the monetary authorities to falsify the inflationary expectations) will be sufficient to induce the public to hold much smaller average cash balances. While we would not expect a widespread "flight from cash" unless a severe inflation were well underway, a modest increase in interest rates will result in an immediate increase in the opportunity cost of holding idle cash balances, and so may well inspire a shift of funds from checking deposits to a relatively more lucrative form of investment such as a savings account. And, it is important to note that shifts from demand to time deposits increase the expansive potential of the banking system significantly in that time deposits enjoy lower reserve requirements.

Another way in which the existing money supply can be utilized more fully by the private sector is via sales of government securities from one segment of the non-bank sector of the economy to another. An important development in post-World War II America has been the phenomenal increase in the volume of government obligations held by both financial and non-financial corporations, and the growth of an active market in which to exchange these securities. An important consequence of this development is that many non-financial concerns may meet an increased need for cash balances by selling a part of their portfolio of Governments in the open market. Similarly, financial corporations (such as insurance companies) may unload Governments in an effort to increase their ability to make loans. And, households and unincorporated enterprises faced with a particularly dire need for cash may also sell Governments to other non-bank investors that happen to be more amply supplied with cash reserves. In all these cases it seems reasonable to assume that relatively "idle" balances are translated into relatively "active" balances— that is, that the average velocity of circulation is increased.

A final, broader reason why a restrictive monetary policy may be hampered by velocity increases is that the private sector of the economy seems to possess great ingenuity for discovering new institutional arrangements by which the existing money supply can be used more efficiently. This point can be illustrated by noting three financial developments that have occurred during the 1954-1957 period. (1) Large non-financial corporations have taken on many of the functions of banks in order to come to the aid of smaller concerns. Big business has not only taken over much of the load of inventory financing by such techniques as carrying on their own books stocks actually located in the storerooms of dealers, but has also extended short-term, intermediate, and even long-term credit for other needs as well.[17] (2) The use of monthly payment plans to finance the acquisition of equipment as well as additions to working capital has mushroomed. The C.I.T. Financial Corporation showed a 28 per cent growth in "other" installment receivables—largely industrial equipment loans—during the 1957 calendar year.[18] (3) Sales and repurchase agreements with non-financial corporations have become a major source of funds for government bond houses. In this way banks have been freed of much of their responsibility for financing the inventories of these institutions and so have been able to make more business loans on the basis of a given amount of reserves.[19]

While the possibility that new institutional arrangements of this sort *may* continue to develop certainly con-

[17] *New York Times*, April 27, 1958, Sec. 3, p. 1.
[18] *New York Times*, March 9, 1958, Sec. 3, p. 1.
[19] H. Minsky, "Central Banking and Money Market Changes," *Quarterly Journal of Economics*, LXXI (May 1957), pp. 176-181.

stitutes additional grounds for a healthy skepticism concerning the rigidity of the link between the money supply and the size of the spending stream, a more fundamental basis for skepticism lies in the intriguing possibility that a tight money policy, in and of itself, *encourages* such evolutionary developments. After all, higher interest rates and an increasing demand for credit provide the stimulus for the discovery of new ways to economize a given money supply. Thus higher interest rates not only lead to an increase in velocity directly within a stable institutional framework, but also operate indirectly by stimulating institutional innovations, which in turn permit a still more intensive utilization of cash balances.[20]

Our inquiry into the techniques by which the banking system and the rest of the private sector of the economy escape the need to ration credit is now complete. The main implications of this inquiry can be summarized briefly as follows: There is no magic mechanism that enables the monetary authorities to prevent aggregate spending from rising by the simple expedient of controlling bank reserves and the money supply; the commercial banking system will usually be able to increase its loans via an alteration in the composition of its assets even though it cannot increase its reserves; the non-banking sector will also be able to find ways of utilizing the given money supply to support a higher volume of spending; and the final consequence of this financial maneuverability is that the restrictive pressure of a fixed money supply will be offset to a considerable extent by a variety of actions that will show up statistically as an increase in the income-velocity of circulation.

However, this emphasis on the expansiveness of the velocity factor must not be overdone. While there are good reasons for expecting the application of a restrictive mon-

[20] This hypothesis has been developed at some length by Minsky (*ibid.*, pp. 171-187).

etary policy to bring about *some* increase in velocity, there is no reason to suppose that all the financial needs of a high-employment economy can be met in this manner. Even allowing for the more intensive utilization of the existing money supply, businesses may still demand more credit from the banking system than can be supplied. Thus the banks may still be forced to ration their limited credit capacities in some way, and so we must now return to the important issue of the *form* this rationing is likely to take.

The Significance of Price vs. Non-Price Modes of Credit Rationing

As noted above, Roosa, Ellis, and others have suggested that the nature of the banking business encourages non-price credit rationing.[21] That is, instead of letting the interest rate be bid up until the excess demand for funds has disappeared, bankers may prefer to permit the continuance of an excess demand at the going interest rate and simply turn down a higher proportion of credit applications. This conception of lender behavior has, in turn, been attacked by others. Samuelson, for instance, has questioned the length of time over which such an increase in credit stringency would last and has argued that, "after the shortest run," a banker will respond to a tightening credit situation by doing "what any normal, prudent, commercially-minded man would do: namely, if a thing is in short supply, he will gradually raise the interest charges on it, and let the higher price help him do the rationing."[22]

[21] See the references cited in n. 8.

[22] P. A. Samuelson, Joint Committee on the Economic Report, *Hearings on Monetary Policy*, 1952, p. 696. A bit later in the *Hearings* (pp. 741-742), Samuelson reiterates this point and emphasizes that the credit rationing argument relies on increased imperfection in the loanable funds market. This argument has since been picked up by Tobin (James Tobin, "Monetary Policy and the Management of the Public Debt," *Review of Economics*

This question of the reaction of lenders to an excess demand for credit is, of course, at bottom an empirical issue that cannot be resolved by additional speculation on our part. However, without pretending to have a complete answer to this question, we can (in fact, are obligated!) to move on to the much more neglected—but by no means less important—issue of the *significance* of various modes of credit rationing. What difference does it make whether bankers employ price or non-price credit rationing?

At the outset, it is necessary to observe that the prevalence of non-price credit rationing has implications for a number of important questions including the "perfection" of the loanable funds market and the "equity" of credit restraint. However, for the moment, it is useful to concentrate our attention on the implications of the mode of credit rationing for the over-all impact of a restrictive monetary policy on the dollar magnitude of loans made by the commercial bank. And, viewed from this perspective, the important point to note is that the popularity or lack of popularity of non-price rationing *need not* have *any* strong and direct impact at all.[23]

---

and Statistics, xxxv [May 1953], p. 123) and Kareken (John H. Kareken, "Lenders' Preferences, Credit Rationing, and Effectiveness of Monetary Policy," *Review of Economics and Statistics*, xxxix [August 1957], pp. 292-302). Unfortunately, it is far from clear what precise meaning is to be attached to this notion of the "degree of imperfection" in the loanable funds market. The complexity of the loan transaction certainly suggests that it may be misleading to identify the degree of imperfection with the sluggishness of interest rates in response to variations in the excess demand for credit.

[23] Samuelson, without addressing himself directly to this question, implies that he holds a view contrary to the one expressed in the following paragraphs. See Samuelson's own summary of his conception of the mechanism of monetary policy (Joint Committee on the Economic Report, *Hearings on Monetary Policy*, 1952, pp. 741-742). In brief, he suggests that: (a) ". . . in the

To be a bit more precise, the significance of the mode of credit rationing for the issue of how responsive the volume of bank loans is to a restrictive monetary policy depends to a considerable extent on the nature of supply conditions in the loanable funds market. If the supply schedule of loanable funds were quite interest-elastic at whatever interest rate resulted from the interplay of central bank policy and commercial bank behavior, the impact on the volume of bank loans would then depend on (a) the interest-elasticity of the demand for loanable funds; and (b) the extent to which bankers actually choose to let interest rates be bid up rather than to ration credit by other means.[24]

In fact, however, it would seem that the supply schedule of loanable funds does not conform to the above picture. The obvious point here is that with their authority to alter reserve requirements and to influence the volume of bank loans the monetary authorities can exert a direct impact on the supply of loanable funds and can impose a fairly rigid ceiling on the ability of the commercial banking system to make loans. Consequently, the loanable funds supply schedule (assuming a situation in which the banking system has negligible excess reserves) probably comes closer to being perfectly *inelastic* with respect to

intermediate- and longer-run, the central bank can depress the flow of current spending primarily by the single device of raising the interest cost to spenders enough to discourage their spending by the desired amount . . ."; (b) ". . . its [the central bank's] open-market operations have no effect upon the commercial banks different in kind from its effects on insurance companies and all other institutions and persons generally"; and (c) it is the interest-elasticity of consumption and investment spending that determines the effectiveness of monetary policy.

[24] It is in this context (and only in this context) that Samuelson's conception of how monetary policy works (*ibid.*) seems helpful.

changes in interest rates than perfectly elastic. The existence of statutory reserve requirements means that banks are *not* just like insurance companies, other institutions, and individuals. No matter how high interest rates may rise, the central bank can impose a legal limit on the ability of the commercial banking system to satisfy the private sector's demand for credit.

Returning now to the original question of the significance of price versus non-price credit rationing, let us suppose that banks act in accord with Samuelson's conception of lender behavior and let interest rates rise sufficiently to restrict the over-all volume of deposits to the level permitted by reserve requirements and the reserve positions of individual banks. What does the magnitude of this increase in the interest rate signify? If the supply of loanable funds is relatively inelastic, it signifies mainly the "stubbornness" with which borrowers resist the curtailment of their requests for funds—or, in more precise terms, the rise in interest rates *measures* the elasticity of demand for loanable funds. The important point to note is that in this case the extent to which the demand for loanable funds is inelastic does not determine the reduction in the volume of loans brought about by the restrictive actions of the monetary authorities, but instead determines the extent to which interest rates must rise in order to allocate the limited loan capacity of the banking system by means of the interest rate mechanism.

Consequently, it would appear that the significance of the alternative modes of credit rationing (price rationing *vs.* non-price rationing) is confined to determining the magnitude of the increase in interest rates which will *accompany* the reduction in the volume of credit brought about by the restrictive actions of the monetary authorities. In short, the fundamental question that emerges from the ashes of this lender-behavior-credit-rationing controversy is whether or not it makes any difference how high interest rates must rise in order to achieve a certain amount of restraint on the aggregate spending stream. If one is prepared to argue that the purpose of monetary policy is to achieve price stability and that changes in interest rates are an incidental and rather unimportant by-product of efforts to achieve this end,[25] it follows that this whole issue of whether lenders ration credit by price or non-price means is basically rather academic and insignificant.

Actually, however, there are a number of good reasons why we dare not be indifferent to the magnitude of the increase in interest rates brought about by a given action of the Federal Reserve. First, and perhaps most important, the impact of a given Federal Reserve action (say an increase in reserve requirements of a few percentage points) on the aggregate spending stream is not independent of the associated change in interest rates. This is because: (a) As we have seen above, the volume of loans banks can make is not rigidly determined by their reserve positions but can be adjusted to some extent by shifts in the composition of assets. And, the larger the increase in the return obtainable on loanable funds, the greater the incentive of lenders to accommodate borrowers. In more precise terms, the supply schedule of loanable funds presumably possesses some interest-elasticity, and so the magnitude of the reduction in the volume of loans engendered by central bank action will vary directly with the interest-elasticity of the demand for loanable funds.[26] (b) Higher

[25] This position is represented by Friedman's comments (Joint Committee on the Economic Report, *Hearings on Monetary Policy*, 1952, especially pp. 732, 736).

[26] It is obvious that only if the supply schedule of loanable funds is perfectly inelastic will the quantitative impact of a shift in this supply schedule be unaffected by the shape of the demand function. Kareken has used a number of supply-demand diagrams to illustrate the importance of demand-elasticities under various conditions (*Review of Economics and Statistics*, August 1957, pp. 292-302).

interest rates not only encourage banks to scrape up more funds with which to make loans, but they also encourage the non-banking sector to economize on cash balances and to utilize a given stock of money more fully.

A second way in which rising interest rates complicate the job of the monetary authorities is via the attitude of the public toward this accoutrement of a restrictive monetary policy. There seems to be a general aversion on the part of the public towards rising rates of interest, partly because of the understandable distaste which we all feel for any price increase, and partly because increasing yields (and thus declining bond prices) impose a capital loss on those who may wish to dispose of existing holdings of government securities. Consequently, a restrictive monetary policy that can be carried off without much of an accompanying rise in rates probably stands a better chance of gaining and holding public favor.

The extent to which the monetary authorities can tighten credit without bringing about a severe decline in the prices of government securities is also likely to influence directly the support for a restrictive monetary policy which can be mustered within the government itself. In addition to the public clamor against rising interest rates, there is the effect of rising yields on the cost of servicing the public debt to be considered. And, even if the Treasury and Congress do not object too strenuously to paying higher yields on per se grounds, there is the fear that significant increases in interest rates might set off a cumulative unloading of Governments and eventually impair the government's credit.

These considerations probably serve to limit the range of permissible rate fluctuations. Consequently, monetary actions that cannot achieve their ends without causing interest rates to move outside this range will presumably not be undertaken. It is in this very important sense that the effectiveness of monetary policy can be said to depend on the existence of either credit rationing or a demand schedule for credit that is not overly interest-inelastic. The response of interest rates to a "given" monetary action may well help determine whether further monetary manipulation is attempted.

The behavior of interest rates is also significant in that rising rates put additional upward pressure on costs and may well result in an increase in certain types of prices, such as public utility rates. Thus, a part of the downward pressure on prices exerted by the restriction on the supply of funds that brought about the increase in interest rates may be offset by the cost effects of the higher interest charges.

For all the above reasons it seems safe to conclude that the impact of monetary policy on interest rates is of considerable importance. In general, it seems reasonable to assert that the greater the extent to which interest rates must rise in order to achieve a given amount of monetary restraint, the more difficult it will be for the central bank to exert downward pressure on the spending stream. And, this is not all. It is also important to note that the behavior of interest rates is significant in yet another, more obvious respect—whether or not interest rates rise as a consequence of pressure on bank reserves determines the criteria on which the allocation of the limited supply of bank credit is based. That is, our discussion of the credit-rationing debate leads naturally into the broader question of the incidence of a restrictive monetary policy.

Impact of a Restrictive Monetary Policy on Various Classes of Borrowers

While a detailed inquiry into the incidence problem would certainly be inappropriate here, it is necessary to comment briefly on the question of *which* spending plans are especially prone to suffer at the hands of a restrictive monetary policy. And, it may as well be admitted at the outset that this is one of the many subjects about which economists know far too little; nonetheless, there are some generalizations that can be made.

Looking at this question from the vantage point of the dilemma model, the first and most important point to be noted is that the initial brunt of the restrictive monetary policy is *not* likely to fall on those companies or individuals that face an immediate need for higher transaction balances as a consequence of increases in prices and costs. It seems much more likely that the direct or primary effects of monetary restriction will fall mainly on certain types of investment spending.

Within the investment category, there seems to be general agreement that housing or residential construction is especially responsive to changes in the monetary environment.[27] Producer durables may also be affected to some extent. However, both the increasing predominance of internal financing and the relatively small fraction of total costs represented by interest charges suggest that expenditures on new plant and equipment are somewhat more immune from a tight money policy than is housing. Certain long-range projects undertaken by utilities may constitute an exception to this generalization. Changes in business inventories constitute another segment of investment which is heavily dependent on borrowed funds and thus might be expected to be quite responsive to rising

[27] An important corollary to this general observation is that there seem to be good grounds for suspecting that all segments of the housing market are not affected uniformly. Specifically, the existence of rigid ceilings on the interest rates charges on government-supported loans tends to bring about a disproportionate reduction in that part of residential construction financed by FHA and VA mortgages. This point has been strongly emphasized by Whittlesey (*Review of Economics and Statistics*, February 1957, pp. 31-39) and Smith (Joint Economic Committee, *Compendium on Prices and Economic Stability*, 1958, pp. 499ff.).

interest rates. However, the fear that lower inventories will result in the loss of customer allegiance—coupled with the fact that at a time of rising prices inventory accumulation is profitable in spite of rising interest rates—suggests that here again the magnitude of impact may not be very great.[28]

Turning now from private investment to government spending, there seems to be general agreement that whereas the expenditures of the Federal Government are fairly immune to variations in interest charges, state and local governments may not be so well insulated. Spending by states and municipalities may be rather seriously affected by rising interest rates as a consequence of the very perceptible effect of higher interest charges on local tax rates.

The final component of the spending stream whose magnitude may be directly reduced by rising interest rates is the group of purchases (mainly durables) financed by consumer installment credit. However, a recent study by the Federal Reserve[29] suggests several reasons for doubting that a general tightening of credit will have a terribly significant impact on this type of purchase: (1) the issuance of consumer credit is a very profitable business, and lenders are therefore extremely reluctant to curtail this aspect of their operations; (2) the demand for consumer credit is notoriously interest-inelastic, and for this reason finance companies have very little difficulty in passing higher interest charges on to their customers; and (3) passing on higher interest charges is facilitated by the

[28] This is the conclusion of Friedrich Lutz ("The Interest Rate and Investment in a Dynamic Economy," *American Economic Review*, xxxv [December 1945], pp. 812-814).

[29] Board of Governors of the Federal Reserve System, *Consumer Instalment Credit* (6 vols.; Washington: U.S. Government Printing Office, 1957). The implications of this study for the problem at hand have been drawn from Warren L. Smith's excellent review article ("Consumer Installment Credit," *American Economic Review*, xlvii [December 1957], pp. 966-984).

fact that the consumer credit contract contains many facets, and higher interest rates can therefore be offset somewhat by relaxing downpayments and lengthening maturities.

Thus far, we have tacitly assumed that the restricted supply of credit is rationed solely by means of higher interest rates. If, however, a part of the rationing is accomplished by non-price means (by the adoption of more stringent credit standards, for example), interest-elasticities of demand cease to be the sole allocator of credit. While it is very difficult to generalize about the characteristics of those who will be deprived of credit on non-price grounds, there are several reasons for thinking that small business may be hit somewhat harder than the large firms.[30] This is because (a) there is a considerable body of statistics which suggest that small firms not only have less funds available from internal sources but also are generally less "liquid" than the larger companies,[31] and so are more dependent on others for additional financing; (b) furthermore, smaller firms have much less opportunity to secure funds by selling their debt obligations in the open market; and (c) the generally lower profitability of the smaller firms coupled with the understandable inclination of banks to avoid disappointing their larger customers suggests that the smaller concerns are most likely to be refused accommodation.[32]

However, it must also be noted that "there are small firms and there are small firms"—the heterogeneity of

[30] The thesis that a tight money policy discriminates against small business has been developed by a number of people. Perhaps the most forceful exposition is by Galbraith in *Review of Economics and Statistics*, May 1957, pp. 130-133.

[31] See Aschheim, thesis, 1954, pp. 69-70, and references cited therein.

[32] See Aschheim, *ibid.*, pp. 74-75; and Smith, Joint Economic Committee, *Compendium on Prices and Economic Stability*, 1958, pp. 505-507.

this rather amorphous category makes it hazardous to draw sweeping generalizations. Furthermore, it is exceedingly difficult to assess the quantitative significance of whatever tendency towards discrimination against smaller firms does in fact exist.[33]

Let us now summarize our brief inquiry into the incidence of credit restraint. On the basis of the fragments of evidence which are available it would seem that the direct effects of a restrictive monetary policy will be concentrated on investment spending and, more particularly, on residential construction (especially the part financed by government-supported mortgages), the expansion plans of public utilities, and the spending programs of state and local governments. In addition, small business seems somewhat more likely to be deprived of funds than its larger counterpart. A widely-discussed implication of these conclusions is that the direct effects of monetary control may well not be so "neutral" and "impersonal" as has often been argued.

Before going any further it is very important to remember that the above discussion concerns only the *direct* or *apparent* effects of a tight money policy. The point to be noted here is that there may well be a considerable discrepancy between the "apparent" and the "actual" victims of monetary manipulation. That is, it is very danger-

---

[33] A recent Federal Reserve Board inquiry into this question has certainly not yielded very conclusive answers. See Board of Governors of the Federal Reserve System, *Financing Small Business; Report to the Committees on Banking and Currency and the Select Committees on Small Business*, 85th Cong., 2d Sess., 1958. Part of the difficulty is that over the 1955-57 period the increased demand for accommodation by large firms greatly exceeded the requests of small firms, and so it is very hard to tell how much of the relative increase in the volume of loans made to large firms is attributable to this differential credit-rationing effect and how much to a differential increase in the rate of demand.

ous to assume that the refusal of a bank to grant credit for a specific venture means that that particular venture will not be carried out. The firm may be so determined to go ahead with the particular project in question that it will divert funds away from some other intended use. In short, that segment of spending most immediately affected by a restrictive monetary policy will depend on the over-all financial resources and priorities of individual decision-making units and need not coincide with the group of proposals rejected at the banker's desk.

And, of course, the allocation of the over-all impact of a restrictive monetary policy will also depend on numerous secondary and tertiary repercussions. For instance, if the demand for loanable funds is rather interest-inelastic, higher interest charges will at least temporarily redistribute money income in favor of a segment of the economy whose spending propensities may be quite different from the segment at whose expense the redistribution occurred. Furthermore, the intended recipients of whatever spending is immediately curtailed suffer a loss of income, which will in turn presumably engender a reduction in their own spending and thus in the incomes of other folk, and so on down the line. The moral of this story is simply that what might be termed the "total incidence" of a tight money policy is exceedingly difficult to unravel and can only be estimated in a very rough way on the basis of data describing the types of projects initially curtailed as a consequence of the general shortage of funds.

Price vs. Employment Effects of a Restrictive Monetary Policy

We have now considered in some detail the mechanism by which a restrictive monetary policy influences the behavior of various segments of the economy and thereby exerts an eventual impact on the aggregate spending stream. However, the ultimate objective of a restrictive monetary policy is surely not control of aggregate spending for its own sake, but rather as a means of restraining upward movements of the general price level. Consequently, we are now obligated to say a few words about the last link in the chain of events, which depicts the *modus operandi* of a restrictive monetary policy—namely, how and to what extent a reduction in aggregate dollar spending can be expected to prevent price increases.

The reason why it is so very important to recognize the existence of this link is, of course, that there is no law requiring the general price index to move in perfect harmony with aggregate spending. Let us suppose that the monetary authorities have now succeeded in imposing a ceiling on the size of the aggregate spending stream. The all-important question is whether this limitation will bring about price level stability without reductions in the rate of output or whether rising prices and declining real output can be expected to coexist—at least for a time. Anything resembling a full answer to this question would necessitate a much more complete recapitulation of our earlier analyses of wage and price determination than is appropriate here. For our present purposes, it is sufficient to note that there are several reasons for thinking that price stability can only be purchased at the cost of some reduction in the volume of sales.

First of all, our earlier analysis of the factors influencing wage decisions warns us not to expect a modest reduction in aggregate demand concentrated in certain sectors to prevent unit labor costs and unit total costs from rising. The *threat* of reduced output and employment is not likely to be sufficient to offset the upward pressure on the level of costs. And, as we have seen, firms have a very strong inclination to translate higher costs into higher prices.

Furthermore, even if costs did hold steady in certain sectors, our discussion of price behavior suggests that

369

many firms will be reluctant to cut prices in response to a modest decrease in incoming orders. And, it must be remembered that the initial impact of a restrictive monetary policy will probably fall on those industries which produce construction materials and capital goods of various sorts— not an area of the economy in which prices are generally thought to be particularly responsive to fluctuations in demand.

Consequently, since costs and prices do not seem particularly flexible in the downward direction, the initial impact of a restrictive monetary policy is likely to be concentrated on output and employment within those sectors which are most directly affected by the actions of the monetary authorities. It is layoffs and reduced incomes in these areas which then transmit the restrictive effects of a tight money policy throughout the economy by exerting downward pressure on the demand for other products. The next question is how these other sectors will react to a leveling off in the monetary demand for their products. Again, it seems likely that costs and prices are insufficiently flexible in response to changes in demand conditions to preclude the possibility of further reductions in output and employment.

This is not to suggest that the ceiling on aggregate spending imposed by the tight money policy will fail to bring about *any* diminution of the upward pressure on the overall price level. Some measure of price relief may occur right along, and there is little doubt but that, if the restrictive money policy is pursued with unswerving devotion, unemployment will eventually succeed in giving us stable prices. However, to accomplish this objective it may first be necessary to bring about a considerable amount of unemployment.

And, since the appearance of unemployment cannot be treated as a passive and unimportant by-product of the fight against inflation, but must be recognized as a serious problem in its own right, it is by no means clear that the monetary authorities either will or should carry a restrictive monetary policy far enough to achieve price stability.

That is, the monetary authorities and the Federal Government in general may well decide that unemployment has become a more important problem than inflation and thus abandon the restrictive monetary policy in favor of measures designed to put people to work. In short, the adoption and effective implementation of a restrictive monetary policy is quite likely to lead almost inexorably to the need for counter measures—our appraisal of the *modus operandi* of a restrictive monetary policy thus requires, as a final step, that we examine the probable monetary-fiscal reactions to the appearance of unemployment. However, before considering the implications of anti-unemployment policies, it may be helpful to summarize the main conclusions that emerge from the preceding analysis of anti-inflation policies.

Conclusions

The main general conclusion is simply that the monetary authorities possess no magic wand that can be used for quick and painless manipulation of the price level. Our analysis suggests that a restrictive monetary policy is beset with many difficulties, the most important of which are enumerated below.

1. It is highly doubtful that the monetary authorities can accomplish very much by raising the discount rate and by issuing express and implied pronouncements condemning the evils of inflation. Consequently, the central bank must rely heavily on its power to engage in open-market operations and to alter reserve requirements.

2. The apparent insensitivity of saving to mild changes in interest rates—coupled with the relative insensitivity of investment—suggests that desired changes in aggregate

spending are quite unlikely to be brought about by the initial thrust given to the interest rate structure by open-market operations. Hence, the monetary authorities must depend on their ability to force the banking system to ration credit via central bank control of member bank reserves and the money supply.

3. But, it is one thing to be able to control aggregate bank reserves and the quantity of money and quite another to be able to control the volume of bank loans—much less private spending *in toto*. The commercial banking system possesses both the incentive and the capacity to minimize the need for credit rationing by altering the distribution and composition of its collective assets. The most important technique by which commercial banks can at least partially and temporarily frustrate the aims of the central bank consists simply of reducing holdings of government securities—the so-called "locked-in" effect notwithstanding—and using the deposit-creating capacity thereby acquired to make new loans. In this way the ratio of loans to deposits is raised and the ratio of "active" to "idle" deposits presumably increased to some extent.

4. Furthermore, the private non-banking sector of the economy can also be expected to contribute to the increase in velocity not only by purchasing Governments from the banking system but also in a whole host of other ways, including: shifting savings from demand deposits to time deposits where a lower reserve requirement is in effect; exchanging government securities among themselves so that those individuals and institutions most anxious to spend will have cash; and, possibly most important of all, conjuring up ingenious new institutional arrangements whereby the existing money supply can be utilized much more fully and efficiently. The link between aggregate spending and the volume of loans is at least as weak as the link between member bank reserves and the volume of loans.

5. The unattractiveness to bankers of increased non-price credit-rationing as anything but a quite temporary adjustment coupled with the relative inelasticity of demand for loanable funds suggests that, when the above escape hatches are finally closed, the control of aggregate spending by monetary policy is likely to necessitate a considerable increase in interest rates. And, rising interest rates cannot be dismissed as an altogether unimportant by-product of credit restraint. While the strong tendency of interest rates to rise most certainly does not render monetary policy ineffective, it does hamper a restrictive monetary policy by (a) inducing additional increases in velocity, (b) raising costs to producers, and (c) lessening public and governmental support for a tight money policy.

6. Whether credit is rationed by price or non-price means, the immediate or initial impact of a restrictive monetary policy is not spread evenly throughout the economy, but is concentrated on investment spending in general, and on residential construction (especially the part financed by government-supported mortgages), public utility expansion, state and local government spending, and small businesses of various sorts in particular. Consequently, the equity of credit restraint has been strongly challenged.

7. Most serious of all, there are no grounds for expecting a rigid one-to-one correspondence between aggregate money spending and the price level. In fact, it seems quite likely that the initial impact of a restrictive monetary policy will fall more heavily on output and employment than on prices. It may well take a larger amount of unemployment to halt upward movements of costs and prices than either the public or the monetary authorities themselves are prepared to tolerate.

The final conclusion to be drawn from all this is that a restrictive monetary policy *can* quell a cost-price spiral, but that such a policy is apt to (a) take quite a while to exert its impact, (b) require a significant increase in interest rates, (c) exert a rather concentrated effect on certain sectors and activities within the economy, and (d) necessitate the appearance of more than frictional unemployment.

20. Impact of an Anti-Unemployment Policy

It is useful to distinguish between two main ways in which a cost-price spiral can call forth a sufficient increase in money incomes and spending to permit its indefinite continuance. First, upward pressure on costs can lead to what has been termed an "automatic" or "natural" increase in spending.[1] This will happen (a) if increased costs encourage firms and individuals to either increase their borrowings (and thus the money supply) or to economize on the use of the existing money supply (and thus increase the velocity of circulation) in order to permit themselves to make the same amount of real purchases as before, and (b) if the banking system is either unable or unwilling to prevent such an occurrence. It is this means of financing a cost-price spiral that a restrictive monetary policy can eventually prevent in the way described in the previous chapter.

The second way in which aggregate monetary spending can increase sufficiently to prevent unemployment from interfering with the orderly development of a cost-price spiral is through the direct intervention of the government. That is, if restrictive monetary policies threaten to prevent the "natural" financing of higher costs, it is still possible for the government to permit the continuance of the cost-price spiral by the simple expedient of creating sufficient monetary demand to render it profitable for firms to hire available manpower, even though wages and costs in general are still rising. And, it is this latter possibility which must now be examined.

At the outset, it is necessary to note that the existence of this second source of monetary demand depends entirely on a certain conception of government economic policy—namely, that Congress is committed to the goal of main-

[1] See Hicks, *Economic Journal*, September 1955, p. 393.

taining a high level of employment and will make every effort to attain this objective. It has been argued that, whereas the secular stagnationists of but a few years ago assumed that the functions of government are limited in both scope and scale, the secular inflationists of today envision a government that will always act to provide sufficient aggregate monetary demand to maintain a high level of employment.[2] Whether one wishes to attribute this acceptance of government responsibility for the level of employment to advances in economic analysis, to humanitarian concern, to a basic change in political philosophy, to the requirements of foreign policy, or to a very mundane desire on the part of elected representatives to stay in office, there is no denying the active interest of Congress in preventing—and, if this fails, in combatting—widespread unemployment.

Paralleling this alteration in the attitude of government toward the unemployment problem has been the development of a fear on the part of many economists that various sorts of full-employment guarantees may not be unmixed blessings in that they are likely to be accompanied by one of two unwanted offspring: (a) the problem of continued inflation; or (b) direct controls over wages and prices. Within this broad area of concern, some writers have chosen to argue that an overly-ambitious full employment goal will produce inflation directly, regardless of the behavior of unions and corporations, whereas others have emphasized the increase in the bargaining strength of workers that will accompany a high level of employment.[3]

[2] See Martin Bronfenbrenner, "Some Neglected Implications of Secular Inflation," *Post-Keynesian Economics,* ed. Kenneth K. Kurihara (New Brunswick, N.J.: Rutgers University Press, 1954), p. 37.

[3] Perhaps the strongest spokesman for the viewpoint that certain definitions of full employment are inherently inflationary is Walter A. Morton ("Keynesianism and Inflation," *Journal of*

There can be little doubt that a full-employment policy can be embraced so strongly as to produce inflation (whether it will also produce "full" employment is more open to question). However, the fact that such an "unlimited commitment" on the part of the government to the full-employment objective is inconsistent with price stability need cause no immediate concern. This is because governments have simply not been willing to accept this sort of unlimited commitment to a single goal, but have been prepared to tolerate varying amounts of unemployment in order to avoid deviating too far from certain other policy objectives.[4] While the exact nature of these other policy objectives has not always been terribly clear, it would appear that the government's willingness to fight unemployment has been tempered by (a) the fear of inflation, and (b) a strong antipathy towards a rising national debt.

Whether for the above reasons or simply as a consequence of the rather long time lag involved in implementing a counter-cyclical fiscal policy, the record shows that both Democratic and Republican administrations have reacted rather cautiously to moderate downturns in business activity. Unemployment stood at 6.0 per cent in June 1949, and at 5.1 per cent in July 1954.[5] The experience during the recession that commenced in 1957 affords perhaps the best evidence that Congress is apt to refrain from

---

Political Economy, LIX [June 1951], pp. 260-261). Edward S. Mason represents the school of thought that prefers to stress the effect of a full employment guarantee on wage behavior (*Economic Concentration and the Monopoly Problem* [Cambridge, Mass.: Harvard University Press, 1957], pp. 191-193).

[4] The phrase "unlimited commitment" belongs to Harry G. Johnson ("The Determination of the General Level of Wage Rates," *Theory of Wage Determination*, ed. Dunlop, 1957, pp. 37-38).

[5] These data are taken from Kenyon Poole's article (*American Economic Review*, May 1955, p. 586).

taking strong actions at the first sign of unemployment. The reluctance of Congress to enact a tax cut is of particular interest. If the present behavior of Congress can be projected, it would seem that anti-unemployment fiscal policies will, at least initially, be confined to moderate increases in spending and to the passive acceptance of a government deficit as a consequence of "automatically" declining tax revenues. Tax cutting seems to be considered an "ultimate weapon," which should be reserved for action only in case of dire emergency.

While positive fiscal actions are apt to be enacted only after a considerable delay, we may expect somewhat quicker action on the part of the monetary authorities. After all, one of the traditional arguments in favor of a flexible monetary policy is that it can be adapted to changed circumstances in very short order. And, there are good grounds for thinking that the Federal Reserve will elect to use its discretionary authority in order to combat unemployment.

For one thing, it is just as well to admit that the Federal Reserve System is not nearly such an "independent" agency as is sometimes thought. Its ability to survive in its present form rests squarely on the continued allegiance of both Congress and the public to the basic policies it enunciates. Thus, since Federal Reserve officials are certainly not unaware of the source of their discretionary power, it is unrealistic to regard central bank policies as immune from the strong pressures for a high level of employment that are so prevalent in our society. And, it may be suggested in passing that the Federal Reserve is apt to be especially anxious to do all in its power to cure a recession which some think was brought about by the perverse policies of the monetary authorities themselves.

Actually, it may be overly cynical to explain the likelihood that the central bank will adopt an anti-unemployment policy on the basis of political pressures. Federal

Reserve officials may simply feel that at certain times a high level of employment becomes a more paramount economic objective than price stability.[6]

Consequently, it seems reasonable to suppose that the central bank will seek to contribute to the elimination of non-frictional unemployment, and that in order to achieve this aim the various restrictive monetary policies described earlier will be reversed. That is, the Federal Reserve is likely to lower the discount rate and to ease the pressure on the reserve position of banks by whatever combination of open-market purchases and lowered reserve requirements seems most appropriate.

Thus far we have considered the *nature* of the actions that Congress and the Federal Reserve System are likely to take in response to the appearance of unemployment. The final question which requires comment concerns the probable combined impact of credit ease and a modest counter-cyclical fiscal policy on the economy. Without becoming unduly embroiled in the multitude of detailed problems involved in carefully assessing the impact of an anti-unemployment policy, it is possible to make a few general observations.

Looking first at the fiscal policy side, it is reasonable to suppose that whatever increase occurs in the amount of direct government purchases of goods and services will tend to increase employment both directly and via the in-

[6] This interpretation of Federal Reserve policy is reflected in a *Business Week* editorial (May 31, 1958, p. 100) reporting a speech made by Alfred Hayes, president of the New York Federal Reserve Bank: "Refuting those who fear that the Fed's easy money policy is inviting inflation, he bluntly stated that 'during recent months the immediate dangers of recession had come to outweigh the dangers of inflation, and still outweigh them.' And though inflation may again be a threat, he explained that 'it would have been inexcusable to let this consideration prevent our doing all we could do to combat the recession and provide an atmosphere of money and credit ease conducive to recovery.' "

duced increases in private money incomes. And, increases in transfer payments (for example, unemployment compensation) will also serve to raise money incomes. However, there is certainly no reason to suppose that the moderate sort of counter-cyclical fiscal policy described above will be sufficient to eliminate all non-frictional unemployment. Not only is there the question of the magnitude of the government program, but there is also the possibility that a part of the increase in money incomes will bring about higher prices and costs rather than increased real output. This "leakage" is apt to be especially large if the higher consumer incomes are spent mainly for products for which demand has held up fairly well through the recession. For example, increased money incomes may well be spent largely on such items as food and medical bills, while unemployment may be concentrated in durable goods and producer goods industries.

An easing of credit conditions is, of course, less likely to have a sudden and direct effect on the volume of employment. While declining interest rates may be of immediate benefit to such activities as residential construction, the economy as a whole does not seem particularly sensitive to easier credit conditions at a time of uncertainty and general underutilization of existing capacity. In such circumstances, potential borrowers may well be reluctant to avail themselves of the easier credit conditions. It is this reasoning which has led to the widespread feeling among economists (and central bankers) that monetary policy is generally less effective in combatting unemployment than inflation. As far as the actual magnitude of the impact is concerned, much depends on the timing of the monetary authorities—that is, the expansionary effect of credit ease will presumably be much greater if the monetary authorities make additional reserves available to the banking system shortly after the appearance of unemployment than if action is delayed until layoffs have spread throughout the economy.

Thus it would appear that while both a moderate counter-cyclical fiscal policy and an easing of credit conditions will contribute towards recovery, it would be surprising if all vestiges of unemployment were speedily removed. There is apt to be a considerable hiatus between the adoption of these policies and the sought-after pick-up in employment. Consequently, we must reject the assertion that the government itself will insure the uninterrupted progression of cost-price increases by acting quickly and decisively to eliminate all non-frictional unemployment. The fear that "full" employment policies would always stand ready to provide any increase in aggregate spending that did not come about "naturally" and yet was necessary for the financing of cost increases seems to have been considerably exaggerated. There is little evidence to suggest that the government will play the role of "financier of last resort" with sufficient determination or success to preclude the possibility that rounds of cost-price increases will culminate in non-frictional unemployment.

However, this is certainly not to suggest that anti-unemployment policies make no contribution at all to the propagation of the inflationary process. For one thing, they do serve to moderate the downward pressures on employment, and in this way lessen the downward pressures on costs and prices. And, perhaps of greater long-run importance is the impact of anti-unemployment policies on the composition of the assets held by both the banking system and the private sector of the economy in general.

A significant alteration in private asset holdings occurs as a by-product of both fiscal and monetary anti-unemployment policies. First of all, the combination of a drop in anticipated tax revenues (as personal and corporate incomes level off or decline) and an increase in government payments means an increase in the government deficit and in the volume of government obligations outstanding. The final impact of the net increase in new offerings is influenced, of course, by the identity of the purchasers. If the Federal Reserve acquires some of the new government securities offered for sale by the Treasury, the result will be an increase in both the money supply and member bank reserves.

The easy money policy of the central bank constitutes an even more direct and obvious source of increased reserves for the banking system. Not only may the Federal Reserve purchase a portion of the newly issued obligations of the Treasury, but it may also go into the open market and buy bonds previously held by the private sector of the economy. Furthermore, the Federal Reserve may lower reserve requirements and in this way improve the reserve position of the banks without engaging in open-market operations. These reductions in reserve requirements may then permit the banking system to increase its holdings of government securities and in this way "store-up" liquidity for later use. This seems to be exactly what happened during the latter part of 1954. Between June 30, 1953 and December 31, 1954 commercial and savings banks strengthened their liquidity positions by adding $9.6 billions to their holdings of government securities.[7]

In brief, one of the main consequences of a larger government deficit and an easy money policy is likely to be a considerable increase in the expansionary potential of the banking system and a strengthening of the liquidity position of the economy in general. And, this legacy of liquidity may then permit not only an increase in the money supply, but also an economizing of the given (larger) money supply and thus an increase in velocity when economic activity and the demand for loans picks up. In this

[7] Warren L. Smith, "On the Effectiveness of Monetary Policy," *American Economic Review*, XLVI (September 1956), p. 603.

way continued rounds of cost-price increases may be financed by increases in the money supply during the latter stages of contractions and the start of recoveries and by increases in velocity during the high-employment stage.

The important point here is that the appearance of unemployment is significant not only in that it may interrupt the pursuit of a restrictive monetary policy before price stability is achieved, but also in that the anti-unemployment policies called forth pave the way for future increases in both the size and velocity of the monetary stock and in this way accentuate the difficulties of monetary authorities in combatting subsequent rounds of inflation.

This is not, of course, to suggest that the monetary authorities are unable to reverse their policies and in this way offset the consequences of anti-unemployment policies. It is just that the necessity for such offsetting actions further complicates and magnifies an already arduous task. In order to restrain subsequent upward movements of costs and prices, the monetary authorities will have first to "wear down" the new legacy of liquidity that the private sector has inherited. And, as emphasized in the preceding chapter, such a "wearing down" is time-consuming, difficult, and not altogether popular.

PART V
Conclusions

21. THE DILEMMA MODEL RE-EXAMINED

The aim of this book has been to make a limited contribution towards a fuller understanding of the so-called "wage-price issue"—a phrase used throughout the preceding pages as a short-hand expression for the whole complex of questions involved in the allegation that the wage- and price-setting institutions of the contemporary American economy impart an upward bias to the price level. Express recognition of the *limited* nature of the intended contribution stems not so much from any sense of false modesty on the part of the author (although investigation of this subject certainly does inspire humility) as from the inescapable fact that there are three broad sets of questions involved in the wage-price issue—namely, a theoretical set, an empirical set, and a public policy set—and that this study deals only with the theoretical set.

By way of pursuing the above objective, this inquiry has passed through two main stages. The first stage was devoted to describing the importance and evolution of the topic, to exploring the nature and origins (or "types") of inflation, and to investigating in some detail one particular model of the inflationary process—the familiar "dilemma model," in which it is asserted that "spontaneous" increases in labor costs instigate a train of events that force society to choose between inflation and unemployment.[1] The second, and much lengthier, stage has been devoted to analyzing the questions raised by the three assertions that comprise the dilemma model—the wage

[1] At this point it is appropriate to emphasize that concentration on this one model of the inflationary process precludes this study from qualifying as a general inquiry into the origins and characteristics of inflations. Other potential sources of inflationary pressure (such as a sudden increase in defense spending attendant upon a national emergency) are not considered here.

determination, cost and price determination, and monetary policy assertions.

Organizationally, the concluding Part of this study is divided into two chapters, each of which is intended to serve a specific purpose. In the present chapter, an attempt is made to draw together the main findings which stem from the preceding analysis of the dilemma model; and then, in the next chapter, a few final observations are hazarded concerning the implications of this analysis for the dual problem of isolating the "cause" of inflation and finding a "solution" to the inflation-unemployment dilemma.

However, before plunging into the main business of this chapter and re-examining the dilemma model, one final comment is in order. The reader is hereby duly warned that these final two chapters do *not* purport to restate all the detailed conclusions that are contained in the preceding pages. There are several reasons for this. First of all, these detailed conclusions have already been gathered together with some care, are readily accessible at the end of individual chapters, and so need not be reproduced here. More important is the ever-present need to balance the advantages of tying together a long piece of work such as this against the disadvantages of over-summarization— which, incidentally, are particularly pronounced in the case of the present study. One of the main themes that runs throughout this inquiry is that the laudatory desire to simplify has been carried to unnecessary and undesirable extremes in many discussions of wage-price relationships. It is entirely possible that whatever contribution this book may make is to be found primarily in the detailed analyses which constitute certain individual chapters rather than in the more general conclusions which follow.

Turning now to the dilemma model proper, the main general conclusion to be drawn from the preceding analysis is that this model suffers from two closely-related weaknesses. First, each of the individual assertions that comprise the model leaves something to be desired. These assertions all appear to be half-truths, which at best are somewhat misleading and at worst provide a highly dangerous basis for public policy decisions. Second, the way in which these assertions interact is unduly neglected in the basic dilemma model.

Both the rationale behind this rather sweeping indictment and the more positive picture of the dilemma process that emerges from the foregoing discussion can best be described with the aid of Figure 3, which appears below, on page 391. The function of this figure is to provide an over-all view of the way in which the various parts of the model interact, and where within the dilemma framework other factors and considerations exert their influence.

The solid heavy lines that appear in the center of the figure identify the main events that make up the basic dilemma model described in Chapter 3.[2] The solid heavy arrows illustrate the sequence of events usually emphasized in this model: wage determination is followed by an increase in unit labor costs and unit total costs; these higher costs are then mediated through the price determination process and transmuted into upward pressure on the price level; and, the monetary-fiscal authorities then decide whether this trend of events is to culminate in inflation or unemployment. The dotted heavy lines show the aggregate money income and spending links, which are given less attention in the basic dilemma model. The remaining lines and arrows indicate both the points in the dilemma process at which various factors exogenous to the basic model exert their impact and the ways in which various endogenous factors interact. The specific links or lines of impact are discussed below. The arabic numbers that appear on the arrows serve only to facilitate the exposition, and have no substantive significance.

[2] The skeleton of this model is described on pp. 35-38 of Part I.

It is convenient to organize the following conclusions concerning the over-all dilemma model around the same three assertions that have provided the framework for the body of this study. And, it is again useful to begin with the wage determination assertion.

The Wage Determination Assertion

The first and most basic conclusion about this aspect of the dilemma model that emerges from the preceding discussion is that the empirical sort of wage determination assertion frequently encountered—to wit, that so long as unemployment does not rise above some "critical" level wages will in fact increase more rapidly than productivity in general can advance—is both unsatisfactory and unnecessary. It is unsatisfactory for two reasons: first, the magnitude of wage adjustments is dependent on many facets of the economic environment and is not nearly such an independent variable as implied in the empirical type of assertion; and, second, an understanding of the determinants of wage adjustments is absolutely imperative if wise public policies are to be formulated and costly mistakes avoided.

The empirical type assertion is also unnecessary because, while admittedly complex, the wage determination process is not totally undecipherable. All of Part II—and particularly Chapters 10 and 11 are devoted to supplying a framework and developing certain hypotheses with which to understand the behavior of both specific and general wage adjustments. On the basis of this analysis, it is possible to single out six factors that seem especially crucial for determining the general magnitude of wage adjustments. The arrows illustrating the impact of these wage-determining factors are grouped at the extreme left of Figure 3, and bear numbers 1 through 6.

It would, of course, be extremely naïve to think (and un-

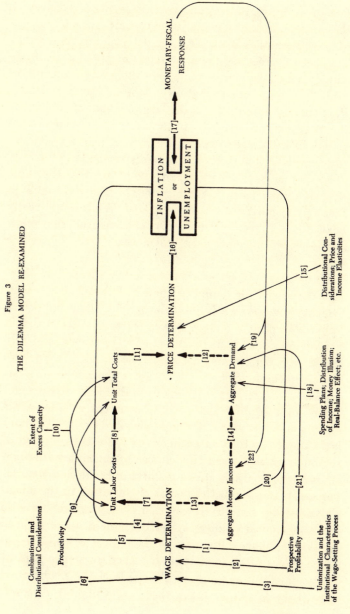

Figure 3

THE DILEMMA MODEL RE-EXAMINED

391

fair to suggest) that existent writings on the subject of
the wage-price issue have failed to consider the significance
of these factors. The single wage determining factor that
has probably received the most attention is the level of unemployment (the arrow connecting the level of unemployment with wage determination is labeled 1 in Figure 3).
Particularly noteworthy is the large number of quests for
the "critical" volume of unemployment at which wage
pressures will cease to exceed the rate of productivity improvement. Without intending to disparage the efforts of
these searchers, it is necessary to point out that the value
of such a parameter (assuming, for the moment, that it in
fact exists) must not be overestimated. What would really
be useful is a nice, well-defined, *continuous* function relating levels of unemployment to movements of aggregate
wages.

Unfortunately, however, there are a number of theoretical reasons for doubting the existence of such a convenient function: (a) The existence of other important
wage determining factors makes it very unlikely that a
precise relationship between wage adjustments and any
single wage determining factor can be found. (b) The volume of unemployment is *not* always a good index of labor
market pressures, since it tells us nothing about the number of unfilled jobs that exist concurrently with people
seeking job openings. Unemployment data are particularly unsatisfactory as an index of the total situation in
the labor market when the number of unemployed is low,
since in such periods striking shifts in the demand for labor can take place with little or no variation in the unemployment figures. (c) Even when unemployment data do
serve as accurate indices of shifts in the demand for and
supply of labor, there may not be a close correlation between such shifts and changes in either the wages paid by
particular firms or the general wage level. This is because:
(i) within particular firms, there are a number of sound

reasons for thinking that certain changes in labor market pressures will often have little or no direct effect on wages;[3] and (ii) within the economy as a whole, there is the additional complication introduced by the fact that the distribution of a given volume of unemployment among various sectors and industries may be extremely important.

This is not, of course, to deny that high levels of employment are conducive to substantial wage increases, and that "enough" unemployment will moderate the magnitude of wage adjustments. However, it should be pointed out that this may be more a consequence of the *associated effects* of the employment situation than of the alteration in labor market pressures per se.

More precisely, the apparent importance of the employment situation may stem to a large extent from the fact that the volume of unemployment serves as a very rough index of movements in a second wage-determining factor—namely, the *prospective profitability*[4] of firms (labeled 2 in Figure 3). One of the main wage determination hypotheses developed in the course of this study is that prospective profitability coupled with the opportunity cost of the proposed wage adjustment serves as an important determinant of (a) the reaction of firms possessing unilateral wage-setting power to the wage pressures they encounter, and (b) both the magnitude of the proposed wage adjustment and the resistance of the firm to the wage demand in cases where collective bargaining is the mode of wage determination. It must be emphasized that prospective profitability is most certainly not an exog-

[3] For a detailed discussion of these reasons and the factors which influence the nature of the response a firm makes when faced with a shortage of labor, see Chapter 6.

[4] Prospective profitability is defined and discussed in some detail in Chapter 7. The role played by prospective profitability in the over-all determination of wage adjustments is outlined in Chapters 10 and 11.

enous variable, but is dependent on such factors as the level of aggregate demand—and, for this reason, arrow 21 links aggregate demand and prospective profitability together.

A composite wage determining factor that has received at least as much attention as the amount of unemployment is the institutional characteristics of the wage-setting process (arrow 3). In particular, the question of the impact of the union has been the subject of heated debate. Without pretending to have resolved the complex methodological problems that beset anyone brave enough to attempt to unravel the independent significance of this institution, it can be suggested that the visible and dramatic nature of union activities has resulted in some exaggeration of the importance of this whole question. It must be remembered that the trade union is but one of the parties to a collective bargaining agreement—trade union wage policy most emphatically cannot be identified with wage determination—and that, to some extent at least, the union mediates economic pressures which would have taken their toll in its absence. This is not to deny that unions probably exert some upward pressure on wages, but rather to warn against an uncritical exaggeration of union impact. The ability of the union to increase the cost to the employer of not agreeing to a hypothetical wage increase would certainly suggest, on a priori grounds, that in most circumstances unions encourage upward wage adjustments.[5] However, the empirical magnitude of this impact must be classed as an unsolved problem.

This preoccupation with the impact of the union per se has diverted attention from certain other institutional characteristics of the wage- and price-setting process that may serve to impart added upward thrust to the over-all

[5] A group of hypotheses concerning the circumstances especially amenable to a strong union impact is presented in Chapter 8.

wage level. These characteristics include: (a) the strength of non-price competition in product markets, the accompanying incentive to maintain production at almost any cost, and the concomitant reduction in employer resistance to union wage demands; (b) the growth of longer-term contracts which, coupled with the importance of inter-union and inter-firm wage comparisons, may serve to lessen the tendency for wage adjustments to be moderated by mild recessions; and (c) the existence of an apparent tendency for workers to expect a significant wage increase each year as the "normal" thing—annual wage increments have come close to achieving an "habitual" status.

By following arrow 4 back to its origin, another wage-determining factor which has received considerable attention is identified—namely, inflation itself, or movements of the cost-of-living index. There is little doubt but that this wage-determining factor magnifies upward price adjustments which have received their impetus elsewhere, and that workers will make every effort to see that their wages at least keep pace with the cost of living so that real wages are maintained. However, it must also be remembered that wage changes attributable to increases in the price level constitute a "play back" effect and cannot instigate an upward movement of wages and prices. At the same time, it is equally important to recall that *ex post* statistics showing that wages and prices have increased at the same rate prove absolutely nothing concerning the direction of impact. Such equivalent increases are perfectly compatible with either a wage→price model or with a price→wage model, and in no way demonstrate that the wage-setting institutions have merely reacted passively to price changes originating elsewhere rather than instigating the upward movements of wages and prices themselves.

The fifth wage determining factor portrayed in Figure 3 is productivity itself. One of the key questions raised—but left unanswered—in the basic dilemma model is whether wage adjustments and changes in productivity are independent or functionally related. The only general answer which can be given to this question is that wages and productivity are both partly interrelated and partly independent. Remembering that productivity is defined as the ratio of output to labor input, it is first necessary to recognize that there are a number of ways in which an increase in productivity can come about, and that not all of these sources of productivity gains have the same implications for wage determination.[6]

It is also necessary to recognize that, except in cases where workers are paid on a piece-rate basis, there is no visible link between productivity changes and wage adjustments. Productivity usually exerts its impact indirectly, by influencing other wage determining factors. It is generally thought that the main link through which productivity changes are transmitted is the demand for labor—however, closer examination has suggested that it is rather difficult to predict the impact of a change in output per man-hour on the firm's demand for labor; and, as already pointed out above, whatever change in the demand for labor does occur will often have a minimal effect on wages. Instead, it appears that the more important link between productivity improvements and wage adjustments is the profit position—or, more precisely, the prospective profitability—of the firm.

In short, while an increase in productivity is likely to lessen the upward pressure on the price level to some extent, this cost-reducing impact will be moderated by the tendency of productivity gains to call forth still larger wage adjustments.

[6] The early part of Chapter 5 contains a discussion of both the problems involved in defining productivity and the various sources of productivity improvements. The wage-determining implications of these various sorts of productivity increases are discussed in the second half of Chapter 5.

This brings us to arrow 6, which identifies the final wage determining factor depicted in Figure 3—namely, "combinational and distributional considerations." The inclusion of this somewhat nebulous-sounding category is intended to emphasize that the magnitude of wage adjustments cannot be adequately understood by considering each of the other wage-determining factors individually. The important points to be noted here are: (a) within the individual firm, the *combinations* in which these factors appear are vitally important for determining the magnitude of the resultant wage adjustment; and (b) throughout the economy as a whole, the *distribution* of various factors—such as unemployment and profitability—among sectors, areas, and industries cannot be neglected.

While it is impractical to summarize the detailed characteristics of the schema developed to take account of these interrelations,[7] it is still possible to emphasize the central point of this analysis—to wit, the real source of significantly large wage increases is the existence of certain "potent" or "deadly" groupings of wage-determining factors. To illustrate, large productivity increases by themselves may not be overly significant, but when they are combined with an aggressive union, a high capital-to-labor ratio, and little price competition in the product market, but sufficient non-price competition to encourage the maintenance of production at almost any cost, sizeable wage increases are likely to result.

The Cost and Price Determination Assertions

At this point, it is appropriate to note that, as Figure 3 indicates, any change in the general level of money wages affects both costs and aggregate money incomes;

[7] A more complete discussion of the way in which the individual wage determination factors interact to determine the magnitude of wage adjustments within the individual firm is provided in

consequently, the decision to continue along the main route laid out by the basic dilemma model and consider wages-as-cost prior to wages-as-income constitutes a somewhat arbitrary—albeit convenient—procedure.

Proceeding along the upper branch of Figure 3, the links initially encountered are those which join wage determination to unit labor costs (arrow 7) and unit labor costs to unit total costs (8). The first thing to note about the wages→ unit-labor-cost link is that the behavior of productivity is, as the dilemma model explicitly recognizes, an important determinant of the extent to which upward wage adjustments are translated into higher unit labor costs. And, apart from certain detailed problems involved in computing a useful labor cost index (such as the proper treatment of salaried personnel and fringe benefits), there is little else to be said about this link.

The link between unit labor costs and unit total costs is, however, much more complex, and there are several significant points to be made here. The basic point is simply that the connection between unit labor costs and unit total costs cannot normally be expected to be as "tight" or rigid as has often been implied in discussions of the dilemma model. This is primarily because considerations associated with changes in productivity may bring about changes in non-labor costs. And, it is in recognition of this possibility that link 9 in Figure 3 joins productivity to unit total costs as well as to unit labor costs.

More specifically, a given change in unit labor costs will necessarily result in an equal absolute increase in unit total costs only if (a) the proportions in which labor and non-labor variable factors are combined do not vary as relative factor prices and technology change; (b) the prices of non-labor factors do not change; and (c) there is no change in capital costs per unit of output as a con-

Chapter 10; the fusion of individual wage adjustments into movements of the general wage level is discussed in Chapter 11.

sequence of technological innovations. In addition, it should be observed that so long as unit labor costs and unit total costs are thought of as arithmetic ratios, their actual magnitudes will also vary with changes in the rate of output—unless, of course, the cost schedules turn out to be perfectly horizontal. Hence, arrow 10 indicates that the extent of excess capacity must also be recognized as a factor influencing both per unit cost figures.

While it is certainly worthwhile knowing that the unit-labor-cost → unit-total-cost link is likely to be somewhat elastic, there is a still more interesting and useful conclusion to be noted here: in most cases it is reasonable to expect changes in unit labor costs to be *smaller* than the associated changes in unit variable costs and unit total costs. This is because the pressure of rising labor costs would normally encourage firms to substitute other factors for labor, and this increased demand may well bring about an increase in the per unit price paid for these other factors as well as an increase in the number of units employed.

Turning now to the impact of unit costs on prices (arrow 11), we immediately run head-on into the price determination assertion of the dilemma model—namely, that changes in the general price level are geared mainly (if not exclusively) to changes in unit costs. Here the central issue is the validity of the cost-plus pricing doctrine.

Since in our economy changes in the general price level are the result of a myriad of individual price decisions, it is necessary, in the first instance, to look at this question from the vantage point of the individual firm and to evaluate the famous cost-plus pricing controversy. The main conclusion that we can draw from this controversy is that available evidence does not justify dethroning traditional price theory and replacing it with a rigid cost-plus formulation. And, the most important corollary to this finding is that demand considerations still play some role in the price-setting process. Hence, it is necessary to picture demand (arrow 12)—along with costs—as a determinant of the magnitude of price adjustments.

However, restoration of demand to its accustomed position in the price determination process fortunately does not exhaust the conclusions of this study germane to the price determination assertion. The depressing aspect of the entire cost-plus controversy is that so much time has been invested in attacking and defending various people's conceptions of "traditional theory" rather than in fusing the insights of traditional theory and the cost-plus investigations into a more useful model of price behavior. Such a fusion has been attempted in Part II of this study, and, while it would be impractical and unwise to condense the resulting formulation still further in order to summarize it here, certain conclusions stemming from this analysis can be listed.[8]

The first conclusion is that changes in costs are in general more likely to inspire a price adjustment than are shifts in demand, and that rising costs are especially likely to lead to a price increase of approximately the same dollar amount per unit and possibly the same percentage magnitude. The rationale for this conclusion includes the following points: (a) the "usual" shape of cost and demand functions suggests that a firm seeking only to maximize short-run profits will receive clearer and sharper instructions from an increase in costs than from a shift in demand; (b) the existence of uncertainty encourages price increases based on rising costs because of the strong desire to maintain profit margins and because cost increases are relatively knowable, predictable, and permanent; (c) cost increases are often fairly uniform among industries and competitors, and price increases based on rising costs are

[8] The final synthesis is described at the end of Chapter 15; the spade work which lies behind this synthesis is contained in Chapter 14 and the first part of Chapter 15.

not terribly likely to upset relationships among firms or to start a price war; and (d) price increases based on higher costs are fairly acceptable on "ethical" grounds and are easier to "justify" before Congress and the public than price adjustments geared to "what the market will bear."

A second conclusion is that decreasing costs are not nearly so likely to bring about price reductions as rising costs are to precipitate price increases. And, there are some grounds for suspecting that it is downward shifts in demand rather than in costs which are the key element in inspiring price reductions. This may be because decreases in demand are "unfavorable" events; consequently, once a certain action threshold is passed, the firm may succumb to the pressure to "do something," and price cuts may thus result.

A third, closely related point, is that the existence of a "turnover lag" coupled with the desire of firms for security imparts a certain upward bias to price decisions even apart from long run tendencies for costs to rise and governments to prevent serious deficiences of demand from lasting for an extended period of time.

It is important to remember that these comments pertain to price-setting within the individual firm. In order to arrive at a picture of the behavior of the general price level—which, after all, is the main concern of the dilemma model—several additional observations are required.[9] For one thing, it is necessary to recognize the existence of more than a single mode of price determination. Agricultural prices, for example, are very important in the Consumer

[9] At this juncture it should be noted that at the macro-economic level the interdependence of costs and demand can no longer be completely ignored. That is, the existence of arrows 13 and 14 must now be recognized, even though a discussion of the determination of aggregate demand and aggregate money income is postponed until later. For the present, only the proximate determinants of price level changes are being considered.

Price Index and yet are determined quite differently from the prices of such durable goods as automobiles. And, a general weakness of the price determination aspects of the dilemma model is that price behavior in the "competitive" sectors of the economy is unduly neglected.

The main implication resulting from the addition of explicit recognition of the sectored nature of the economy to the preceding analysis of micro-economic price determination is that neither the strict cost-plus pricing doctrine of the dilemma model nor the aggregative excess demand (inflationary gap) model provides a satisfactory framework within which to study changes in the general price level. The difficulty with both these hypotheses is that they are able to deal only with special cases and cannot serve as useful general descriptions of macro-economic price behavior. The cost-plus model not only suffers from certain difficulties when applied to the "administered price" sector of the economy, but is totally inapplicable to other sectors such as agriculture and the service trades. The excess demand model, on the other hand, is useful only in dealing with the competitive sector of the economy.

Thus, it is necessary to turn to a less aggregative approach which recognizes the sectored nature of the economy and which supplements an understanding of micro-economic price behavior with an appreciation of the importance of the composition or distribution of changes in aggregate demand and aggregate cost indices (these distributional considerations are represented by arrow 15 in Figure 3).

The importance of distributional considerations is illustrated by the fact that the impact of a given increase in an aggregate index of unit costs[10] will depend on: (a)

---

[10] It is necessary at this point to append a comment concerning the need for a clear definition of any aggregate cost index used in making cost-price comparisons. Unless the cost index is constructed in the same manner as the price index, very misleading results may be obtained.

the distribution of cost increases among modes of price determination—the immediate price reaction will be strongest if rising costs are concentrated in sectors where cost-plus pricing is prevalent and weakest if most of the cost increases occur in the competitive sector; (b) the distribution of cost increases vis-à-vis the demand situation in various sectors and industries—an adverse situation in the product market may force firms that "usually" set prices on a cost-plus basis to depart from this policy; and (c) the uniformity of the cost increase among sectors—the tendency of prices to respond more quickly to cost increases than cost reductions suggests that a given increase in aggregate costs comprised of a great number of moderate price increases may lead to less pressure on prices than a combination of cost reductions and larger cost increases.

Distributional considerations are at least equally important in determining the impact of shifts in demand. It seems reasonable to suppose that a given decrease in aggregate demand will exert more downward pressure on prices in general the more heavily it is concentrated in the "competitive" sectors of the economy. Conversely, the general price index will increase more rapidly in response to an increase in the demand for such items as farm products than in response to an increase in orders for structural steel. At the root of shifts in the distribution of demand are, of course, price and income elasticities of demand as well as shifts in the distribution of income and secular changes in tastes. The preceding analysis suggests that these rather unexciting and frequently neglected considerations may be important determinants of price level movements.

The Monetary Policy Assertion

The links in Figure 3 that still remain to be considered are all related to the third and last assertion contained in the dilemma model—namely, the monetary policy assertion, which states that the awesome responsibility for deciding whether the wage and price behavior of individual economic units is to culminate in inflation or unemployment rests with the monetary authorities (or, more precisely, with the monetary-fiscal authorities). The arrows numbered 16 and 17 indicate the relationships usually envisioned in discussions of the dilemma model. Arrow 17 points in both directions in order to show that the initial pressures on prices and the level of employment influence the monetary-fiscal authorities, who in turn help determine whether inflation or unemployment finally results from the dilemma process.

The fundamental objection to the conception of the role of the monetary authorities embodied in the dilemma model is that it is seriously incomplete—there is no explanation of the mechanism whereby monetary policy affects wage, price, and employment decisions. It is to remedy this deficiency that links 18-22 have been added to Figure 3, and an examination of the characteristics of these links included in the following discussion of the monetary policy assertion.

However, before looking at specific links, it is necessary to have a clear understanding of the general role played by the monetary authorities. In this connection, the first point to be noted is that the dilemma model is entirely correct in emphasizing the importance of the monetary environment as a determinant of price level movements. It is clearly improper to ignore monetary considerations by arguing (as some have done) that what is cost to one man is income to another, and so a cost-induced price increase is self-financing and self-sustaining in that money incomes are automatically raised in tune with rising prices. The difficulty with this rigid linking of wages to aggregate money income to aggregate demand (links 13 and 14) is that the monetary authorities *may* inhibit such self-financing by keeping the supply of money under tight control and letting the increasing demand for transactions balances bid up interest rates (or reduce the "availability" of credit) sufficiently to dampen some spending plans.

However, this point must be counterbalanced immediately with a second observation. It is equally improper to move from this laudatory recognition of the significance of the monetary environment to the position that price level movements can best be understood by concentrating attention solely on the money supply and the behavior of the monetary authorities. The difficulty with this purely monetary approach is that it leaves unanswered too many fundamental questions such as: (a) What is the probability that changes in velocity will offset changes in the stock of money? (b) What factors influence the size of the money supply, and to what extent is the quantity of money dependent on wage and price behavior, rather than the other way around? and (c) What is the mechanism whereby changes in the money supply exert their impact, and what are the social and economic costs involved in controlling the level of prices and employment in this manner? In order to answer these questions it is necessary to examine the interactions of monetary policy and wage-price behavior—concentration on either to the exclusion of the other precludes the possibility of finding satisfactory answers.

Furthermore, it is necessary to note the existence of still a third set of factors (in addition to wage-price behavior and monetary-fiscal policy) which affect the outcome of the dilemma process—namely, the group of factors which affect private decisions to spend out of a given level of aggregate income and which are linked to aggregate demand by arrow 18 in Figure 3. An unfortunate consequence of the dilemma model's concentration on the production side of the economic process is the tendency to forget that aggregate income and aggregate spending are *not* rigidly bound together, and that a cost-price spiral can be either interrupted or hastened by a change in

405

private spending plans due to: (a) exogenous factors such as the world political situation or the climate; (b) the possible existence of a money illusion; (c) the so-called "real-balance effect"; (d) redistribution of aggregate income; (e) temporary disparities between the composition of plans to spend and plans to produce; and (f) price expectations. An important implication of the existence of such factors is that it is by no means obvious that an "elastic" or "easy" money policy is sufficient to insure the uninterrupted progression of a series of cost-price increases.[11]

Having bounded the significance of monetary policy somewhat, it is now possible to concentrate on the two basic questions here: (a) What actions are the monetary-fiscal authorities likely to take in the face of upward pressures on the general price level? and (b) What will be the impact of these actions?

The first of these questions falls at least as much in the province of the political scientist as it does in the province of the economist; however, at the risk of transgressing, it seems reasonable to suppose that the monetary authorities will not support an on-going inflation indefinitely, but instead will make an effort to preserve price level stability. The weapons used in this anti-inflation campaign may range all the way from a simple refusal to supply additional reserves to the banking system (such a "do nothing" policy will eventually put pressure on the banking system because of the need for increasing transactions balances that accompany rounds of cost and price increases) to more overt actions such as raising the discount rate, selling Governments in the open market, and raising reserve requirements.

[11] At this point it should be noted that, in addition to the above factors, the existence of both a progressive federal income tax and a foreign component in aggregate demand may also serve to slow up an on-going inflation.

The next question is *where* within the dilemma model this response of the monetary authorities exerts its impact. In very general terms, this question is answered by arrow 19—the initial and direct impact of a restrictive monetary policy will be on aggregate demand. A restrictive monetary policy will exert a direct impact on the wage and price determination processes proper *only* if the "anticipatory" or "announcement effects" impinge significantly on individual wage and price decisions—and, earlier discussions have suggested that it would be unwise to pin much hope on this possibility. Hence, there are no arrows that lead directly from monetary-fiscal policy to wage and price determination; as will be seen below, these processes feel the impact of a restrictive monetary policy only in a more circuitous manner.

This brings us to the important and exceedingly complex issue of *how* monetary policy affects aggregate demand. A quite detailed analysis of the questions involved here has already been presented in Chapter 19 and need not be repeated *in toto*. For our present purposes, it is sufficient to note three of the main conclusions that stem from this analysis.

First, it is extremely important not to exaggerate the speed and the ease with which the central bank can control aggregate spending. The monetary authorities have to rely on control of bank reserves and the quantity of money to achieve their objectives—and, both the banking system and the private sector in general possess the incentive and the capacity to bring about increases in velocity that will offset (at least partially and temporarily) central bank control of the money supply. It may take considerable time and effort for the central bank to "wear down" the liquidity of the private sector sufficiently to permit effective control of aggregate spending.

Second, the attempt to control aggregate spending by monetary policy is quite likely to necessitate a significant increase in interest rates, which will in turn hamper a restrictive monetary policy both by inducing additional increases in velocity and by lessening public and governmental support for a tight money policy.

Third, the initial impact of credit restraint will not be felt with equal severity by all sectors of the economy and all types of spending, but will be concentrated on private investment in general, and on such categories as residential construction, public utility expansion, and state and local government spending in particular.

So much for the link between a restrictive monetary policy and aggregate demand. The next question is how whatever diminution in aggregate spending does result from a restrictive monetary policy affects prices and employment. Our earlier analysis suggests that a restrictive monetary policy is much more likely to lead, in the first instance at least, to a reduction in output and employment within the sectors especially susceptible to monetary restraint rather than to much of a reduction in the upward pressure on the price level. Hence, we have now traversed the route by which the adoption of a restrictive monetary policy can precipitate unemployment; however, to see how such an anti-inflationary policy can actually halt inflation, a few additional steps are needed.

The initial reduction in employment will in turn lead to both a reduction in aggregate money incomes (arrow 20) and some tendency for the magnitude of wage adjustments to be reduced (arrow 1). The distribution of the initial volume of unemployment and the effect of the reduced aggregate demand on prospective profitability (arrow 21) will both be important determinants of the speed with which labor costs respond to the beckoning of the monetary authorities. The key question now is whether this combination of less upward pressure on costs and a further reduction in aggregate demand (due to the appearance of unemployment and possibly to continued pres-

sure from the monetary authorities as well) will be sufficient to bring about price stability. If it is *not* sufficient,
unemployment will continue to increase and will in turn
induce another round of reductions in money incomes and
demand as well as a bargaining climate less and less favorable to substantial wage increments.

If the monetary authorities are resolute in their determination to achieve price stability, this cycle will have
to continue until either (a) the downward pressure on aggregate demand has been disseminated widely enough to
bring price level stability even though the aggregate cost
index may still be rising, or (b) the pressures exerted by
unemployment, excess capacity, and lower prospective
profitability have become strong enough to eliminate the
upward pressure on prices attributable to rising costs. It
must be emphasized that it is only by operating through
these channels that a restrictive monetary policy can hope
to halt the inflationary process.

However, it is far from certain that a restrictive monetary policy will in fact be carried this far. The monetary
authorities (or the Federal Government in general) may
become so concerned over the rising level of unemployment that they will seek to halt the above cycle by rescinding the anti-inflation policy—and, it is this latter possibility that still remains to be considered.

The point here is simply that in our society the continuous attainment of high-level employment is at least as important a goal as price level stability, and that when the
two conflict, high-level employment may well receive preference. Arrow 22 illustrates the possibility that the monetary-fiscal authorities will react to the appearance of non-
frictional unemployment by adopting tax and expenditure
programs designed to bolster private incomes directly.
And, while the oft-voiced fear that "full" employment
policies will operate to remove all barriers to inflation
seems to have been considerably exaggerated (primarily

409

because governments in fact have not been willing to adopt such unlimited commitments to a single goal), it is reasonable to expect that unemployment will be countered with at least a moderate anti-cyclical fiscal-monetary policy.

Anti-unemployment policies will, of course, increase inflationary pressures. For one thing, the direct impact of such policies on the level of employment and money incomes is bound to lessen downward pressures on costs and prices. Perhaps of greater long-run importance is the effect of anti-inflationary monetary and fiscal policies on the composition of private asset holdings and on the liquidity of the banking system and the public in general. That is, the by-product of attempts to fight unemployment may be a legacy of liquidity which, by paving the way for future increases in both the size and velocity of the money supply, will in turn accentuate the problems faced by the monetary authorities in combatting subsequent periods of inflation.

In short, to predict the eventual outcome of the dilemma process it is necessary to know not only the initial monetary-fiscal policy adopted and the way in which the private sector reacts to this policy, but also to what lengths the monetary-fiscal authorities are prepared to carry their initial policy decision.

Our re-examination of the dilemma model is now complete. In the above, all-too-sketchy synopsis an attempt has been made to point out some of the more significant weaknesses of this model—namely, an inadequate picture of the wage determination process; neglect of the differences between labor costs and total costs; an overly rigid price determination schema; undue neglect of the spending side of the inflationary process; and a failure to consider the *modus operandi* of monetary policy—and to indicate how some of the more important gaps may be filled. This analysis has, of necessity, been critical—perhaps overly critical—and at this juncture it is appropriate to redress the balance somewhat. For all its weaknesses, the dilemma model does serve a very worthwhile function in that it focuses our attention on an important macro-economic problem and then encourages us to think about this problem from the vantage point of the ultimate decision-making units involved.

22. Some Final Observations on "Causes" and "Solutions"

The discussion of the wage-price issue has been so replete with attempts to single out "the cause" of inflation and to "solve" the inflation-unemployment dilemma that it would be inappropriate to end this study without commenting briefly on these broader questions. However, it would be equally inappropriate to conclude too much from this kind of theoretical inquiry. That is, it would be a grave error to try to "squeeze out" conclusions of a sort which are simply not deducible from the type of analysis contained in the preceding chapters. Hence, the following discussion does not purport to supply substantive answers to the questions of causation and solution but instead is confined to a few simple, common-sense observations on how and how not to go about looking for such answers.

Identifying "Causes" and Fixing "Responsibility"

It would be very nice indeed if, on the basis of the preceding analysis, it were possible to supply a clear, unequivocal answer to the question of who or what is the "cause"[1] of upward price adjustments, and thereby settle the seemingly endless controversy over the "responsibility" for inflation. However, this is clearly *not* possible—and, it is rather important to see why.

The first and most obvious reason is that the preceding discussion has been concerned solely with theoretical is-

---

[1] The word "cause" has been encased in parentheses long enough. In the present chapter, this troublesome word is used in the usual sense of: "That which occasions or effects a result. . . . *Cause* applies to any circumstance, condition, event, etc., or to any combination thereof that necessarily brings about or contributes to a result. . . ." (*Webster's New Collegiate Dictionary* [2d ed.; Springfield, Mass.: G. & C. Merriam Co., 1949], p. 132).

sues and has not crossed over into the realm of empirical analysis. However, if this were the only source of difficulty, the outlook at least would be hopeful, since this is a short-coming which presumably can be surmounted by intensive spade work. Unfortunately, this avenue of hope is dashed by the existence of a more fundamental barrier to the identification of causes—namely, the inherent characteristics of the dilemma process itself.

As Figure 3 and the discussion in the preceding chapter indicate, we have here a process which is circular or continuous and in which almost all the significant economic variables are mutually interdependent. Hence, the end result of the dilemma process must be classed as the joint product of the whole complex of factors involved. And, in such circumstances, it is simply not possible to single out any one aspect of the dilemma model and stamp it as "the" cause. A statement by Rees illustrates the pitfall to be avoided here:

> An expansion of the money supply as a consequence of wage increases is possible if in fact the monetary authorities permit it or assist it. However, it is not correct to argue that the cause of inflation in this case is wage increases. The real cause of inflation is the abdication by the monetary authorities of their responsibility for maintaining stable monetary conditions.[2]

[2] Rees, *McGill Industrial Relations Conference*, 1953, pp. 100-101. For a rather similar point of view see Morton, *Journal of Political Economy*, June 1951, pp. 258-259. The direct quotation of the comment made by Rees is certainly not meant to imply that he is in any way especially guilty on this score. In fact, his recent contribution to the Congressional study of wage-price relations (Albert E. Rees, "Price Level Stability and Economic Policy," Joint Economic Committee, *Compendium on Prices and Economic Stability*, 1958, pp. 651-663) is quite probably the best paper that has been written on the policy aspects of the wage-price is-

Unless Rees is using the word "cause" in some special sense (and, it is suggested below that this may well be the case), it is difficult to see on what grounds the monetary authorities can be singled out as "the real cause of inflation." It would be equally possible (and equally improper) to say that since the monetary authorities would not find themselves in such an uncomfortable position if unions and corporations had refrained from negotiating wage increases in excess of productivity gains, it is the wage-setting parties that are "the cause" of the difficulties.[3] And, pursuing the same erroneous line of reasoning a bit further, it is even possible to attribute inflation to the engineers, since if productivity had risen at a sufficiently rapid rate, wages could have gone up without an accompanying increase in unit costs. To repeat: the main point here is simply that in the case of the dilemma model the constituent elements are so interdependent and inter-related that it is hard to see what good can result from arguing over which factor or behavior pattern is "the real cause" of inflation.

---

sue. What the above quotation is meant to do is illustrate that even as careful and competent an economist as Rees can slip into methodological difficulties when it comes to assessing "the cause" of a particular inflationary episode.

[3] E. H. Chamberlin has recently written (*Economic Analysis of Labor Union Power*, 1958, p. 29): "To deal with wage-push inflation by monetary or fiscal policies is certainly not to deal with causes. . . . An obvious alternative is to diminish in some measure the degree of economic power in the hands of unions, so that the pressure may be reduced at its source." It should be noted that Professor Chamberlin actually goes farther than the statement in the text in that he singles out not the entire wage-determination process as "the cause" but only the unions. This tendency to attribute all of whatever wage increases that occur via the collective bargaining process to the unions has been decried earlier (see Chapter 8) and represents a secondary manifestation of this same problem of identifying causation.

Furthermore, there is an important corollary to the above point—the difficulties besetting anyone trying to pinpoint the cause of inflation are not resolvable simply by locating the factor which initiated the dilemma process. That is, even if one succeeded in surmounting the serious methodological difficulties involved in identifying the origins of an inflation, it would still be improper to claim that "the cause" of inflation had now been isolated. This is because the resultant price increases are a function not just of the nature and magnitude of the disturbing factor, but also of the factors and behavior patterns that condition the response of the economy to the initial disturbance. It is for this reason that in our earlier discussion of the origins of inflation (Chapter 2), the word "cause" was carefully avoided. Origins and causes are by no means identical.

So far we have talked mainly about identifying the causes of inflation, and have said little about assigning "blame" or fixing "responsibility." Actually, it is in some ways easier (at least conceptually) to mete out blame than it is to identify causes. The reason for this is that when we talk about blame or responsibility we must have in mind some norms or standards of behavior against which to compare actions—and, when any individual or group violates one of these norms, blame can be readily assessed. For example, if we are prepared to make the value judgment that the job of the monetary authorities is to preserve price level stability no matter what the by-products of this action, then it makes considerable sense to hold the monetary authorities responsible for the outcome of the dilemma process. There is, of course, nothing inherently wrong with this procedure so long as the value judgments that undergird the assessment of responsibility are both stated clearly and recognized to be value judgments. The real danger is that someone will forget the key role played by value judgments and will think (mistakenly) that blame and responsibility can be determined solely by "objective" or "factual" means.[4]

Actually, the difference between identifying causes and assessing responsibility may not be so great in practice as is suggested above. It is not totally unreasonable to assume that some sort of implicit value judgment lies behind many of the attempts to find the "causes" of inflation as well as behind attempts to assess responsibility. In short, there seems to be a strong temptation to pick out whatever behavior element in the dilemma process one happens to disapprove of (whether it be the activities of trade unions or the reticence of the monetary authorities to pursue a policy of price stability with proper vigor) and then to identify this element as "the cause" of inflation. Yielding to this temptation can be particularly dangerous in that the "objective" or "scientific" connotations of the word "cause" obscure the significance of the underlying value judgments. When value judgments as to the propriety of certain actions become so closely intertwined with analysis, it is just as well to admit explicitly that we have passed over into the realm of public policy formulation.

Finding "Solutions"

The search for "solutions"[5] to the inflation-unemployment dilemma has grown naturally out of attempts to find

[4] In a letter to all members of Congress urging a Congressional investigation into wage-price-profit relationships, Mr. Reuther commented as follows: "In his State of the Union message yesterday, President Eisenhower dealt at some length with the problem of inflation. This time, with seeming impartiality, he blamed both industry and labor. But is it really impartial to blame both if only one is guilty? We have been seeking a Congressional investigation to establish, on a *factual* basis, where the fault really lies so that the innocent will not be condemned for the sins of the guilty." (*News from the UAW*, January 13, 1957, p. 1 [italics mine].)

[5] In the present context we are using the word "solution" to

416

causes or fix responsibility and has proven to be at least as popular an undertaking. This concern with public policy facets of the wage-price issue is, in and of itself, altogether proper and highly commendable. However, there are certain aspects of the way in which this search has been conducted which are not so commendable and which require comment.

The first and most important point to be made here is that there has been some tendency to construct too tight a link between "types" of inflation and appropriate public policy solutions. The following statement by Lerner is indicative of this tendency:

> All this brings us to the perhaps only too obvious conclusion that sellers' inflation can not be cured or prevented by measures directed against excess demand by buyers. It can be successfully treated only by attacking the pressure on prices by sellers.[6]

The thing to note about this quotation is not the conclusion itself—Lerner may be entirely right in suggesting that it is unwise to use demand depressants to combat "sellers' inflation"—but rather the way in which the conclusion is reached. That is, Lerner's conclusion is by no means as "obvious" as his statement suggests.

Quite apart from the serious conceptual shortcomings of such distinctions as "sellers' inflation" versus "buyers' inflation" and "cost inflation" versus "demand inflation" (which are enumerated in Chapter 2), it simply does not follow that ability to insert a particular inflation into a

---

mean simply the optimal way of dealing with a given situation. If the word "solution" is interpreted to mean the discovery of some arrangement whereby all aspects of a given situation regarded by anyone as "undesirable" are eliminated, we may as well abandon hope of "solving" the wage-price issue.

[6] Joint Economic Committee, *Compendium on Prices and Economic Stability*, 1958, p. 261.

particular category is sufficient to prescribe public policy remedies. While the identification of a new "type" of inflation (assuming for the sake of argument that such an identification can and has been made) most certainly should make us wary of applying in a blunderbuss fashion tools intended for different situations, there is certainly no reason to think that our economic tools are so specialized that they should not be used to deal with any situation other than the one for which they were initially designed.

To take the case in point, the preceding analysis of the dilemma model suggests clearly that demand depressants *can* halt "sellers' inflation"; whether such policies constitute the optimal way of dealing with this type of inflation is another question, and can only be decided after a careful weighing of the advantages and disadvantages of all available modes of attack. The view that policy can be determined in a semi-automatic way by simply placing inflations in various categories is but one manifestation of the general tendency to try to find overly simple solutions to the problems raised by the wage-price issue.

This last comment leads directly to a more general series of observations. The process of formulating any public policy decision must include four steps: (1) an attempt to identify the basic functional relationships involved and to develop—with the aid of existent tools and writings— a set of hypotheses or presumptions concerning the nature of these relationships; (2) an analysis of these hypotheses and presumptions in the light of empirical evidence; (3) a clear statement of the social values or preferences which must provide the basis for the ultimate decision; and (4) an evaluation of the relative desirability of the alternative modes of action available. Unfortunately, a rather large— in fact, discouragingly large—proportion of the attempts to find solutions to the wage-price issue have skipped over at least one of the above steps either entirely or much too hurriedly. While the complexity of the dilemma process provides at least a partial explanation for such impatience, the fact remains that none of the above steps can be handled in a cavalier fashion if the wage-price issue is to be dealt with adequately.

The basic need for theoretical analysis and a systematic investigation of the relevant behavior patterns has, of course, provided the motivation for this entire study, and need not be dwelt on here. It is sufficient to note that, while the type of analysis attempted in the preceding chapters is an essential part of the policy formulation process, it would be folly to pretend that this brand of theoretical inquiry represents more than a necessary first step.

The need for careful empirical analysis of the relationships highlighted by the foregoing discussion is no less apparent. It would certainly be foolhardy to embark on a program designed to "reform" some of our more important socio-economic institutions without first assessing the *magnitude* of the problem in order to see if such strong measures are really needed.

Similarly, it is essential that at least some effort be made to decide just how "bad" any given amount of inflation actually is, and how much of other objectives (such as high-level employment) our society is prepared to sacrifice in the pursuit of price stability. However, it is also essential to remember that answers to questions of this type require the expression of social values as well as economic analysis, and so no economist—*qua* economist—has either the responsibility or the right to make ultimate pronouncements.

Finally, it is mandatory that a careful study of the advantages and disadvantages of *alternative* public policies precede the decision to adopt any given program. And, the word "alternative" requires special emphasis. It is not enough to assess the social costs involved in permitting the *status quo* to continue. Even if these costs seem rather high, the adoption of reform proposals may prove to be still more costly; and, in this case, the optimal "solution" would consist of avoiding the temptation to make major changes. To assume that whenever the existing conglomeration of institutions provides less than "perfect" results some modification must be made is surely to misunderstand the nature of the world in which we live.

It is true that computing and comparing the costs of maintaining the *status quo* against the costs of various alternative programs can be an arduous, time-consuming, and even somewhat unexciting way of proceeding. However, no acceptable shortcut has as yet been found.

SELECTED BIBLIOGRAPHY*

Books

Andrews, P. W. S. *Manufacturing Business*. London: Macmillan & Co., Ltd., 1949.

Bach, G. L. *Inflation: A Study in Economics, Ethics, and Politics*. Providence, R.I.: Brown University Press, 1958.

Backman, Jules. *Steel Prices, Profits, Productivity, and Wages*. New York: Public Relations Department, United States Steel Corporation, 1957.

Baumol, William J. *Economic Dynamics: An Introduction*. New York: Macmillan Co., 1951.

——. *Welfare Economics and the Theory of the State*. Cambridge, Mass.: Harvard University Press, 1952.

Beveridge, Sir William H. *Full Employment in a Free Society*. New York: W. W. Norton & Co., 1945.

Brown, A. J. *The Great Inflation; 1939-1951*. London: Oxford University Press, 1955.

Cartter, Allan M. *Theory of Wages and Employment*. Homewood, Ill.: Richard D. Irwin, Inc., 1959.

Chamberlain, Neil W. *Collective Bargaining*. New York: McGraw-Hill Book Co., 1951.

Chamberlin, E. H. *The Economic Analysis of Labor Union Power*. Washington: American Enterprise Association, January 1958.

——. *The Theory of Monopolistic Competition; A Re-orientation of the Theory of Value*. 6th ed.

* N.B. It must be emphasized that this is a *selected* bibliography. That is, not all works referred to in the process of preparing this manuscript are included. Only those sources expressly cited in the preceding pages are listed below.

Cambridge, Mass.: Harvard University Press, 1948.

Chandler, Lester V. *The Economics of Money and Banking.* Revised ed. New York: Harper & Brothers, 1953.

Conference on Economic Progress. *Consumption—Key to Full Prosperity.* Washington: Conference on Economic Progress, 1957.

Due, John F. *Government Finance: An Economic Analysis.* Homewood, Ill.: Richard D. Irwin, Inc., 1954.

Duesenberry, James. *Income, Saving, and the Theory of Consumer Behavior.* Cambridge, Mass.: Harvard University Press, 1949.

Dunlop, John T. (ed.). *The Theory of Wage Determination.* London: Macmillan & Co., Ltd., 1957.

Fabricant, Solomon. *Employment in Manufacturing, 1899-1939: An Analysis of Its Relation to the Volume of Production.* New York: National Bureau of Economic Research, 1942.

Fellner, William J. *Competition Among the Few.* New York: Alfred A. Knopf, 1949.

Galbraith, John K. *The Affluent Society.* Boston: Houghton Mifflin, 1958.

Halm, George N. *Monetary Theory: A Modern Treatment of the Essentials of Money and Banking.* 2d ed. Philadelphia: Blakiston Co., 1946.

Hansen, Alvin H. *Monetary Theory and Fiscal Policy.* New York: McGraw-Hill Book Co., 1949.

Hansen, Bent. *A Study in the Theory of Inflation.* New York: Rinehart & Co., 1951.

————. *The Economic Theory of Fiscal Policy.* Translated by P. E. Burke. Cambridge, Mass.: Harvard University Press, 1958.

Hart, A. G. *Defense Without Inflation*. New York: Twentieth Century Fund, 1951.

————. *Money, Debt and Economic Activity*. New York: Prentice-Hall, Inc., 1948.

Hart, A. G., and Brown, E. C. *Financing Defense*. New York: Twentieth Century Fund, 1951.

Hawtrey, Ralph George. *Cross Purposes in Wage Policy*. London: Longmans, Green and Co., 1955.

Hicks, J. R. *The Theory of Wages*. London: Macmillan & Co., Ltd., 1935.

————. *Value and Capital: An Inquiry into Some Fundamental Principles of Economic Theory*. 2d ed. Oxford: Clarendon Press, 1946.

Hill, Samuel E., and Harbison, F. H. *Manpower and Innovation in American Industry*. Princeton, N.J.: Industrial Relations Section, Princeton University, 1959.

Income, Employment and Public Policy: Essays in Honor of Alvin H. Hansen. New York: W. W. Norton & Co., 1948.

Keynes, John Maynard. *A Treatise on Money*. Vol. I. New York: Harcourt, Brace, and Co., 1930.

Kuhn, Alfred. *Labor: Institutions and Economics*. New York: Rinehart & Co., 1956.

Kurihara, Kenneth K. (ed.). *Post-Keynesian Economics*. New Brunswick, N.J.: Rutgers University Press, 1954.

Lang, Theodore (ed.). *Cost Accountants' Handbook*. New York: The Ronald Press, 1952.

Lester, Richard A. *Adjustments to Labor Shortages; Management Practices and Institutional Controls in an Area of Expanding Employment.* Princeton, N.J.: Industrial Relations Section, Princeton University, 1955.

Lester, Richard A. *Hiring Practices and Labor Competition.* Princeton, N.J.: Industrial Relations Section, Princeton University, 1954.

Lester, Richard A., and Robie, Edward A. *Wages Under National and Regional Collective Bargaining: Experience in Seven Industries.* Princeton, N.J.: Industrial Relations Section, Princeton University, 1946.

Lester, Richard A., and Shister, Joseph (eds.). *Insights into Labor Issues.* New York: Macmillan Co., 1948.

Lindblom, Charles E. *Unions and Capitalism.* New Haven, Conn.: Yale University Press, 1949.

Markham, Jesse W. *Competition in the Rayon Industry.* Cambridge, Mass.: Harvard University Press, 1952.

Mason, E. H. *Economic Concentration and the Monopoly Problem.* Cambridge, Mass.: Harvard University Press, 1957.

Money, Trade, and Economic Growth: Essays in Honor of John Henry Williams. New York: Macmillan Co., 1951.

Morgenstern, Oskar (ed.). *Economic Activity Analysis.* New York: John Wiley & Sons, 1954.

Myers, Charles A., and Shultz, George P. *The Dynamics of the Labor Market.* New York: Prentice-Hall, Inc., 1951.

National Bureau of Economic Research, Conference of the Universities–National Bureau Committee for Economic Research. *Business Concentration and*

Price Policy. Princeton, N.J.: Princeton University Press, 1955.

National Bureau of Economic Research, Conference on Price Research, Committee on Price Determination. *Cost Behavior and Price Policy*. New York: National Bureau of Economic Research, 1943.

National Industrial Conference Board. *Wage Inflation: A Discussion by the Conference Board Economic Forum and Guests*. ("Studies in Business Economics Number fifty-six.") New York: National Industrial Conference Board, 1957.

Patinkin, Don. *Money, Interest, and Prices*. Evanston, Ill.: Row, Peterson & Co., 1956.

Reynolds, Lloyd G. *The Structure of Labor Markets: Wages and Labor Mobility in Theory and Practice*. New York: Harper and Brothers, 1951.

Robinson, Joan. *The Economics of Imperfect Competition*. London: Macmillan & Co., Ltd., 1933.

———. *Essays in the Theory of Employment*. London: Macmillan & Co., Ltd., 1937.

Roosa, Robert V. *Federal Reserve Operations in the Money and Government Securities Markets*. New York: Federal Reserve Bank of New York, 1956.

Ross, Arthur M. *Trade Union Wage Policy*. Berkeley: University of California Press, 1948.

Samuelson, Paul A. *Economics: An Introductory Analysis*. 4th ed. New York: McGraw-Hill Book Co., 1958.

Scitovsky, Tibor. *Welfare and Competition: The Economics of a Fully Employed Economy*. Chicago: Richard D. Irwin, Inc., 1951.

Stonier, Alfred W., and Hague, Douglas C. *A Textbook*

of Economic Theory. London: Longmans, Green and Co., 1953.

Taylor, George W., and Pierson, Frank C. (eds.). *New Concepts in Wage Determination.* New York: McGraw-Hill Book Co., 1957.

Triffen, Robert. *Monopolistic Competition and General Equilibrium Theory.* Cambridge, Mass.: Harvard University Press, 1949.

Twenty-five Economic Essays, in English, German, and Scandinavian Languages, in Honor of Erik Lindahl. Stockholm: Ekonomisk Tidskrift, 1956.

Wiles, P. J. D. *Price, Cost and Output.* Oxford: Basil Blackwell, 1956.

Wilson, T., and Andrews, P. W. S. (eds.). *Oxford Studies in the Price Mechanism.* Oxford: Clarendon Press, 1951.

Woytinsky, W. S. *Labor and Management Look at Collective Bargaining.* New York: Twentieth Century Fund, 1949.

Wright, David McCord (ed.). *The Impact of the Union.* New York: Harcourt, Brace & Co., 1951.

Public Documents

United States Board of Governors of the Federal Reserve System. *Consumer Instalment Credit.* 6 vols. Washington: U.S. Government Printing Office, 1957.

————. *Financing Small Business: Report to the Committees on Banking and Currency and the Select Committees on Small Business.* 85th Cong., 2d Sess., 1958.

United States Congress, Joint Committee on the Economic

Report, Subcommittee on General Credit Control and Debt Management. *Monetary Policy and the Management of the Public Debt: Hearings.* 82d Cong., 2d Sess., 1952.

——. *Monetary Policy and the Management of the Public Debt: Replies to Questions.* Part i, 82d Cong., 2d Sess., 1952.

United States Congress, Joint Economic Committee. *Employment, Growth, and Price Levels: Hearings.* 86th Cong., 1st Sess., 1959.

——. *January 1957 Economic Report of the President: Hearings.* 85th Cong., 1st Sess., 1957.

——. *January 1959 Economic Report of the President: Hearings.* 86th Cong., 1st Sess., 1959.

——. *Productivity, Prices, and Incomes.* 85th Cong., 1st Sess., 1957.

——. *The Relationship of Prices to Economic Stability and Growth; Compendium of Papers Submitted by Panelists Appearing Before the Joint Economic Committee.* 85th Cong., 2d Sess., 1958.

United States Senate, Committee on the Judiciary, Subcommittee on Antitrust and Monopoly. *Administered Prices: Hearings.* Part i: *Opening Phase—Economists' Views.* 85th Cong., 1st Sess., 1957.

Articles and Periodicals

Ackley, Gardner. "A Third Approach to the Analysis and Control of Inflation," Joint Economic Committee, *Compendium on Prices and Economic Stability,* 1958, pp. 619-636.

Adelman, M. A. "The Consistency of the Robinson-Patman Act," *Stanford Law Review,* vi (December 1953), pp. 3-20.

Bambrick, James J. Jr., and Dorbandt, Marie P. "The Trend to Longer-Term Union Contracts," *Management Record*, xviii (June 1956), pp. 206-208.

Baumol, William J. "Price Behavior, Stability, and Growth," *Joint Economic Committee, Compendium on Prices and Economic Stability*, 1958, pp. 49-59.

Bissell, Richard. "Price and Wage Policies and the Theory of Employment," *Econometrica*, viii (July 1940), pp. 199-239.

Boulding, Kenneth E. "Collective Bargaining and Fiscal Policy," *American Economic Review*, xl (May 1950), pp. 306-320.

Bowen, William G. " 'Cost Inflation' Versus 'Demand Inflation': A Useful Distinction?" *Southern Economic Journal*, xxvi (January 1960).

Broehl, Wayne G. "Trade Unions and Full Employment," *Southern Economic Journal*, xx (July 1953), pp. 61-73.

Bronfenbrenner, Martin. "Potential Monopsony in Labor Markets," *Industrial and Labor Relations Review*, ix (July 1956), pp. 577-588.

———. "Some Neglected Implications of Secular Inflation," *Post Keynesian Economics*, ed. Kenneth K. Kurihara (New Brunswick, N.J.: Rutgers University Press, 1954), pp. 31-58.

Business Week, May 31, 1958, p. 100.

Chandler, Lester V. "The Impact of Low Interest Rates on the Economy," *Journal of Finance*, vi (June 1951), pp. 252-263.

Dale, Edwin L., Jr. "Inflation Linked to Pay Increases in New U.S. Study," *New York Times*, May 19, 1957, Sec. i, pp. 1, 48.

————. "Living Cost Rise Laid to Services, Rent, and Transit," *New York Times*, March 10, 1957, Sec. I, pp. 1, 54.

Dorfman, Robert. "Mathematical or 'Linear' Programming: A Nonmathematical Exposition," *American Economic Review*, XLIII (December 1953), pp. 797-825.

Dow, J. C. R., and Dicks-Mireaux, L. A. "The Excess Demand for Labour: A Study of Conditions in Great Britain, 1946-56," *Oxford Economic Papers*, X (February 1958), pp. 1-33.

Dunlop, John T. "Allocation of the Labor Force," *Proceedings of the Conference on Industry-wide Collective Bargaining, May 14, 1948* [sponsored by the Labor Relations Council of the Wharton School of Finance and Commerce], ed. George W. Taylor (Philadelphia: University of Pennsylvania Press, 1949), pp. 34-46.

————. "Productivity and the Wage Structure," *Income, Employment and Public Policy: Essays in Honor of Alvin H. Hansen* (New York: W. W. Norton & Co., 1948), pp. 341-362.

————. "Wage-Price Relations at High Level Employment," *American Economic Review*, XXXVII (May 1947), pp. 243-253.

Edwards, Ronald S. "The Pricing of Manufactured Products," *Economica*, XIX (August 1952), pp. 298-307.

Ellickson, Katherine Pollak. "Labor's Recent Demands," *Annals of the American Academy of Political and Social Science*, CCXLVIII (November 1946), pp. 6-10.

Ellis, Howard S. "The Rediscovery of Money," *Money, Trade, and Economic Growth: Essays in Honor of John Henry Williams* (Macmillan Co., 1951), pp. 253-269.

Enthoven, A. C. "Monetary Disequilibria and the Dynamics of Inflation," *Economic Journal*, LXVI (June 1956), pp. 256-270.

Farmer, Guy. "What's Ahead in Collective Bargaining?" *Management Review*, XLV (June 1956), pp. 509-516.

Fellner, William J. "Average-cost Pricing and the Theory of Uncertainty," *Journal of Political Economy*, LVI (June 1948), pp. 249-252.

————. Letter to the Editor, *New York Times*, March 25, 1957, p. 24.

Friedman, Milton. "Comment" [on paper by Caleb Smith], National Bureau of Economic Research, *Business Concentration and Price Policy*, 1955, pp. 230-238.

————. "Comment" [on paper by Lloyd Ulman], *Review of Economics and Statistics*, XXXVII (November 1955), pp. 401-406.

————. "Some Comments on the Significance of Labor Unions for Economic Policy," *The Impact of the Union*, ed. David McCord Wright (New York: Harcourt, Brace and Co., 1951), pp. 204-234.

————. "The Supply of Money and Changes in Prices and Output," Joint Economic Committee, *Compendium on Prices and Economic Stability*, 1958, pp. 241-256.

Galbraith, John Kenneth. "Market Structure and Stabilization Policy," *Review of Economics and Statistics*, XXXIX (May 1957), pp. 124-133.

Garbarino, Joseph W. "Unionism and the General Wage Level," *American Economic Review*, XL (December 1950), pp. 893-896.

Hague, Douglas C. "Summary Record of the Debate," *Theory of Wage Determination*, ed. John T. Dunlop (London: Macmillan & Co., Ltd., 1957), pp. 337-430.

Hall, R. L., and Hitch, C. J. "Price Theory and Business Behavior," *Oxford Economic Papers*, ii (May 1939), pp. 12-45.

Hansen, Bent. "Fiscal Policy and Wage Policy," translated from Danish by R. Spink, *International Economic Papers*, i (1951), pp. 66-83.

———. "Full Employment and Wage Stability," *Theory of Wage Determination*, ed. John T. Dunlop (London: Macmillan & Co., Ltd., 1957), pp. 66-78.

Hansen, Bent, and Rehn, Gösta. "On Wage-Drift: A Problem of Money-wage Dynamics," *Twenty-five Economic Essays, in English, German and Scandinavian Languages, in Honor of Erik Lindahl* (Stockholm: Ekonomisk Tidskrift, 1956).

Hazard, Leland. "Management Action on Wage Inflation," *Management Record*, xix (August 1957), pp. 287-288.

———. "Wage Theory: A Management View," *New Concepts in Wage Determination*, ed. George W. Taylor and Frank C. Pierson (New York: McGraw-Hill Book Co., 1957), pp. 32-50.

Heflebower, Richard B. "Full Costs, Cost Changes, and Prices," National Bureau of Economic Research, *Business Concentration and Price Policy*, 1955, pp. 361-392.

Hicks, J. R. "Economic Foundations of Wage Policy," *Economic Journal*, lxv (September 1955), pp. 389-404.

Johnson, Harry G. "The Determination of the General Level of Wage Rates," *Theory of Wage Determination*, ed. John T. Dunlop (London: Macmillan & Co., Ltd., 1957), pp. 31-38.

Kahn, R. F. "Oxford Studies in the Price Mechanism," *Economic Journal*, LXII (March 1952), pp. 119-130.

Kareken, John H. "Lenders' Preferences, Credit Rationing, and the Effectiveness of Monetary Policy," *Review of Economics and Statistics*, XXXIX (August 1957), pp. 292-302.

Kerr, Clark. "Governmental Wage Restraints: Their Limits and Uses in a Mobilized Economy," *American Economic Review*, XLII (May 1952), pp. 369-384.

———. "Labor Markets, Their Character and Consequences," *American Economic Review*, XL (May 1950), pp. 278-291.

———. "Labor's Income Share and the Labor Movement," *New Concepts in Wage Determination*, ed. George W. Taylor and Frank C. Pierson (New York: McGraw-Hill Book Co., 1957), pp. 260-298.

———. "The Short-run Behavior of Physical Productivity and Average Hourly Earnings," *Review of Economics and Statistics*, XXXI (November 1949), pp. 299-309.

Kerr, Clark, and Fisher, Lloyd H. "Multiple-Employer Bargaining: The San Francisco Experience," *Insights into Labor Issues*, ed. Richard A. Lester and Joseph Shister (New York: Macmillan Co., 1948), pp. 25-61.

Knowles, K. J. G., and Winsten, C. G. "Can the Level of Unemployment Explain Changes in Wages?" *Bulletin of the Oxford University Institute of Statistics*, XXI (May 1959), pp. 113-120.

Kuhn, Alfred. "Market Structures and Wage-Push Inflation," *Industrial and Labor Relations Review*, XII (January 1959), pp. 243-251.

Lerner, Abba P. "Inflationary Depression and the Regulation of Administered Prices," Joint Economic Committee, *Compendium on Prices and Economic Stability*, 1958, pp. 257-268.

Lester, R. A. "Economic Adjustments to Changes in Wage Differentials," *New Concepts in Wage Determination*, ed. George W. Taylor and Frank C. Pierson (New York: McGraw-Hill Book Co., 1957), pp. 206-235.

Lutz, F. A. "Inflation in Europe," *South African Journal of Economics*, xxv (December 1957), pp. 233-238.

————. "The Interest Rate and Investment in a Dynamic Economy," *American Economic Review*, xxxv (December 1945), pp. 811-830.

Machlup, Fritz. "Marginal Analysis and Empirical Research," *American Economic Review*, xxxvi (September 1946), pp. 519-554.

Maclaurin, W. Rupert. "Wages and Profits in the Paper Industry," *Quarterly Journal of Economics*, lvii (February 1944), pp. 196-228.

Markham, Jesse W. "The Nature and Significance of Price Leadership," *American Economic Review*, xli (December 1951), pp. 891-905.

Mason, E. S. "Competition, Price Policy, and High-level Stability," *Economic Concentration and the Monopoly Problem*, ed. E. S. Mason (Cambridge, Mass.: Harvard University Press, 1957), pp. 168-181.

Menger, Karl. "The Laws of Return, A Study in Meta-Economics," *Economic Activity Analysis*, ed. Oskar Morgenstern (New York: John Wiley & Sons, 1954), pp. 419-481.

Minsky, H. "Central Banking and Money Market Changes," *Quarterly Journal of Economics*, lxxi (May 1957), pp. 171-187.

Morton, Walter A. "Keynesianism and Inflation," *Journal of Political Economy*, LIX (June 1951), pp. 258-265.

————. "Trade Unionism, Full Employment and Inflation," *American Economic Review*, XL (March 1950), pp. 13-39.

Mullendore, W. C. "Are Wages Inflationary?—II," *Management Record*, XIX (August 1957), pp. 272-273.

Myers, Charles A. "Labor Market Theory and Empirical Research," *Theory of Wage Determination*, ed. John T. Dunlop (London: Macmillan & Co., Ltd., 1957), pp. 317-326.

New York Times, March 9, 1958, Sec. 3, p. 1.

New York Times, April 27, 1958, Sec. 3, p. 1.

New York Times, January 10, 1959, p. 6.

News from the U.A.W., January 13, 1957.

Ozanne, Robert. "Impact of Unions on Wage Levels and Income Distribution," *Quarterly Journal of Economics*, LXXIII (May 1959), pp. 177-196.

Papandreou, A. G. "Comment" [on paper by R. B. Heflebower], National Bureau of Economic Research, *Business Concentration and Price Policy*, 1955, pp. 394-396.

Pen, J. "Wage Determination Revisited," *Kyklos*, XI, Fasc. 1 (1958), pp. 1-28.

Perroux, François, and Lisle, Edmond A. "Structural Inflation and the Economic Function of Wages: The French Example," *Theory of Wage Determination*, ed. John T. Dunlop (London: Macmillan & Co., Ltd., 1957), pp. 251-263.

Phillips, A. W. "The Relation Between Unemployment and the Rate of Change of Money Wage Rates in the United Kingdom, 1861-1957," *Economica*, XXV (November 1958), pp. 283-299.

Pierson, Frank C. "Discussion" [of paper by Kenyon E. Poole], *American Economic Review*, XLV (May 1955), pp. 601-604.

Pitchford, J. D. "Cost and Demand Elements in the Inflationary Process," *Review of Economic Studies*, XXIV (February 1957), pp. 139-148.

Poole, Kenyon E. "Full Employment, Wage Flexibility, and Inflation," *American Economic Review*, XLV (May 1955), pp. 583-597.

Rees, Albert. "Collective Bargaining, Full Employment, and Inflation," Industrial Relations Centre, *Fifth Annual Conference* (Montreal, Quebec: McGill University, Industrial Relations Centre, 1953), pp. 93-120.

———. "Discussion" [of papers by Slichter and Christenson], *American Economic Review*, XLIV (May 1954), pp. 363-365.

———. "Labor Unions and the Price System," *Journal of Political Economy*, LVIII (June 1950), pp. 254-263.

———. "Price Level Stability and Economic Policy," Joint Economic Committee, *Compendium on Prices and Economic Stability*, 1958, pp. 651-663.

———. "Reply" [to a comment by Lloyd Ulman on an earlier paper by Rees], *American Economic Review*, XLVIII (June 1958), pp. 426-433.

———. "Wage Determination and Involuntary Unemployment," *Journal of Political Economy*, LIX (April 1951), pp. 143-153.

"Resolution on Long-term Contracts," *Ammunition*, XI (April 1953), pp. 28-29.

Reynolds, Lloyd G. "The General Level of Wages," *New Concepts in Wage Determination*, ed. George W. Taylor and Frank C. Pierson (New York: McGraw-Hill Book Co., 1957), pp. 239-259.

Reynolds, Lloyd G. "Toward a Short-run Theory of Wages," *American Economic Review*, XXXVIII (June 1948), pp. 289-308.

Roberts, B. C. "Trade Union Behaviour and Wage Determination in Great Britain," *Theory of Wage Determination*, ed. John T. Dunlop (London: Macmillan & Co., Ltd., 1957), pp. 107-122.

Robinson, E. A. G. "The Pricing of Manufactured Products," *Economic Journal*, LX (December 1950), pp. 771-780.

Roosa, Robert V. "Interest Rates and the Central Bank," *Money, Trade, and Economic Growth: Essays in Honor of John Henry Williams* (New York: Macmillan Co., 1951), pp. 270-295.

Ross, Arthur M. "The External Wage Structure," *New Concepts in Wage Determination*, ed. George W. Taylor and Frank C. Pierson (New York: McGraw-Hill Book Co., 1957), pp. 173-205.

Ross, Arthur M., and Goldner, William. "Forces Affecting the Interindustry Wage Structure," *Quarterly Journal of Economics*, LXIV (May 1950), pp. 254-281.

Ruggles, Richard. "The Nature of Price Flexibility and the Determinants of Relative Price Changes in the Economy," National Bureau of Economic Research, *Business Concentration and Price Policy*, 1955, pp. 441-495.

Samuelson, Paul A. "Recent American Monetary Controversy," *Three Banks Review*, XXIX (March 1956), pp. 3-21.

Schlesinger, James R. "Market Structure, Union Power, and Inflation," *Southern Economic Journal*, XXIV (January 1958), pp. 296-312.

————. "The Role of the Monetary Environment in Cost-Inflation," *Southern Economic Journal*, XXIV (July 1957), pp. 12-27.

Schouten, D. B. J. "The Wage Level, Employment, and the Economic Structure," translated from the Dutch by L. Katzen, *International Economic Papers*, II (1952), pp. 221-232.

Selden, Richard T. "Cost-Push Versus Demand-Pull Inflation, 1955-57," *Journal of Political Economy*, LXVII (February 1959), pp. 1-20.

"Sharing the Gains of Productivity," *Labor's Economic Review*, II (June-July 1957), pp. 41-48.

Shultz, George P., and Myers, Charles A. "Union Wage Decisions and Employment," *American Economic Review*, XL (June 1950), pp. 362-380.

Slichter, Sumner H. "Do the Wage-Fixing Arrangements in the American Labor Market Have an Inflationary Bias?" *American Economic Review*, XLIV (May 1954), pp. 322-346.

————. "How Bad Is Inflation?" *Harper's Magazine*, CCV (August 1952), pp. 53-57.

————. "Thinking Ahead: On the Side of Inflation," *Harvard Business Review*, XXXV (September-October 1957), pp. 15ff.

Smith, Warren L. "Consumer Installment Credit," *American Economic Review*, XLVII (December 1957), pp. 966-984.

————. "Monetary Policy and the Structure of Markets," Joint Economic Committee, *Compendium on Prices and Economic Stability*, 1958, pp. 493-511.

————. "On the Effectiveness of Monetary Policy," *American Economic Review*, XLVI (September 1956), pp. 588-606.

Smithies, Arthur. "The Control of Inflation," *Review of Economics and Statistics*, XXXIX (August 1957), pp. 272-283.

Soffer, Benson. "The Effects of Recent Long-Term Agreements on General Wage Level Movements; 1950-1956," *Quarterly Journal of Economics*, LXXIII (February 1959), pp. 36-60.

Sproul, Allan. "Changing Concepts of Central Banking," *Money, Trade, and Economic Growth: Essays in Honor of John Henry Williams* (New York: Macmillan Co., 1951), pp. 296-325.

Steiner, Peter O. "Collective Bargaining and the Public Interest," *Labor Law Journal*, IV (June 1953), pp. 410-416.

————. "The Productivity Ratio: Some Analytical Limitations on Its Use," *Review of Economics and Statistics*, XXXII (November 1950), pp. 321-328.

Stigler, George J. "The Kinky Oligopoly Demand Curve and Rigid Prices," *Journal of Political Economy*, LV (October 1947), pp. 432-449.

————. "Production and Distribution in the Short Run," *Journal of Political Economy*, XLVII (June 1939), pp. 305-327.

Tobin, James. "Monetary Policy and the Management of the Public Debt," *Review of Economics and Statistics*, XXXV (May 1953), pp. 118-127.

Turner, H. A. "Inflation and Wage Differentials in Great Britain," *Theory of Wage Determination*, ed. John T. Dunlop (London: Macmillan & Co., Ltd., 1957), pp. 123-135.

Turner, Robert C. "Relationship of Prices to Economic Stability and Growth: A Statement of the Problem," Joint Economic Committee, *Compendium on Prices and Economic Stability*, 1958, pp. 671-684.

Ulman, Lloyd. "Marshall and Friedman on Union Strength," *Review of Economics and Statistics,* XXXVII (November 1955), pp. 384-401.

————. "The Union and Wages in Basic Steel: A Comment," *American Economic Review,* XLVIII (June 1958), pp. 408-426.

"The Uneasy Triangle," *The Economist,* August 9, 1952, pp. 322-323; August 16, 1952, pp. 376-378; August 23, 1952, pp. 434-435.

United States Department of Labor, Bureau of Labor Statistics. "Major Agreement Expirations or Reopenings in 1957," compiled by Cordelia T. Ward, *Monthly Labor Review,* LXXX (January 1957), pp. 37-49.

Wagner, Harvey M. "A Unified Treatment of Bargaining Theory," *Southern Economic Journal,* XXIII (April 1957), pp. 380-397.

Wagner, Valentin F. "Wage Policy and Full Employment," *Theory of Wage Determination,* ed. John T. Dunlop (London: Macmillan & Co., Ltd., 1957), pp. 79-90.

Weintraub, Sydney. "A Macroeconomic Approach to the Theory of Wages," *American Economic Review,* XLVI (December 1956), pp. 835-852.

White, W. H. "Interest Inelasticity of Investment Demand—The Case From Business Attitude Surveys Re-examined," *American Economic Review,* XLVI (September 1956), pp. 565-587.

Whittlesey, C. R. "Monetary Policy and Economic Change," *Review of Economics and Statistics,* XXXIX (February 1957), pp. 31-39.

Other Sources

Aschheim, Joseph. "Central Banking and Wage-Induced Inflation." Unpublished Ph.D. dissertation, Department of Economics, Harvard University, 1954.

Blough, Roger M. *The Great Myth.* (Statement of Blough before the Subcommittee on Antitrust and Monopoly of the Senate Committee on the Judiciary, 85th Cong., 1st Sess., August 8, 1957; reprint supplied by: Public Relations Department, United States Steel Corporation.)

Rees, Albert E. "The Effect of Collective Bargaining on Wage and Price Levels in the Basic Steel and Bituminous Coal Industries, 1945-1948." Unpublished Ph.D. dissertation, Department of Economics, University of Chicago, 1950.

Reuther, Walter P. *Price Policy and Public Responsibility.* (Statement prepared for presentation to the Subcommittee on Antitrust and Monopoly of the Senate Committee on the Judiciary, 85th Cong., 1st Sess., January 28, 1958; reprint supplied by the United Automobile Workers.)

Samuelson, Paul A. "Wages and Prices in the United States." Paper prepared at the request of the Financial Editor of the *Sydney Morning Herald* for its annual Financial Supplement, 1957.

Schlesinger, James Rodney. "Wage- Cost- Price- Relationships and Economic Progress." Unpublished Ph.D. dissertation, Department of Economics, Harvard University, 1955.

"The Trend Toward Longer-Term Contracts." ("Selected References," No. 73.) Princeton, N.J.: Industrial Relations Section, Princeton University, 1957.

United Steelworkers of America. *Facts on Steel: Profits, Productivity, Prices and Wages; 1956.* (Reprinted as an exhibit in United States Congress, Joint Economic Committee, *January 1957 Economic Report of the President; Hearings,* 85th Cong., 1st Sess., 1957, pp. 187-233.)

INDEX

Ability-to-pay, defined, 86n, 114–
119, 123; effect of productivity
on, 86-89, 90; as "principle" of
wage determination, 113; effect
on wages, 113-124. *See also* Profits; Prospective profitability
Ackley, Gardner, 34
Adelman, M. A., 281n
Administered prices, and "types"
of inflation, 21, 22, 23n
Aggregate demand, role in dilemma model, 44-45, 54; and transmission of wage increases, 220;
role in inflationary process, 318-
321, 328-337; and aggregate
money incomes, 328-337, 405-
406; importance of distribution
of, 334-335. *See also* Demand
Aggregate spending, *see* Aggregate demand
Agriculture, price determination
in, 300-302, 401-402
Andrews, P. W. S., 251n, 253n,
277n
"Announcement effects" (of monetary policy), 341-342, 371, 407
Annual improvement factor, 128n,
176, 180
Anti-inflationary monetary policy,
see Restrictive monetary policy
Aschheim, Joseph, 325n, 366n
Automobile, Aircraft and Agricultural Implement Workers, United, 176-177, 179n. *See also* Reuther, Walter
Average hourly earnings, as index
of "wages," 233-234

Bach, G. L., 15, 16n
Backman, Jules, 72n, 122n
Balanced-budget multiplier, 328n
Bambrick, James J., Jr., 174n
Bargaining, *see* Collective bargain-
ing
Bargaining power, 104n
Baumol, William J., 146n, 282n,
320n
Beveridge, William H., 38

Bissell, Richard, 333n
Blough, Roger M., 183
Bottleneck inflation, 26
Boulding, Kenneth E., 175n
Bowen, William G., 29n, 30n
Broehl, W. G., 172n
Bronfenbrenner, Martin, 376n
Brown, A. J., 93n, 125n, 248n, 351,
352n
Brown, E. Cary, 24
Buyers' inflation and sellers' infla-
tion, 25-28

Capital costs, 239, 243
Cartter, Allan M., 65n
Chamberlain, Neil W., 65n
Chamberlin, E. H., 144, 260n, 298,
414n
Chandler, L. V., 16n, 345n
Collective bargaining, wage determination under, 103-108, 111,
118-123, 124, 126-129, 134-137,
142-168, 170-186, 195-204, 205-
206; geographical scope of, 171-
174; public nature of, 181. *See
also* Employer wage policy;
Union wage policy
Collective bargaining contracts, duration of, 121, 174-179, 186, 395
Competition in product market,
and wage determination, 115-116,
148-150; and price determination,
289-293, 296-297
Consumer Price Index, 16, 124,
300, 310, 401-402
Consumer spending, effect of restrictive monetary policy on,
365-366
Consumption function, effect of
inflation on, 331-333
Cost, as determinant of individual
prices, 251, 261-270, 274, 280-281,
287-289, 292-295, 301-303, 399-
401; as determinant of general
price level, 309-313, 401-403.
See also Cost-plus pricing; Unit
labor costs
Cost accounting, 234, 288

441